Contemporary Italian Diversity
in Critical and Fictional Narratives

Contemporary Italian Diversity in Critical and Fictional Narratives

Edited by Marie Orton, Graziella Parati, and Ron Kubati

FAIRLEIGH DICKINSON UNIVERSITY PRESS
Vancouver • Madison • Teaneck • Wroxton

Published by Fairleigh Dickinson University Press
Copublished by The Rowman & Littlefield Publishing Group, Inc.
4501 Forbes Boulevard, Suite 200, Lanham, Maryland 20706
www.rowman.com

6 Tinworth Street, London SE11 5AL, United Kingdom

Fairleigh Dickinson University Press gratefully acknowledges the support received for scholarly publishing from the Friends of FDU Press.

British Library Cataloguing in Publication Information Available

Library of Congress Cataloging-in-Publication Data

Names: Orton, Marie, 1965–, editor. | Parati, Graziella, editor. | Kubati, Ron, editor.
Title: Contemporary Italian diversity in critical and fictional narratives / edited by Marie Orton, Graziella Parati and Ron Kubati.
Description: Madison : The Fairleigh Dickinson University Press ; Lanham, Maryland : Copublished by The Rowman & Littlefield Publishing Group, Inc., [2021] | Series: The Fairleigh Dickinson University Press series in Italian studies | Some work translated from the original Italian; some work in the orignal Italian with English translations. | Some text in Italian with English translation. | Summary: "Contemporary Italian Diversity in Critical and Fictional Narratives brings together creative literary works and scholarly articles. Both address the changes and challenges to identity formation in an Italy marked by the migrations, populism, nationalism, and xenophobia, and analyze diversity and the affirmation of belonging"—Provided by publisher.
Identifiers: LCCN 2021017395 (print) | LCCN 2021017396 (ebook) | ISBN 9781683933144 (cloth) | ISBN 9781683933168 (paperback) | ISBN 9781683933151 (epub)
Subjects: LCSH: Italian literature—21st century—History and criticism. | Mass media—Italy—History—21st century. | Italian literature—21st century—Translations into English. | Italy—In mass media. | Multiculturalism in literature. | Multiculturalism in mass media.
Classification: LCC PQ4089 .C66 2021 (print) | LCC PQ4089 (ebook) | DDC 850.9/0092—dc23
LC record available at https://lccn.loc.gov/2021017395
LC ebook record available at https://lccn.loc.gov/2021017396

In loving memory of our friend and colleague, Lidia Curti.

Contents

Acknowledgments   vii

Introduction   1

Part 1: Diversity in Italy   **13**

Ero fra calda gente in un caldo paese / I was among warm folk in a
warm country   15
Vera Lúcia de Oliveira / Translated by Ashna Ali

"Stran(i)ero nella mia nazione": Hip-Hop from Southern Alie-
Nation to Afro-Italian Nation-Hood   23
Clarissa Clò and Enrico Zammarchi

Reading "Albania" in Italy: Reception of Elvira Dones's *Piccola
guerra perfetta* and Ron Kubati's *La vita dell'eroe*   43
Daniele Comberiati

Migration, the Novel, and the Power of Fear: A Dialogical
Perspective from Bakhtin to Lakhous   53
Lucia Re

Clash of Civilizations Over an Elevator in Piazza Vittorio   69
Amara Lakhous

Gendering the *Giallo*: Gender Roles in the Opus of Amara Lakhous   75
Ryan Calabretta-Sajder

The Phoenix   95
Ubah Cristina Ali Farah Translated by Silvia Guslandi

Creativity as a Feminist Practice: Intercultural Women's
Associations in Italy   103
Wendy Pojmann

"Arriving Too Soon Is a Mistake": Amnesia in the Postcolonial
    Archives: The Antonaros Case   117
    Fulvio Pezzarossa

When Jacopo da Fiore Watched the Monkeys in the Treetops   129
    Adrián N. Bravi / Translated by Kevin Regan-Maglione

Part 2: Diversity in Diversity   **137**

Le Mandorle Amare / The Bitter Almonds   139
    Basir Ahang Translated by Ashna Ali

Defying the Chromatic Norm: Strategies of Invisibility and Italian
    Transdiasporic Blackness   147
    Caterina Romeo

Reconfiguring "la donna del Sud": Trans-Mediterranean Narratives   159
    Marta Cariello

The Guest   171
    Shirin Ramzanali Fazel

Questions of Authoriality and Literary *Meticciato* in *Scrivere di*
    Islam: Raccontare la diaspora   179
    Simone Brioni

Albania Mon Amour: Tales of Female Love and Duty in the Italian
    Writings of Vorpsi, Dones, and Ibrahimi   199
    Lidia Radi

Chiodi dell'esilio / The Nails of Exile   215
    Gëzim Hajdari / Translated by James Walker

Beyond the Canon: Women's Italian Writings of Migration   223
    Lidia Curti

Kinships: Relations of Care and Experiences of Locality in
    Transnational Italian Narrative   237
    Jennifer Burns

The Two of Me   249
    Gabriella Kuruvilla / Translated by Eleanor Paynter

Translingual Literature and Multi-Belonging   263
    Ron Kubati

Index   277

About the Contributors   283

Acknowledgments

We would like to express our first and greatest thanks to the writers, scholars, and translators who collaborated on this project. Their support and enthusiasm for this volume brought it to life, and their diverse experiences embody its ideas.

For the funding that made it possible to remunerate the creative writers, we thank the Dickey Center of Dartmouth College and the Humanities College at Brigham Young University. We also give special thanks to Brent Orton and to colleagues from the BYU English department for their editorial advice: Spencer Hyde, Kimberly Johnson, and Stephen Tuttle.

We thank Europa Editions for granting permission to reprint excerpts from the English translation of Amara Lakhous's novel *Clash of Civilizations over an Elevator in Piazza Vittorio* by Anna Goldstein.

Introduction

Migration impacts every nation across the globe, and Italy's peninsular geography casts it as first responder in the migratory waves aimed at Europe. Its location as a peninsula that extends into the Mediterranean made it a destination for people across the century. Italy as a crossroads signifies Mediterranean culture as a shared culture, the result of complex imbrications that have shaped a contemporary world that flourishes thanks to its hybridity.

Although Italy's European identity has been artificially privileged in official discourses, the peninsula is the result of people's movements, which makes it a very special kind of South. Migration from Italy to western countries as well as to other geographical South(s) such as Tunisia and Egypt, renders Italy a crucial object of study that helps us understand both the local—Italy—and the global, namely the changes that migrations have brought to specific contexts. Migrations to Italy in the last thirty years have radically transformed the nation's economic, political, and cultural profile; they have transformed what diversity is in Italy, as well as the impact of diversity within the country. Whereas internal migration (from rural to urban, and from south to north) as well as a distinction between those locations once defined difference, more recent migrations into Italy demand Italy's contribution to more complex debates about difference.

Migrating to Italy means migration to a South that is a result of the way in which other countries and their colonial agendas have inflected it. Spanish Italy, French Italy, and Austrian Italy have defined its political and geographical profile and made Italy what it is today. Italy as defined by other cultural imaginations has impacted what the country has become. Narratives of travel to Italy have contributed to the definition of the country as a South to be admired for its ruins but disparaged for its perceived backwardness and for the non-whiteness of its inhabitants. Post-unification Italy struggled to whiten its citizens through transformations that looked at Northern European countries as models to be imitated in order to make the country less southern, less other within a Europe to which it belongs geographically and politically. Contemporary migrations to Italy add to the complexity of defining what Italy is and enrich its future by creating innovative connections that challenge the traditional definition of North and South.

This volume explores the issues raised by the transnational and transcultural phenomena of a changing Italy whose cultures can only be addressed in the plural. That nation's reaction to these changes functions as a test case, a kind of canary in the mine for other locations adapting to cultural shift. Italy's colonial past, its renewed nationalism, populism, and xenophobia, and its shifting national identity are reactionary phenomena relevant to societies worldwide. Thus, we believe that the issues explored by the writers collected in this volume will be relevant and timely for other cultures, other contexts. The implications of discussing migration and diversity in one geographical location means bringing to the fore the importance of difference and migration as a fundamental actor of change all over the world.

Writers that experienced migration in person or through familial postmemory stress that difference matters in all its nuanced characteristics. They also stress that the identities of contemporary Italy and of Italians are constitutively grounded in difference and so is their future. A number of volumes have explored contemporary multicultural Italy; the editors of this volume want to accentuate literatures' contribution in changing the country.

The literature and the scholarship presented here are thematically transnational. Just what constitutes "transnational" can be, and indeed has been, defined both rather narrowly and much less restrictively. Ours is the wider net, gathering together not only those works that are firmly based in a national idiom from which they then depart, but also those works which question the implications of "the national" altogether. This volume does not attempt to define or delineate what exactly constitutes transnational in literature. Rather, this study adds the more personal (identity, homelessness, belonging, multiple-belongings) into the discussion of the range of global issues (politics, national identity, race, dehumanization, colonialism). This is what literature can accomplish: it brings private and public experiences together in order to signify the present for a diverse readership.

This volume brings together eight creative works with thirteen scholarly articles which analyze various aspects of the literature of migration. The choice to assemble creative and critical pieces together arose naturally from our desire to mitigate the potentially damaging hierarchy separating those who study from those who are studied. Especially in politically charged matters, and issues of race, identity, and nationalism, it is easy for the theorist's voice to usurp the dialogue. Therefore, the ethos of this volume recalls the approach of Marianne Hirsch and Nancy Miller, "In placing [these writings] alongside each other, we are putting forward a *connective* rather than *comparative* approach," in order to put them in conversation with one another and the reader (*Rites of Return* 8).

About thirty years ago, people who experienced migration to Italy began to share their knowledge about their geographical and cultural journeys. Their stories challenged and expanded the concept of both Italian culture and Italian literature in particular. Today, literary Italy is a realm in which difference cannot be erased. The narrative of difference has radically transformed the way in which Italian literature is experienced within and outside the confines of the country. This volume wants to celebrate the transformative power of diversity and the authors that sustain it.

The critical voices in this volume echo the particular way in which literature is interpreted from an academic point of view. This volume is also certainly an invitation to challenge that standpoint, as institutional voices may become complacent at times. We did our best in inviting a number of colleagues to contribute and wish we could have included many others whose approach to contemporary literature would have certainly enriched this volume. Restrictions in length dictated and limited our choices, but we hope other volumes will continue the dialogue and expand our limited contribution. We recognize that the group of critical writers here is not as diverse as could be hoped. While the academy recognizes diversity and declares its commitment to it, the reality remains that professors, literary critics, and journalists in the Italian and Italianist context are predominantly white. This is reflected in the voices contained in our imperfect volume. As a profession, we need to do better, for today we are not doing enough.

The creative and critical voices assembled in this volume all emphasize how individuals both reflect and enact societal change and evaluate the power of individuals as social agents of change. Contributions have been organized thematically into two parts: the first is "Diversity in Italy," and the second is "Diversity in Diversity." This volume is unapologetically a proponent of diversity. Inclusivity is its unifying ethos. However, just as the pieces in the first section on "Diversity in Italy" confront the resistance to the inclusion of migrants and their children as "Italian," so the idea of inclusion itself might result in its own ghettoization of others who do not fit existing accepted forms of diversity. For that reason, categories and presuppositions must be continuously reexamined and checked; this motivated our formulation of the second part on "Diversity in Diversity." Many of the pieces in this second section extend and challenge the ways in which we have been prepared to encounter diversity in the past, ways that have been codified as recognizable forms of diversity, because they have represented majority forms, and have entered the thinking of the academic status quo.

For instance, we have developed ways of thinking about the interstitial migrant, who has belonging neither in the homeland, nor in the host country.

But what about the transnational migrant who does not seek home in a homeland or belonging in a place? Or, we have perhaps grown comfortable with the discomfort of Italian law denying citizenship to the offspring of migrants—the so-called g2 population. Or, the aftermaths of colonialism and decolonization have made us aware of some of the types of dislocation that can happen even in the "home" space. But what of revolutions, religious and political, that are currently transforming the concept of home for those affected in parts of the world? And what of migrants whose departures lie outside the usual Mediterranean points of origin? We find that we must evolve new ways of thinking, enlarging or abandoning categories with which we may have only recently become familiar in order to attempt to understand the changing situations of individuals in a changing world.

PART 1: DIVERSITY IN ITALY

The suite of poems by Vera Lúcia de Oliveira, collectively titled "I was among Warm Folk in a Warm Country," all deal with universal themes of love, death, nature, and movement. The reassuring title, however, stands in contrast to elements in the poems that talk of the loss that attends leaving, the complications of feeling, and the complexities of belonging. The poetry leaves the reader to somehow reconcile that distance between the warm folk and warm country of the title and the loss brought by leaving. Clarissa Clò's and Enrico Zammarchi's article "'Stran(i)ero nella mia nazione': Hip-Hop from Southern Alie-Nation to Afro-Italian Nation-Hood" focuses on the success of hip-hop in Italy, where a similar rags to riches trajectory that has characterized the genre in the United States was further enriched with specific and important local connotations. While in its early Italian stages it was produced by white, Italian-born artists, the genre has later been adopted by new generations of Black Italians like the Italian-Egyptian rapper Amir Issaa who in 2016 released "Straniero nella mia nazione," the first hip-hop song to engage with the discrimination faced second-generations of migrants in Italy, and the Italian-Nigerian Tommy Kuti who in 2015 turned Issaa's "straniero" into "stra-nero" (super Black). Clò and Zammarchi discuss how the work of this new generation of rappers challenges traditional notions of Italianness. While Italian hip-hop artists have drawn substantially from global black hip-hop, they have also contributed to global hip-hop by producing cross-fertilization between Italians and African Americans.

Daniele Comberiati examines the circulation and reception of translingual authors in his article, "Reading 'Albania' in Italy: Reception of Elvira Dones's *Piccola guerra perfetta* and Ron Kubati's *La vita dell'eroe*." He employs Stuart Hall's concepts of decoding and coding a work to interrogate how these works are positioned in the Italian cultural and literary landscape.

"There is no uniformity of reception," he asserts, and suggests that the adoption of a cross-analysis of sociological, literary, cultural, and political elements helps to investigate the process of the legitimization and canonization of this literature.

In "Migration, the Novel and the Power of Fear: A Dialogical Perspective from Bakhtin to Lakhous," Lucia Re investigates how fear can turn to social aggression and how literature by and about migrant writers can "counter and debunk the work of fear and anxiety." Analyzing Amara Lakhous's novels, Re suggests that his dialogical textual strategies may be able to reappraise and refute the media-generated speculative societal fear. Lakhous's novels, concludes Re, are not as much about the fear of immigration as they are about the constantly changing Italy, where "what is taking place is not a fearful clash of civilizations, but, yet again, an encounter of cultures."

From Amara Lakhous's best-selling novel, *Scontro di civiltà per un ascensore in Piazza Vittorio* (Clash of Civilization Over an Elevator in Piazza Vittorio), we have included the "Ninth Wail" and "The Truth According to Abdallah Ben Kadour." In these selections, the tension between past, present, and future is expressed in the figure of the protagonist, Amedeo/Ahmed, whose present identity (Amedeo) is in love with Stefania, while his past (Ahmed) is in love with Bagia. These pages become an opportunity to reflect on the problem of the categorization of identity, which Amedeo considers "a stupid question," for Amedeo sees translation as a journey, and himself as a smuggler of words, ideas, images, and metaphors. In this section, Lakhous quotes from Amin Maalouf's novel *Leo Africanus* whose protagonist does not identify with Africa, Europe, or Arabia, but with perpetual travel and movement: "I'm the son of the road."

Ryan Calabretta-Sajder's "Gendering the *Giallo*: Gender Roles in the Opus of Amara Lakhous" discusses the author's female characters who break from the typical gender binaries set both in the *giallo* tradition and in Italian culture. Calabretta-Sajder points out how the characters in Lakhous's novels manipulate the concepts of space and place in order to open a dialogue around diversity, following closely in the evolution the *commedia all'italiana* (alla Pietro Germi). Lakhous, like Germi, employs Pirandellean *umorismo* while composing unique narrative voices and analyzing new cultural rules, questions the etiquette of gender and sexuality in Italian society.

Ubah Cristina Ali Farah's short story "The Phoenix" compares women from two different generations who meet in the estuary of a naval base. The elder, Jeanne, had lived in the area for many years and forms a tenuous friendship with a young migrant woman. Jeanne looks back at her own life to better understand the unspoken story of the young woman. Being hopeful when young is seen in this dense short story as an essential and timeless human right. The connection between the two women, which is not based in the communication of facts but on the common events of their lives, is cast as both light and dark.

Wendy Pojmann begins her article, "Creativity as a Feminist Practice: Intercultural Women's Associations in Italy," with a series of questions: To what extent can migrant and native women join forces? Can they, or should they, construct a common agenda? If so, what form should it take? Are there new practices still to be envisioned in building a multicultural feminism that can be applied to the particular characteristics of Italy and extended to other parts of the Mediterranean? Pojmann addresses these questions by evaluating the effectiveness of several intercultural women's associations in central Italy, demonstrating how the most successful are those whose creative forms of integration still respect cultural diversity and allow their members to connect across distinctions of ethnicity, class, and nationality, and construct new feminist practices.

Fulvio Pezzarossa's "'Arriving Too Soon Is a Mistake': Amnesia in the Postcolonial Archives: The Antonaros Case" reflects on the complications involved in attempting to define the literature known and studied in Italy as "postcolonial." The author debates "the silence around the male writers of the Italian postcolonial period," which he responds to by delineating the career of Alfredo Taracchini Antonaros, author, playwright, and journalist, born in 1950 to an Italian father and a mother of Greek and Eritrean origins. Pezzarossa highlights the contradiction in Antonaros's prolific literary contributions, visibility, and high level of integration with the difficult path of translingual and transnational writers to integration into the Italian national canon.

The protagonist of Adrián Bravi's short story "When Jacopo da Fiore Watched the Monkeys in the Treetops" is inspired by Joachim of Fiore (Jacopo da Fiore, ca. 1135–1202), the controversial, apocalyptical writer and abbot of a Cistercian monastery who later moved to Fiore, Calabria. Bravis's Jacopo da Fiore discovers a dead monkey floating near the riverbank in the middle of a jungle and wonders if the monkeys are able to contemplate the sense of life and death. He eagerly tells Sandoval of "a half-naked savage covered in necklaces and painted skin," explaining how the nature of the universe and all its creatures were made by erudite quotes from Scotus Eriugena, Albertus Magnus, and Saint Augustine. Sandoval responds by sharing his son's drawings with Jacopo to show "that both he, Sandoval and the boy, had realized that everything can be represented, all you need is a little pen in your hand."

PART 2: DIVERSITY IN DIVERSITY

The creative and critical contributions in the second part exemplify practices by writers and scholars that complicate and problematize issues of identity, how belonging is assigned, and how belonging is expressed. Basir Ahang's poetry reflects on the classic themes of migration such as identity and belonging. With direct and limpid verses, he depicts with sincerity and simplicity the migrant condition. In Milan, where "the human being is just a machine," he is not permitted to feel Italian because of his Persian surname and because his somatic traits make him look like a "Buddha of Bamiyan Quano." The city's alienating gaze freezes the poet, who, since a country is a place that makes one feel secure, has nowhere to go and turns into "an uprooted tree." There are no countries for exiled poets, from whose verses, oozes the dark fear of not belonging. He spends his days looking at the swallows who are not able to find the way back home, sharing their loss.

Caterina Romeo's article, "Defying the Chromatic Norm: Strategies of Invisibility and Italian Transdiasporic Blackness," explores the intersection of Blackness and Italianness in two memoirs: *The Skin Between Us* (2006) by African Italian American author Kym Ragusa and *La mia casa è dove sono* (2010, My Home Is Where I Am) by Igiaba Scego, an Italian author of Somali origin. While they write from different standpoints, both authors outline how their Italianness and Blackness were frequently coded socially as mutually exclusive and undesirable. Romeo, however, analyzes the relationship between race, "chromatic norm," and mobility, as the families of both writers are part of the Italian diaspora and delineate how the hypervisibility of their Blackness leads both writers to adopt complex strategies of invisibility. At the same time, these two writers' exploration of Blackness push back against systematic erasure of difference and "instead demand its inclusion into the process of shaping Italian and European identities."

Marta Cariello's article traces the tradition of the woman of the south, "la donna del Sud." She shows how, paradoxically, this figure is devoid of agency due to the limitations imposed by patriarchal tradition, and yet she is also terrifyingly powerful. Though relegated to private spaces and constrained domestic roles—she is frequently a metaphor for the household—"she carries on her body not only social disorder but also the possibility of claiming and taming such disorder. The southern woman embodies an intimidating form of power and a territory that must be controlled." As Cariello's title, "Reconfiguring 'la donna del Sud': Trans-Mediterranean Narratives," explains, this trope has been intentionally rewritten and complicated, specifically by Italian Somali writer Igiaba Scego.

Shirin Ramzanali Fazel's short story "The Guest" is not a translation but was written directly in English. The title immediately recalls Camus' *Guest*, and readers familiar with James Joyce's short story "Araby" will appreciate the beginning of Fazel's story. Ayah, an adolescent girl, narrates in first-person the complex presence—and absence—of a series of guests: many family members are guests, frequently from her mother's side, and once a year from her father's side. The most dramatic guest is the narrator's cousin, Hilal, whose visit is initially seen as a sign of reconciliation with the paternal relatives, and he is a welcomed guest and a potential suitor for Ayah. However, when Ayah becomes pregnant and he disappears, the unborn child becomes the family's final, complicated guest. Simone Brioni's article, "Questions of Authoriality and Literary *Meticciato* in *Scrivere di Islam: Raccontare la diaspora*," discusses the advantages, complications, and stakes of direct collaboration between writers and scholars. Specifically, he outlines the creative process involved in the creation of the hybrid text named in his title, which Shirin Ramanzali Fazel and he wrote together "a quattro mani." Brioni sees this kind of collaboration as a powerful, decolonial practice. Brioni's article exemplifies the ethos of this entire volume. It is a call for more participative, collaborative practices between creative writers and scholars that will promote "methodological enrichment, the development of new theoretical standpoints, a better ethical and cultural awareness, and a new attention to the needs expressed in diaspora and postcolonial literature, so that academic research and public engagement can successfully contribute to the pursuit of social justice."

Lidia Radi chooses the three most successful Albanian female writers of what she calls "Italian transnational literature" to explore Albania's painful past and its more recent encounters with the Western world. Her article, "Albania Mon Amour: Tales of Female Love and Duty in the Italian Writings of Vorpsi, Dones, and Ibrahimi," traces how all three writers evaluate the patriarchal traditions that characterize Albania as distant from Italy (though geographically only 45 miles from the Italian coast). She reads these authors' works as potential defense against the dangers of adopting a monocultural and monolingual perspective, and her analysis serves as an invitation for readers to rethink national otherness from a multicultural outlook.

Gëzim Hajdari's poem "The Nails of Exile" is a dark family saga of three generations intertwined with regional geography, history, and folk traditions. There is the civil conflict between the right-wing Balli Kombtar (The National Front) and the Communist Party during the anti-Nazi-fascist resistance years. There are the years of the communist dictatorship. There is the geography of Albania hinted at through the family's story of internal migration—due to the centuries-old vendetta inscribed in the northern Kanun—from the Bjeshkët e Namuna (Cursed Alps) of the north to the hills of the south. There are the codes and beliefs that regulate people's lives. There are clairvoyants, snakes, and magical beliefs against the backdrop of the rough, Balkan landscape. Then there is nature, with which people's lives are one but which is often—if not always—harsh, cold, and malignant, as if to reinforce the curse of human history. There is also the distant gaze of the poet who, from the vantage point of exile, tells of the Fridays with his family, when "the Ancient Romans used to carry out death sentences." He does so in two languages, Albanian but also Italian, which both filters out a little pain of the tragic life and makes visible the conditions of his exile. The poet knows his destiny: he will die on a (metaphoric) Friday, when all the members of his family died, but far away and alone, "crucified hands and feet with the nails of exile."

Lidia Curti's article, "Beyond the Canon: Women's Italian Writing of Migration" delineates how female migrant writers have been doubly excluded from the canon of Italian literature (as women and as non-national writers). She considers works by several female authors—Gabriella Ghermandi, Ubah Cristina Ali Farah, Igiaba Scego, Francesca Melandri, the Wu Ming 2 collective, and Antar Mohamed—and discusses how they write against patriarchal limits. "Female and feminist literatures occupy a space with their own specificities," she explains, a space where linguistic or cultural homogeneity is impossible. Curti sees the tradition of canon formation as a way of drawing national barriers and the works of female authors as a way to resist colonialism's authoritarian rule and form an alternative tradition.

Jennifer Burns, in her "Kinships: Relations of Care and Experiences of Locality in Transnational Italian Narrative," reflects on the notion of kinship through the lens of feminist theory and inquiry into the posthuman. According to Burns, the idea of the family as the core unit as represented in the European novel in the last two centuries is being displaced by new forms of relations between individuals which explore more inclusive and expansive forms of intimate and social relations. The author investigates these aspects in migrant and diasporic communities where they become even more evident, particularly in Gabriella Kuruvilla's writings and her polycentric narrative, which Burns compares to Lakhous's *Scontro di civiltà*.

Gabriella Kuruvilla's short story "The Two of Me" (Io siamo in due) plays with multiple ambiguities. As the title hints, the "I" who relates the first-person narrative is doubled, so there are "two of me." This ambiguity plays out on more than one level, generating narrative uncertainties that further complicate the typical, teenage process of identity construction of the conflicted adolescent protagonist, Laura. The "two of me" can refer to Laura's best and only friend to whom she confides everything, a stuffed animal named Bear. The "two" could likewise refer to Laura's conflicted identity: she insists she is adopted, but her parents insist on calling her "daughter." Still, she remains troubled by the differences in their appearances: "I'm very dark brown and that Kamala and Prabir are dark brown. It's a matter of gradation, but it's important . . . ." Laura's attempts at self-identification take place largely through internal dialogue. She insists that she is African, but her parents are Indian: "There's the matter of our hair. Mine is curly and frizzy, but theirs is straight and soft." But the process of identity construction by contrasting herself with her parents becomes conflated with her childlike imaginations: "The truth that supersedes all others is that we're really different, them and me. Except that none of us is black. Bear and I are quite different, too." The continuous ambiguous interplay in Laura's narration between fantasy and reality, perception and experience emphasize how uncertain the process of identity construction is.

Ron Kubati's "Translingual Literature and Multi-Belonging" focuses on writers such as Schneider, Lahiri, Haidari, and Kundera. The trauma of their origins is a common feature of Schneider's (2001) and Hajdari's (2001, 2011) works. Schneider, for example, writes in Italian to distance herself from her German side, which she feels connects her to Nazism and to her ex-SS mother. However, so as not to entirely cut the ties to her mother and her mother tongue, Schneider moves from one language to another, from one belonging to another, according to need. Hajdari calls the motherland Medea without idealizing Italy, which confines him to the margins. Horrified by the abyss of not belonging, the poet entrusts the construction of his condition precisely to the bilingual writing. The metaphor of the bad mother is very present in both authors. The bad (step-)mother in Hajdari, however, is not nature (as in Leopardi) but the motherland, as if to emphasize the shift from the "Natural Man" to the "National Man" first and to the transnational poet afterward. The hyphenated literature of multi-belonging writers concretely shows their cultural contexts of belonging. Today the legal bridge, the hyphen of multi-belonging after having accompanied the difficult process of the building of the European Union, preserves its importance.

The poetry and short stories written originally in Italian are rendered here in English translation, along with all the citations from other literary works referenced in the scholarly articles. Umberto Eco (2003) insists that translation is fundamentally an act of negotiation. Ideally, it is an edifying collaboration between author and translator but also between idea and idiom. Even so, meaning must inevitably shift somewhat between one idiom and another. Just as a bridge connects and at the same time marks the distance between that which is bridged, so translation makes evident the distance between its two distinct linguistic (and cultural) moorings. As Eco affirms, "Translation is always a shift not between two languages but between two cultures. . . . A translator must take into account rules that are not strictly linguistic but, broadly speaking, cultural" (82). Thus, translation enacts a cultural shift. But when the subject of the translation is itself cultural shift, the translator's role as collaborator rather than fixer becomes doubly important. We hope our offerings are true to this credo of collaboration.

REFERENCES

Eco, Umberto. 2003. *Mouse or Rat? Translation as Negotiation*. London: Weidenfeld & Nicolson.

Hirsch, Marianne, and Nancy K. Miller, eds. 2011. *Rites of Return: Diaspora Poetics and the Politics of Memory*. New York: Columbia University Press.

Part 1

Diversity in Italy

Ero fra calda gente in un caldo paese / I was among warm folk in a warm country

Vera Lúcia de Oliveira / Translated by Ashna Ali

Un sogno di bellezza un dì mi prese.
Ero fra calda gente in un caldo paese.
* * *
One day I was taken by a dream of beauty
I was among warm folk in a warm country.
—Sandro Penna, *Appunti*, Edizioni della Meridiana, 1950, p. 172

c'è una ballerina in me
pronta a occupare il mio corpo
per vederla bisogna andare a fondo
infilare la mano con delicatezza
nella pancia di Dio
* * *

se è stato per il colore del vento
che sono nata, per il rumore delle
foglie accese di luce, l'aria che si
muove fra i panni bianchi sui fili

la sera che sembra non scorrere

there's a dancer in me
ready to occupy my body
to see her you must go deep
delicately thread your hand
into the belly of God

if it was for the color of the wind
that I was born, for the sound
of leaves alive with light, air that
moves between laundered sheets on the line

the evening that seems unable to move

il midollo del tempo, questa vita	the marrow of time, this ardent body
in estasi, questo corpo ardente	this clear gaze
questo sguardo lucido	on the nucleus of everything
sul nucleo di tutto	

* * *

l'amore è vissuto in me	love has lived inside me
con tutto il suo fiore di velluto	with its full flower of velvet
un'estate in cui ero stata rapita	a summer in which I was taken
dal dio della bellezza del mondo	by the god of worldly beauty
e ho avuto parole	and I had words
come un panetto di farina	like a tray of flour
da impastare imburrare	to knead and butter
mettere nel forno per i giorni	leave in the oven for the days that are
peggiori	hardest

* * *

valeva la pena	it was worth it
in quella mattina	that morning when
il bianco spalancato	whiteness thrust itself onto
sulle finestre di giugno	the June windows
e tutto quel colore	and all that color
acceso in ogni cosa	ignited every object
perché non avrei dovuto	why shouldn't I have
volerlo perché non avrei	wanted it why shouldn't I
dovuto amarlo?	have loved?

* * *

sdraiata nel buio e nel freddo	stretched out in the darkness and the cold
sentiva dall'altra parte del mondo	she listened from the other part of the world
la voce del figlio distante che dentro	for the voice of the distant son that came in the night
la notte veniva a svegliarla mamma	to wake her up mommy

ti va di parlare con me oggi?

do you feel like talking to me today?

* * *

non si fa poesia sulla morte

There's no making poetry on death

ma se l'amore permane

but if love persists

oltre la morte se l'amore

beyond death if love

rimane anche la morte

remains even death

vissuta da viva

lived while alive

valeva la pena

was worth it

* * *

in queste sere ancora fredde

in these still cold evenings

ho visto una piccola rondine

I saw a small swallow

si era messa in viaggio troppo presto

she put herself in flight too soon

i battiti delle ali non bastavano

the beat of her wings didn't suffice

per riscaldarle il corpo stanco

to warm her tired body

ho fatto di tutto per salvarla

I did everything to save her

ma non si faceva avvicinare

but she wouldn't let anyone near

voleva morire sola

she wanted to die alone

in quella terra straniera

in this strange land

* * *

non sono mie le guglie

the peaks of illuminated mountains

di montagne illuminate

are not mine

non sono miei gli orti

the vegetable gardens perfumed with rose and resin

profumati di resina e rose

are not mine

erba fresca recisa

the fresh cut grass

non sono mie le orme

the footprints on the winding streets of a city

su vie ritorte di una città

sculpted by time

che il tempo ha modellato

are not mine

non sono miei gli occhi

the eyes that keep vigil from the windows

che vegliano dalle finestre

polished by the winds and the rains

levigate da venti e piogge	are not mine
non sono nata qui	I was not born here
ma i muri mi annusano	but the walls sniff me
quando m'incontrano	upon each encounter

* * *

apriva la bocca	she opened her mouth
e a sorsi e a morsi	and swallowed the light
ingoiava la luce	in sips and bites
sapeva di vento e resina	she knew of the winds and resin
cicale canterine	sing-song cicadas
muri di pietra	marble walls
tronchi ritorti	twisted trunks
e foglioline argentee	and little silvering leaves
che suonavano mute	that mutely play
la musica dell'universo	the music of the universe

* * *

per quelle vie odorose	along those odorous streets
due poeti commossi	passed two verklempt poets
erano passati	they had loved the universe
avevano amato l'universo	because the forests knew
perché i boschi sapevano	of berries eaten
di bacche mangiate	by small animals
da piccoli animali	because the light rained on the fields
perché la luce pioveva sui campi	which rustled the grain
ed essi crepitavano il grano	just ruffled by wind
appena mosso dal vento	because the olive trees shone
perché gli ulivi brillavano	under the full moon like
sotto la luna piena come	silver jewelry
gioielli d'argento	because the flowers blanketed
perché i fiori coprivano	the unplowed fields with color
di colori i campi non arati	because the swallows flitted about
perché le rondini svolazzavano	thumping their own heads

in picchiata sulle loro teste

perché erano ubriachi

di ogni cosa ed essere

creati da Dio

* * *

because they were drunk

on each thing and from being

creatures of God.

girava per sentieri e la luce pareva

dilatarsi e confluire e mescolarsi in una tavolozza

di gialli e arancioni che grondavano dalle siepi

sui prati e sulle colline e monti

in lontananza era come camminare in

una tela di Van Gogh in mezzo ai campi

incendiati dalle spatole di colori attenti solo

a non risvegliare

i corvi

* * *

she wandered around paths and the light seemed

to dilate and merge and blend in a palette

of yellows and oranges that spilled from the fences

onto the pasture and on the hills and mountains

in the distance it was like walking in one of

Van Gogh's paintings in the middle of fields

set ablaze by the palette knifed colors

careful only to not wake

the crows

sotto la luce anche la morte

in quel piccolo cimitero

sembrava meno spoglia

sotto la luce

la città in lontananza

luccicava nella sera

e pareva che si potesse

essere felice persino

nella pena

* * *

under the light even death

in that small cemetery

seemed less nude

under the light

the faraway city

glimmered in the evening

and seemed as if it could

be happy even within

suffering

venite a vedere la notte

che si accende di colori

come and see the night

that lights up with color

è possibile abitare la notte	you can inhabit the night
se porti un filare di sillabe sconnesse a penzoloni	if you bring threads of disjointed, dangling syllables
cammini e loro si inoltrano e nel filo cominciano	you walk and words propel themselves on a thread and they begin
a separare il buio da quel lumicino che porti in mano	to separate the darkness from that little light you carry in hand
per non perderti	to not get lost

* * *

la fame ferisce diceva, avrei dato chissà cosa	hunger harms, he would say, who knows what I would have given
per vedere me stessa attendere mio padre e poi	to see myself wait for my father and then
baciarlo abbracciarlo, avrei dato chissà cosa per	kiss him embrace him, who knows what I would have given
offrirgli quel pezzo di pane, aveva tanta fame	to offer him that piece of bread, he was so hungry
è morto in guerra portando con sé la fame	he died in war carrying hunger with him

* * *

pensava al vento e alle sue distanze	I was thinking of wind and its distances
pensava alle ali degli uccelli migratori	I was thinking of migratory birds
pensava alle foglie staccate dai tronchi	I was thinking of leaves unstuck from branches
pensava alle farfalle alle rondini	I was thinking of butterflies of swallows
a tutti quelli che tornano	at all those who return
dopo aver varcato	after having crossed
qualche porto distante	some distant port

* * *

se tocca morire	if this is the turn to die
che sia sotto il sole	may it be under the sun
che il caldo s'infili	may the heat thread itself

fra il cuore e le costole	between the heart and ribs
forse risveglia	perhaps reawaken
un po' di forza	a bit of strength
e la morte deraglia	to derail death

"Stran(i)ero nella mia nazione"

Hip-Hop from Southern Alie-Nation
to Afro-Italian Nation-Hood

Clarissa Clò and Enrico Zammarchi

Hip-hop is arguably the most recognizable and commercially successful musical genre today around the world. Its dominance is affirmed by the global popularity and ubiquity of familiar names of the entertainment industry whose tracks top billboard charts and hit parades. Born in the 1970s in New York's South Bronx, hip-hop, among other things, represented a form of art and a style of protest and resistance enacted by African Americans and more in general by artists and activists of the Black diaspora, rebelling against oppressive living conditions and disenfranchised citizenship (Lipsitz 1996, 26; Rose 1994, 21). While the term is often used to refer only to rap music, hip-hop is fundamentally a transmedia practice comprising b-boying (break-dancing), graffiti writing, DJing, and MCing (emceeing). The relatively few technical resources needed to create and produce hip-hop in the early days—compensated by extraordinary levels of ingenuity, skill and craftsmanship—made it a street art accessible to American inner-city youth prior to its explosion into the mainstream. In the 1980s, the international circulation of U.S. movies where hip-hop was a central element of the plot—such as *Wild Style* (1983) and *Beat Street* (1984)—favored its global diffusion, and hip-hop started to be imitated and performed by youths worldwide.

The history of hip-hop in Italy, like elsewhere, unfolded with decidedly local connotations but followed a similar trajectory from rags to riches that has characterized the genre in the United States. Initially embraced by restricted and, in some cases, highly politicized youth subcultures, it was quickly seen as lucrative and appropriated by famous DJs and talent scouts.

23

Its best expressions, however, remained defiant even in the face of market and public acceptance. If in the early days hip-hop was produced by (white) Italian-born youth voicing their own grievances against a state indifferent to their own plight and needs, the genre has since been adopted by new generations of Black Italians primarily of African descent and it has progressively become their platform for both social contestation and artistic expression.

In 2006 Italian-Egyptian rapper Amir Issaa released "Straniero nella mia nazione," considered the first hip-hop song to expose the predicament of second-generations, children of immigrants who are born or raised in Italy but not considered fully Italian whether they are citizens or not. A decade later, in 2015, Italian-Nigerian Tommy Kuti adapted Amir's concept proudly and playfully rapping that he was not "straniero," a foreigner in Italy, but rather "stra-nero," super-black, thus fully embracing and flaunting his blackness as distinctive of his Italian identity. In this essay we consider the work of Afro-Italian hip-hop artists and their increasing visibility on the national music scene. Quite aware of the perils and potentials of their diversity, today's rappers—who include established talents like Italian-Tunisian Ghali—capitalize on it, while also moving beyond confining categorizations. We argue that their work belongs as much to recent international music trends as to an Italian lineage that can be traced back to historic 1990s groups like Sangue Misto (Mixed Blood), all the while challenging traditional notions of Italianness and re-imagining a new nation-hood.

Unlike American hip-hop, where the issue of race has always been central, the limited academic literature on Italian hip-hop initially demonstrated little attention to questions of racial and ethnic diversity, and the problematization of the notion of *italianità* (*Italianness*) was not usually considered a relevant element of discussion.[1] We believe that the study of Italian hip-hop, from early origins to later developments, has much to contribute to the understanding of Italian identity today, one defined simultaneously, if controversially, by multiple overlapping factors, including Italy's contested North/South divisions, its recent history as a country of immigration, and its older but enduring pasts of colonialism and emigration (Fiore 2017; Gabaccia 2000; Lombardi-Diop and Romeo 2012; Parati 2005; Parati and Tamburri 2011; Verdicchio 1997).

"STRANIERO NELLA MIA NAZIONE"
PART 1: SOUTHERN ALIE-NATION

In Italy the 1990s were without a doubt the most important decade for the development and affirmation of hip-hop culture. In a few years, hip-hop moved from the radically militant arena of the *centri sociali* to a more mainstream legitimization, marked by its acceptance by national media, major record labels, and by the increasing economic revenues that came with both (Mitchell 2001). In a transitional and turbulent period typified by operation *Mani pulite* (*Clean Hands*)—the nationwide judicial investigation into Italy's political corruption that led to a massive turnover in the ruling class—and the subsequent emergence of Milanese entrepreneur Silvio Berlusconi on the political stage, hip-hop proved initially to offer oppositional youth subcultures, especially those tied to the radical Left, creative ammunition to contest the status quo. Meanwhile, the increasing arrivals of African and Middle Eastern migrants in the mid-1980s started to gradually challenge traditional notions of *italianità* that would be reflected in the music repertoire of Italian hip-hop and reggae groups, especially from the South (Scarparo & Sutherland Stevenson 2018). By the mid-1990s the presence of migrant communities was visible in many parts of Italian society. Substituting Italians in jobs that they no longer wanted to perform, migrants provoked the angry reaction of conservative right-wing movements, and were often accused of stealing jobs and undermining the white, Christian roots of European culture.[2] In the face of this shifting social and political situation, music, and hip-hop in particular, became an important site of counter-discourse.[3]

In its early iterations, Italian hip-hop, often written and performed in local dialect, was mobilized by Southern Italian crews to question the myth of national unification and homogeneity. Official historiography describes the process of nation-building as an epic tale where the country's unification represents the ending point of a process initiated during the Italian Renaissance; in this respect, Italy often stands as the birthplace of Western modern humanistic values (Forlenza and Thomassen 2016). This idealistic representation has often been questioned by Italian studies scholars and historians (Dainotto 2007; Dickie 1999; Guerri 2010; Lumley and Morris 1997; Schneider 1998), who described the process of unification as traumatic and violent, rather than romantic and harmonious. Similar critiques emerged in the arts, and in the regional music scenes, where the use of local dialects implied the willingness to affirm a separate, "countercultural" identity (Vacca 2012), proudly perpetrated by "internal others" (Verdicchio 1997, 100) who did not want to surrender to the hegemonic imposition of the Italian standard language.

In the early 1990s, Southern Italian hip-hop artists were fully invested in this battle, and rapping in dialect quickly became one of the points of major scholarly interest.[4] Not only did Southern Italian rappers manifest their alienation with respect to the rest of the Italian society: their refusal became a way to seek solidarity with those non-European migrants who were and are still being similarly mistreated by Italian institutions. Southern Italian groups like Nuovi Briganti, Almamegretta, Comitato, and 99 Posse, all strongly tied to the Italian experience of *centri sociali*,[5] noted the similarities between the process of racialization that had previously been applied to Southern Italian internal migrants, and the rhetorical strategies used to single out African migrants. In songs like "Unificazione = falsificazione" (Unification = Falsification), "Sono siciliano" (I Am Sicilian) and "Fottuto terrone" (Fucking Southerner), Sicily-based Nuovi Briganti rejected the importance of national figures like Giuseppe Garibaldi and Vittorio Emanuele II, while simultaneously demystifying the self-awarded purity of Northern Italians. Instead, Nuovi Briganti drew an alliance between Southerners and non-European migrants by stating: "Nero amico, qua la mano. Solidale con l'uomo africano, sono un fottuto terrone fiero" (My Black friend, shake my hand. In solidarity with the African man, I'm a proud, fucking *terrone*.)" Much like the n-word—which has historically been re-appropriated by African Americans to express racial and social camaraderie—the derogatory term applied to Southern Italians, *terrone,* was taken by Nuovi Briganti, who transformed it into a proud statement of Southern identity, using it in solidarity with African migrants.

The same year, a rap crew from Milan called Comitato released an album titled *Immigrato* (1993), where the band criticized the short memory of those Italians of Southern origins who had forgotten what being a migrant had meant for their ancestors, and who were now themselves insulting African migrants. In the title-track, Comitato sang:

> If we have good memory, [we can remember that] many came from Africa to our *Belpaese*. The reason is the same: dreams, hopes, and very few demands. [. . .] That son [of a Southern immigrant] has almost forgotten the wrongs he suffered as an immigrant, because in this society he has integrated himself, together with his sons. He forgot the rest: bad indifference that unleashes violence, disdain [. . .] [The African migrant today] is subject to more offenses, marginalized, left in smaller and smaller ghettoes; then people start calling him *vu cumprà, vu lavà, terroni* and Africans. [. . .] We Italians used to be mistreated, teased, disliked when abroad. What did those past years teach us? Let's think about what we used to be . . . a population of immigrants!

The importance of these examples stands both in their lyrics and in the musical style that they exhibited. While Comitato's music drew heavily from U.S. East Coast hip-hop styles, sampling beats that made them sound like an Italian answer to Public Enemy, bands like Nuovi Briganti and the Neapolitan Almamegretta mixed music traditions that originated in Southern Italy—such as the *tamurriata* and the *tarantella*—with Northern African percussions and Arabic vocal techniques (Inserra 2017, 124–126). As Dawson and Palumbo (2005, 170) emphasize, by "recuperating such relics of the pan-Mediterranean cultures of the past, [these bands] lay claim to the African roots of regional culture in Italy."

The juxtaposition of Southern subalternity with the one of non-European migrants is not limited to the cases of Nuovi Briganti and Comitato. Indeed,

Tom Behan (2007), Joseph Pugliese (2008), and Marcello Messina (2016) have explored the politics of Neapolitan band 99 Posse, concluding that while the band's early songs articulated Southern alienation, "in the wider context of global and national social problems," in more recent years "the condition of Naples and Southern Italy appears to be the main prism through which the global social problems are observed" (Messina 2016, 132), with obvious references to the so-called migrant crisis of the new millennium, but also to the emergence of Italy's second-generations. All groups discussed so far have played an important role in the history of Italian oppositional hip-hop and in linking different national and international musical, social, and political experiences, but one that more than the others proved to be influential for the emergence of a new generation of Afro-Italian hip-hop artists is Sangue Misto.

Formed in the multicultural university town of Bologna in the early 1990s, Sangue Misto's debut album *SxM* was released in 1994 under the local record label Century Vox. The significance of the album for the Italian hip-hop scene stemmed not only from how it sounded, but rather from the fact that it was released immediately after the disbandment of the *Pantera*, a nationwide student movement that conducted months-long occupations of universities across Italy in protest against the Italian government's education reform (Simeone 2010). In their lyrics, Sangue Misto communicated the idea of a youth that was feeling unwelcome in its own city, crushed by the repression that young people in Italy were facing against the *Pantera* student movement and, more widely, in the *centri sociali* scene. In songs such as "Clima di tensione" (Tense Times) Sangue Misto claimed to be in a state of constant threat where the "state" was certainly psychological and, symbolically, a reference to the oppressive nature of the Italian nation-state. The most iconic anthem in Sangue Misto's record was "Lo straniero" (The Foreigner) a song that was later sampled and re-signified multiple times by Afro-Italian rappers.[6]

In "Lo straniero" Sangue Misto's MC Neffa raps: "At school, as a kid, my classmates called me Moroccan, *terrone*. [They'd say] Shut up! Go back to where you came from!" Once again, identified as a *terrone*, and associated with North Africans, Neffa is subsequently insulted because of his Southern origin, revealing how the divisions and hierarchy between different regional populations within Italy are still very acute. In the verses that follow, Sangue Misto's distrustful attitude becomes the main reason for the lack of participation in the life of the nation. Juxtaposing his role in Italian society with the one of a generic "they," MC Neffa states:

> I'm number zero. [They have] cautious faces when the foreigner comes in. [They are] freaking out, [they are] really nervous. [I] dress with dark clothes and bang my head against the wall. I'm nobody's friend, rest assured: I'm not

into fashion, I don't go to the [soccer] stadium, I'm not in any political parties, and you can be sure that I'm not the average Italian.

MC Neffa frames his alienation with respect to the rest of Italian society, marking a clear distance from the norm and choosing instead to stay on the margins. This self-imposed exile proved prophetic not only for Southern or inner-city youth, but also for second-generations kids.[7]

MC Neffa's introspective verses serve to set the stage for bandmate MC Deda's critique of the resulting institutional reactions: namely, repression. Deda raps:

> Repression gets me down, [it] crushes me, when the cop punches me in the face. For me, the [Italian] State is just a state of menace. When I see the Tunisian selling drugs on the street corner, the black [prostitute] smacked by the pimp, I know it's all "made in Italy." So, don't ask me if I vote for Forza Italia. My position: I'm a foreigner in my own nation.

In just a few verses, MC Deda points out some of Italy's major contradictions. On the one hand, institutions limit freedom of expression by violently repressing discordant opinions (represented here by the cop who punches MC Deda in the face). On the other hand, the same institutions turn a blind eye to underground social problems such as drug dealing and prostitution; indeed, as MC Deda denounces, for the Italian state those issues are secondary, or even convenient. Since drug dealing and prostitution are crimes that tend to be associated with foreigners—because of the conditions of structural racism and unemployment silently imposed by the Italian state—the latter will gain in prestige and national authority when the foreigner turns out to be the one who is guilty. In this respect, the involvement of Italian organized crime—as MC Deda speculatively hints at when he raps that he knows "it's all *made in Italy*"—further emphasizes the ambiguities within the Italian state. In contrast with the nation's majority—who, as MC Deda correctly predicted, voted for Silvio Berlusconi's *Forza Italia* in the 1994 general election—Sangue Misto recognized itself as closer to foreigners, ultimately declaring its sense of estrangement, and becoming strangers in its own nation.

Just like any other musical genre, Italian hip-hop has been facing the same changes that affected Italian society in the last two decades. One of these major changes can be seen in the increasing number not only of immigrants, but also of people who were born from immigrant families and were raised in Italy, the so-called second-generation Italians. The inherently non-Italian origins of hip-hop made this subculture more welcoming towards inputs coming both from foreigners and second-generation Italians. The next section of the paper will discuss original forms of artistic production developed by second-generation Italians, focusing on hip-hop and on the prominent case of Italian-Egyptian artist Amir Issaa.

"STRANIERO NELLA MIA NAZIONE"
PART 2: AMIR ISSAA IN-BETWEEN GENERATIONS

Approaching the development of rap among non-white Italian artists from a chronological perspective, the first rapper to meet some public success outside of underground circles is Amir Issaa. Born in Rome in 1978 from an Egyptian father and an Italian mother, Amir has been active as a graffiti writer and rapper since the early 1990s, but he released his debut solo album, *Uomo di prestigio* (*Prestigious Man*) only in 2006. Amir's lyrics have often revolved around the topic of citizenship for second-generation Italians, but equally important as his contribution to the Italian hip-hop scene is Amir's personal history, narrated in a recently published autobiography entitled *Vivo per questo* (*This is What I Live For*, Issaa 2017).

To Amir, the mixed ethnic origins that he carries were only marginal while growing up in Rome in the early 1980s. Indeed, Amir's childhood was much more marked by the repeated incarcerations of his father, who was accused and jailed multiple times for drug dealing, a situation that forced his mother to work several jobs to maintain the family. Spending his days between the peripheral neighborhood of Torpignattara and Piazzale Flaminio—a more central square of Rome and, in the late 1980s, a hotspot for the development of alternative subcultures—Amir grew up surrounded by the kind of multicultural youth that was unknown to other, smaller and more provincial realities in Italy. Discussing the youth in Piazzale Flaminio, Amir reports:

> Some of the kids came from Francophone African countries like Gabon. [. . .] they spoke two or three languages and knew more about hip-hop culture than we did. [. . .] Skin color was not an issue in Piazzale Flaminio: what mattered was how much you knew about hip-hop, what you could do, and what your contribution was with respect to the artistic ecosystem that was developing. I had spent all my life feeling different, and suddenly I was way less different than the others. (Issaa 2017, 102)

Amir's interest in hip-hop culture was initially favored by his friendship with other kids who had hobbies such as skateboarding and graffiti writing, which were not yet popular among the Italian youth in the late 1980s. One of his best friends and mentor, Napal, was "twice an immigrant," an Italian who had emigrated with his parents first to Germany and then Australia, where he was considered a "*wog*," a sort of "terrone," only to experience the same sense of foreignness and non-belonging upon his return to Rome (Issaa 2017, 60).

Interestingly enough, Amir's alias in the world of graffiti writing was "Er Cina" (*The Chinese*), a nickname given to him by his friends because of his almond-shaped eyes (Issaa 2017, 55). This is particularly significant because it signals that, even within the more liberal and welcoming environment of the emerging Roman graffiti and hip-hop scene, Amir's physical appearance stood as a sign of racial difference that would later become central in his career as a rapper. In several songs, Amir discusses the idea of feeling alien-ated in Italian society. For example, Amir's "Straniero nella mia nazione" (2006) plays with the legacy of Sangue Misto's "Lo straniero," reinterpreting its meaning in light of the condition of second-generation Italians. As a spokesperson for those second- and third- generation kids who see their legal status as Italian citizens indefinitely postponed or denied, Amir boasts his father's immigrant origin, rapping that he is "proud of my name and my mixed blood." In line with hip-hop's traditional braggadocio, he foresees himself being elected as the mayor of Rome, residing at the Campidoglio, because "I want to make money like all the presidents."

In 2014, Amir further reprised Sangue Misto's denunciation, partially shifting its significance. No longer just a generic sense of alienation ex-pressed by the (white) Italian youth, the sense of exclusion was now directed at migrants and second-generation Italians, denouncing the institutional re-strictions imposed by the Italian law on citizenship based on *jus sanguinis*, right of blood and lineage.[8] The title-track for Amir's 2014 mixtape *Ius Music* sparked controversy among Italy's right-wing parties because the lyr-ics were considered aggressive and anti-patriotic (Issaa 2017, 207; Janeczek 2014). In the song, Amir raps:

> My brothers are proud Africans, Maghrebians, Chinese, and Filipinos who have their feet here, and their blood from other countries. [. . .] Mine is not a race: mine is a tribe. Those who are always at gunpoint: that is my crew. My people are tired of being accused, of being considered dangerous. [. . .] And there's no excuse when ignorance is vast, if being Italian is only on paper, if you feel out of place in this situation, and you become a foreigner in your own nation.

The track describes the frustration of second-generation Italians—and, in particular, the youngest ones—who are tired of waiting for legislative actions from the Italian institutions and are not considered fully Italians even when they have the correct papers. Later in the song, Amir brings his frustration one step forward, refusing the definition of hyphenated Italian and denounc-ing the insensibility of Italian politics vis-à-vis such an urgent issue. In the video clip, Amir is shown in the context of his former school, acting in the role of a professor who, after having walked past pictures of Martin Luther

King, Gandhi, Malcolm X, and Rosa Parks, proceeds to lecture before a class of multiracial students. The clip also features Italian-Moroccan member of parliament Khalid Chouki acting in the role of the school principal. Chouki had been in charge of following second-generations demands on behalf of the Italian Partito Democratico (PD) and his cameo in *Ius Music*, along with Amir's forceful rap, provoked quite a few negative reactions on social media, reversing the original message with a barrage of accusations of fear mongering and trafficking in anti-Italian hate, which Helena Janeczek aptly labelled "squadrismo 2.0," a fascist squad tactic for the digital era (Issaa 2017, 207).

Sobering lessons like this have prompted Amir to shift his activism in a different direction, not necessarily shying away from taking strong stands against racism, especially when perpetrated by official institutions, such as the decision to deny public school meals to children of immigrants by the League-led municipality of Lodi,[9] but more geared toward a form of "conscientization" through song writing workshops in schools and colleges in Italy and around the world, including the USA, teaching rap lyrics in Italian to new generations of global citizens.[10] In the wake of the killing of George Floyd in police custody in Minneapolis and the subsequent Black Lives Matter protests across the U.S. and the world during the summer of 2020, Amir penned the lyrics for "Non respiro" (I Can't Breathe). The song was created in collaboration with Afro-Italian artists David Blank and Davide Shorty and was accompanied by a sobering video in which diverse subjects look directly into the camera in close-up shots while being progressively choked by a black cloth wrapped around their faces.[11]

FROM "STRANIERO" TO "STRA-NERO": AFRO-ITALIAN HIP-HOP IS THE NEW BLACK

While Amir belongs to an "in-between" generation of rappers and his experience bridges old school Italian rap with a more contemporary and contaminated one, younger second- and third- generation artists growing up in Italy in the new millennium have taken different approaches. An interesting case came from a now-defunct independent record label called *Mancamelanina Records*. The name of the record label translates to *Lack-of-Melanin Records*, and its members' sarcastic motto is "Non sono straniero, sono solo stra-nero!" (I'm not a foreigner, I'm just extra-black!) Founded in 2015 in the city of Brescia, this label was the first example of an all-Afro-Italian project, and its mission, according to its website, was to "portare un po'" di "Melanina lì dove manca."[12] The artists of this label tended to mix different music genres, going from hip-hop and rap to reggae and dancehall, with the idea of crafting a sound that was modern and yet brought together the various influences of African and Caribbean music.

The most successful artist within the label was an Italian-Nigerian rapper called Tommy Kuti (né Tolulope Olabode Kuti). Born in Nigeria in 1989, Tommy Kuti moved to Italy at the age of two, growing up in northern Italy before taking part in a series of educational exchange programs that led him to study in the United States and in England, where he obtained a degree in Communication Science. Upon his return to Italy, Kuti—who was known at the time as Mista Tolu—released a few songs and video clips via YouTube where he raps in Italian. In "Welcome to Italy," Tommy Kuti starts the song stating: "I talk about the discomfort that I witness in every city, I feel like I'm the son of Italy, even though I wasn't born here." In a more sarcastic and upbeat track called "Faccio rap" (I Do Rap), he samples the intro sequence from the 1967 Walt Disney animated movie *The Jungle Book*. Dressed up as a baby in a cradle that has "Made in Italy" written on it, in the video clip Kuti compares the silence of the jungle being broken by the unfamiliar sound of Mowgli in the Disney movie to the impact he is about to have on the Italian music scene. Over the course of the song, Kuti both shows his pride for being black—claiming that he knows Italians would love to have "a darker skin tone"—and then he goes back to affirm that Black Italians exist, rapping in English that he is a "n**** made in Italy."

In 2017, Tommy Kuti released a new video on YouTube. The song was simply titled "#AFROITALIANO," and it was regarded as the contemporary musical manifesto for Afro-Italians and, in part, for second-generation Italians. In the lyrics of the song, Tommy Kuti references some of the clichés identifying the Italian population; he discusses how he cheers every time Black Italian-Ghanaian soccer player Mario Balotelli scores a goal, and states that he cannot eat his pasta without sprinkling some Italian Parmesan cheese on it. Moreover, he declares his love for Italy by claiming that he celebrates Italy's National Day (on June 2), sending pictures to his Nigerian relatives surrounded by Italian flags while eating pizza. The black-and-white video clip for the song features not just Kuti, but also scenes taken from multiracial classrooms in Italian schools; here we see once again how the hope for integration—for lack of a better term—and recognition of the complex identities embodied by Afro-Italians starts from a very young age, within the walls of Italy's public schools. In the ending scenes of the video clip, Kuti is shown lying on a sofa, in what appears as a typical psychotherapy session. The psychologist—interpreted by Italy's most popular contemporary rapper, Fabri Fibra—asks Tommy Kuti one of the most common questions: "Do you feel you are more African or Italian?" Kuti avoids what seems like an absolute dichotomy answering: "I'm Afro-Italian, because I'm sick and tired of having others deciding what I am and what I am not. I'm too African to be just Italian, and too Italian to be just African."[13] Kuti has recently published a new autobiography entitled *Ci rido sopra* (*I Laugh About It*, 2019) in which he deploys the same decisive ironic tone to define his experience as an Afro-Italian in the face of the racist injuries inflicted on his generation by the likes of Matteo Salvini, leader of the xenophobic League party, and his followers.

Among the most well-known Afro-Italian rappers today is undoubtedly Ghali, born in Milan in 1993 of Tunisian parents. Raised primarily by his mother, his story resonates, at least biographically, with Amir's. In "Ninna Nanna" (Lullaby)—the first of his songs to reach stratospheric views on YouTube, currently more than 110 million, and the track opening his first album, simply entitled *Album*, as in a collection of carefully curated photographic snapshots—he calls himself "son of a janitor with a father in jail." If absolutely mind-boggling, Ghali's extraordinary success in the past few years is also completely homegrown. After a disappointing run-in with the Italian institutional music industry when he was part of a group called Troupe d'Elite, Ghali decided to pursue a solo career, self-producing his work and attending to his music business with entrepreneurial flair surrounded only by trusted close friends, like the producer Charlie Charles (né Paolo Monachetti) and the writer Antonio Dikele DiStefano. Distinguished by genuine, heartfelt, often autobiographical lyrics, chiseled with understated and perhaps deceivingly easy skill, mixing Italian with Arabic, French, and the language of Tunisian immigrants to create a singular patois, Ghali's commercial feat is also the product of a savvy use of social media (YouTube, Instagram, Facebook, Twitter, Spotify, TikTok), a series of highly original, polished and professionally executed music videos, and a maniacal attention to fashion, style, and aesthetics.

Practicing a subgenre of hip-hop defined as trap—a sort of gangsta rap originated in Atlanta in the early 2000s—Ghali's musical style encompasses pop and world music influences beyond the confines of a single category. *Album*, whose cover was created by the internationally renowned Italian street artist Ozmo, is proudly and unapologetically dedicated, like many of his lyrics and singles' covers, to his mother, with such tenderness and vulnerability that reveal the extent of the respect and gratitude for the sacrifices she made: "I thank my mother, the person who gives me strength in the most fragile moments and light in the dark ones [. . .] Growing up she made sure that I wouldn't miss what I did not have. She taught me to love and respect women who are my greatest source of inspiration." It is hard to imagine a twenty-something youth, let alone a rapper, so secure in his identity and masculinity to take such emotional risks. This is not to say that he cannot also be playfully manipulating hip-hop's stereotypes and self-referentiality, or act his age, with frequent allusions to smoking pot and hanging out with his "frate" (bros).

In "Ninna Nanna" Ghali raps, "I came out of dirt/from a stable to a star/ I'll buy a villa for my mom/ and then I will think of Africa." In "Ricchi dentro" (Rich Inside), the second track in his album, he sings, "Mother, seriously, did you expect all of this?/ We were already rich inside/ But, God, it feels great to say to you: I told you so!" Questions of racism, intolerance, and immigration are not necessarily dealt head-on in *Album*, where Ghali's flows speak of his day-to-day snippets of life and already includes a hybridized experience made of Arabic and Italian, Western and Islamic cultures mixing together, as in "Habibi" ("I love you" in Arabic) and "Pizza Kebab," where he drops the lines "the last ones will be the first [. . .]/ Black or white race/ what's a VISA in the middle of the galaxy?" Perhaps "Ora d'aria" (Outdoor Time) gets closer to including some militant lines, when Ghali replies to a seemingly customary question directed his way: "Are you asking me if I am Italian or Muslim? [. . .] Either we are terrorists or parasites."

While *Album* is personal and introspective, leaving politics aside for the most part, other singles like "Cara Italia," "Wily Wily," and "Dende," are far more overt and militant. In "Cara Italia" (Dear Italy), originally written for a Vodafone commercial, and which became "the most watched music video of all time on the nation's YouTube" (Mackay 2018), he asks, "what kind of politics is this/what is the difference between left and right?/ Ministers change, but not what they feed us." The most effective line is the tongue-in-cheek jingle, "oh eh oh, when they tell me to go home/ oh eh oh I answer: I am already here/ oh eh oh I love you dear Italy/ oh eh oh, you are my other half."

It was Ghali himself to provide the exegesis of these lyrics for his fans in a post on Instagram, accompanied by a picture of himself smiling with his face covered by two hands, one white and one black, revealing all his love and respect for his country, but also expecting Italy to rise to the occasion on the global stage and its domestic affairs.[14] Mixing different languages and idiomatic expressions, "Wily, Wily," an exclamation of disapproval in Tunisian Arabic, is more forceful in contesting facile stereotypes against "others"[15] ("Io sono un negro terrorista/culo bianco, ladro bangla, muso giallo") perpetrated by the media and the institutions with "the Italian people who let themselves be swindled." Accompanied by an evocative video filmed by director Martina Pastori in Jordan, Ghali's words represent a sort of "j'accuse": "You think that Islàm equals Isis." In "Dende," titled after a manga and anime character from the animated series *Dragon Ball*, he is at its most explicit when he provocatively challenges a rival by arguing: "You will beat me the day that you'll see Salvini [the leader of the xenophobic League] at my concerts."

In a famous Facebook post a month preceding his first interview with the "trapper" for *La Repubblica* in the summer of 2017, writer Roberto Saviano provocatively called Ghali "one of the major poets in the Italian language, a rap poet" because "in his verses there is a rare poetic style, the echo of words' poetic and ritualistic sacrality."[16] It is a compliment to Ghali's skillful use of the Italian language and his contamination with other jargons, but it is also a reminder that, "Italy is changing and its rappers are telling its new reality in far deeper and complex ways than its politicians, journalists, commentators" (Saviano 2017a). In *La Repubblica*'s article, Saviano and Antonio Dikele DiStefano agree that without being didactic and pedantic, Ghali's poetic rap will tell more about Islam to Italian youth and kids who are growing up with his music than any other media and outlet (2017). In his work Ghali's intention remains subtle, ludic, spirited, and nuanced. In interviews he is reluctant to be pigeonholed in a political category, what he has to say, he says it in his flows, for him "music is a weapon" (Alovisi 2017, 28) and should be used wisely, because it can change lives, his and those of his listeners.

NEW KIDS IN THE HOOD

There is no question that the music and transmedia production of Afro-Italian rappers and trappers in Italy today are trendy and influential and are having an impact as much in the way in which they are created and delivered outside the confines of the established channels and control of the cultural industry as in the way they are received and re-circulated by youth and kids as young as tweens (Contrino 2017). The contested victory of rapper Mahmood at the 2019 Sanremo Music Festival—the country's most popular song contest and the bastion of Italian musical tradition—may be considered the industry caving in to hip-hop, but it also serves to reaffirm larger postcolonial transformations already in motion in Italian society (Ardizzoni 2020). And yet, the rap and trap music of this new generation is significant on its own merits and not simply on account of the multiracial and multicultural Italian identities that these artists embody within the nationhood.

The examples provided by Tommy Kuti, Ghali, and others, including a small but steady cohort of female rappers,[17] are critical because they have proven capable of circumnavigating "the barriers often erected by Italian mainstream media" (Fusaro 2017). Instead, they take advantage of the possibilities created by social media to develop a new type of DIY attitude. Unlike the ultimately self-segregating DIY style embraced in the 1990s by Southern posses (Branzaglia, Pacoda, & Solaro 1992), second-generation Italian rappers have been "quick to capitalize" on their own diversity and to use it as a new tool of promotion via the help of the Internet (Fusaro 2017). The self-managed, entrepreneurial nature of these artists is definitely a consequence of the extraordinary economic success met by hip-hop culture in the past four decades both in the United States and abroad. While in some cases hip-hop has become "the lingua franca for popular and political youth culture around the world" (Morgan and Bennett 2011, 179), its assimilation by the entertainment industry has also been crucial for hip-hop's own evolution both in terms of sound and style. Because of its capacity to connect with marginalized ethnic minorities across the official borders of the nation-state, hip-hop has developed a global nation-hood where artists and audiences easily communicate regardless of geographical and institutional limitations.

While Afro-Italian artists' inspirations and references come from a larger transnational context encompassing a global "hood" that has seen the prolife-ration, imitation, reproduction, appropriation, and remixing of Afrocentric and "black-identified" cultures (Osumare 2007, 62). Nonetheless, it is impor-tant to understand their contributions also within a historical national arc. Their relation to previous rap music in Italy, which represented different sets of experimentations, creativities, and rebellions (Ivic 2010), may not always be explicit, but the symbolic significance of such hip-hop archival genealogy is helpful in order to identify commonalities and departures and trace the changes and continuities that have occurred within Italian society and its various "others." Indeed, popular music and hip-hop in particular can provide us with more and different insights about Italy's transformations since the 1980s than other genres and media which have received more attention, like literature and cinema, and constitute an important resource.

Beyond the confines of the nation-hood strictly defined by territorial boundaries, it is useful to also situate second-generation Italian hip-hop, like its combative 1990s predecessor, in a diasporic framework that accounts for both previous transmigrations, material and cultural, and current cross-polli-nations. In this respect, it is notable that one of the most important specialists of early Italian hip-hop vernaculars has been Italian-American scholar Joseph Sciorra, whose transcultural work in connecting, transmitting, and preserving this genre through international gatherings and personal archives is invalu-able and recognized among fans and artists across continents (Sciorra 2002, 2011).[18] Italian hip-hop, old and new, has drawn substantially from global black hip-hop, but the other way around is also true. Italian hip-hop artists collaborate with their peers around the world and command their own influ-ence. Atlanta-based trap music claimed to be influencing Afro-Italians and other Italian trappers include artists like Gucci Mane and Donald Glover Jr.'s Childish Gambino, whose names clearly allude to the allure of Italian gang-ster luxury lifetyle. The cross-fertilization between Italian and African Americans is a well-documented love affair (Gennari 1996, 2017; Cinotto 2014), which continues and amplifies in the diaspora as much as on Italian soil. Ghali's success in Tunisia and elsewhere in Europe and the Middle East (Alovisi 2017, 29; Al Habash 2017) is indicative of the complex cultural circuits of knowledge production and dissemination. These works reach where politics cannot, and journalistic as well as scholarly interest for these artists has been gradually emerging (Ardizzoni 2020; Dolesinski 2021; Giuli-ani 2019, 224–240). The savvy use of digital and social media has generated networks, influences, and conversations among artists and their fans that are not limited by the vagaries and restrictions of politics or the traditional music industry, but that transcend them both.[19] The example of second-generation Afro-Italian rappers is one of artistic entrepreneurship and initiative beyond the narrow boundaries of institutional music industry and political structures. They are interested in building their own transborder contacts and collaborations to bring back home. Like Ghali in "Cara Italia," who is "happy to make music for kids,"[20] they are proud to reach younger audiences. Future generations have already intuited their value. Perhaps these kids will save the world next or save us from ourselves.

NOTES

1. Most of the early academic studies on Italian hip-hop preferred instead to focus on the phenomenon of the *posses* and its development within the realm of the *centri sociali*. See Branzaglia, Pacoda, & Solaro 1992; Canevacci et al. 1993; Mitchell 1995; Mitchell 2001; Plastino 1996; Wright 2000.

2. For a sharp criticism of this attitude in favor of an inclusive approach to account for "European others" see El-Tayeb 2011.

3. See Mitchell (1995; 2001) and Pacoda (1996; 2000).

4. See, for instance, Androutsopoulos and Scholz (2003), Mitchell (2000), and Scholz (2005 and 2006).

5. Following Santoro and Solaroli's definition, *centri sociali* can be described as an especially European reality consisting of: "abandoned urban sites such as government buildings [. . .] that [once squatted] were consequently converted into community-based laboratories of cultural innovation and artistic creativity, offering concerts, films, dance courses and a variety of informational services such as discussion circles on political antagonism or drug use and language classes for immigrants" (2007, 482).

6. "Straniero" in Italian could be translated either as "stranger" or "foreigner," depending on the meaning intended by users, and can indicate someone feeling alienated from their own country, or someone who comes from another country. We have chosen to retain Santoro and Solaroli's translation of Sangue Misto's song "Lo straniero" as "foreigner" (2007, 478).

7. The importance of Sangue Misto's influence on second-generations is also affirmed by Afro-Italian writer Antonio Dikele DiStefano who cites "Lo straniero" and rap music in general as fundamental during difficult periods in his childhood and adolescence. See https://youtu.be/Yo3hhv47u18.

8. For a discussion of second-generation children of immigrants in Italy, their legal predicament and cultural activism, see Clò 2012 and Thomassen 2010.

9. See Polchi 2018.

10. In recent years Amir has travelled frequently to colleges in the United States. Though the East Coast remains closer, last year he also travelled to Ohio, Colorado, and California.

11. The video is available at https://youtu.be/GB4MngjiiBY. On the making of the song and the biases of the Italian music industry regarding race see Amir Issaa's July 2020 interview in *Griot* (Affricot 2020).

12. "Bring some melanin where it is lacking." While the website is not accessible anymore, the description of the project can still be found on their Facebook page: https://www.facebook.com/mancamelanina/

13. The absurdity of such questions, meant to force bicultural children into making an impossible choice has been explored in literature as well. In her famous short story "Salsicce" (Sausages), Somali-Italian writer Igiaba Scego unmasks a similar nonsensical conundrum: "Quella domanda odiosa sulla mia identità del cazzo! Più somala? Più italiana? Forse ¾ somala e ¼ italiana? O forse è vero tutto il contrario? Non so rispondere! Non mi sono mai 'frazionata' prima d'ora." (That horrible question about my fucking identity! Am I more Somali? Am I

more Italian? Maybe ¾ Somali and ¼ Italian? Or maybe the opposite is true? I can't answer! I have never "fractioned" myself before.) (2005, 28). See Clò 2012, 278–279.

14. On January 24, 2018 Ghali wrote on Instagram: "Cara Italia,/ Ti dedico questa canzone che ho ideato tornando dal mio primo viaggio in America./ Non hai nulla da invidiare a questi grandi Paesi che vediamo nei film./ Spero però che tu non ti offenda per aver risaltato i tuoi difetti, sappiamo tutti che sei bellissima ma questo serve a migliorarsi. / Cara Italia,/ Ho scritto 'sei la mia dolce metà' perché è davvero così./ Tu mi hai visto nascere, mi hai cresciuto e ora che in ogni tuo angolo gridano il mio nome come posso voltarti le spalle?/ Tu che sei la dimora dei miei desideri, il letto dei miei sogni./ Infinite le giornate di dolore tra le tue mura e infinite le notti di rabbia ma come potrei voltarti le spalle senza rimpianto?/ Cara Italia,/ Ti chiedo solo tre cose: /NON PARLARMI più di confini e non ti parlerò più con diffidenza. /NON SENTIR-TI inferiore e io mi sentirò all'altezza. /NON VEDERMI come un nemico e io ti vedrò come una sorella, un'amica, una mamma. /Spero che tu possa prendere in considerazione le mie parole. /Io T.V.B Cara Italia." (Dear Italy,/ I dedicate to you this song, which I created as I was coming back from my first trip to America. /You are every bit as good as these great countries we see in movies. / I hope you won't be offended because I highlighted your flaws, we all know you're beautiful but this helps you become better./ Dear Italy,/ I wrote:— you are my better half because it is true. / You saw me being born, you raised me and now that from every corner people scream my name, how can I turn my back to you?/ You, the abode of my desires, the bed of my dreams./ Infinite painful days within your walls and infinite angry nights, but how could I turn my back without regretting it?/ Dear Italy,/ I ask of you only three things: /NEVER TALK TO ME again of borders and I will no longer speak with skepticism./DON'T FEEL inferior and I will measure up./ DON'T LOOK AT ME as an enemy and I will look at you as a sister, a friend, a mom./ I hope you will take my words into consideration. /I love you, Dear Italy). We have chosen to use Michela Ardizzoni's translation from her article "On Rhythms and Rhymes" (2020, 6). All other translations are our own, unless noted. For Ghali's post, see Schettino 2018.

15. "Io sono un negro terrorista/culo bianco, ladro bangla, muso giallo" (I am a black terrorist/ white ass, Bangladeshi thief, yellow face).

16. See Roberto Saviano's May 4, 2017 Facebook post: https://www.facebook.com/ 17858286863/posts/10154596887936864/. Saviano's subsequent article in La Repubblica was published on June 4, 2017 as "Ghali, il ragazzo della via rap che canta l'Islam e i migranti."

17. Second-generation female hip-hop artists include Karima 2G, Chadia Rodriguez, Wii Houbabi, Doris, Lina Simons, and others. This is a topic that would require a full-length analysis, which is still lacking. Indeed, the contribution of women to Italian hip-hop has been historically disregarded. For a discussion of the work of Karima 2G in a feminist Afrofuturism perspective see Fabbri 2020.

18. See Amir Issaa's personal tribute to Joseph Sciorra on the rapper's Instagram: https:// www.instagram.com/p/Bkc4FSpgzcb/. Dr. Joseph Sciorra's website *italianrap.com*, was for years the reference point of Italian hip-hop fans worldwide. This site and other parts of his personal archive, including all issues of the historic 1990s Italian underground hip-hop maga-zine *Aelle/AL*, are now housed in the San Diego State University's Special Collections.

19. For an insider's critique of the Italian music industry and its obsolete system see Zukar 2017.

20. See also Amir Issaa's post in support of immigrant children in public schools: https:// www.instagram.com/p/Bo3VOkuC8PD/.

REFERENCES

Affricot, Johanne. 2020. "Non respiro: Amir Issaa su Floyd, errori degli afroitaliani, mancanza di genere, indifferenza dell'industria." *Griot*, 2 July. http://griotmag.com/it/people-musica-amir-issaa-non-respiro-intervista-mamma-non-respiro-floyd-david-blank-davide-shorty-afroitaliani-rap/

Androutsopoulos, Jannis and Scholz, Arno. 2003. "Spaghetti Funk: Appropriations of Hip-Hop Culture and Rap Music in Europe." *Popular Music and Society* 26.4, 463–479.

Al Habash, Nur. 2017. "Ghali: Arrivederci Habibi Ciao." 19 June, https://www.rockit.it/ghali-intervista-album/

Alovisi, Elia. 2017. "Ghali: Per un rap inclusivo e contemporaneo." *Rumore* 305, June, 26–29.

Ardizzoni, Michela. 2020. "On Rhythms and Rhymes: Poetics of Identity in Postcolonial Italy." *Communication, Culture & Critique* 13.1, 1-16.

Behan, Tom. 2007. "Putting Spanners in the Works: the Politics of the 99 Posse." *Popular Music*, 26.3, 497–504.

Branzaglia, Carlo, Pacoda, Pierfrancesco, and Solaro, Alba. 1992. *Posse italiane: centri sociali, underground musicale e cultura giovanile degli anni '90 in Italia*. Firenze: Tosca.

Canevacci, Massimo, Alessandra Castellani, Andrea Colombo, Marco Grispigni, Massimo Ilardi, and Felice Liberi, eds. 1993. *Ragazzi senza tempo: immagini, musica, conflitti delle culture giovanili*. Genova: Costa & Nolan.

Cinotto, Simone. 2014. "Italian Doo-Wop: Sense of Place, Politics of Style, and Racial Crossovers, in Postwar New York City." In *Making Italian America: Consumer Culture and the Production of Ethnic Identities*, ed. Simone Cinotto, 163–177. New York: Fordham University Press.

Clò, Clarissa. 2012. "Hip Pop Italian Style: The Postcolonial Imagination of Second-Generation Authors in Italy." In *Postcolonial Italy: Challenging National Homogeneity*, ed. Cristina Lombardi-Diop and Caterina Romeo, 275–291. New York: Palgrave.

Comitato. 1993a. *Immigrato*. Black Out.

———. 1993b. "Immigrato." *Immigrato*. Black Out.

Contrino, Luca. 2017. "The 'New Italians' Are Finding Their Voice at a Tense Moment in the Debate on Italian Identity." *Europa United*, 28 October, https://europaunited.eu/2017/10/28/the-new-italians-are-finding-their-voice-at-a-tense-moment-in-the-debate-on-italian-identity/

Dainotto, Roberto. 2007. *Europe (in Theory)*. Durham: Duke University Press.

Dawson, Ashley, and Palumbo, Patrizia. 2005. "Hannibal's Children: Immigration and Antiracist Youth Subcultures in Contemporary Italy." *Cultural Critique* 59.1, 165–186.

Dickie, John. 1999. *Darkest Italy: the Nation and Stereotypes of the Mezzogiorno, 1860–1900*. New York: Palgrave Macmillan.

Dolasinski, Lisa. "'In Between' Ethnic Heritage and Italian Identity: The Global Hip-Hop of Mahmood and Ghali." *The Italianist*, forthcoming.

El-Tayeb, Fatima. 2011. *European Others: Queering Ethnicity in Postnational Europe*. Minneapolis: University of Minnesota Press.

Fabbri, Giulia. 2020. "L'afrofuturismo tra Stati Uniti e Italia: dalla memoria storica ai viaggi intergalattici per re-immaginare futuri postumani." *California Italian Studies*, 10.2: 1-16. https://escholarship.org/uc/item/4551s41r

Fiore, Teresa. 2017. *Pre-Occupied Spaces: Re-Mapping Italy's Transnational Migrations and Colonial Legacies*. New York: Fordham University Press.

Forlenza, Rosario, and Thomassen, Bjørn. 2016. *Italian Modernities: Competing Narratives of Nationhood*. New York: Palgrave Macmillan.

Fusaro, Francesco. 2017. "Twisting Cultural Codes: Trap in Italy." *Norient: Network for Local and Global Sounds and Media Culture*, 4 July, https://norient.com/stories/italian-trap/

Gabaccia, Donna. 2000. *Italy's Many Diasporas*. Seattle: University of Washington Press.

Gennari, John. 1996. "Passing for Italian." *Transition* 72, 36–48.

———. 2017. *Flavor and Soul: Italian America at Its African American Edge*. Chicago: University of Chicago Press.

Ghali. 2017a. *Album*. Sto Records.

———. 2017b. "Dende." *Lunga vita a Sto*. Sto Records.

———. 2017c. "Ninna nanna." *Album*. Sto Records.

———. 2017d. "Ora d'aria." *Album*. Sto Records.

———. 2017e. "Pizza Kebab." *Album*. Sto Records.

———. 2017f. "Ricchi dentro." *Album*. Sto Records.

———. 2017g. "Wily Wily." *Lunga vita a Sto*. Sto Records.

———. 2018. "Cara Italia." Sto Records.

Giuliani, Gaia. 2019. *Race, Nation and Gender in Modern Italy: Intersectional Representations in Visual Culture*. Basingstoke, Hampshire: Palgrave Macmillan UK.

Guerri, Giordano Bruno. 2010. *Il sangue del Sud: antistoria del Risorgimento e del brigantaggio*. Milano: Mondadori.

Inserra, Incoronata. 2017. *Global Tarantella: Reinventing Southern Italian Folk Music and Dances*. Urbana: University of Illinois Press.

Issaa, Amir. 2006. *Uomo di prestigio*. Emi/Virgin.

———. 2014. "Ius Music." *Ius Music*.

———. 2017. *Vivo per questo*. Milano: Chiarelettere.

Ivic, Damir. 2010. *Storia ragionata dell'hip hop italiano*. Roma: Arcana.

Janeczek, Helena. 2014. "Ius Music." *Nazione Indiana* July 4 https://www.nazioneindiana.com/2014/07/04/ius-music/

Kuti, Tommy. 2018. "#AFROITALIANO." Italiano vero. Universal.

———. 2019. *Ci rido sopra: Crescere con la pelle nera nell'Italia di Salvini*. Milano: Rizzoli.

Lipsitz, George. 1996. *Dangerous Crossroads: Popular Music, Postmodernism, and the Poetics of Place*. London: Verso.

Lombardi-Diop, Cristina, and Romeo, Caterina, eds. 2012. *Postcolonial Italy: Challenging National Homogeneity*. New York: Palgrave.

Lumley, Robert, and Morris, Jonathan, eds. 1997. *The New History of the Italian South: the Mezzogiorno revisited*. Exeter: University of Exeter Press.

Mackay, Jamie. 2018. "Countering Italy's Far-Right Nationalism With Pop Music." *Frieze* 31 August. https://frieze.com/article/countering-italys-far-right-nationalism-pop-music

Messina, Marcello. 2016. "*Cattivi guagliuni*: The Identity Politics of 99 Posse." In *Keep it Simple, Make it Fast! An Approach to Underground Music Scenes*, eds. Paula Guerra, Tânia Moreira, 131–136. Porto, Portugal.

Mista Tolu. 2014. "Welcome to Italy." Single.

———. 2015. "Faccio rap." Single.

Mitchell, Tony. 1995. Questions of Style: Notes on Italian Hip-Hop. *Popular Music 14*, 333–348.

———. 2000. "Doin' Damage in My Native Language: The Use of 'Resistance Vernaculars' in Hip Hop in France, Italy, and Aotearoa/New Zealand." *Popular Music and Society* 24.3, 41–54.

———. 2001. "Fightin' da Faida: The Italian Posses and Hip-Hop in Italy." In *Global noise: rap and hip-hop outside the USA*, ed. Tony Mitchell, 194–221. Middletown, CT: Wesleyan University Press.

Morgan, Marcyliena, and Bennett, Dionne. 2011. "Hip-Hop & the Global Imprint of a Black Cultural Form." *Daedalus* 140.2, 176–196.

Nuovi, Briganti. 1993a. *Fottuto terrone*. Cyclope / Polydor.

———. 1993b. "Fottuto terrone." *Fottuto terrone*. Cyclope / Polydor.

Osumare, Halifu. 2007. *The Africanist Aesthetic in Global Hip-Hop: Power Moves*. New York: Palgrave Macmillan.

Pacoda, Pierfrancesco. 1996. *Potere alla parola: antologia del rap italiano*. Milan: Feltrinelli.

———. 2000. *Hip hop italiano: suoni, parole e scenari del posse power*. Torino: Einaudi.

Parati, Graziella. 2005. *Migration Italy: The Art of Talking Back in a Destination Country*. Toronto: University of Toronto Press.

——— and Tamburri, Anthony J., eds. 2011. *The Cultures of Italian Migration: Diverse Trajectories and Discrete Perspectives*. Madison: Fairleigh Dickinson Press.

Plastino, Goffredo. 1996. *Mappa delle voci: rap, raggamuffin e tradizione in Italia*. Roma: Meltemi.

Polchi, Vladimiro. 2018. "Lodi, 'Dite a quei bambini che non sono soli e un'altra Italia esiste.'" *La Repubblica* 14 October. https://www.repubblica.it/solidarieta/immigrazione/2018/10/14/news/lodi_dite_a_quei_bambini_che_non_sono_soli_e_che_un_al   tra_italia_esiste_-208941794/?refresh_ce

Pugliese, Joseph. 2008. "Whiteness and the Blackening of Italy: La guerra cafona, Extracomunitari and Provisional Street Justice." *PORTAL Journal of Multidisciplinary International Studies 5*.2, 1–35.

Rose, Tricia. 1994. *Black Noise: Rap Music and Black Culture in Contemporary America.* Hanover, NH: Wesleyan University Press.

Sangue Misto. 1994a. SxM. Century Vox.

———. 1994b. "Lo straniero." SxM. Century Vox.

Santoro, Marco, and Solaroli, Marco. 2007. "Authors and Rappers: Italian Hip Hop and the Shifting Boundaries of Canzone d'Autore." *Popular Music* 26.3, 463–488.

Saviano, Roberto. 2017. "Ghali: Vi presento il ragazzo della via rap." *La Repubblica* (Robinson insert) 4 June 4–6. (Updated as "Ghali: il ragazzo della via rap che canta l'Islam e i migranti") https://www.repubblica.it/spettacoli/musica/2017/06/04/news/ghali_il_ragazzo_della_via_rap_che_canta_l_islam_l_isis_e_i_migranti-167196276/

———. 2017a. May 4 Facebook Post, https://www.facebook.com/17858286863/posts/10154596887936864/

———. 2017b. "Ghali, il ragazzo della via rap che canta l'Islam e i migranti." *La Repubblica,* June 4, https://www.repubblica.it/spettacoli/musica/2017/06/04/news/ghali_il_ragazzo_della_via_rap_che_canta_l_islam_l_isis_e_i_migranti-167196276/

Scarparo, Susanna, and Sutherland Stevenson, Mathias. 2018. *Reggae and Hip-Hop in Southern Italy: Politics, Languages, and Multiple Marginalities.* New York: Palgrave Macmillan.

Scego, Igiaba. 2005. "Salsicce." In *Pecore nere*, ed. Flavia Capitani and Emanuele Coen, 23–36. Bari: Laterza.

Schettino, Gabriele. 2018. "Cara Italia di Ghali, esce oggi il video ufficiale." January 27, *The Giornale*, https://www.thegiornale.it/2018/01/27/ghali-cara-italia-lattesa-e-finita/

Scholz, Arno. 2005. *Subcultura e lingua giovanile in Italia: hip-hop e dintorni.* Roma: Aracne.

———. 2006. "L'aspetto quantitativo dell'impiego del dialetto nel rap italoromanzo fra il 1992 e il 2004." In *Giovani, lingue e dialetti*, ed. Gianna Marcato, 447–453. Padova: Unipress.

Schneider, Jane, ed. 1998. *Italy's 'Southern question': Orientalism in One Country.* Oxford: Berg.

Sciorra, Joseph. 2002. "Hip Hop from Italy and the Diaspora: A Report from the 41st Parallel." *Altreitalie 24*, 86–104.

———. 2011. "The Mediascape of Hip Wop: Alterity and Authenticity in Italian-American Rap." In *Global media, culture, and identity: theory, cases, and approaches*, eds. Rohit Chopra, Radhika Gajjala, 33–51. New York, NY: Routledge.

Simeone, Nando. 2010. *Gli studenti della Pantera: storia di un movimento rimosso.* Roma: Alegre.

Thomassen, Bjørn. 2010. "'Second Generation Immigrants' or 'Italians with Immigrant Parents'? Italian and European Perspectives on Immigrants and their Children." *Bulletin of Italian Politics* 2.1, 21–44.

Vacca, Giovanni. 2012. "Music and Countercultures in Italy: the Neapolitan Scene." *Volume!* 9.1, 67–83.

Verdicchio, Pasquale. 1997. *Bound by Distance: Rethinking Nationalism Through the Italian Diaspora.* Madison: Farleigh Dickinson University Press.

Wright, Steve. 2000. "A Love Born of Hate: Autonomist Rap in Italy." *Theory, Culture & Society* 17.3, 117–135.

Zukar, Paola. 2017. *Rap. Una storia italiana.* Milano: Baldini & Castoldi.

Reading "Albania" in Italy

Reception of Elvira Dones's Piccola guerra perfetta *and Ron Kubati's* La vita dell'eroe

Daniele Comberiati

Although migration and postcolonial Italian literature studies have closely examined authors' works, and applied multiple theoretical approaches, the issues of circulation and reception of works have not yet been amply developed (Lombardi-Diop and Romeo 2014; Parati 2005). Analyzing the circulation of the works of Italian migrant writers means reflecting on the cultural context in which they are perceived and received. This analysis also provides the possibility of considering the eventual cultural transference that the work produces and the reasons for the success or failure of a single text. The critical and theoretical literature on the circulation and reception of literary works is today very extensive. The present article will take into consideration Stuart Hall's reflections, which are particularly appropriate for analyzing texts which—although written directly in Italian (and sometimes also conceived in Italy)—always propose a meaningful negotiation between two or more cultures.

As Stuart Hall contends, from a Marxist point of view (Hall 1974, 61–79), in order to decode a work, we first need to distinguish the various moments of production and circulation to be able to analyze the transition from one form to another. Hall identifies four different moments of this process: the production of the work, the circulation, the distribution or consumption, and the possible reproduction (even concerning visual or technological cultural works). Hall refers here mainly to non-literary cultural works (particularly media works), but his theories are very useful for understanding the "global travel" of a literary work. This attention to the distribution and circulation processes is even more important in the context of literary objects. Stuart Hall speaks explicitly of a coding (message of the writer) and of a decoding (message received by the reader) that may not be identical, and indeed very often it is not. It is precisely from this non-uniformity of reception of the text that an important fissure opens up: it concerns the translation of the message, the interpretation and the reception of the text itself. Elements emerge from this asymmetrical space showing how, even today and almost three decades after the earliest texts by migrant authors, some clichés and stereotypes of migrant literature are still present in the Italian cultural context. While in Italy many literary works have been produced by migrant, postcolonial, and/ or second-generation writers, it is more complex to grasp whether these texts are really understood or if, due to their circulation and reception, they are still victims of a cultural-oriented point of view.

Here I will analyze different typologies of circulation and reception of two recent novels: *La vita dell'eroe* (The Hero's Life) by Ron Kubati (2016) and *Piccola guerra perfetta* (Little Perfect War) by Elvira Dones (2011). These texts have common points that are useful in understanding the process of reception of migrant literature in Italy. At the same time, these novels also display important differences that can elucidate their diverse receptions by the public and the literary critic. Both novels were published recently within a limited time frame; their authors are from Albania, though each has a different story of migration. Both authors were already well-known when their books were published, and they had previously published several novels. Elvira Dones had a great success with her *Vergine giurata* (Sworn Virgin) (2007b); Ron Kubati had published *Il buio del mare* (The Darkness of the Sea, 2007) with the important publisher Giunti, and was one of the five finalists for the "Strega" Prize, the most important literary award in Italy. Both books were written directly in Italian, a not so obvious choice, especially in Elvira Dones's case whose previous books were written in Albanian. Finally, both novels confront the subject of war: for Kubati, the Albanian civil war during World War II, and for Dones, the 1999 war in Kosovo. While both wars could seem unrelated to contemporary Italy, in reality, both are closely linked to past and present Italian politics.

Despite the similarities the novels share, their circulation, and above all, their reception show the distinctiveness of the books and their authors. The following section will analyze the reception of Elvira Dones's *Piccola guerra perfetta*, and the subsequent section will examine the context of Ron Kubati's *La vita dell'eroe*. In addition to Stuart Hall's theoretical approach to the circulation and reception of literary works, I will also use the theories of Pascale Casanova from *The World Republic of Letters* (1999). In particular, she analyzes the context of circulation and reception employing Pierre Bourdieu's studies concerning authorship (Casanova 1999, 34–57). For Casanova, the positioning of the book in the market and in this "Republic of Letters" is fundamental. Therefore, special attention will be given to the collection or series in which the books were published, as well as to elements of their public presentation.

I chose to not consider the books' sales data, because in Italy the data provided by the publishers are often incomplete and include only books sent to bookstores, but not the number actually sold. Therefore, in addition to the positioning of the books in the editorial series and any eventual translation, my data will also include: books reviews, interviews or programs on the authors, and any literary prizes. The cross-analysis of these data makes it possible to obtain a more complete point of view of the context of the production, circulation and reception of these novels.

ELVIRA DONES'S *PICCOLA GUERRA PERFETTA*

The first striking element in the publication of Elvira Dones's *Piccola guerra perfetta* is the change of publisher. The author started publishing in Albanian and her works were translated into Italian by medium-sized publishing houses (Dones 1998, 2001, 2007a). At that time she lived in the Italian area of Switzerland, a cultural and geographical position that could be defined as "marginal" to the center of the linguistic context in which she worked. Although she lived in an Italophone context, she wrote in Albanian, so her works were simply translated into Italian. The change from being translated into Italian to Dones writing directly in Italian coincides with a change of publisher: with the publication of *Vergine giurata* by the Feltrinelli publishing house in 2007, Elvira Dones gained great international success, increased by the film version directed by Laura Bispuri (2015) (reviewed in *The New York Times* and presented at the Berlin Film Festival) and translations in multiple languages (2014). The success of this novel, due in part to social media discussions on the female figure in Albania, has certainly contributed to the legitimacy of Dones as author in Italy and internationally, and contributed to her move from Feltrinelli to Einaudi, arguably the most important publisher in Italy. The novel was published in the "Stile libero Big" series, which mainly welcomes well-known contemporary Italian writers. The specific goal of the publisher was to position the novel within great contemporary literature, without distinction related to its Albanian origin or to the fact that Dones had recently changed language. The author's "international" status is therefore immediately highlighted: even Dones's career path—she worked in the Albanian public television and was one of the few people who could leave the country during the dictatorship—helped to create this structure. If the image of the renowned and well-known publisher Feltrinelli was linked in the cultural imagination to the personality of its founder and to a precise notion of engagement and idea of literature, with Einaudi publisher, the position of the author goes further, aiming to enter the "contemporary classic novels" through a global novel. In 2019 the novel was republished with the newspaper *La Repubblica* in the special collection "La biblioteca del mondo. Grandi autori contemporanei ti raccontano l'anima più autentica del loro paese" (The Library of the World. Great contemporary writers tell you about the most authentic soul of their country). The novel was published with the intention to describe and present Kosovo to the Italian public, but there was no mention that the text was written directly in Italian. Dones was associated with other important contemporary writers like Mo Yan, Tahar Ben Jelloun, and Chimamanda Ngozi Adichie.

Pascale Casanova identifies in literary apparatuses (prefaces, introductions, afterwords, fourths or cover laps) the decisive elements to establish the legitimacy of the author within a given literary context and to propose a precise positioning (Casanova 1999, 78–83). Her famous example of Gide's preface to the French edition of Yukio Mishima is symbolic of the endorsement attempt of the Japanese author in the world of French letters, through a specific point of view and a specific scale of values (Casanova 1999, 97). To highlight the international character of *Piccola guerra perfetta* and its author, the publisher Einaudi chose Roberto Saviano, probably the best known Italian contemporary writer abroad, as the author of the preface to Elvira Dones's novel. The international success of Saviano's *Gomorrah* (2006, 2007) and the emotion aroused by the death threats to the author by the Camorra have made Saviano much more than just an author: he is considered—and presented—as the spokesman of a new way of writing "committed" literature, as well as the repository of the truth of literary and journalistic investigations against illegal organizations and corrupt politicians and media. Obviously, the presence of such an important author for the preface, in addition to giving further prestige to Elvira Dones, also has the function of directing the public to a precise type of reading. Saviano's endorsement aims to position the novel in that hybrid territory between fiction and non-fiction (on closer inspection, the same territory that has partly caused the success but also the controversy of *Gomorrah*), which is the same space occupied by the stylistic and ethical figure of the Neapolitan author. Saviano's words in the beginning of the preface are very clear in this sense: "Not a novel about war, nor a war novel. No, this novel is instead directly the war. It is the assumption of war in the compassionate eye of the victim who does not judge, does not condemn, but communicates his vision to everyone. A clear, classic look that does not twist anything" (Saviano 2011, 1. The translation is mine).

The proposed reading path is explicit: more than underlining the construction of the characters or the structure of the story based on the role of memory and on women's relationships, Saviano focuses on the analytical eye of the author who describes the war. The function of literature, typical of contemporary Italian non-fiction novels (Serkowska 2011), would therefore be to describe the hidden truths of reality, and to adhere to this truth more than to conventions of style and plot. Obviously, Elvira Dones never claimed that hers was a non-fiction novel, nor has the publication of the novel sparked controversy over the reality of the "sources," like those that emerged after the publication of *Gomorrah*. What is interesting here is the prospect of reading and therefore of reception that Saviano's endorsement proposes and that certainly has a great value in the perception of the book by the Italian reader. This would be a case of the difference between coding and decoding, according to Stuart Hall: the reader is brought by Saviano to read the novel as if it were a true story and the Albanian origin of the author guarantees internal knowledge of the war in Kosovo, at least on the level of linguistic and cultural codes. Therefore, the author's story of migration, "hidden" by the publisher in the general presentation of the novel, acquires a specific weight in the construction of its legitimacy as a witness to the war in Kosovo, a legitimacy that would certainly have been lacking in an Italian author.

Piccola guerra perfetta tells the story of three generations of women, hidden during the 1999 conflict, who face the war differently. One narrative thread follows the story of war, its development and aftermath; the other emphasizes the female figure as twice victimized: first from suffering because of wartime conflict, and second, because this conflict is the result of a patriarchal society. Given the success of *Vergine giurata*, readers familiar with the earlier text would approach the centrality of the female figure in the later novel attuned to the issues of gender relations. Furthermore, the political importance in Italy of the war in Kosovo should not be forgotten: when the left-wing government chaired by Prime Minister Massimo D'Alema chose to join NATO's attack in Belgrade in 1999, public opinion was very shaken by the incident. Together with the first Gulf war of 1990–1991 and the siege of Sarajevo, the war in Kosovo was the most controversial topic in Italy, due to its geographical and cultural proximity and the fact that a left-wing government had participated. The double positioning of the work is noteworthy: on the one hand, it was framed as an "international" text, with themes that can be understood by readers of different cultures and countries, as with *Vergine giurata*; on the other, the latter novel has very precise references to a local reality, with close ties to the recent past and to Italy's involvement.

With the publication of the novel in the Einaudi series and with an apparatus of this kind, we have the "construction" of a "glocal" author, who should be able to speak to an audience close to her as well as to a distant one. The novel was in fact translated into Albanian in 2012 (along with Saviano's preface) and into French in 2013 for the publisher Métailié, specialized in the translation of contemporary Italian writers. The Albanian translation is understandable in a certain sense, given the origin of the author and the subject matter, but it is interesting that in the French translation, Elvira

Dones is presented directly as an Italian-language author, without any mention of the linguistic "passage" from Albanian to Italian and her previous migration. Probably for the French public, accustomed to Francophone authors, it is not necessary to reiterate the author's migratory path, which however is important in the original Italian context of the novel.

An analysis of the novel's reviews reinforces this idea of a "glocal" work. *Piccola guerra perfetta* has obtained national and local reviews and in different media. A few days after its publication, the novel was reviewed by Tiziana Lo Porto, a well-known cultural journalist for the national newspaper *La Repubblica*, the best-selling newspaper in Italy. Lo Porto focuses her review on the specific point of view of the author and the protagonists: how the text recounts the war from the female point of view becomes the main object of the review, more than the description of the war itself (Lo Porto 2011, 32). The review also comes out in the insert of the newspaper *La Repubblica* named "D," initially conceived for a predominantly female audience. Already from this brief information, we notice how the gender analysis of the review is important in order to understand how the text was received and perceived. Another well-known cultural journalist, Nello Ajello, wrote a review in the weekly magazine *L'Espresso,* which belongs to the same publishing group as *La Repubblica*, emphasizing the description of the war and the quality of Dones's writing style (Ajello 2011, 36). The author was also invited to the television program *Che tempo che fa* (What's the Weather Like), conducted by the well-known TV journalist Fabio Fazio, a cultural entertainment program that was broadcast on the national networks during weekend evening primetime.

In addition to these reviews in major national news outlets, other national newspapers with strong local roots such as *Il Piccolo* of Trieste and *Il Mattino* of Naples have devoted attention to the book. In the case of *Il Piccolo,* we can think that the proximity of Trieste and Friuli to the Balkans amplifies the attention to works that deal with issues about this area, while *Il Mattino* is the newspaper in which Roberto Saviano began his political and economic investigations. Other reviews like the one published in the monthly magazine of the Italian National Union of Writers, *Le reti di Dedalus*, though having a smaller audience, have the merit of analyzing the literary qualities of the work. Hence, the ways of reading and receiving the novel are varied: at the national level, the gender and "political" aspects are highlighted, while at the local level, the most immediate cultural aspects are emphasized (the relationship with Balkans, investigative narrative). Other magazines instead focus on the literariness of the work, showing that it is not just a novel with a sociological interest, but also with a great literary value.

While the novel has not had the success of *Vergine giurata*, also because it still lacks the English translation that contributed so much to the international spread of Dones's earlier book, the French translation has been a first step towards the internationalization of the text. In addition to positive reviews in major French literary inserts (*La quinzaine littéraire*, *Le Monde des livres*) and in the most popular magazines such as *L'Express*, *Piccola guerra perfetta* was mentioned for the "Jeunes Européens" (Young Europeans) award, which represents a further confirmation of this process of internationalization of the author and of the work.

RON KUBATI'S *LA VITA DELL'EROE*

This novel was released in 2016 and tells the story of Sami Keçi, one of the leaders of the Albanian resistance against the fascist invasion and later a member of the communist secret service. Through its protagonist, the author speaks about several years of Albanian history, constantly relating it to Italy and to the Albanian perception of Italy.

Analysis of the editorial positioning of the book helps us to understand the circulation and reception it has had. The novel was published by the Besa publishing house, which over the years has specialized in Albanian and Balkan authors and has a special proximity to Albanian culture and literature. Besa's catalogue of published authors includes Ismail Kadaré, the best-known contemporary Albanian writer, and the name "Besa" itself in Albanian means "given word." Elvira Dones had also published a novel (1998) with Besa, and also Kubati published the novels *M* (2002) and *Va e non torna* (Goes and Doesn't Come Back, 2000) with Besa. In addition, the publisher, which has its registered office in Nardò, near Lecce, is very rooted in the region of Puglia, where Kubati has lived and worked for many years, and where, thanks to his writings, university teaching, and collaborations with newspapers, he is a recognized intellectual figure. The local context in this case is very important, because most of the reviews of the novel appeared in magazines or newspapers in Puglia: in addition to the activity of the publishing house, Puglia, for its recent history and for its geographical position, is particularly attentive and interested in relations with Albania. In fact, the Albanians arrived in Bari with the Vlora in 1991 and important Albanian communities developed in the region. The collection in which the novel is included, called "Nadir," is a fairly recent series of "mixed" literature: there are Italian and foreign authors (especially from the Balkan context, but not only), modern and contemporary, with particular attention to currently living authors. Besa has no specific collection or series for Italian migration literature, nor for Albanian literature. *La vita dell'eroe* becomes directly part of the contemporary narrative series of the publisher, as had happened to the novel by Elvira Dones.

An analysis of the reviews received by Kubati's novel directs our understanding of the reception of the text along two parallel paths. The particular union between local and global that constituted the attempt to present Elvira Dones as "global writer" and her novel as a "global novel" is here delineated in a completely different way. With Kubati's *La vita dell'eroe,* the same union exists, but the dynamics are completely different: first, the relationship with the so-called Italian migration literature, almost completely absent with Dones, is very evident in Kubati's case. One example is the review published in the online magazine *El-Ghibli,* one of the most authoritative journals dealing with Italian literature on migration, with an editorial staff composed largely of migrant writers and critics (Taddeo 2016). The author of the review focuses on the relationship between modernity and secular traditions, considering this aspect as typical in the writings of migrant authors of Albanian origin.

Two other reviews came out on *Il gioco degli specchi* (The Mirror's Game), a portal that reviews works related to migration (Camilotti 2016), and on the website (balcanicaucaso.org), which is specifically interested in these areas (Mura 2016). The element of migration and the linguistic change of the author are always important in these reviews (balcanicaucaso.org also mentions the fact that the author lives permanently in the United States, adding a further element of migration in his biography). Silvia Camilotti, for example, talks about the proximity of the themes of the novel to those of the New Italian Epic theorized by the collective of writers Wu Ming: the absence of the typical postmodern irony, the use of precise sources such as archives or historical memories, the will to analyze the story from a marginal point of view are all characteristics that the New Italian Epic theorized since 2008. Maria Rosa Mura instead emphasizes the "linguistic voyage" of the author and his Italian to which he grafts Albanian terms which are decisive to the understanding of the work.

Other reviews have been published in local or regional magazines or newspapers, in Lecce or Puglia. This is not coincidental, because the publisher is based in Puglia, and Kubati lived many years in Puglia, collaborated with the University of Bari, and is an intellectual figure recognized in those areas. These elements explain the radically "local" feature of the work, a concept of "local" obviously very different from the one observed in Elvira Dones. In Kubati's case, this is not merely an intellectual construction, but the physical presence of the author. On the other hand, Dones, having lived for many years in the Italian area of Switzerland, also positions herself indirectly in relation to Italy, because, apart from the use of Italian (and as we have seen, a belated use), the Italian political and cultural context is not directly concerned.

Compared to Dones's, Kubati's novel lacks translations in foreign languages (at least for the moment) and reviews in large national newspapers—even an interview in the newspaper *La Repubblica,* the day after the release of the novel, focuses more on opinion about the Albanian football team at the

2016 European Championships than on an in-depth analysis of the novel. It would be easy to attribute these disparities in circulation, diffusion, and reception to the different weight of the two publishers: Einaudi represents an indispensable reference point for the national literary context; Besa is linked to a significant but niche reality, focused on Balkan literature. The advertising media for each are therefore different and as a result, there is also a different diffusion. While these disparities do not fully explain the different reception methods, they partially elucidate the different reaction of the public. In this case too, Stuart Hall's reflections on "not identical coding" between the message of the writer and the message received by the reader can be very useful. According to Hall's idea, reception is never neutral, since the message is always distorted by the receiver's ideology and way of thinking. In Hall's ideas, encoding and decoding may not coincide at all: thus there would be a partial separation between the original idea of the message and the ways in which it is received, as we actually observe in Kubati's novel.

The novel by Kubati does not speak only of resistance in Albania and of the successive disillusionments of the revolutionaries. The message of the book is much deeper and more universal than a mere review of Albanian history. Kubati discusses the role of minorities and of gender relations in World War II-era Albanian society, and the persistence, even today, of racist attitudes, despite the fact that the struggle against Nazi-fascism has been won. The novel highlights the figure of the protagonist and the struggle against the foreign oppressor, as well as the change the revolutionaries undergo once they have taken power. These themes could be difficult for contemporary Italians to confront, as they impinge on delicate contemporary issues surrounding immigrants, minorities, and racial and cultural identity, which hint perhaps that the "real" defeat of fascism within society is still missing. Post-war Albania, in fact, makes the fight against Nazi-fascism and the consequent victory an identiary pillar, which even justifies an attitude in open contrast with this struggle. The Italian situation, although radically different, presents some common elements in this sense: this is why in my opinion the reading was more difficult than the novel by Dones. In this case there was simply not the narration of a past war, but a reflection on our contemporary society and on identity and cultural impostures. It is precisely in this gap of reception that a fundamental element of the text is hidden.

CONCLUSION

The analysis of the circulation and reception of Dones's and Kubati's texts shows profound differences about the positioning of the works in the contemporary Italian cultural and literary landscape. These differences reveal how fundamental it is to take into consideration the plurality of elements that constitute the literary work. The sociology of reception is particularly useful, as the success or failure of a work cannot simply be attributed to the greater or lesser quality of writing, to the standing of the author, or to the prestige of the publishing house. In this process—which is also a process of legitimization and canonization—specific cultural, political, and literary resistances come into play, as shown in the case of Kubati's novel. Only a cross-analysis between cultural, sociological, literary, and political elements can give as complete a picture as possible of the literary panorama of migrant authors, whose complexity goes beyond the mere study of the corpus as an element independent from the context in which they operate.

REFERENCES

Ajello, Nello. 2011. "Recensione a *Piccola guerra perfetta*." *L'Espresso*. October 31, 36.
Bispuri, Laura. 2015. *Vergine giurata* (movie). Vivo film.
Camilotti, Silvia. 2016. Review of *La vita dell'eroe*. http://www.ilgiocodeglispecchi.org/libri/ scheda/la-vita-delleroerecensione. Accessed 12 November 2018.
Casanova, Pascale. 1999. *La République mondiale des lettres*. Paris: Gallimard.
———. 2007. *The World Republic of Letters*. London: Harvard University Press.
Dones, Elvira. 1998. *Senza bagagli*. Lecce: Besa.
———. 2001. *Sole bruciato*. Milano: Feltrinelli.
———. 2007a. *I mari ovunque*. Novara: Interlinea.
———. 2007b. *Vergine giurata*. Milano: Feltrinelli.
———. 2011. *Piccola guerra perfetta*. Milano: Feltrinelli.
———. 2012. *Luftë e vogël e përkorë*. Tiranë: Botimet Dudaj.
———. 2013. *Une petite guerre parfaite*. Paris: Métailié.
———. 2014. *Sworn Virgin*. London: And Other Stories Publishing.
Hall, Stuart. 1974. "A reading of Marx's 1857 Introduction to the Gundrisse." *WPCS*, 6: 37–59.
Kubati, Ron. 2000. *M.* Nardò (Lecce): Besa.
———. 2002. *Va e non torna*. Nardò (Lecce): Besa.
———. 2007. *Il buio del mare*. Milano: Giunti.
———. 2016. *La vita dell'eroe*. Nardò (Lecce): Besa.
Lombardi-Diop, Cristina and Romeo, Caterina (eds.). 2014. *Postcolonial Italy: Challenging National Homogeneity*. New York: Palgrave Macmillan.
Lo Porto, Tiziana. 2011. "Recensione a *Piccola guerra perfetta*." *La Repubblica delle donne*, Supplement of *La Repubblica*, November 19, 32.
Mura, Maria Rosa. 2016. Review of *La vita dell'eroe*. https://www.balcanicaucaso.org/aree/ Albania/Ron-Kubati-la-vita-dell-eroe-173278. Accessed 12 November 2018.
Parati, Graziella. 2005. *The Art of Talking Back in a Destination Culture*. Toronto: University of Toronto Press.
Saviano, Roberto. 2006. *Gomorra*. Milano: Mondadori.
———. 2007. *Gomorrah*. Translated by Virginia Jewiss. New York: Palgrave Macmillan.
———. 2011. "La guerra delle donne." In *Piccola guerra perfetta*, ed. Elvira Dones. Milano, Feltrinelli.
Serkowska, Hanna (ed.). 2011. *Finzione, cronaca, realtà. Scambi, intrecci e prospettive nella narrativa italiana contemporanea*. Massa: Transeuropa.
Taddeo, Raffaele. Review of *La vita dell'eroe*. 2016. http://www.el-ghibli.org/la-vita-delleroe/, (accessed 13 November 2018).

Migration, the Novel, and the Power of Fear

A Dialogical Perspective from Bakhtin to Lakhous

Lucia Re

I intend to look more deeply into the question of the Italian imaginary, because I think that in Italy there is an imaginary that needs to be healed, to be soothed. There is a beautiful phrase by Nietzsche that is relevant here—and by the way, it was in Turin that Nietzsche went mad, after living there for two years. There is a passage in *Ecce Homo* in which he speaks of the role of the doctor, that is that of soothing the imagination of the sick, because what scares a sick person in reality are not the symptoms of the illness, but rather the troubled imaginary that develops around the illness. I use this metaphor to say that I think in Italy there is a troubled imaginary that developed with regard to the encounter with the Other. There are baseless fears in this country. (Ruta 2008)

ITALIANS: THE MOST AFRAID

Much has been written about the relationship between immigration and fear. Fear of immigrants and fear felt by immigrants—fear as a component of what Abdelmalek Sayad has called *The Suffering of the Immigrant* (Sayad 2004). Scholars such as Giovanni Giulio Valtolina have pointed out that, paradoxically, feelings of insecurity, fear of crime, and a sense of unsafety and general anxiety related to immigrants, are most widespread in some of the European countries, such as Italy, that are in fact the safest. Citizens are fearful not because they are unprotected, but rather because they "feel" un-protected, as they face economic problems and societal changes—changes for which they are not emotionally prepared (Valtolina 92). This fear in turn feeds a form of social aggressiveness that may lead to scapegoating. The

53

2008 killing in Milan of 19-year-old Abdul Guibre, the son of immigrants from Burkina Faso, beaten to death by a coffee bar's father-and-son proprietors (allegedly for having stolen a pack of cookies), is an example of how such fears may escalate (Gramigna 2008). The rise to power of Matteo Salvini's populist Lega Party (along with the Movimento 5 Stelle) in 2018, whose campaign and then government rhetoric made a pointed and instrumental use of anti-immigrant fear, coincided with a new wave of racist violence.[1]

Italians, according to studies by the European barometer of social reality (which compares feelings of insecurity in twenty-five countries) and according to Italian national research units, are among the "most afraid"; more so than the Greek, the Portuguese, the German, the French, the Dutch, and so on. Only the Danish, Austrians and Spanish are more afraid than Italians. And more than most other Europeans, Italians perceive immigration, along and in connection with criminality, to be one of the very top reasons for feeling unsafe (Valtolina 101; Bonomi and Majorino 2018). Italians also turn out to be the least amenable in Europe to having an immigrant as a next-door neighbor. Immigrants may indeed be involved in criminal acts, but statistically they are hardly the principal subjects responsible for crime in Italy. Furthermore, statistics of the Ministry of the Interior show that there has been no real variation in crime rates in the last couple of decades (Tabar 2014, 87; Bordi 2010).

In his analysis of "unsafety perception studies" and polls, however, Omid Firouzi Tabar, sociologist at the University of Turin, has shown how such studies and polls often use a type of language and a line of questioning that in their very structure and phrasing—usually general and abstract—reproduce and heighten the very fears they seek to document. As soon as polls shift from the more abstract to the concrete, however, seeking specific answers about the perception of fear and unsafety in everyday reality (in other words the lived experience of individuals and their immediate neighborhoods, streets and homes, and personal behavior), the levels of anxiety about immigration and crime rapidly decline (Tabar 2014), as does their sense of fearful hostility towards immigrants. For example, individuals who fear immigrants and crime in the abstract, in practice do not feel the need to put extra locks on their doors or bars on their windows and state that they walk confidently at night in their neighborhoods and cities.

Furthermore, in analyzing these studies and polls over time, Tabar shows how in Italy the collective fear of criminal acts in connection to the fear of immigrants (and this includes Islamophobia and the fear of terrorist acts when dealing with Muslim immigrants), are shaped by politics and the media. He charts in detail how public fear peaked during periods of electoral campaigns, such as fall 2007 and then 2008, and then rapidly declined (Tabar 85). Indeed, according to studies conducted by the renowned Italian political scientist Ilvo Diamanti, the Italian media are "at the top" in Europe in terms of production of anxiety-inducing discourse. Episodes of micro-criminality in connection with immigrants are in fact over-represented by a percentage of about 64.9 per cent, in contrast to media coverage related to other factors that contribute to overall feelings of unsafety and insecurity, such as the economic crisis, public welfare and the degradation of the environment (Diamanti 2010). This discursive construction and circulation of the fear of immigrants, then, serves to crystalize—to use sociologist Zygmunt Bauman's term—the more fluid, generalized anxiety, the seemingly "liquid fear" (Bauman 2006) that afflicts Italians, and also serves to justify the attempts by Matteo Salvini and his League Party—among others—to create a new securitarian and anti-immigrant paradigm of governance.

The specific question I would like to pose here is: does literature, and specifically narrative literature by and about immigrant writers, tell us something about the relationship between immigration and fear that is somehow different; and something that may make a difference? I wish to explore this question through a reading of the immigrant writer Amara Lakhous, and try and think about how and why it is the specifically literary dimension or function of his work that may indeed make a difference.

AMARA LAKHOUS, IMMIGRATION, AND THE QUESTION OF FEAR

When Lakhous first arrived in Italy in 1995, he was twenty-five and fleeing his native Algeria, where, after earning a degree in philosophy at the University of Algiers, he had started writing fiction and working as a radio journalist. His non-traditional views on religion, gender roles, and Algerian identity caused him to receive harsh criticism and even death threats, and as he himself put it, he decided not to wait for an assassin to materialize. Starting in 1993, the civil war in Algeria produced more than 150,000 victims; Lakhous was able to travel back to Algiers only in 2003. His first novel (written in Italian on the basis of an earlier version in Arabic), entitled *Scontro di civiltà per un ascensore a piazza Vittorio* (*Clash of Civilizations over an Elevator in Piazza Vittorio*), published in 2006, became a best seller in Italy, and the translation into English by Ann Goldstein published in 2008 by Europa Editions has also done very well, as have all of Lakhous's novels thus far.[2] All of his novels revolve around immigration and the question of fear in today's Italy and in Europe, yet they are all to a large extent comic and decidedly unsentimental novels. He has thus far published three more novels in Italian, all very successful: *Divorzio all'Islamica a Viale Marconi* (2010; *Divorce Islamic Style*, 2012); *Contesa per un maialino italianissimo a San Salvario* (2013; *Dispute Over a Very Italian Piglet*, 2014), and *La zingarata della verginella di via Ormea* (2014; *The Prank of the Good Little Virgin of via Ormea*, 2016, translation by Antony Shugaar), which is about the Italian fear of the Rom, or gypsies. In this essay I will limit my discussion to *Clash of Civilizations* and *Divorce Islamic Style,* though such an analysis could encompass all of Lakhous's novels set in Italy.

Lakhous grew up speaking Berber, and Algerian Arabic as well as French, the language of instruction in school. He also learned classical Arabic as a child by studying the Koran in religion school. His mother spoke only Berber and—although she grew up in Algeria under French colonialism—received no schooling and was illiterate. Yet she was a very intelligent and cultivated woman who raised nine children (Ruta 2008). Lakhous's father also spoke a limited amount of Arabic, with a strong Berber accent. He had been for a number of years a migrant worker employed in a Citroen plant near Paris, and according to Lakhous himself, his life as a migrant in France was very difficult. Upon arriving in Rome, Amara Lakhous spent two years in a center for immigrants and refugees, many from Islamic countries such as Pakistan and Bangladesh, sharing with them space, time, as well as fears and other emotions. It was a formative experience that became an inspiration for his writing.

In Rome, Lakhous immediately started studying Italian, taking courses for immigrants taught by volunteers. Even after leaving the center, he lived until 2001 in the multiethnic working class neighborhood of Piazza Vittorio, near the Termini train station and the Università di Roma La Sapienza, where he proceeded to earn a second college degree, in cultural anthropology. In 2002, Lakhous settled in another multi-ethnic Rome neighborhood, viale Marconi, where he lived until 2006. Viale Marconi became the setting for *Divorce Islamic style.*

Lakhous lived as an "extracomunitario" for thirteen years before he was able to become an Italian citizen in 2008. In the meantime, not only did he become fluent in Italian, but he also turned into a non-professional linguist of sorts, as anyone who reads his novels in Italian can attest, with a keen ear for idiolects, regional inflections, and dialects. Lakhous is an interesting case of "migrant" Mediterranean writer in that his process of writing takes place as a kind of zigzag, a movement back and forward across languages and between different codes, places and voices that brings them into contact, creating new situations and—as we will see—his particular brand of novelistic dialogism.

Before going back to Lakhous, I will try and explain in more specific critical, transnational and theoretical terms how I approach the question of fear. Rather than approach fear in Lakhous from a psychoanalytic perspective (Burns 2013), I am interested in looking at it from the vantage point of the cultural and political history of emotions.

FEAR TODAY

Most cultural critics and social analysts today agree that fear—always a powerful force in the history of humanity—has become the norm, and the principal emotion through which public life is administered in the West. The role that the mass media have played in inciting and fomenting waves of panic since the interwar years has been repeatedly scrutinized internationally. The historian Joanna Bourke, for example has looked at Britain and the United States. Since 2001, the specter of "the terrorist" has, according to Bourke, seemingly taken on a divine power, equivalent to the plague in early modern history (Bourke x–xii). The persecution of immigrants and their fearful lives are among the results of this transnational panic.

Fear, it has been argued, has become effectively a *technology* used for governance; a tool, and a system of modern life itself (Ahmed 72). In *The Cultural Politics of Emotion* ,Sarah Ahmed has studied the emotionality of texts, and the work of fear in particular, in contemporary websites, newspaper articles, government reports and political speeches in the US and Britain. Jef Huysmans, on the other hand, in his 2006 volume entitled *The Politics of Insecurity,* about fear, migration and asylum in the European Union, has analyzed the construction and circulation of fear and the politics of knowledge in Europe, showing how since 2001 fear has become an instrument for reasserting an authoritarian kind of sovereignty, and for establishing a new securitarian paradigm. The politicization of migration as danger in the European Union, and the silencing of refugees and immigrants and their stories, have increasingly made dialogue very difficult, Huysmans writes (58–64). "Personal histories of immigrants and refugees are submerged in images, such as flood or invasion, representing a mass that endangers," or "images of criminality" that must be feared (58). Like all emotions, fear is fundamentally about the body, but emotions are also always cultural artefacts (Geertz 1973; 2000, 81). Indeed, most scholars and historians of emotions agree that there is no clear line between fear felt and recognizable immediately in the body and fear as something that is culturally produced and mediated; and something that historically develops and mutates over time, though in a non-linear fashion. The emotional body itself produces multiple signs that constitute a kind of textuality. And the work of fear in particular, argues Sarah Ahmed, involves sticky signs, and the sticking of signs to bodies (4).

Although we think fear is distinct and recognizable when we feel it or witness it, the boundaries between fear and other emotions, such as shame and anger, are never clearly marked. Yet fear is indisputably, as anthropologist Mary Douglas and others have shown, about boundaries and about borders, and about difference (Douglas and Wildavsky 1982). It is about the awareness of unclear or unsafe borders: borders of the material body (what is outside and what is inside; what brings illness and death), identity (self and other) and society (belonging and not belonging) (Bourke 389). It is about difference between ethnicities, social groups and even genders. Fear is not just about the defense of borders, however: fear, argues Ahmed, effectively *makes* borders (67). Zygmunt Bauman has suggested that the object of our fear tells us more about the epoch we live in than the substance of the fear itself (Bauman 1995, 2000). Throughout his work, he has often returned to the concept of "strangerhood" and of the apparently "deviant other" (Bauman 2004) in connection with fear. Immigrants and refugees tend to appear as strangers, "ambivalent people" who "are, as it were, neither close nor distant." They are "neither friends nor foe . . . [and therefore] they cause confusion and anxiety" (Bauman 1990, 55). Strangers become objects of fear because they make social, cultural and physical boundaries emerge as porous and unstable; rather than reinforcing boundaries, these "ambivalent people" make them tenuous and problematic (Bauman 1991, 55). They threaten the insider/host's identity; the hybrid stranger disturbs the pre-existing, familiar social and cultural boundaries.

Immigrants and refugees as hybrid strangers appear as a threat to national "emotional communities" because of their ambiguous position. In the case of Italy, the immigrant stranger today is all the more uncanny and fearful in that it evokes the history and reawakens the repressed, frightening collective memory of Italians themselves as migrants, outsiders, deviant criminals and "strangers" in the US and even within Italy itself, in the great postwar migration from the impoverished south to the industrial north.

The hybrid and uncanny stranger not only questions the opposition between friend and enemy, self and other, but also the very principle of monological opposition. While at one level hybrid strangers unmask the tenuous artificiality of division, at another level they are also threatened by the very same order that they question. From objects of fear, they are in fact forced to become fearful subjects themselves. Bauman (2004), Huysmans, and others have argued that political power and governance have increasingly become dependent in the West on how governments deal with immigrants, particularly recent arrivals, who are often represented by politicians as "ideal deviant others." The fear of "strangers" becomes visible in public spaces where immigrants become the targets of racism and find their cultural and religious expression, and even the way they dress, censored or suppressed.

FEAR AND LITERATURE

Can literature help understand, contain and even master or defuse this fear thus defined? Do literary texts and in particular literary narratives deal with emotions, and fear in particular, in ways that differ from the general "emotionality of texts"—non-literary texts, that is, and discursive flows such as those studied by Sarah Ahmed?

Since at least Aristotle's *Poetics*, it is a common place of literary criticism that literature, in and of itself, is a repository and an endless source of emotions, fear and pity being prime examples. Yet many literary critics seem no longer to have much interest in the aesthetic function of literature, its specifically literary quality, and seem altogether to have abandoned literature and moved more towards a sociological type of cultural studies. A growing number of political theorists and public relations scholars, on the other hand, not to mention sociologists and philosophers, have been studying literature to gain a different view of the political and the social. The 2009 book entitled *Aesthetics and World Politics*, by Roland Bleiker, professor of International Relations at the University of Queensland in Australia, published by Palgrave in their *Rethinking Peace and Conflict Studies*, is an example of this trend, although his specific interest is what poetry can do.

In terms of narrative, one of the more influential approaches has been that of ethicists such as Martha Nussbaum, whose method is basically neo-Aristotelian. In her *Upheavals of Thought: The Intelligence of Emotions* and more recently in *The New Religious Intolerance*, Nussbaum claims that literary novels can provide imaginative insight into human beings and their emotions that other sources of representation fail to capture. For Nussbaum, narrative works have a crucial role in human self-understanding and the mastering of emotions. Stories and novels (and the play of narrative in particular) are connected to the role of the imagination in the human psyche, and to the need for imagination in the cultivation of love and compassion. Literary narrative, and in particular the novel, Nussbaum claims, serves to promote intense concern and acknowledgment of "a common humanity" (Nussbaum 2001, 438).

From the perspective of collective fear, according to Nussbaum, "immigrants, rather than being seen as full people [are] seen as missiles attacking the homeland" (2012, 56). The empathetic imagination promoted by literary narratives allows us, on the other hand, to see the world from another's point of view. It allows us to overcome fear and understand people at a distance from ourselves in ethnicity, religion or race (146).

As helpful as this vision of the power of narrative is, it also has some problems. Nussbaum's readings of novels, even as they claim to engage with the very language and discourse of literature, are often over-determined and look at characters and plots merely as models for real human situations and moral problems. The specific subtleties, ambiguities and ironies of narratives as literary texts, and of literary language itself, are barely visible and secondary in her work.

A DIALOGICAL PERSPECTIVE

In order to gain some insight into how some novels are able creatively to address the question of fear, and specifically the fear of the immigrant other as "stranger" that has become commonplace in Italy and much of Europe, I will turn to the ideas of a critic and theorist who, having himself lived through the terrors of dictatorship, knew a great deal about fear. I mean the Russian critic Mikhail Bakhtin.

For Bakhtin, just having captivating characters and dialogues in a novel is not what makes it dialogical. Bakhtin sees the dialogical novel as a multi-voiced text, whose internal and diversified dialogism engages the reader in hermeneutical work, reflection and questioning of him or herself and her own beliefs, even as he or she is made aware of the playful fictionality of the novelistic texts. Bakhtin argues that the dialogical novel necessarily draws upon multiple languages and discourses and puts them into relationships with each other. It is this dialogue among languages and kinds of discourse that in turn becomes a critical and imaginative dialogue among worldviews and ideologies.

According to Bakhtin, the reader of the dialogical novel is endowed with an essential power and freedom of creative response. The dialogical or poly-phonic novel, as opposed to the monological novel (Michel Houellebeq's 2015 novel *La Soumission*—"Submission" in English—may be cited as a relevant example of the monological), is therefore structurally anti-authori-tarian. In a monological text, all the characters' voices and perspectives are subordinated to the voice and ideology of the author. The dialogical novel, on the other hand, recognizes competing and juxtaposed voices without mak-ing any single voice normative for the reader. This type of novel thus gives a voice to the other, making possible not just empathy or compassion, but an imaginative dialogue. Bakhtin's novelist in fact attempts to "speak in an alien language" or to represent "another's speech in another's language" (287, 324). Bakhtin's notion of "hybrid construction"—an utterance combining two speech types or styles—allows multiple languages a shared space. The novel therefore serves to "sharpen [. . .] our perception of socio-linguistic differentiations" (287, 366). This shared textual space is a radical form of preserving—rather than fearing or abolishing—differences.

CLASH OF CIVILIZATIONS

All of Amara Lakhous's Italian novels deal with fear and fearful subjects, immigrants, strangers and deviant others who are both afraid themselves and a source of fear in others. They deal in narrative terms not only with the emotion, but also with the question of fear. *Clash of Civilizations* revolves around the murder of a violent man and xenophobic fanatic from Rome, Lorenzo Manfredini, better known as Gladiator, whose body is found in an elevator of a building in a multi-ethnic neighborhood, and the disappearance at the same time of the man who is initially wanted for the killing—Amedeo, whose original name was Ahmed. He is an immigrant from Algeria who knows Rome inside out and speaks Italian well enough to pass for southern Italian even with his Roman wife, and now hides because he is afraid of being unmasked and denounced not only as a killer, but as a fraud.

Amedeo/Ahmed worked as a volunteer, an Italian who—like the novel's author—translated, mediated and helped immigrants with their applications for residence permits and jobs and was universally loved. Through a colorful cast of characters, all of whom are called upon by the police to give their deposition about the missing man, and through Amedeo/Ahmed's own first-person recorded voice diary, we learn about the lives and perspectives of several different individuals, and about their diverse yet overlapping and complementary fears and anxieties. For example, we hear about the abject fear and desperation of a refugee (Parviz) whose petition is rejected by Italian authorities and potentially faces death upon his return to Iran; the fear of the police who treat immigrants and refugees as criminals (24); the fear of being insulted and abused (25); and the immigrant's fear of forgetting one's food traditions, one's identity and even one's own name (28, 49–50). Yet Ahmed/Amedeo also especially fears remembrance. Haunted by nightmares, he is afraid of reliving in his mind the traumas that led to his fleeing abroad. He even fears schizophrenia (100–101).

We hear about a Peruvian female undocumented immigrant's fear of being raped, her fear of pregnancy, and of losing her job (68). Lakhous contrasts this with the media-instigated (and now also apparently government-instigated) anxiety Italians feel of becoming extinguished as a people while immigrants take over: "The Italian is doomed to die out," and the opposite, complementary fear of native Italians: the fear to have children in circumstances felt to be precarious, unsafe and insecure (101). And we learn about impoverished Italians' fear that immigrants are in fact stealing their jobs (36, 38) and that they will be contaminated and made sick by illnesses imported by immigrants.

We hear throughout the novel about the abstract, generalized panic instigated by the media against immigrants represented as criminals (48–49). Yet, as Amedeo/Ahmed comments wryly in his journal recalling how Italian immigrants had been both feared and fearful in the United States, "Italians don't seem to have learned anything from the lessons of history" (54).

If, as the historian of emotions Jean-Jacques Courtine has argued, individual and collective emotions—even without needing necessarily to postulate (or assume) the existence of a collective national unconscious or a collective imaginary—bear the sedimented traces of past emotions from one's national past, or from the past of one's community (Courtine 2016), then the work of novels such as those of Amara Lakhous has been and continues to be that of making us aware of those emotions, and of the emotional past we think we may have forgotten, or that we would like to forget, or that some of our politicians would like us to forget. The act of remembering and recollecting the emotions and particularly the fears of our past, for Lakhous, is essential in order to dispel the misunderstandings and misconceptions that fuel our paranoia today in relation to migrants.

DIVORCE ISLAMIC STYLE

Divorce Islamic Style, whose epigraph from Machiavelli's *Prince* reads, "it is much safer to be feared than to be loved," tells in alternate chapters two stories that overlap and develop into a potential love story; one is the story of a Sicilian translator and interpreter, Christian Mazzari. He is a young man who "looks like an Arab" and is co-opted by the Italian Secret Services, in collaboration with the CIA and other international agencies, to pass as Tunisian in order to infiltrate and expose an alleged terrorist cell among recent Muslim immigrants in Rome, and thus join in the new international "war on terror."

The second novel tells the story of Sofia, a young Muslim woman who has emigrated to Rome from Egypt with her new husband, hoping to fulfill her dream of becoming a hairdresser and having her own beauty salon. She soon learns, however, to fear her husband, who turns out to be very observant, forces her to wear the veil, and forbids her to work. Even as she experiences the fear and potential shame of repudiation and divorce, she suffers the frights of the immigrant in multiple ways. She sees Italians look at her with suspicion and dread in their eyes because she wears the veil, she becomes the target of racist abuse, and in an open market in central Rome— where she particularly likes shopping because bartering with the vendors reminds her of her father and of her native Egypt—she becomes the victim of a physical attack that terrifies her along with her small daughter, Aida:

> I have to go to the market to do the shopping. I like to wander among the fruit and vegetable stalls. Shopping is a career, in fact an art, my father always says. There are important rules to follow. First, examine the goods very patiently. Second, don't respond immediately to the solicitations of the vendors. Third, take the time necessary to choose what you want. Fourth, buy exclusively on the basis of the quality-price relationship. You have to be like a good hunter: strike at the right moment in order not to make a mistake. Maybe I've found my prey. This vendor has the best apples in the market. There are two people ahead of me. After a couple of minutes, it's my turn. As I'm about to speak a man of around fifty emerges out of nowhere and asks to be served first. I

thought he hadn't seen me, a simple and innocent lack of attention. I was wrong. And in a big way. The man looks at me disdainfully and says:

"I was here first. Do you understand Italian?"

"I understand Italian perfectly. You are rude."

"Look at this! A speaking mummy! Why don't you go back to your own country! Why do you come here to make trouble, to spread fanaticism and plant bombs, eh?"

"You are an imbecile."

"Go back to Afghanistan in your burka, or else I'm gonna get really pissed off and give you a beating."

The imbecile gives me a shove, and I lose my balance and fall down. Aida starts crying. I feel a knot in my throat. I can hardly breathe. People gather in a circle around us to enjoy the show entitled, "The Veiled Maya and the Racist Idiot." Someone reaches out a hand to help me up.

Now I can't keep from crying. (104–105)

The episode is told with near-cinematic immediacy in Sofia's own voice, yet this voice is in itself already double-voiced. Sofia is in fact an Egyptian woman who speaks and relates (or in a sense "translates") the incident into Italian in her putative diary. At the same time, she retains in what she says and communicates to us as readers the mental image and the linguistic and cultural background of her Cairo upbringing. Lakhous thus succeeds in putting the reader effectively in Sofia's shoes without, however, fostering complete or unreflective identification—the way a more traditional realist or sentimental novel might do when the reader is led instinctively and emotionally to identify with a character.

Through Sofia's own voice and words, we are able to experience directly the dramatic turn of her emotions from joyful expectation to surprise, anger, resentment and then fear and trembling, even as we are able at the same time to retain a certain distance of vision, gaining thoughtful appreciation of her being her own individual in a specific cultural predicament.

The physical symptoms of fear in her body are communicated in a simple, yet highly effective and immediate way: "I feel a knot in my throat. I can hardly breathe." Here her voice is represented as effectively taken out of her. Her attacker has rendered her voiceless and breathless. Nonetheless, it is in her own pained yet proud voice that she recounts this traumatic moment of fear, suffering and public humiliation that ironically reverses and undermines her initial feelings of pleasure and control of the situation, based on her father's lessons. The insults proffered in genuine romanesco dialect by her attacker ("sennò m'incazzo e te meno pure" [I'm gonna get really pissed off and give you a beating]) are felt all the more powerfully by being reported and "quoted" in Sofia's own voice.

Yet this powerful scene is neither direct nor immediate in its emotionality. Indeed, the scene—though vivid—has no voyeuristic or sadistic dimension. It is in fact a recollection, filtered through the perspective of a subsequent moment in time, when the narrator (Sofia herself), who has by now experienced the helpful hand of Christian (who has come to her rescue in the market and has lifted her back on her feet), has been able to recollect herself and to gain a critical and even ironic perspective on the whole incident.

She is no longer fearful, and she is critically aware—and makes us aware—of how the violence of the incident was experienced by most of the witnesses merely as a harmless and even entertaining spectacle: "People gather in a circle around us to enjoy the show entitled, 'The Veiled Maya and the Racist Idiot.'" In the chapter that follows, the same episode will be narrated by Christian (who for his secret mission uses the name Issa) from a very different vantage point, comically infused with Orientalism, and in a distinctly Sicilian voice. All of Lakhous's novels are effectively (and self-consciously) double-voiced and polyphonic in the Bakhtinian sense. Even at a basic linguistic level, they are designed to evoke and recall to memory another voice and another language, and to dispel the myth of the alien, fearful stranger.[3]

For his Italian novels, Lakhous uses a highly original, innovative process of writing and establishing his characters' voices and perspectives, based in part on actual dialogic exchanges—live and in person or by e-mail—with friends and correspondents—both men and women—across Italy. As he composes his novels, Lakhous often shares his fictional dialogues—the things his characters say, and in particular the ways they say them (the idioms or turns of phrase they use), with multiple readers-critics, who are often his own friends. These readers and friends, including for example the anthropologist Roberto De Angelis,[4] advise him as to the likelihood and believability—from their point of view and the perspective of their own diverse experiences and local knowledge—of the scenes and conversations and speech patterns that Lakhous uses to build his stories and his characters. They even sometimes recommend alternatives or reject them altogether as false, misplaced or far-fetched. The point of this type of creative process is not so much accuracy or even verisimilitude, but rather—in Bakhtinian terms—the rejection of authorial monologism, and the construction of a truly dialogical text.

All of Lakhous's novels are effectively dialogical in that they are built on speech diversity. They incorporate a rich plurality and multiplicity of voices, styles and points of view, creating a genuine polyphony. One of the many intertextual and linguistic references in his multi-voiced novels is film comedy Italian style, *commedia all'italiana*, with its mix of the comic and the satirical with the dramatic, and its linguistic vitality. *Divorce Islamic Style*, for example, quotes and plays with Pietro Germi's classic *Divorce Italian Style* (1961), set in Sicily. Classic Italian cinema provides in fact a vast repertoire of images, voices and situations embedded in the minds of many Italians—and presumably part of a genuine collective cultural memory of sorts—that Lakhous uses in order to lead his readers to remember Italy's own past as a nation of migrants, and to see the new migrants as similar to them rather than alien.

In *Divorce Islamic Style*, when during his undercover mission Christian meets the new migrants and shares a place to live with some impoverished, exploited and fearful illegal street sellers pejoratively dubbed *vu cumprà* in Italy, he is reminded of the voices and predicament of poor Italian migrants after World War II who tried to make a living by working as illegal vendors of second-hand clothes and cloth abroad in West Germany in Francesco Rosi's classic film *I magliari* (1959), starring the *romanesco*-speaking Alberto Sordi (Totonno) as the illegal gang's leader.[5] In addition to evoking and using a variety of Italian regional inflections, and the language of classic Italian cinema, Lakhous inserts words and short phrases in Arabic into the novel, with the surprising effect of de-familiarizing "Italian" for his readers while re-familiarizing them with Arabic. One of Lakhous's prime motivations in his novels has been in fact to re-awaken in Italian readers the long-forgotten or repressed historical memory of Italy's connection and reciprocal fertilization with Arabic culture and civilization, especially in Sicily and southern Italy. In Lakhous's novels, the immigrant other becomes not a fearful stranger, but an uncanny mirror in which to contemplate and reflect on one's own complex and changing identity.

In conclusion, in my discussion of Amara Lakhous's best-selling novels, I have tried to show how a certain kind of narrative, through its dialogical textual strategies, may be able to counter and debunk the work of fear and anxiety generated by the media and other political and social discursive flows in Italy and Europe, and the "emotionality of texts" that tend to turn immigrants into deviant others and perpetual strangers, and thus heighten and manipulate our fears and rationalize the securitarian paradigm.

Finally, Amara Lakhous's Italian novels are not so much about the fear of immigration per se, as about Italy, as a place that is constantly changing and where what is taking place is not a fearful clash of civilizations, but, yet again, an encounter of cultures.

NOTES

1. Although there are no comprehensive official statistics and data on racist violence and hate crimes in Italy (unlike, for example, in France and Great Britain), the Italian NGO Associazione Lunaria publishes online the quarterly report *Cronache di ordinario razzismo*, http://www.cronachediordinariorazzismo.org/, based for the most part on data they collect from the Italian news media. Twelve shootings, two murders and thirty-three physical assaults were recorded in the two months after Matteo Salvini entered the government in 2018.

2. Lakhous has also published Arabic versions of all of his novels written in Italian.

3. In an interview, Lakhous explained what I call his linguistic double-voicedness as follows: "I chose to write in two languages; each novel has two versions, one in Arabic and one in Italian. I hope to continue like this and the goal is a very ambitious one: to Italianize Arabic and

to Arabize Italian. [. . .] To live in two cultures means to hold, as it were, different keys for different doors. [. . .] To Arabize Italian [. . .] means also to take the imaginary from one shore of the Mediterranean to the other, not only in the sense of the encounter between cultures, but also in the sense of the rediscovery of a mutual memory. [. . .] As an Arab author who writes in Italian I do not come but rather I return to Italy, which is a place that for many centuries was inhabited by Arab culture" (Sandri 2007).

4. De Angelis is cited many times by Lakhous in his novels' acknowledgements, along with several other interlocutors.

5. See *Divorce Islamic Style* 74–75: "I recall Francesco Rosi's film, *I magliari*, with Renato Salvatori and the great Alberto Sordi. The story is set in Germany in the fifties and recounts the adventures of a group of illegal, crooked fabric merchants, in other words, Italian street peddlers."

BIBLIOGRAPHY

Ahmed, Sarah. 2015. *The Cultural Politics of Emotion*. New York: Routledge (second edition).
Bakhtin, Mikhail. 1981. *The Dialogic Imagination. Four Essays*. Ed. Michael Holquist; translation by Caryl Emerson and Michael Holquist. Austin: University of Texas Press, 1981.
Bauman, Zygmunt. 1990. *Thinking Sociologically. An introduction for Everyone*. Cambridge, Mass.: Basil Blackwell, 1990.
———. 1991. *Modernity and Ambivalence*. Ithaca, N.Y.: Cornell University Press.
———. 1995. "Making and Unmaking of Strangers." *Sage Journals*. 43. 1: 1-16.
———. 2000. *Liquid Modernity*. Cambridge: Polity Press.
———. 2004. *Wasted Lives. Modernity and its Outcasts*. Cambridge: Polity Press.
———. 2006. *Liquid Fear*. Cambridge: Polity Press.
Bleiker, Roland. 2009. *Aesthetics and World Politics*. New York: Palgrave.
Bonomi, Aldo and Pierfrancesco Majorino. 2018. *Nel labirinto delle paure. Politica, precarietà e immigrazione*. Turin: Bollati Boringhieri.
Bordi, Alberto. 2010. "Più stranieri, più criminalità. Un'equazione che non torna." *Libertà Civili. Bimestrale di studi e documentazione sui temi dell'immigrazione* 6, 10: 115–120.
Bourke, Johanna. 2005. *Fear: A Cultural History*. London: Virago Press.
Burns, Jennifer. 2013. "*Lupus in Fabula*: The Workings of Fear in Italian Migration Narratives." *Italian studies* 68, 3: 429–48.
Comito, Chiara. 2013. Interview with Amara Lakhous. http://www.arabismo.org/questa-italia-alle-prese-con-la-paura-dellaltro-intervista- con-amara-lakhous/?i=1
Corbin, Alain, Jean-Jacques Courtine, Georges Vigarello. 2016. *Histoire des émotions: Tome 2, Des Lumières à la fin du XIXe siècle*. Paris: Seuil.
Courtine, Jean-Jacques. 2016. "The History of Fear in the Age of Anxiety: Historical Perspectives." Paper delivered at the September 2016 conference, "What are we afraid of? Local Fears, Global Perspectives." University of Auckland, New Zealand.
Diamanti, Ilvo. 2010. *La sicurezza in Italia: Significati, immagini e realtà*. http://www.demos.ir1200S/pdflsicurezza_italiic200S.pdf.
Douglas, Mary and Aaron Wildavsky. 1982. *Risk and Culture: An Essay on the Selection of Technical and Environmental Dangers*. Berkeley: University of California Press.
Geertz, Clifford. 2000. "The Growth of Culture and the Evolution of Mind" (1973) in *The Interpretation of Cultures*. New York: Basic Books.
Gramigna, Agostino and Gianni Santucci. 2008. "Abdul e quell'offesa che non sopportava." *Il corriere della sera* . September 15. http://www.corriere.it/cronache/08_settembre_15/abdul_offesa_che_non_sopport ava_f68a431c-82ea-11dd-a6c8-00144f02aabc.shtml
Houellebeq, Michel. 2015. *La Soumission*. Paris: Flammarion.
Huysmans, Jef. 2006. *The Politics of Insecurity. Fear, Migration and Asylum in the EU*. London: Routledge.
Lakhous, Amara. 2006. *Scontro di civiltà per un ascensore a piazza Vittorio*. Edizioni E/O.
———. 2008. *Clash of Civilizations over an Elevator in Piazza Vittorio*. Translated by Ann Goldstein. Europa Editions, 2008.

————. 2010. *Divorzio all'Islamica a viale Marconi.* Rome: Edizioni E/O.

————. 2012. *Divorce Islamic Style.* Translated by Ann Goldstein. New York: Europa Editions.

————. 2013. *Contesa per un maialino italianissimo a San Salvario.* Rome: Edizioni E/O.

————. 2014. *Dispute Over a Very Italian Piglet.* Translated by Ann Goldstein. New York: Europa Editions.

————. 2014. *La zingarata della verginella di via Ormea.* Rome: Edizioni E/O.

————. 2016. *The Prank of the Good Little Virgin of via Ormea.* Translated by Antony Shugaar. New York: Europa Editions.

Nussbaum, Martha. 2001. *Upheavals of Thought: The Intelligence of Emotions.* Cambridge University Press.

————. 2012. *The New Religious Intolerance. Overcoming the Politics of Fear in an Anxious Age.* The Belknap Press and Harvard University Press.

Ruta, Suzanne. 2008. Interview with Amara Lakhous. http://www.wordswithoutborders.org/article/scheherazade-cest-moi-an-interview-with-amara-lakhous/

Sandri, Chiara. 2007. Intervista con Amara Lakhous. *Italian Espresso 2, Caffè Culturale.* Firenze: Alma Edizioni: 110–111.

Sayad, Abdelmalek. 2004. *The Suffering of the Immigrant.* Translation by David Macey. Cambridge: Polity Press.

Tabar, Omid Firouzi. 2014. "Una rassegna di ricerche sulla percezione dell'insicurezza in Italia: Forza e vulnerabilità del 'paradigma securitario.'" *Studi sulla questione criminale* 3: 73–92.

Valtolina, Giovanni Giulio. 2010. "I cittadini europei e l'immigrazione: gli italiani sono i più preoccupati." *Libertà Civili. Bimestrale di studi e documentazione sui temi dell'immigrazione* 6, 10: 92–102

Clash of Civilizations Over an Elevator in Piazza Vittorio

Amara Lakhous

NINTH WAIL

Sunday June 4, 10:33 P.M.

I'm like a newborn, I need milk every day. Italian is my daily milk. Stefania is life; that is, the present and the future. I love Stefania because she is closely attached to life, I adore her memory free of nightmares. I want to be infected by life, love, future, and a happy wail. Auuuuuuuuu . . .

Monday November 17, 11:57 P.M.

So many people consider their work a daily punishment. Whereas I love my work as a translator. Translation is a journey over a sea from one shore to the other. Sometimes I think of myself as a smuggler: I cross the frontiers of language with my booty of words, ideas, images, and metaphors.

Wednesday September 29, 11:09 P.M.

Poor Stefania, she's worried about me, she thinks I'm suffering from stomach pains. The problem is that the stomach of my memory hasn't yet digested everything I swallowed before coming to Rome. Memory is just like a stomach. Every so often it makes me vomit. I vomit memories of blood nonstop. I have an ulcer in my memory. Is there a cure? Yes: wailing! Auuuuuuuuu . . .

Sunday March 9, 11:17 P.M.

Today I finished reading Amin Maalouf's novel *Leo Africanus*. I reread this passage over and over until I knew it by heart: "I, Hassan, son of Muhammad the weigh-master, I, Jean-Leon de' Medici, circumcised at the hand of a barber and baptized at the hand of a Pope, I am now called the African, but I am not from Africa, nor from Europe, nor from Arabia. . . . I'm the son of the road. My country is the caravan. My life the most unexpected of voyages." It's marvelous to be able to free ourselves from the chains of identity. Which lead us to ruin. Who am I? Who are you? Who are they? These are pointless and stupid questions.

Thursday November 18, 10:51 P.M.

Stefania is very pleased at having started teaching Italian to the Bangladeshi women. Yesterday she said to me, "Soon we'll establish the first Bangladeshi feminist organization in Italy!" I told her that that wasn't the agreement. She laughed, adding, "Don't you remember that Louis Aragon quote? 'Woman is the future of man.'" I said, "Soon I'll be like *le fou d'Elsa*: Stefania's mad-man." I love Stefania because she is my future.

Thursday February 2, 11:13 P.M.

Today I started reading the aphorisms of Emil Cioran. I was struck by this one: "We inhabit not a country but a language." Is the Italian language my new dwelling place? Auuuuuu . . .

Saturday October 24, 10:45 P.M.

Stefania is never tired of seeing *The Sheik*, with Rudolf Valentino. I've seen her weep sometimes, with emotion. Maybe it reminds her of her father, who died in a drilling accident in Libya several years ago. Her father was an expert at finding oil. Stefania believes that the word "expert" was his curse. She always says to me that the Sahara has no pity for those who do not show respect for it.

Thursday June 24, 10:57 P.M.

The damn nightmare is pursuing me. Stefania told me this morning that I cried out in my sleep and that I kept repeating the name Bagia. I didn't want to tell her the details. It's pointless for her to join the game of nightmares. My memory is wounded and bloody: I have to heal the wounds of the past in solitude. A shame, Bagia shows up only in nightmares, wrapped in a bloodstained sheet. Oh, this open wound that will never heal! I have no consolation but wailing. Auuuuuu . . .

Sunday March 30, 11:48 P.M.

This morning I reread the novel *The Invention of the Desert* by the Algerian writer Tahar Djaout. I paused for a long time on this sentence: "Happy people have neither age nor memory, they have no need of the past." I'm going to wail all night long in search of consolation: Auuuuu . . .

THE TRUTH ACCORDING TO ABDALLAH BEN KADOUR

Why did he call himself Amedeo? That's the question that leaves me so perplexed. His real name is Ahmed, which is a precious name, because it's one of the names of the prophet Mohammed—it's mentioned both in the Koran and in the Gospels. Frankly I don't much appreciate people who change their name or deny their origins: for example, my name is Abdallah, and I know perfectly well that it's a difficult name for Italians to pronounce, but in spite of that I've sworn not to change it as long as I live. I don't want to disobey my father, who gave me this name, or God, who forbids us to disobey our parents. Changing your name is a capital crime, like murder, adultery, bearing false witness, like stealing from orphans. Many Italians I know have tried to persuade me to change my name, proposing a series of Italian names like Alessandro, Francesco, Massimiliano, Guido, Mario, Luca, Pietro, and others, but I have resolutely refused. The problem doesn't end there. Some have used a trick that's very common in Rome, which consists of eliminating the first or second part of a name. So I've been called Abd, which means "slave," or even Allah! I've asked forgiveness from God because He forgives all sins except polytheism. I've tried to keep my composure as I explain to them that all men, including the prophets and messengers of God, are His servants, and so my name has nothing to do with the kind of slavery that was everywhere in the time of Kunta Kinte. So I found myself caught between two fires: either fall into the trap of polytheism every time someone called me Allah or endure the insults of those who called me Abd. Finally I found a way out of this impasse, thanks to my Egyptian friend Metwali, who advised me to make a small change in my name. He told me that the Egyptians have a custom of calling Abdu people whose name begins with Abd: Abdrahman, Abdalkarim, Abdkader, Abdrahim, Abdjabar, Abdhakim, Abdsabour, Abdaraouf. I agreed, because this solution avoided the problems I've mentioned. Unfortunately there are some people who have first and last names steeped in polytheism. Take Iqbal, the Bangladeshi. I've told him many times that his last name, Amir Allah, is polytheistic. If he knew Arabic, he would understand that there is no difference between Amir Allah and Amir "superior to Allah." God save us from Satan!

I will not change my skin, or my religion, or my country, or my name, for any reason. I'm proud of myself, I'm not like those immigrants who change their name to please the Italians. Take the Tunisian who works in the restaurant Luna at the station. His real name is Mohsen, but he's had himself called, or they called him, Massimiliano. God says in the Koran: "Jews and Christians will not accept you until you follow their religion." God the Great is right. I can't bear it when people 'deny their origins.' You know the story of the donkey, who when he's asked "Who is your father?" answers "The horse is my uncle"? You know about the crow that wanted to imitate the dove's way of walking and, after various futile attempts, decides to go back to his natural way and at that point discovers that he no longer remembers it?

Amedeo is from my neighborhood. I know him very well, just as I know his whole family. His younger brother was one of my dearest friends, my schoolmate and playmate. Ahmed was a person who was loved and respected in the neighborhood. I don't recall that he ever fought, although there were frequent brawls among gangs, which are a widespread phenomenon in the neighborhoods of Algiers. Ahmed's troubles began when his fiancée, Bagia, died; she was the neighbors' daughter. Ahmed had loved her since he was a child, and wanted to marry her, but unfortunately things turned out differently. Bagia, which in Arabic means "joy," is a female name, and a name, too, for Algiers.

One day Bagia went to see her sister in Boufarik, not far from Algiers, and on the way back the bus was stopped by terrorists who had set up a fake checkpoint, passing themselves off as police. They cut the throats of all the passengers except the girls. Bagia tried to flee, to avoid being raped, so they shot her in a burst of machine-gun fire. Ahmed couldn't accept that tragedy. He shut himself in the house for days, then he disappeared. In the neighborhood various hypotheses made the rounds: some said that he had enlisted in the army, seeking revenge against the fundamentalists, some maintained that he had joined the armed fighters in the mountains as a sign of rejection and condemnation of the state, some said that he had gone off to join a Sufi sect in the Sahara and live like the Tuareg, and finally someone said that Ahmed had gone mad and was wandering, naked, through the streets. One neighbor even assured his family that he had recognized Ahmed at the station in Annaba, in the eastern part of the country, waiting for a train to Tunisia. I never understood why his family didn't resort to a well-known television show, *Everything Is Possible*, which looks for missing people. One day I asked his mother, Aunt Fatma Zohra, for the news of Ahmed, and she said sharply, "He's outside." The word "outside" has a thousand meanings: outside of reason, outside of Algiers, outside the law, outside the charity of his parents, outside the grace of God. I preferred not to insist and left the cover on the well, as our old proverb goes.

Then one day I saw him in the market in Piazza Vittorio, where I sell fish: I called to him, "Ahmed! Ahmed!" but he didn't respond. It seemed to me that he was pretending not to recognize me. Finally he greeted me, but coldly. He was with an Italian woman, only later did I find out that she was his wife. We met often at the Bar Dandini. He wasn't enthusiastic about hearing the latest news from Algeria, so I decided to avoid talking to him on subjects that had to do with our country—I didn't want to upset him. I didn't even dare to advise him to give up the name Amedeo and return to his original name, Ahmed, which is the name of the Prophet, peace be upon him. It's said that returning to one's origins is a virtue!

Ahmed or Amedeo—as you call him—worked at the Supreme Court in Algiers as a translator from French into Arabic. He had bought an apartment in Bab Azouar for him and Bagia to live in after their marriage, but destiny held another life in store for him. As you see, the story of Ahmed Salmi is simple, it's not that complicated. The truth is different, it's not what you thought up to now. There are no particular secrets, no twisted events in his life before he settled in Rome.

I've sold fish for years, and I find no difference between the lives of fish and the lives of immigrants. I know a proverb that the Italians often repeat: "Guests are like fish, after three days they stink." The immigrant is a guest, no more or less, and, like fish, you eat him when he's fresh and throw him in the garbage when he loses his color. There are two types of immigrants: the fresh ones, who are exploited inhumanly in the factories of the north or the agricultural lands of the south, and the frozen, who fill the freezers and are used only in an emergency. You know what Gianfranco, the owner of the shop where I work, calls the girls from Eastern Europe who sell their bodies for a little money: fresh fish!

Gianfranco is over sixty, he is married and has four children older than me. His favorite hobby is to drive out on the Appia Antica at night in search of girls from Nigeria or Eastern Europe, girls who are at most twenty and often much younger. So he spends a peaceful hour with the fresh fish—so he calls the girl of the moment—before returning to the arms of his wife, whom he makes fun of with his friends, calling her a frozen fish, who always needs a little time to thaw and warm up before being consumed. Gianfranco, or the Pig—as his friends call him—likes to sit in front of the shop all day with them and, before the astonished gaze of his customers, recount in detail his adventures of the night before. Often enthusiastic laughter greets him, followed by obscene comments like "Gianfranco, you're a pig! Gianfranco, you're a fat pig!" And the cad isn't bothered by that odious nickname, because the pig is the symbol of virility in Italy. In fact, he's proud of it!

I haven't changed the subject. I'm still talking about Ahmed. If I heard someone call me Pig I would cut out his tongue, because the pig or *halouf*— as we call it—is hateful and has nothing to do with virility and masculinity. In fact, it's the worst insult. The pig is a dirty animal, it lives in the garbage. I don't understand why there hasn't been an outbreak of mad-pig disease. Why has that dangerous disease affected only cows? It's a perplexing question.

In Rome there is the Termini station. "Termini" means terminal, the journey is over. There's something strange about this city. It's very difficult to leave. Maybe the water in the fountains is mixed with a special substance that has magical origins.

Have you seen the difference between us and them? Ahmed hasn't grasped the substantial differences between our religion and Gianfranco's. I can still remember the fear that struck me when I heard people call him Amedeo. I was afraid he had renounced Islam. I didn't hesitate an instant, I asked him with distress and concern, "Ahmed have you converted to Christianity?" And he answered serenely, "No." I sighed deeply and said aloud, "Praise be to God! Praise be to God!" My fears were legitimate, because usually someone who changes his name has embraced a new religion, like the famous English singer Cat Stevens who had people call him Yousef Islam right after his conversion.

Don't you see what the newspapers are saying about Ahmed? As soon as they discovered that he was an immigrant and not an Italian they didn't hesitate to accuse him of murder. Certainly, Ahmed made a mistake by swimming outside his natural harbor. His disappearance reminds me so much of his disappearance years ago, which caused such dismay in our neighborhood. The question is the same today: what happened to Ahmed, or Amedeo—as you call him?

Gendering the *Giallo*

Gender Roles in the Opus of Amara Lakhous

Ryan Calabretta-Sajder

As a literary art form, the *giallo* arrives in Italy rather late, compared to the Anglo-American and French traditions. Its formal introduction was born out of Mondadori's 1929 interest in translating British and American detective stories, such as those of Sherlock Holmes and Edgar Allan Poe, for an Italian audience.[1] The Italian form boasts a rich and intricate foundation, experimentation, and evolution, and some scholars have traced characteristics of detective fiction in the historical novel of the *Risorgimento*.[2] Unfortunately, detective fiction, in general, has received serious critical attention only during the last fifty to sixty years; until recently, Italianists have traditionally given even less attention to this genre, both in literature and cinema.[3] Within the last fifteen years, Italianists have turned their attention to the genre of the *giallo*, particularly to its relationship with the New Italian Epic with writers like those of the Wu Ming collective.[4]

Historically, the *giallo* has often been associated with the subgenre of mafia fiction, established by Leonardo Sciascia's *Il giorno della civetta* (The Day of the Owl), considered to be the first mafia novel. The Italian *giallo* continues to evolve and encapsulate diverse themes and subgenres. The most noted *giallo* writers—Leonardo Sciascia, Carlo Emilio Gadda, Umberto Eco, and Andrea Camilleri—are also among Italy's most prominent contemporary authors, and who have solidified its importance within the Italian canon. Present-day scholarship on the *giallo* focuses on various aspects of the genre and pushes the discourse beyond the realm of literary studies, combining the humanities with the social sciences through sociological criticism. The *giallo* provides a sociopolitical commentary on contemporary society. Through his satire, Amara Lakhous's *gialli* bring the treatment of migrants into the critical discussion. Lakhous's writings address numerous sociopolitical issues that accompany the migrant experience, such as language, culture, and religion. This article examines how Lakhous's characters break from typical gender binaries of the *giallo* tradition and Italian culture at large.

Graziella Parati considers the concept of the migrant body concerning his/her/their newfound space in Lakhous's first novel *Scontro di civiltà per un ascensore a Piazza Vittorio* (Clash of Civilizations over an Elevator in Piazza Vittorio, 2006).[5] She employs philosophy and sociology and applies Affect Theory to explain how these two approaches are linked. Although she does not directly address the genre of the *giallo*, it has a pertinent place within this larger discussion. Aligning with the discourse of space within the *giallo*, Luca Somigli points out that

> murder and investigation take place within the confines of a very specific environment [. . .] The closed environment is certainly not an invention of De Angelis: from country houses on the moors to international trains, the Anglo-American tradition had already thoroughly explored the murderous possibilities of almost all the spaces of the bourgeois society that it took as its main subject. In the fiction of the Italian writer, however, these closed spaces become something more: they seem to provide an alternative to the metropolis that surrounds and encroaches on them like a suspension fluid. (2005, 77)

The spatial context is critical for Lakhous, who sets his tales in specific neighborhoods of Italy. His first two novels, *Scontro di civiltà per un ascensore a Piazza Vittorio* (2006) and *Divorzio all'islamica a viale Marconi* (Divorce Islamic Style, 2010), take place in two specific migrant areas of Rome, while his next two novels, *Contesa per un maialino italianissimo a San Salvario* (Dispute Over a Very Italian Piglet, 2013) and *La zingarata della verginella di Via Ormea* (The Prank of the Good Little Virgin of Via Ormea, 2014), are set in Torino.[6] Most of the action in each novel revolves around one or two main physical spaces within the specific neighborhood.

These microcosms are critical for Lakhous because he manipulates the concepts of space and place to open a dialogue around diversity, acceptance, and integration. The author thus constructs a metaphor for a commentary on our global society. In *Scontro di civiltà*, the concept of space, both physical and philosophical, is intertwined in each character's perspective. The novel is divided into eleven chapters, each subdivided into two sections: the first entitled "La verità di X" (The Truth According to X), X being a character's name, immediately followed a numbered "Ululato" (Wail) section. Each "verità" section represents a different character's point of view, as well as that character's opinion of the protagonist, Amedeo. Each "wailing" section assumes Amedeo's voice and functions as a foil for the other characters' perspectives. Unclear until the very end of the novel, these chapters function as a series of interviews conducted by Detective Mauro Bettarini, creating a log or chronology, similar to a detective's notes in traditional detective fiction. However, each section is independent; although there is a connection between interviews and an anticipated movement to find the killer, the chapters also offer individual truths. These varying conceptions of the truth prove prudent because of the objective of the genre—to find the killer. Although the reader expects to clue-gather through the various "La verità di X" chapters, Lakhous instead plays with the spectator's expectations, using these pieces more often to expose stereotypes and racism rather than offer clues to the mystery. Despite the fact that little truth derives from those chapters directly, the conceptualization of truth, or better yet "truths," and how its forms remain the satirical focus of the chapters and novel as a whole.

The main occupants of the building include: Amedeo/Ahmed and his partner Stefania Massaro, who was Amedeo's Italian professor when he first arrived in Rome; Benedetta Esposito, who is extremely proud to be Neapolitan and works as the concierge; Elisabetta Fabiani, an elderly lady who dotes on her dog, Valentino (he is accused of peeing in the elevator and eventually goes missing); Maria Cristina Gonzalez, originally from Peru, works as the caretaker for the elderly Signora Rosa; Antonio Marini, a professor at one of the universities in Rome but who is originally from Milan, considers Rome to be Southern Italy and therefore, feels it is a horrible place to live; and Johan Van Marten, who is a young Dutch student in Rome studying filmmaking. The only illegal migrant is Maria Cristina Gonzalez, who is afraid of being deported. Amedeo is amicable to all, including those not living in his building: Parviz Mansoor Samadi, a friend whom Amedeo helps to get a job as a cook since Parviz owned a restaurant in Shiraz; Igbal Amir Allah, who owns a local shop that Amedeo often frequents; Sandro Dandini, who owns the local caffè where Amedeo often meets the previously mentioned characters; Abdallah Ben Kadour, the only character who knows Amedeo's past; and Mauro Bettarini, the local detective. The diverse, multi-ethnic backgrounds of our protagonists all living close to each other will help underscore Samuel Huntington's 1992 theoretical concept, "The Clash of Civilizations?"[7]

The first chapter, "The Truth According to Parviz Monsoor Samadi," reveals that Lorenzo Manfredini, otherwise known as "The Gladiator," was murdered in the elevator of Amedeo's building, located within walking distance of Piazza Vittorio in Rome, where most of the characters work. After Amedeo's mysterious disappearance, rumor suggests that he is not Italian and that his legal name is Ahmed Salmi. Because the culprit remains at large, people begin questioning Amedeo's innocence. In the end, however, the truth sets Amedeo/Ahmed free. The unfolding of the narrative underscores the hyper-racial tensions that exist in the community, from the previously mentioned organization of the novel to its characters and their ethnic backgrounds. Almost every main character partakes in systematic racism: the Italian characters, particularly Benedetta Esposito and Professor Antonio

Marini, are regionalist and express racist sentiments not only towards migrants but also other Italians depending on the region of origin.[8] Although Benedetta recalls the racism that she faced as a Southerner moving to Rome, she continually derides all the migrants, particularly Parziv and Maria Christina. Moreover, the ethnically diverse microcosm of the building in Piazza Vittorio acts directly as a metaphor for Rome. Yet the metaphor is not confined to Rome or even Italy; the building in Piazza Vittorio acts as an analogy for any community.

While the novel breaks from the traditional *giallo* in several ways,[9] here, I will examine the concepts of community and gender, which serve as one social commentary on Italy. In a 2014 interview, Lakhous explains:

> My *gialli* are not traditional *gialli*; in my novels, little importance is given to the assassin. My main objective is to use the novel to address a context: the clash of civilizations, daily life. The principle question is not who killed "The Gladiator," rather to understand the stories of those who live in the building, to understand how these diverse protagonists live together in close vicinity. (Calabretta-Sajder 2016b, 822)

By examining the principles of intercultural competence, community, integration, and even humor, Lakhous's works aim to disrupt issues of prejudice in Italy.

The title of Lakhous's novel is a direct reference to Huntington's rather racist and narrow conceptualization of society.[10] Huntington's text lists six reasons that civilizations clash, including language, history, culture, traditions, and religion, but he downplays the importance of local communities and economies. Huntington's conservative theory of modernism is openly challenged by Lakhous: the main character, a foreigner who is more Roman than the seventh generation Romans, is not the killer; instead, the Roman *pensionata* Elisabetta Fabiani is. Moreover, not one character within the novel believes that Amedeo is the killer.

On the concept of community, Benedict Anderson's *Imagined Communities: Reflections on the Origin and Spread of Nationalism* (1983) challenges the ways scholars conceive of communities and how they function within the nation-state.[11] Anderson argued, "In contrast to the immense influence that nationalism has exerted on the modern world, plausible theory about it is conspicuously meagre" (3). Anderson attempted to integrate principles of Marxism and nationalism, in the hope of challenging the preconceived Western European notions of national identity. Lakhous first confronts the concept of the imagined community in *Scontro di civiltà* by the vicinity which exists amongst the characters within the *palazzo* and nearby areas, "It is *imagined* because the members of even the smallest nation will never know most of their fellow members, meet them, or even hear of them, yet in the minds of each lives the image of their communion" (Anderson, 6; original emphasis).

Within the novel, then, what exactly would be the "imagined community" as theorized by Anderson? If we assume his definition, the imagined community would be Italy as a whole. Although a bit problematic due to the country's unique history, in theory, it conforms to Anderson's definition. If we want to scale the concept down one level, the imagined community can even become Rome. Yet, Lakhous's *palazzo* serves as a metaphor for Italy and by returning to Huntington, we cannot ignore the "clash of civilizations" present within the *palazzo* itself and its surrounding neighborhood. The second layer of difficulty arises with the complexity surrounding the Southern Italian characters. Benedetta, the concierge, is first and foremost Neapolitan: "I'm from Naples, I'll shout it out, I'm not ashamed. But then why should I be? [. . .] My name is Benedetta, but a lot of people like to call me la Napolitana. That nickname doesn't bother me" (Lakhous 2006, 30). Benedetta proudly displays and accepts her Neapolitan origins as she continues to speak in her dialect and cites San Gennaro and the actor Totò, all obvious references to the "City of the Sun."

Yet, Benedetta simultaneously, and seemingly indirectly, attempts to align herself with the Italian nation-state through cinema. In discussion with Johan, "He calls me Anna Magnani! I've told him many times that Anna Magnani was born in Rome, she's Roman, whereas I was born in Naples, I speak Neapolitan. He asked me to be in a movie. [. . .] I'm a concierge, not an actress! [. . .] he looked at me seriously: 'You're the new Anna Magnani!'" (Lakhous 2006, 32). The comparison to Anna Magnani works on two levels: Anna "*nannarella*" Magnani, indeed represents the Eternal City, but Magnani was known on an international level as a representation of Italy, in part due to Tennessee Williams's play and later film adaptation of *The Rose Tattoo* (1955).[12] The reader encounters Benedetta's struggle to create her imagined community where she no longer remains outside but becomes part of mainstream culture in Piazza Vittorio, as Antonio Marini suggests. As Marini excludes Benedetta from his nationalistic imagined society when stating, "For example, the Neapolitan concierge, Sandro Dandini, and Elisabetta Fabiani are symbols of the south, with their sadness, their chatter, their underdevelopment, gossip, credulousness, superstition. I'm not a racist" (92). Both characters argue against including the newly arrived migrants in their community. Sandro and Elisabetta are not even Southerners in the true sense, rather they are Roman, but Marini is so prejudiced in that he includes even them because he equivalates laziness with Southernness/Otherness: "To me there is no difference between immigrants and people from the south. . . . I'm an attentive observer, I can distinguish between someone who is lazy and someone who wants to work" (92). For Marini, therefore, anyone who is not a Northern Italian cannot participate in the imagined community of Italy.

Lakhous's use of Marini's very close-minded character is the problematic epitome of Anderson's conceptualization, and simultaneously the social clash contemporary Italy is still fighting to grasp.

When examining *Scontro*'s physical surroundings, the novel revolves around the *palazzo* and nearby Piazza Vittorio. The only other spatial reference point within the novel is Santa Maria Maggiore, a space which does not conform to Anderson's theory, rather functions on the contrary, as the public space where all the migrants happily convene to converse with each other. In fact, it is a space in which Maria Cristina spends her free time as it is one of the only places she finds comfort in Rome due to being populated by other migrants. The *palazzo* is a closed, private space; to enter, people must confront Benedetta, the concierge. Returning to Anderson's framework, thus, the *palazzo* needs to be considered as a microcosm, representing Italy as a whole. To a certain extent, however, this mini-nation has borders around it, and passage is not necessarily controlled but, at the very least, regulated. Once granted passage, another prominent space, that of the elevator, is a closed space with hidden characteristics; once the doors shut, no one from the outside is privy to what happens inside. Even though each character is theoretically allowed entry into the elevator, the connotations connected with ethnic identity and Culture with a capital "C" reign. The elevator is treated as a princely space, allotted for royalty, aka Italians, rather than migrants. As we will explore, the Italians create the regulations around the elevator, while the migrants are treated as second-class citizens to its use.

Therefore, each character within the novel claims his/her/their relationship with the elevator, which seems at times itself to function as a character. Indeed, each character's relationship with the elevator underscores an aspect of his/her/their personality. For example, Benedetta, the Neopolitan, tries to assert the little power she has over the residents concerning the elevator; she insults them for using it and strives to keep it pristine. When Amedeo's friend Parviz, the Persian immigrant, comes to visit, he enjoys the elevator ride even though Benedetta attempts to block him from entering it: "I adore the elevator, I don't take it because I'm lazy—I meditate in it. You press the button without any effort, you go up or descend, it could even break down while you're inside. It's exactly like life, full of breakdowns [. . .] The elevator is a tool for meditation" (Lakhous 2006, 16). In this regard, Parviz embarks on a quasi-spiritual/philosophical relationship with the elevator.

Another Italian occupant of the *palazzo*, Elisabetta Fabiani, creates drama over the elevator as she allows her dog, Valentino, to constantly pee inside, upsetting all the characters in the novel. Because she is Italian, however, Fabiani is never reprimanded; if she had been a migrant, she would have been banned from its use. Yet for the Milanese professor, the elevator is a question of civilization:

> I've tried quite a few times to organize tenants' meetings to deal once and for all with some serious problems, especially the problem of the elevator. I repeated that the elevator is a matter of civilization, and that we must establish clear rule for using it: tossing our cigarette butts is prohibited, eating is forbidden, writing obscenities is prohibited, urinating is forbidden, and so on. I proposed putting a sign on the door of the elevator: "Please keep the elevator clean!" But the proposal did not win a majority vote, and afterward the Dutch student Van Marten went off saying, "Such a sign should only be at the entrance to a public toilet!" (76)

Marini's tirade begins on a practical level but eventually includes a class-structure argument; however, his imagined community, for him that of Northern Italy, clearly does not match his reality, for, within the exchange, we observe Johan Van Marten's logical response. The same sentiment can be noted in an interview with the author:

> In *Clash of Civilizations over an Elevator in Piazza Vittorio* I chose the elevator because I wanted to reflect on the question: how do we live together? The elevator is a place in which one has to remain in close contact with others, a place in which one observes the scent of others, positive and negative, a place where people look each other in the eye and have an urge to say something [my translation].[13]

The elevator *should* be a neutral entity, yet in the novel, it never is. Essentially, the elevator morphs into the most uncivilized space within the entire novel, serving as the focal point of the plot since "The Gladiator" was murdered there. While all the Italians suspect one of the migrants to be the culprit because they are generally considered "suspicious," actually an Italian, Fabiani, is the murderer. Yet, something about the murderer is a bit surprising. Within the *giallo* tradition, we traditionally expect the murderer to be one who is innocent or less suspicious. However, it is noteworthy that not only is Elisabetta a native Italian, coming from within the imagined community on every level (Italian, Roman, lived in the *palazzo* her adult life), but also the fact that she assassinates another Italian, again one form within the imagined community (Italian, Roman, and who grew up within the *palazzo*). Her motive is clear: "The Gladiator" stole Valentino and used him in a dogfight and he did not survive.

The astute Fabiani, who follows crime fiction television, first consulted with the police, which were useless, before she took the law into her own hands. Not surprisingly thus, Fabiani learns the tricks of the trade from television, which became a nationalizing agent in Italy during the post-war years, first and foremost regarding questions of broadcasting in Italian standard, and also for the consequences the television brought to regionalism, from language to culture. After learning about the "The Gladiator's" crime, she chooses the elevator "because it's at the center of the conflicts among the building's residents. Then, to avoid suspicion, she used a knife, because it's considered a typically male weapon" (Lakhous 2006, 127). Having learned from Columbo and others, Fabiani knows exactly how to cover her tracks. Moreover, Fabiani launches a nationalistic discourse aimed at quantifying life: "I say that the rights of the native-born come first, and dogs are children of this country. I don't trust immigrants. I read recently in the paper that an immigrant gardener raped an old woman who had given him everything: residency permit, job, place to live, and so on. Is that the reward? Have you ever heard of a dog who raped its owner?" (Lakhous 2006, 69).

Although nationalistic in nature, Fabiani not only weighs the importance of human life, she also compares human relationships with those with animals, glorifying the latter to justify her actions. In her interview with the detective, she directly states a world order: native-born and their children. In her mind, her child, which happens to be a dog, is a child of the *patria*, and as such, she is entitled to revenge, even against a native-born human. This nationalistic, almost fascist mentality demonstrates the strength hate and fear establishes in a community, whether large or small.

Ergo Lakhous "genders" the *giallo* through Elisabetta Fabiani's character. Lakhous is not the first author to adopt a female killer in the detective novel. The French tradition provides a female killer as early as 1969 with Émile Gaboriau's Monsieur Lecoq series in *Seconde Partie: L'Honneur du Nom.* Lakhous's extensive knowledge of the evolution of the *giallo* as represented in both the literary and visual culture traditions, in Italy and internationally, illustrates his self-awareness in constructing the villain within the text. In fact historically when there is a female killer in literature, she usually uses poison. Still, in *Scontro di civiltà,* Fabiani favors the knife since she believes the evidence would not point to her; her own familiarity of the *giallo* tradition empowers the gendered role-reversal she assumes in the murder. Like any prideful assassin, however, Fabiani kept a souvenir, a casebook definition of a serial killer: "The only mistake she made was not to get rid of the murder weapon, which she kept as a trophy. [. . .] The woman wanted to keep something to remind her that Valentino's murderer had got the punishment he deserved. Or maybe she was so sure she had carried out the perfect crime that no one would ever suspect her" (Lakhous 2006, 127). By Fabiani favoring the knife, Lakhous challenges the accepted definition of the *giallo* by swapping the assumed gender roles of the killer, a female, and arming her with a phallic weapon, a unique means to the end.

Through her time invested watching detective television, a nationalist action which was considered earlier, Fabiani adopts her learned behavior to real-life, mimicking the nationalist flair of the imagined community. On yet another level of analysis connecting the television to gender studies, it can be noted that Fabiani learned that gender could indeed be performative through her fandom of *Columbo* and other thrillers: "Our neighbor Elisabetta Fabiani is addicted to two things: dogs and thrillers. It's pointless to talk to her about anything in which there is no mention of a dog or of Hitchcock or Agatha Christie, Colombo or Derrick, Montalbano or Poirot. Elisabetta watches the police shows on TV every day" (73). Thus, following Judith Butler's early theoretical framework, she, at first glance, successfully fooled the police and created a false gender pretense to cover her tracks. In the "Introduction" to *Bodies that Matter*, Butler discusses how "the agency denoted by the performativity of 'sex' will be directly counter to any notion of a voluntarist subject who exists quite apart from the regulatory norms which she/he opposes" (xxiii). She continues with a list of guidelines used to adopt her theory. In short, Fabiani consciously utilizes a learned, masculine-connoted assassination method in hopes to fool others. Although psychoanalytical in nature, one should also note the recurring reference to the phallus, which underscores a gendered reading of the murder. Stereotypical in nature, it is important to move beyond the basic reading and consider rather than a lack of the phallus, a taking over of it. By killing "The Gladiator," heightened by the method in doing so, Elisabetta Fabiani simultaneously destroys Anderson's theory of the imagined community as she, the representative of a nationalist, murders another Italian. Through attempting to blame Amedeo/Ahmed as the killer, and having the truth be told in the end, Lakhous underscores the issues in Anderson's theoretical framework.

Various motifs within gender and sexuality studies connect Lakhous's *Scontro di civiltà* and *La zingara della verginella di via Omera* , including gender performativity and unfortunately, rape. The novel opens with the announcement that Virginia has been raped by "gli zingari," "'The gypsies have raped a young girl from the neighborhood.' 'The gypsies! *All* the gypsies?' I ask, trying to figure out what he's saying. 'No, two Roma twins'" (Lakhous 2014, 15). Enzo Laganà, a journalist and friend of Mario Bellezza, learns of this tragedy, but before accepting the story or sharing the blame, Enzo questions his friend a bit. The language is noteworthy: Bellezza states, "the gypsies," and Enzo retorts, "all the gypsies," underscoring the hyperbolic language to both calm Bellezza and make him realize that there is no place for hasty generalizations. Throughout the tale, Enzo reminds the reader and Bellezza himself that once upon a time, he was treated as "the other" because he is Calabrian and "immigrated" to the North for work after the war. The rest of the story charts Enzo's discovery of the facts, resembling a journalist's report by interweaving the story of Patrizia Pascali, a banker during the economic crash who catches her employer in illegal financial transactions, reports him, and leaves her "Torinese" identity behind to live a life of a gypsy/Roma called "Drabarimos." Along the path to truth, the reader encounters stereotypes present both among Italians and the Roma community. The two accused rapists, Drago and Jonathan, live within the Roma community of Turin, where the story takes place. Halfway through the novel, we learn that the Roma boys are innocent, but the rapist is still unknown. In the end, the reader discovers that Virginia gave her virginity to her cousin Giuliano, who was like a brother to her, for his 18th birthday; however, she was still a minor.

It is important to revisit the truth behind the alleged rape. According to Giuliano, Virginia was the mastermind behind everything, from planning the loss of her virginity to blaming the Rom brothers. As in *Divorzio all'islamica a viale Marconi*, we see a strong female character indulging her sexual appetite, which is healthy but is rarely the story told, especially in Italian society. Even though these characters are cousins, as long as they are consenting adults, the ethical dilemma is theirs to ponder. But when one creates legal and ethical problems for innocent people, especially those already marginalized by society, the issue becomes grave. By the end of the novel, Virginia never confesses the truth; rather, she continues to hide behind her mask and play the victim. Even when she admits that she was not raped, though she is not willing to reveal her lover, she maintains the sexual power. Moreover, by falsely accusing the Rom brothers of sexual assault/rape, she is unable to "undo" the gender/sexuality damage, not to mention legal repercussions, to them. Despite their innocence, there is no "undoing" of the gender and sociopolitical problems caused by her actions. Sadly, her character does not accept any responsibility.

Gender roles are much more pronounced in Lakhous's third novel, *Divorzio all'islamica a viale Marconi* . The novel takes place in 2005 and tells the story of Italian secret police receiving intel about a supposed terrorist attack being organized by a group of migrants in the viale Marconi neighborhood.[14] To learn more about the planned attack, the police send Christian Mazzari, a Sicilian translator fluent in Arabic, to go undercover and collect information. Christian's new identity is Issa, a Tunisian migrant looking for work and a place to stay. In reality, Christian, the secret service agent, does not reside in viale Marconi; only when he morphs into Issa, the Tunisian migrant, does he move into the area as part of his undercover assignment. This detail underscores the challenges of being a migrant in contemporary Italian society or, metaphorically, anywhere. Issa quickly meets Said, otherwise known as Felice, a trained architect who currently works in a pizzeria. Said is married to Safia/Sofia, an Egyptian migrant who longs to be a hairstylist. The novel alternates the voices of Issa and Safia, reminiscent of *La zingarata*, offering a unique narrative voice that attempts to provide an anthropological or sociological perspective through playing on various stereotypes of life in a multicultural and multi-ethnic world. In the final pages of the novel, Issa discovers that the entire terrorist attack was a farce, organized to test his skills and loyalty for the secret police.

In both *Divorzio* and *La zingarata*, much attention is focused on the concept of virginity, a concept with is performative by its very nature.

Through the perspective of a Muslim character in *Divorzio*, we encounter many beliefs about virginity before marriage and even afterward. In *La zingarata,* however, Lakhous transposes the idea of virginity to the Italian characters, underscoring another reoccurring theme in his opus: the migrant characters are not that different from the "native" characters. By creating an entire satire around the conceptualization of virginity, Lakhous is not only making the reader laugh, similar to Luigi Pirandello's *L'umorismo* (1908), but is also doing much more. Our *giallo* author is taking the Pirandellian theory and utilizing it to both forewarn and teach contemporary society to remove oneself from the picture and reassess the scenario. In *L'umorismo*, Pirandello reconsiders the various layers and developments concerning humor and concludes that although something can be satirical, there is a human layer of emotion to be granted the object of the laugh, coined *il sentimento del contrario* (the sense of the opposite). Gender is just one motif that cuts through his opus and serves as an example of one aspect of society that needs reconsideration.

Divorzio all'islamica functions similarly to *Scontro di civiltà* regarding the importance of space, as both novels revolve around select locations. *Divorzio all'islamica*'s plot concentrates on Little Cairo, an international calling center, news center (the news from Al Jazeera seems to be constantly playing), and gossip hub operated by *hegg* Akram. Outside of Little Cairo, the plot focuses on Issa's apartment that he rents from Teresa, where he cohabits with mainly Egyptian migrants, along with one Senegalese, one Moroccan, and one Bengalese migrant. Omar states, "The important thing is that we're all Muslims" (47). Omar attempts to create his imagined reality, one in which only Muslims can reside comfortably together and understand each other. This is a noteworthy point regarding the sociological situation of migration from a class-structure situation. Migrants "with privilege," those educated and who have documents that allow them to move freely for work, are often better equipped to camouflage themselves from certain cultural or religious aspects. Yet a large majority are not offered that luxury, and, as Omar has claimed, "The important thing is that we're all Muslims" because there is a sense not only of unity but also of understanding. Safia, on the other hand, complains that viale Marconi reminds her too much of being in Egypt because of all the Egyptians from the neighborhood. She is the only character in the novel to have a real friendship with an Italian, Giuliana, which underscores her ability to integrate with the community.

As previously mentioned, Amara Lakhous purposely plays with the genre of the *giallo* to call into question societal issues in hopes of change. Lakhous closely follows in the evolution of the *commedia all'italiana* genre, particularly in the vein of Pietro Germi, referenced stylistically throughout his opus, including by mimicking the title of his 1961 film. Lakhous, similarly to Germi, aims at bringing awareness to the ironies present in Italian society through Pirandello's for *umorismo*; the rules of humor in both the author and director stem directly from Pirandello. The attention to gender and sexuality is at the forefront of this critical approach. Through unique narrative voices and new cultural rules, Lakhous returns to questioning the etiquette of gender and sexuality in Italian society and does so through "umorismo"—the situations regarding gender in Lakhous's works make us laugh, but we leave knowing that change is necessary.

Each main character in the novel has a double identity split between the public and private realms: Christian/Issa, Safia/Sofia, and Said/Felice. In this sense, Lakhous returns to the Pirandellian theme of the mask, particularly when related to religion in the public forum. In fact, in public, all three characters proclaim to be devout Muslims, particularly Issa, who the readers know first as Christian, an obvious play on words. One of the main intersections of the public and private spheres materializes over Safia's divorce. Although private, it becomes public because of the nature of the community and Issa's role in reunifying the couple. Through reuniting the couple, the novel proposes another layer of irony—Issa seems interested in pursuing a relationship with Safia; however, his task is to rekindle the couple's relationship. Through the Pirandellian mask, Lakhous plays with the concepts of gender and religion.[15]

Lakhous challenges the definition of the *giallo* in *Divorzio all'islamica a viale Marconi* most directly through the narrative voice, which includes one of our culprits who also happens to be the female voice. Throughout the novel, Safia struggles with her role as a loyal Muslim mother and wife, mainly due to her longing for personal identity, within a new society, Italy, which claims to be freer. She wants her career as a hairstylist, which she already performs covertly, and she does not want to be forced to wear the veil. Sofia's actual name is Safia, but when she introduces herself to Italians they immediately understand "Sofia"; she likes that name and accepts it because it reminds her of Sophia Loren, a woman who she respects and would like to mimic: "The truth is that Sofia Loren is a great dreamer, just like me. What sense does life have with dreams?" (Lakhous 2010, 26 [my translation]). Safia wants to become a respected woman of the community, a woman with a purpose, and an individual identity separate from that of her husband and child. This desire, which again is heightened by geographical place, Italy, underscores José Esteban Muñoz's concept of "disidentification." In *Disidentifcations: Queers of Color and the Performance of Politics*, Muñoz he explains, "The cultural performers I am considering in this book must negotiate between a fixed identity disposition and the socially encoded roles that are available for such subjects" (1999, 6). When she is introduced in the second chapter, she states, "The truth is that I understood early on, even before I read some books on feminism by Nawal Saadawi,[16] that our society doesn't love women and above all doesn't tolerate ambition in them"

(Lakhous 2010, 29). It seems as if Safia wants to change just that. Yet, there is an irony that exists for Safia: the veiled woman wants to style hair for other veiled women but also Italians. In order to succeed, however, Safia must be successful in "disidentifying" with her culture, freeing herself from the connotations associated with being a practicing Muslim woman.

Butler's theory evidences the critical role of Safia's character in *Divorzio*: "The development of a language that fully or adequately represents women has seemed necessary to foster the political visibility of women. This has seemed important considering the pervasive cultural condition in which women's lives were either misrepresented or not represented at all" (1990, 2). Not only does Safia's voice act as a political trumpet protecting all women, regardless of their race, creed, or ethnicity, but also her vocation aims at creating a sense of self-beauty and respect for veiled women. Yet Safia struggles from other gender issues due to her ethnicity. It is appropriate to consider José Esteban Muñoz's approach to performativity for ethnic minorities to better grasp Safia's situation. In "Feeling Brown, Feeling Down: Latina Affect, the Performativity of Race, and the Depressive Position," Muñoz argues, "Feeling brown in my analysis is descriptive of the way in which minoritarian affect is always, no matter what its register, partially illegible in relation to the normative affect performed by normative citizen subjects" (2013, 415). In defining "brown," the critic continues, "Browness is not white, and it is not black either, yet is does not simply sit midway between them . . . browness is a mode of attentiveness to the self for others that is cognizant of the way in which it is not and can never be whiteness" (2013, 415). Although Muñoz's framework is intended for a North American audience, focusing on the Latinx population, it can easily be adopted to Italy and to a certain extent, Safia and all of the Egyptian/Middle Eastern characters can be considered brown, particularly in comparison to the "white" Italians. If read through Muñoz's lens thus, Safia's character has additional layers of performativity in which to respond.

Not accepting the role as a stay-at-home mother and understanding the difficulty, both financially and physically, of hair care, therefore, "I became the underground hairdresser of the poor girls of the neighborhood" starting in Egypt and continuing in Rome (Lakhous 2010, 35). She was excited about the move to Italy since it is a mecca for fashion. She hoped that her life would easily transition with the "freedom," a Western, non-Islamic country would introduce. However, her secret position as a hairstylist quickly became public when Akram, the owner of Little Cairo, indirectly threatens her by asking her about her "lavoro" (Lakhous 2010, 57). For Safia, the hairstylist position is not just a job but a vocation that empowers both her and other women: "I wasn't worried about money, I happily accepted whatever they gave me. Often they gave me small presents: perfume, a shirt, a skirt, a purse, a fashion magazine" (Lakhous 2010, 35 [my translation]). Therefore, fulfilling her vocation provides her confidence and a purpose.

Safia has issues with the veil and tries to convince her husband that it is not necessary, especially in Italy. "Put on the veil? Maybe I hadn't understood. Were we going to live in Italy or Iran? Is the veil compulsory in Rome?" she asks her husband, but he insists on forcing her to wear it, respecting the tradition (Lakhous 2010, 39). She follows up with a rather astute reflection: "I tried very patiently to persuade him to give up this absurd condition, insisting on a fundamental point: the veil is not one of the five pillars of Islam and can in no way be used to measure a woman's conduct. Basically—let's be frank—the veil is just a piece of fabric. While faith is an infinite universe" (Lakhous 2010, 39). Safia's reflection is full of intense meaning. She accepts the five pillars of Islam and claims to be a devout Muslim but argues that man, not the Koran, proposes these silly traditions: "The real problem is that we live in a society where the male is both the opponent, and at the same time, the referee. We women—what can we do? Will we ever win this situation?" (Lakhous 2010, 39). Her issue does not concern the veil, but the real issue of male domination. At the end of that chapter, she returns to this idea, once again highlighting her true concern: "As for the veil: there are women who choose it freely, and their reasons can be various: out of conviction (they believe that the veil is the sixth pillar of Islam); for economic reasons (they save a lot of money on clothes); to avoid physical and verbal molestation in public places" (Lakhous 2010, 41). Although Gayle Salamon focuses primarily on the transgender body, her theoretical framework from *Assuming a Body: Transgender and Rhetorics of Materiality* adds to the discourse of the veiled Muslim woman in that the veil creates levels of interpretation to the outside world. Even within Lakhous's text, Issa's relationship with Safia changes when he views her nude in the video; his perception of her beauty is intensified, and he becomes aggressive, defending her to his captain. [17]

Building off the subject of male dominance, Safia addresses polygamy when stating, "The Koran isn't very clear about polygamy" and

> Polygamy in Islam: what confusion. And so? So what. I should explain. I would agree that the Koran is the word of God but always requires an interpretation. Here is the root of the problem: a woman's interpretation of the Koran still doesn't exist. Not one. It's a male monopoly. Women are excluded from so many things. For example, there's no verse, or *hadith*, that prohibits a woman from being an imam. In spite of that, I've never once in my life seen a woman leading prayers. (Lakhous 2010, 60)

This discourse and longing to be an active participant of Islam demonstrate her religious fervor while Safia demands to be treated as an equal, not as property.

Safia's fight for equality does not end with Islam. She also decries violence against women and expresses her surprise about abuse in Western countries when listening to an Italian radio broadcast:

> In Italy more than six and a half million women have suffered, at least once in their life, some form of physical or sexual violence. More than sixty percent of such women are mistreated by their partner or a person they know, and more than ninety-five percent do not report the violence they suffer, probably out of fear of the consequences. [. . .] To tell the truth, this radio discussion of domestic violence really stuns me. Why? I thought women were victims of violence in way zones, like Afghanistan or Iraq, or in countries where there's racism, like some African Muslim countries, and where poverty and ignorance are widespread. But not in Italy! In other words, isn't Italy still a[n] European country, Western, part of the G-8, and so on, or am I wrong? (Lakhous 2010, 122–23)

Here the reader comprehends Safia's delusion with Italy since it is supposed to be a safe place, one without veils, where women are equals. She is shocked to learn of the victimization Italian woman face in the *bel paese* .

This passage introduces the intense topic of female circumcision, beginning with violence against women from partners or companions and moving on to the worst type of female abuse, circumcision, which she argues is "It's a true crime against humanity, worse than rape, because the instigators are the parents!" (Lakhous 2010, 124). Safia recounts the circumstances of her sisters' circumcisions, first Nadia and then Zeineb, who almost died due to an infection from the unsterilized scissors the local witch doctor used. Luckily, Safia escaped this mutilation thanks to her aunt Amina. The latter created an entire performance to trick Safia's parents: the aunt's friend, a nurse, planned everything perfectly, even using hen's blood to verify the act visually. Eventually, her mother, along with other local woman, learned the truth, but it remained a secret. Safia vows that her daughter will not be circumcised after what happened to her two sisters, and she is happy that they live in Italy. She hopes that "Some time ago I heard on the radio that the Italian parliament is drafting a law against female circumcision, which is still practiced in some immigrant communities in Italy. I'm in favor. It's a further protection for girls like my daughter" (Lakhous 2010, 127). This moment in the novel brings to the forefront two perspectives on the same atrocity—female circumcision in Egypt and in Italy. The commentary presents a sociopolitical stance against this issue and underlines how Lakhous inserts this discourse within the *giallo*.

Towards the end of the novel, Felice gets upset with Safia because he finds a stash of her money and knows that she is somehow working; she refuses to discuss it, and he ends up saying *'Anti tàliq,'* which means, "you are divorced." This is the third time Felice wishes this upon his bride. Felice and Safia are then officially divorced. Initially, Safia is a bit stunned, but she seems to recover quickly. When her Italian friend Giulia learns of the divorce, she not only trashes marriage as an institution but also "'Sofia, now you should throw out those male traditions and take off that damn veil.'" (Lakhous 2010, 170). Safia justly retorts, "Women's freedom can't be reduced to a matter of clothes" (Lakhous 2010, 170–71). Safia is clearly attempting to become an independent woman, yet her traditions are blocking her ability to disidentify with her cultural norms and her emotional affect as "brown" maintains power over her decision making. Safia's point, however, is worthy of discussion. When faced with being a liberated woman, Safia is interested in pursuing Issa and starting a relationship with him rather than following her husband's plan of reuniting with her through a new marriage, consumption of the marriage, and divorce. Safia's intricate manner of examining feminism and being a liberated sexual woman is a focal point of the novel. Moreover, she can consume Issa and blur her vision of the scenario even to the observation of his boss. Even though the terrorist act was a farce, Safia remains feminist, willing to break from the status quo and fight for her own identity, which may be seen by some as a selfish act, serves as a strong example for her daughter so that she will not have to disidentify as her mother had.

Amara Lakhous's literary opus touches on a variety of themes and motifs ranging from language, culture, and geography to deeper questions of gender, politics, religion. Although Lakhous is not Italian by birth, it is challenging to define him as a migrant author as he has to accent according to the framework set forth by Hamid Naficy. [18] Lakhous delves into Italian culture and his knowledge of it, both capital and lower-cased "c" is extraordinary. He challenges the norms of Italian culture, as Pietro Germi did through cinema in the '60s, while paying homage to the director himself. Numerous scholars have shown how Lakhous's style includes allusions to many Italian authors, particularly Carlo Emilio Gadda, demonstrating how truly Italian Lakhous's literary voice is. To call him a "migrant author" seems doubly ignorant: his voice focuses on Italian culture through Italian references, in Italian. His novels satirize cultural norms in hope to have them reconsidered.

When considering the significance of place in *Scontro di civiltà*, Lakhous overtly plays with various tropes from literature and philosophy. Through using the *giallo* and the *palazzo*, truth about nationalism and the desires of migrants to integrate unfold Anderson's theory of imagined communities. Moreover, through applying performative gender theories, we learn the truth about the murder. Similarly, in Lakhous's other works, the performance theories of Butler, Muñoz, and Salamon demonstrate not only new approaches to the *giallo* as gender, but also societal issues Italian culture much face, particularly in the 21st century.

NOTES

1. Detective fiction in Italy was termed "*giallo*" or "*gialli*" because these translated works were published with yellow book jackets. When I refer to the *giallo*, I use it as a general reference for any detective fiction novel in Italian.

2. For a well-thought-out account of the evolution of the Italian *giallo*, see Luca Somgili, "The Realism of Detective Fiction: Augusto De Angelis, Theorist of the Italian *Giallo*," *Symposium* 59, no. 2 (Summer 2005): 70–83. For complete histories of the genre, see Loris Rambelli, *Storia del "giallo" italiano* (1979), and Luca Corvi, *Tutti i colori del giallo* (2002).

3. See Tzvetan Todorov, "The Typology of Detective Fiction," in *The Poetics of Prose* (Oxford: Blackwell, 1977), 42–52. Todorov believes that "detective fiction has its norms. To 'develop' them is also to disappoint them; to 'improve upon' detective fiction is to write 'literature,' not detective fiction" (43). Barbara Pezzotti argues that a *giallo* presence exists as early as the Risorgimento. See *Investigating Italy's Past through Historical Crime Fiction, Films, and TV Series* (New York: Palgrave Macmillan, 2016), 11–62.

4. For a thorough analysis of the *giallo* as it relates to the historical novel *Fascism, and the Years of Lead*, see Pezzotti, *Investigating Italy's Past through Historical Crime Fiction, Films, and TV Series* (New York: Palgrave Macmillan, 2016).

5. See Graziella Parati, *Migrant Writers and Urban Space in Italy: Proximities and Affect in Literature and Film* (2017), particularly "Transitive Spaces."

6. Piazza Vittorio is a unique area of Rome, found in the Esquilino *rione* of the city and serviced by Vittorio Emanuele Metro station. Built after the Unification of Italy, Piazza Vittorio is one of the largest piazzas in Rome, garnished with galleries, usually uncommon in the Roman landscape. Originally, this area was inhabited by the upper class; however, in more recent years, Piazza Vittorio has hosted a variety of migrants, particularly from the Arab and Asian worlds, so much so that "La Sapienza" has its Instituto Italiano degli Studi Orientali housed in that neighborhood. Sandro is the only Roman who inhabits the area.

7. Huntington first introduced this concept in a 1992 lecture at the American Enterprise Institute. In 1993, he expanded his idea into an article for *Foreign Affairs* and later in 1996 wrote the book *The Clash of Civilizations and the Remaking of World Order*.

8. Benedetta is so proud of being Neapolitan that she comes off as prejudiced to other Italians. Additionally, she discusses her experiences of prejudice against her as Neapolitan when first arriving to Rome. On the other hand, Professor Marini, Milanese by birth, considers anything south of Milan as Southern Italy and he consistently complains about Romans for being lazy and ignorant.

9. See Ryan Calabretta-Sajder, "Mediterranean Voices and Amara Lakhous' Accent(s): Arabic, Italian, or Simply Roman," in *Mediterranean Studies: Crossing Boundaries*, eds. Anthony Julian Tamburri and Antonio Vitti (New York: Bordighera Press, 2016), 292–316.

10. For criticism on Huntington, see Edward Said's "The Clash of Ignorance" in *The Nation,* October 2001 and CJ Trystan's YouTube video *Noam Chomsky on The "Clash of Civilizations"*.

11. It is important to note that Anderson did receive severe criticism for this idea, particularly from scholars in geography. See Blaut (1987), Short (1991), West (1996), Said (1993), and one of his biggest adversaries, Chatterjee (1993).

12. For more information, see "About Anna Magnani, Iconic Women of Italian Cinema," https://italicsmag.com/2019/03/01/anna-magnani-italian-cinema/, "Rome, The Second Time," https://romethesecondtime.blogspot.com/2017/03/anna-magnani-rome-icon-possible.html, or Fellini's *Roma* (1972).

13. Daniela Brogi, "Le catene dell'identità: Conversazione con Amara Lakhous." *Between.* I. 1 (2011) 2, www.between-journal.it .

14. Set within the Roman landscape, Viale Marconi is a neighborhood Lakhous inhabited for two years. Located within the San Paolo neighborhood, which extends from the Magliana to viale Marconi, partly within the *rione* of Ostiense and Trastevere, viale Guglielmo Marconi is the longest street in the eternal city. The neighborhood hosts the Università di Roma "Tre," providing neighbors a youthful atmosphere with its diverse student body along with an abun-

dance of newly arrived migrants. The protagonists of *Divorzio all'islamica a viale Marconi* reside here.

15. Omar's observation on a shared sense of faith among the tenants seems to mould the novel. In the end, however, it becomes the core of the satire through which the novel takes form. Everything seems to revolve around religious ardor; yet the crux is that religious beliefs and attitudes drive the plot of the novel, and once they consume the readers' emotions, they erupt. From the book's very title, the Italian reader will make the connection with Pietro Germi's 1961 film *Divorzio all'italiana* and its biting satire. Lakhous's manipulation of both place and space introduces the reader to the non-tourist facades of the eternal city inhabited by a multicultural array of characters, demonstrating the author's Italianness.

16. Nawal El Saadawi (1931-2021) was a physician and psychiatrist from Egypt, and an internationally recognized feminist author and activist. She wrote numerous books concerning the role of women in Islam, focusing on the practice of female genital mutilation in her society. She received numerous peace prizes during her life's work.

17. See Gayle Salamon "Chapter 2. The Sexual Schema: Transposition and Transgender in *Phenomenology of Perception*," in *Assuming a Body: Transgender and Rhetorics of Materiality* (New York: Columbia University Press, 2010).

18. See Hamid Naficy's *An Accented Cinema: Exilic and Diasporic Filmmaking.* He argues that migrant authors, even though they try, cannot completely lose their accents.

Anderson, Benedict. 1991. *Imagined Communities: Reflections on the Origin and Spread of Nationalism* (revised and enlarged edition). London: Verso.

Blaut, James Morris. 1987. *The National Question: Decolonising the Theory of Nationalism.* London: Zed Books.

Butler, Judith. 1990. *Gender Trouble.* New York: Routledge.

_____. 1993. *Bodies that Matter.* New York: Routledge.

Calabretta-Sajder, Ryan. 2016a. "Mediterranean Voices and Amara Lakhous' Accent(s): Arabic, Italian, or Simply Roman." in *Mediterranean Studies: Crossing Boundaries.* eds. Anthony Julian Tamburri and Antonio Vitti. New York: Bordighera Press. 292–316.

_____. 2016b. "Amara Lakhous: da scrittore a rivoluzionario del giallo" *Italica* 93. 4 (Winter): 812–835.

Chatterjee, Partha. *The Nation and its Fragments: Colonial and Postcolonial Histories.* Princeton, NJ: Princeton UP.

Corvi, Luca. 2002. *Tutti i colori del giallo.* Venice: Marsilio.

Germi, Pietro. 1961. *Divorzio all'italiana.* Embassy Pictures.

Lakhous, Amara. 2006. *Scontro di civiltà per un ascensore a Piazza Vittorio.* Rome: Edizioni e/o.

_____. 2008. *Clash of Civilizations over an Elevator in Piazza Vittorio.* Translated by Ann Goldstein. New York: Europa Editions.

_____. 2010. *Divorzio all'islamica a viale Marconi.* Rome: Edizioni e/o.

_____. 2012. *Divorce Islamic Style.* Translated by Ann Goldstein. New York: Europa Editions.

_____. 2013.*Contesa per un maialino italianissimo a San Salvario.* Rome: Edizioni e/o.

_____. 2014. *La zingarata della verginella di Via Ormea.* Rome: Edizioni e/o.

_____. 2016. *The Prank of the Good Little Virgin of Via Ormea.* Translated by Anthony Shugaar. New York: Europa Editions.

Muñoz, José Esteban. 1999. *Disidentifications: Queers of Color and the Performance of Politics.* Minneapolis, MN: University of Minnesota Press.

_____. 2013. "Feeling Brown, Feeling Down: Latina Affect, the Performativity of Race, and the Depressive Position," in *The Routledge Queer Studies Reader* . Donald E. Hall and Annamarie Jagose, eds. New York: Routledge.

Naficy, Hamid. 2001. *An Accented Cinema: Exilic and Diasporic Filmmaking* . Princeton, NJ: Princeton UP.

Parati, Graziella. 2010. "Where Do Migrants Live? Amara Lakhous's *Scontro di civiltà per un ascensore in piazza Vittorio.*" *Annali d'Italianistica* 28: 431-446.

_____. 2017. *Migrant Writers and Urban Space in Italy: Proximities and Affect in Literature and Film.* New York: Palgrave Macmillan.

Pezzotti, Barbara. 2016. *Investigating Italy's Past through Historical Crime Fiction, Films, and TV Series: Murder in the Age of Chaos.* New York: Palgrave Macmillan.

Pirandello, Luigi. 1992. *L'umorismo.* Milano: Oscar Mondadori.

Rambelli, Lois. 1979. *Storia del "giallo" italiano.* Milano: Garzanti.

Said, Edward Wadie. 1993. *Culture and Imperialism.* New York: Vintage.

Salamon, Gayle. 2010. "Chapter 2. The Sexual Schema: Transposition and Transgender in *Phenomenology of Perception.*" In *Assuming a Body: Transgender and Rhetorics of Materiality.* New York: Columbia University Press, 43–68.

Sciascia, Leonardo. 1961. *Il giorno della civetta.* Turin: Einaudi.

Short, John Rennie. 1991. *Imagined Country: Society, Culture and Environment.* London: Routledge.

Somigli, Luca. 2005. "The Realism of Detective Fiction: Augusto De Angelis, Theorist of the Italian *Giallo.*" *Symposium* 59, no. 2 (Summer): 70–83.

Todorov, Tzvetan. 1977. "The Typology of Detective Fiction." In *The Poetics of Prose.* Oxford: Blackwell, 42–52.

The Phoenix

Ubah Cristina Ali Farah
Translated by Silvia Guslandi

"A human migrant may never understand the language in which he dies. When an animal migrates, the return is part of its journey. One could say an animal migrates for the sake of its return." (Anne Michaels and John Berger, *Railtracks*, Counterpoint Press, 2013)

Jeanne always woke up early in the mornings. Not because she was getting old. People think the elderly always wake up early in the morning, as if wanting to drink it to the very last drop, the last drop of a glass that is gradually running out. But Jeanne had always woken up early in the morning. And that dawn was not different from the others, except for the fact that it was Spring, the estuary was embracing the sea and the horizon emanated blowtorch flames streaking the pale cerulean blue sky. Jeanne walked confidently along the shore, her body straight, a cap crooked on her head and her austere face beaten by the sun and the salt. She leaned against an ebony stick, a gift from a sailor grandson who had sailed across the oceans aboard oil tankers.

Jeanne was plunging her feet into the sand, her shadow stretched out toward the West, when she suddenly saw a tuft of seaweed appear indecorously right where the legs meet and, instinctively, she brought her free hand to her pubis, ashamed. But the seaweed was on her shadow, and she knew it and so she started giggling to herself looking around to make sure no one had seen her. It was then that she caught sight of a silhouette coming toward her on the deserted shore: from a distance it looked like that of a young woman and a flock of seagulls encircled her, or maybe they were turtle-doves, although turtle-doves rarely go all the way to the sea.

The silhouette rose and fell and, as it came nearer, Jeanne made out a young woman picking bird feathers: her hair looked like black embers ready to catch fire in the sun. Jeanne nodded to her, a nod the girl responded to with a broad smile pointing, in the basket that hung on her arm, to her loot of feathers. "Well done!" Jeanne said "Although seagull feathers aren't really that pretty, are they. I mean, it depends what you want to make with them, a dress, a pair of wings, a costume for a party? In those cases I think you'd have better luck on the customs agents' path, there are lots of birds there, or better yet, at the swamp."

The young woman was wearing an iridescent green quilted jacket and her wrists were thin, like her legs. Jeanne realized right away from her stunned expression that she was having trouble expressing herself and trying to enunciate her words she repeated "Wings? Dress?" sketching the shape of a bird on the sand, because both wings and dress had shapes that were too abstract to be recognized. The girl made a gesture with her head, as if to nod, and then Jeanne mustered up some courage, rested her hand on her shoulder and added: "Shall we walk along together for a bit?"

The girl didn't say anything, but she certainly understood that Jeanne was not one to easily act familiar, even though in that country people acted familiar even with foreigners, but sometimes this is what happens to old people, they know time too well and young people make them a little uneasy; maybe a bit less when they come from far away.

"Come," said Jeanne, leaning lightly against her shoulder, the estuary fluorescent, its surface rippling into a myriad of waves. And the girl followed her, listening to the murmur of the water, a murmur that sounded like the crackling of flames or the thud of an explosion. They came to the foot of a tall granite pedestal, on which a huge bronze eagle rested, carrying an armed soldier on its shoulders. Jeanne stopped to look at it, shading her eyes with her hand, and held out her ebony stick to point to it: "I remember when they brought Sammy back," she whispered, "The occupying enemies had melted him to make weapons." And the girl gave a start because she too had been told stories of statues melted for the metal, but she had never seen any, in her country no one had ever reinstated the statues. They walked back up from the beach gazing about every step of the way, their gaze fixed to the rocks, each rock speaking about a past in which it had been urgent to clear out debris, to build a shiny new city on top of the ruins. Not to replicate what had been destroyed—inch by inch, lamppost by lamppost, each and every doorway— because it's impossible to dig up the past, one has to learn to live with grief and give up on trying to bring back the dead.

Jeanne remembered the black skeletons of the houses emerging out of the haze, a pile of dirt rising toward the sky like a giant feather, heaps of plaster everywhere. Together with other children, she had been among the first to be evacuated during the bombings and those among them who returned with their families to live precariously in the shacks found the city dead by a violent death: the streets crumbling, a din of cars, cables like ganglia hanging from dull concrete brains. Everything had been dug up to be rebuilt, the men were filling the old swamp with debris and salvaging only what could be reused, wood and zinc, bricks and radiators, slate and lead, faucets and tubs.

It hadn't taken them very long to get the shipyards up and running, Jeanne was young when she attended the launch of the first ship, a masterpiece of grace and balance, the smokestacks red and black, and they had waited for just the right wave to let it glide into the water. They were so used to its imposing mass that it had been strange, afterward, to see the emptiness, once it had left.

Since then, a busy traffic of ships had returned to the estuary, and that coming and going was nice, the estuary seemed to welcome the entire world in its arms. But it hadn't always been that way and the two women knew it: there are times when one is powerless in the face of violence. And this happens because people deeply believe in the power of violence, without understanding that only in clemency can the implicit answer to any conflict be found. Jeanne and the girl walked on to the submarine basecamp: it has been built during the occupation, now, on its roof, a garden had popped up spontaneously, born from the seeds brought by the birds.

Jeanne wasn't sure that her father hadn't worked with the enemy at building the basecamp. "Well, yeah, I've had to work" he had always answered elusively, Jeanne had often wondered how they had managed to build the basecamp in only two years. When she gave it some thought, though, she'd convince herself that her father had not been complicit with the enemy, certainly they had forced him to work, but not to build the basecamp no, she was sure.

The girl was fascinated by the birds' elevated garden and wondered if Jeanne had seen how it was when birds didn't land on that roof. Now, the new city no longer faced the sea and the river like the old one did, but rather turned away from them, surely fearing a new betrayal. Perhaps the girl thought about the betrayal, about the day in which her dreams were shattered by her country's internal war, and pointed to the Ferris wheel.

The Ferris wheel rose up as if wanting to separate the city from the basecamp. She had rarely seen it moving, and yet it had always seemed to her to be waiting for a boost: the wheel's immobility was actually temporary.

Jeanne thought the girl was hungry and was sorry there weren't any fishermen's wives at the harbor anymore, with their parcels of roasted sardines. Sardines reminded her of her mother. When she worked at the cannery, a siren would let the workers know that the load was on its way and the boat would unload many crates of tiny silvery fish and it was hard to grab them among the ice chips, your fingers would freeze. But later the warmed-up sardine on a slice of buttered bread was a real treat.

Actually, Jeanne was tired and the girl noticed. "Tomorrow" was the only word she managed to say to her and Jeanne repeated with a smile, "Tomorrow." She turned away from the Ferris wheel and walked toward the *Building*: the tall building towered over the city and right on one of the highest floors was her nest; the balcony overlooking a drawbridge.

She made herself an open sandwich with cheese, a cup of hot tea and collapsed onto the couch trying to catch her breath. Out of instinct she turned on the news, but then changed her mind, images from the previous night, of war, phosphorus bombs, the wounded, walls extirpated and of evacuees had filled her with infinite sadness.

The sight of one young woman in particular had kept her awake at night, her eyes stunned, a little burnt pile in her arms, it wasn't clear whether of feathers or human remains. Jeanne thought about the girl: how far she'd had to travel to get to the estuary, that same estuary where Jeanne had spent her whole life. She thought about her own youth, full of joy and hope for the future; although she too had experienced war, had escaped with her parents and brothers to the countryside, then they had returned, they had always known that sooner or later they would return. Like swallows returning in Spring, or migratory birds: one might say that they migrate in order to return, that they migrate to make possible their return. Jeanne wondered if the girl would ever return where she came from and if she would trust the future, as she had done at her age.

When she was young like the girl, they had moved into a brand-new apartment, a dream come true for her mother, running water, the modern kitchen purchased from Levitan, and her father had built a long extendable table big enough to fit the whole family and he would salvage old furniture from the ships to repurpose as needed. Soon afterward came the fridge too, the washing machine, and her mother was insanely happy, her father less so because, despite its comforts, life wasn't lived together in the apartments as it had been in the shacks, and he missed his little garden, the workshop and the trading of favors with friends who were plumbers, electricians and craftsmen.

Jeanne's mother was a quiet type, she listened to the radio and loved to read, she, the daughter of fishermen, brought up without a mother. She always brought her children with her to the library because the library was even open on Sundays, they would have wonderful times together, absorbed by their books. Sunday was feast day and on occasion, once they had returned home, she would make them some delicacy, like chicken with chestnuts, even though it was fish that was plentiful at their table. Jeanne's mother always received as gifts crates full of mackerel and sprat from her fishermen cousins and tuna that she cooked and preserved in tankards. Her father had lost his boat under mysterious circumstances and had been forced like many others to find a job at the Construction sites. He had lost his wife too, the poor man, fervent Communist fisherman: Jeanne's grandmother had died of tuberculosis right after giving birth to her only daughter.

Jeanne continued to meet the girl the following days, every time at dawn, and the girl kept learning new words, and it was as if, at every meeting, she brought with her a fistful of her own land, day after day. Almost as if meeting were this, a miracle of rebuilding. At night the girl would come to her in her dreams and whisper, "Come closer" although she was hardly miles away. Their profiles would blend into each other and every time a tuft of seaweed would pop up, each time in a different spot on their shadow, the chest, the pubis, the head.

They both learned that there was no point in piecing together the facts, rather it was more important to ask questions that had no answer, to collect events whose succession was at the same time clear and obscure to them.

Jeanne would have really loved to become young like her again, to take her around on her bike to catch crabs, fish for mussels, roast grey shrimp on the beach and admire the star-shaped island that rose up before them in a great white arc of sand. Perhaps they could have gone to the swamp together: they would have found multicolored birds' feathers, Jeanne's father would have caught some eels and they both would have been scared stiff watching them coiling in the pan, like disgusting snakes among the grass.

They were satisfied with walking together and Jeanne always left some little cookies on the balcony for the robins: they say that this little bird bloodied its breast while trying to remove the crown of thorns from the Savior's head, a noble gesture of mercy, even though robins are famous mainly for their warlike spirit, in matters of territorial protection.

Jeanne always loved to wake up early in the morning and one morning she met the girl as usual: she had built a large bird-shaped sculpture out of the soft sand and, to the sculpture, she had pinned hundreds of multicolored feathers, bluish black, olive-toned yellow, purplish blue, iridescent red, pink-hued grey and cinnamon streaked with white.

She paused to admire her masterpiece and then said: "I'd like to show you something, if you don't mind," and because the girl seemed to agree, she invited her to follow her to the *Building*, which rose not far from where they were: the façade covered by a rhythm of horizontal pillars and vertical stripes, the framework reinforcing the grid.

They stepped into the glass elevator in silence and emerged at the top of the building: Jeanne had never noticed the goldfinch cage on the landing, their subdued and liquid singing.

The girl stopped to look at them, perhaps fascinated by their song, perhaps by their plumage, whatever the case Jeanne thought it best to make plain that she could not free them: "They live in captivity, you'd be sentencing them to death."

The Phoenix

The girl looked at her in shock and they immediately entered the home, took off their coats and began brewing some coffee.

Jeanne was restless and couldn't wait, she immediately set down her ebony stick and rushed into her bedroom: "I need help," she said a few minutes later. So, the young woman who only spoke a few words, but understood everything, followed her, climbed up a ladder and took out a box that held old clothes protected by mothballs and cellophane.

"Here it is!" Jeanne exclaimed, savoring once more the joy of that memory, and in saying so she lay the dress across the girl's shoulders, to admire it in all of its length.

She must have been about her age when she wore it for the first time: her mother had worked very hard at her old pedal Singer machine. She had got hold of an offcut of violet velour, certainly thinking it better to use it for a high fashion post-war dress than for making drapes. Later she had decorated the neckline and hem with pink swan feathers: where she had found them remained a mystery, her mother loved to surprise her, Jeanne was the only girl in a family of sons.

It was winter and going outside in short sleeves was not really ideal, but how memorable had her first dance in that almost-bridal dress been! It was goosebumps cold and raining a thick heavy drizzle and certainly at that time nobody had a car, nor was it possible to go by bike. So, Jeanne's older brothers, the two who were taking her to the dance, had a genius idea. They dug up a beach umbrella to which they safety-pinned a long waterproof tarp, fashioning a moving booth of sorts. And then, while one of the brothers held the umbrella with Jeanne, the other walked up front and led the way with the oil lamp.

It was freezing and Jeanne had to lift her skirt to avoid splashes and was holding her high heels. The badly lit street was practically empty and thanks to this they were able to hide their catafalque behind the courtyard, and enter the party triumphantly. Everyone admired Jeanne in her pink-feathered dress as she strode in between her brothers. And during the dance a couple of times young men that she refused to dance with had resentfully handed her a feather whispering, "Young lady, you've lost something!" Those were the days of Jazz and Breton rock, but they also danced the samba and the cha-cha.

"Young lady, you've lost something!" exclaimed Jeanne picking a pink feather up from the floor, while the girl admired her old dress. "If you like this dress, it's yours, I won't have another chance to wear it any time soon."

The girl gave Jeanne a hug and left her a gift of cinnamon, lavender and myrrh before saying goodbye. As for her, she couldn't accept her gift: that old dress was hers, it belonged to her youth.

Instead, they could sew a new one together. Neither of the two women managed to wake up early the next day. It was pouring rain and watercolor streaks were dripping down the horizon far away. The boundary between earth and sea, tree and weed, cloud and sand was indistinguishable: everything was mixed up.

Later someone said they had seen a great fire rise up that morning along the coast and the shadow of a woman dressed in feathers stoking it in the wind.

They say it is a privilege of the dispossessed—the only one admitted to them—to personalize History. Each time it presents itself like an estuary open to an infinite number of possibilities, of intentions and misfortune, of chance encounters and desires. And yet, this infinite number of possibilities, of intentions, of misfortune, of encounters and of desires gets lost in living, it gets lost in every single life.

Creativity as a Feminist Practice

Intercultural Women's Associations in Italy

Wendy Pojmann

To what extent can migrant and native women join forces? Can they, or should they, construct a common agenda? If so, what form should it take? Are there new practices still to be envisioned in building a multicultural feminism that can be applied to the particular characteristics of Italy and extended to other parts of the Mediterranean?

Part of the problem in attempting to answer these questions stems from limitations of definitions. But it is also the weakness inherent in creating categories that have formed the boundaries of multicultural exchange. If we ask what is meant by feminism and exactly who is a migrant, it becomes obvious that a key conundrum of multicultural feminism is finding ways to incorporate difference without erasing it. Feminism has many forms and its meanings are contextually determined. Similarly, migration follows no universal pattern. It is therefore preferable to trace both the broad and specific meanings of migration and feminism, since women's experiences exist in relation to multiple forms of identity, at different moments, and in diverse cultural environments. I ask for instance, whether it is more accurate to label an Eritrean woman without a high school education who has been in Italy for thirty-five years as a migrant than to use that term to describe a recent arrival from the Ukraine who holds a doctorate in engineering. Would either woman participating in the activities of a women's center call herself a feminist?

From the framework of multiethnic women's associations that have emerged in Italy during the past two decades, it becomes possible to make some claims about the common elements of women activists, while revealing the constraints they face in their work together. I wish to offer some historical and contemporary observations about the limits and potential of a multicultural or, to use the preferred term of women activists, intercultural, feminism in Italy.[1]

I do not want to claim that political, economic, and social obstacles to the integration of migrants have been resolved, however. In fact, Italian immigration policies have become, if anything, more restrictive since the passage of the Bossi-Fini Law of 2002 and 2009 legislation that made undocumented migration a felony. Public discourse on the promises of multiculturalism has been souring for some time throughout Europe and has been more heightened in Italy since the passage of the 2017 Minniti Decree that seeks to distinguish between "legitimate" and "illegitimate" asylum seekers. The new policy is in part the result of a lack of a unified EU policy on migrants and refugees that continues to leave the Italians in a particularly delicate position. According to the United Nations International Organization for Migration, an estimated 600,000 migrants have reached Italy's shores over the past four years (International Organization for Migration 2018). The recent influx of migrants and the political climate tend to mask the fact that migrant women have been a consistent and growing presence in Italy since the 1970s and have utilized available services provided by the state or their own communities to gain a foothold in their new country of residence. At the same time, Italian feminists have been assessing the power imbalances of gender, class, and citizenship that continue to have a negative impact on women. In their shared social and cultural spaces, migrant and Italian women are exploring intercultural exchanges and finding new sources of empowerment that have the potential to transform the multiple communities with which their lives intertwine.

WOMEN'S ASSOCIATIONS IN HISTORICAL CONTEXT

Historically, going as far back as Anna Maria Mozzoni's Lega promotrice degli interessi femminili (1881) and the Gruppi di difesa della donna (1943), which grew out of the Resistance, Italian women's associations can be characterized as *autonomous*, meaning preferring to work outside traditional political structures; *grassroots*, which means reaching out to women at the local level and building from there; and *practical*, which means simply trying to resolve problems of daily life. Migrant women's associations have followed similar patterns. Migrant women from around the world have identified specific needs in their communities and then searched for ways to fill them. This was especially the case in the first national groups of mostly women to migrate to Italy from the Philippines, Cape Verde, Eritrea, and parts of South America in the 1970s who formed their own informal and formal groups to assist the newest arrivals. During the 1980s, several multiethnic migrant women's associations opened to extend their reach to all of Italy's diverse migrant population, including women from smaller migrant populations or those with higher percentages of male migrants.

However, few occasions presented themselves for the meeting of migrant and native women in the Italian women's associations that date to the immediate postwar era, such as the historic leftist Unione Donne Italiane and lay Catholic Centro Italiano Femminile, or in the feminist groups that arose from the social movements of 1968. Italian feminists had very clear political, social, and economic objectives that tended to focus on the native population and the specific challenges women face in Italy. Many women activists viewed access to work outside the home and economic independence as central goals, which some scholars have argued led them to seek migrant women's labor as a partial solution to managing home and work life (Andall 2000; Parreñas 2001). Because of power imbalances and divergent sets of objectives, Italian employers and migrant workers were unlikely to frequent the same political spaces. Moreover, many migrant women did not necessarily view themselves as feminists in the same sense as the Italian women since gender relations in their home countries took different forms and women's movements followed their own historical trajectories.

When they arrived in Italy, migrant women had to face obstacles to their integration as foreigners in addition to contending with the impact of gender discrimination in their lives. The Italian government did not keep pace with growing numbers of immigrants entering Italy and was already struggling to meet the needs of the native population (Calavita 2004; Zincone 2001). As a result, few services were in place for migrants in general and even fewer for migrant women who faced special problems in finding suitable housing, taking care of children, seeking and retaining employment, keeping track of their immigration documents and status, and even confronting sexual abuse. Migrant and native women did not appear to have much in common at first, especially in the 1970s and 1980s, that would have led them to organize together (Pojmann 2008). The development of separate associations, however, means that women lost early opportunities to form relationships that could have potentially enriched both feminist and migrant movements during previous decades.

During the 1990s, as the term *globalization* entered feminist discourse and European feminists became interested in learning about women's lives and women's movements in other parts of the world, migrant and native women began talking to each other. Migrant women's leaders and Italian feminists decided it would be worthwhile to discuss a fuller range of women's experiences and look for ways to work together on specific initiatives. In the mid-1990s, some of them formed multicultural, or intercultural, women's associations as a result. Alma Mater in Turin and Punto di Partenza in Florence were among the earliest and best-known groups of this type that brought together migrant women of several nationalities and Italian women, most of whom had previous experience in feminist or migrants' associations in Italy or a history of activism in their home countries. Cooperation in some of these first associations was not always easy, however. Italian women have sometimes had a tendency to see women's movements in other parts of Europe as more advanced and to view migrant women as oppressed and in need of instruction. Images of veiled women, forced marriages, and female confinement to the home continue to stir the collective imagination. Perhaps such ideas capture their attention because it was not that long ago that Italian women were confronted with similar stereotypes about their own lives in Italy and as migrants and immigrants worldwide (Gabaccia 2000; Tardi 2010). Migration stories, in fact, have often reinforced the winning model of Italian feminism since they tend to highlight the problems that led women to migrate or the patriarchal traditions that sometimes become even more rigid in immigrant communities.

INTERCULTURAL PRACTICES

Despite, or perhaps because of, the difficulties of these early experiments to integrate the spaces of women activists, intercultural women's associations can now point to many successes. In fact, some of the most exciting moments have occurred when the experiences of migrant women collided with those of Italian feminists and from the wreckage emerged a new perspective that was informed, but not determined by, Italian migration history. An integrated intercultural feminism, with all of its discomfort and pain, is offering new insights into the creative practices of foreign and Italian women looking to overcome the constraints of the past. In intercultural associations that have been able to overcome the stopping point of testimonials, the basis of collective action has been gender. On both sides of the migratory experience, the women who participate in the associations have a consciousness of their gendered position and are driven by the desire to improve their own lives and the lives of other women. They recognize that inequalities of all sorts exist among women and use them to build alternative cooperative approaches, including artistic expression and culinary events as well as political action.

Studies in 2009 and 2018 produced by the region of Emilia-Romagna show that migrant associations grew rapidly after 2000 and that a majority include cultural activities in their programming. In 2009, of the sixty-eight associations researchers identified that had a component dealing specifically with migrant women, twenty-eight were composed of Italian and migrant women together. In 2018, that number had grown to fifty-three (Engroba Oberti and Cataneo 2018). The mixed ethnicity associations identified specific cultural initiatives as central to their work, including theatrical, radio, and television productions; artistic exhibitions; poetry readings; dance classes and performances; and cooking classes. Although many associations that work with migrant women continue to offer a number of first-contact services, such as help finding housing, employment, and legal advice, the work of these more recent associations points to a recognition that there are now many other places where women can obtain this sort of assistance. It also marks a more comprehensive approach to the whole woman as an individual who has social and cultural needs as well as political and economic ones. Associations such as Che la festa continui in Casalecchio, near Bologna, got their start, in fact, with the idea of socialization in mind. Following a riverfront party in 2000, a group of Italian and migrant women decided to keep the positive spirit of the get-together alive by forming an association. Italian feminist and co-founder Lucia Berardi points out that "the situation [of immigration] is dramatic. However, this doesn't mean that we need to cry from morning to evening, and I think that in any case keeping your heart open to the possibility of meeting other people and to have fun together and to eat together, is good for all of us" (interview with author, November 16, 2010).[2]

In 2003, several voluntary associations already working with women and migrants in Parma cooperated to open the Rose e Pane drop-in center, which offers women a space where they can socialize, join in a Sunday supper, listen to music, or read a book in the company of Italian and foreign women and their children. Alida Guatri, who has been working with voluntary associations at the local and European levels since 2000, says the center at first especially filled the needs of "women who arrived from the East and didn't have their own homes because they worked in domestic service and so they mostly saw the people they were taking care of. They didn't have their own spaces where they could do things together other than at bars or restaurants, which meant spending money and wasn't very favorable for them" (phone interview with author, November 17, 2010). The idea behind the name Rose e Pane is that although women may need the basic nutrition of bread to survive, they are very much like roses that require attention and care to truly thrive. A 2007 theatrical production of the same name gave voice to the sentiment that "yes, women want bread, but they also look for roses to assure a possibility for a good future" (*Festina Lente Teatro* 2018). Many of the migrant women who frequent the center are employed and otherwise inserted into the local community but are looking for social activities and cultural fulfillment to round out their lives. Others are looking for new opportunities through networking.

Intercultural women's associations appear to represent the next phase of feminist practice, one that challenges traditional notions of assimilation and integration. No longer trapped in the framework of immigration as an emergency or constrained exclusively by an employer/employee or a teacher/student power imbalance, these women have moved beyond some of the limitations that characterized their first encounters. Italian feminists and migrant women have long grappled with meanings and implications of integration but are now exploring them together as they seek ways to negotiate the demands of social life. In the 1970s and '80s, in such feminist groups as the Milan Women's Bookstore Collective, women asked why women had to become like men, or assimilate into male society, to advance (De Lauretis 1987). They proposed to value and incorporate women's difference to change and improve all of society rather than to negate femininity. In a similar sense, migrant and Italian women's associations, such as Annassim in Bologna, argue that the integration of migrants is preferable to their assimilation because the larger society is enriched when it not only allows for the expression of diverse cultural practices but also values reciprocal moments of teaching and learning. In other words, rather than making migrants conform to certain aspects of Italian identity, an intercultural form of integration grants the possibility of an improved society for all. According to a member of Annassim, Italian women have come to realize that knowledge is not imparted to migrant women in a unilateral direction and that they, too, have talents that should be emphasized instead of repressed. "I believe that a strong point of the association is to have worked on this. Not only to try to teach the women new things, but to reinforce those things the women already know how to do well" (Annassim 2018). When Italian women recognize the strengths of migrant women and seek ways to allow for their expression, they enhance the social and cultural experiences of both groups. However, they are also experimenting with complex notions of identity that may require resistance to both feminine ideals and Italian social norms; resistance itself implies taking certain risks that may leave women on the margins.

Feminist theorist Rosi Braidotti has embraced the subject position of the nomad as potentially liberating for women, arguing that it allows for a "kind of critical consciousness that resists settling into socially coded modes of thought and behavior" (1994, 5). Braidotti's nomad is not necessarily a woman on the move, but she is a free-thinker shaped by the disruptions of integration. Braidotti recognized the absence of "effective links . . . between the 'white' intellectual women and the many 'domestic foreigners' that inhabit Europe today," which made her nomadic feminist accessible mainly to European-origin academics (22). Nevertheless, in the more than twenty years that have passed since the publication of Braidotti's *Nomadic Subjects*, evidence of a version of nomadic feminist subjectivity can be identified in relations between Italian and migrant women. Intercultural women's associations in Emilia-Romagna that feature theater and cooking as key elements of their practices demonstrate the ways in which migrant and Italian women can utilize the idea of a femininity constructed by both fixed and unstable concepts of the self that are acted out and even enriched in different physical and imagined locations.

Intercultural theatrical techniques developed by several mixed ethnicity associations throughout Italy, such as Alma Mater in Turin and IRIDE in Siena, have given women tools to use to play with the idea of nomadic subject identities that allow for transformative experiences. If aspects of identity are performed, women can put forward different versions of themselves depending on circumstances. In some cases, women may prioritize national or religious affinities or reject them outright. The Italian intercultural groups thus differ from the Chicana and coalition theater groups founded in the 1970s and 1980s in the United States that primarily sought visibility for minority actors, playwrights, and directors and shared a "common experience of racial oppression which the white women never perceive and cannot comprehend in subtle social situations" (Case 2008, 111). Instead, the women who take part in the Emilian theater groups Vagamonde and Festina Lente Teatro experiment with the transformation of migratory identities by creating fluid characters as actors and expressing them on the stage. The result is a voyage of multiple identities that reflect the special historical context of Italian (im)migrations. As expressed on Vagamonde's web site, "the show could not have been other than a journey, a route, a route of voices, scenes, sensations, bodies. On large white disks we performed a ritual of memory, an initiatory ritual. Doing theater is perhaps the only mode we have to be free, free to change identities" (Associazione Vagamonde 2018). Through performance, even natives of Emilia-Romagna have come to see themselves as more disconnected from the dominant culture than women who came to Italy from thousands of miles away. The women do not intend to say that migration is merely a state of mind, but rather that integration occurs on multiple levels. After all, in a society in which men are the models for normative behavior, the performativity of femininity necessitates integration as well (Butler 1990; Parati and West 2002). Therefore, at times, it may even be more difficult for Italian women to step outside narrow norms of ideal Italian femininity than it is for migrant women to adopt or refuse them.

Vagamonde began organizing multiethnic theater laboratories in 2004 and immediately recognized the positive impact they had on helping women to build bonds with one another while exploring the multiple components of their identities. The contributions of migrant women have been especially crucial to the success of the laboratories. One member recalls, "This project created an exchange of cultures and stories. The migrant women brought their flavors, colors, emotions; acting interculturally was simple and natural" (Associazione Vagamonde 2018). In 2004, the group took its experimental laboratory to the stage and performed *Voci invisibili* at several multicultural festivals and held a related photographic exhibition. The production recounts the many realities of migration, especially highlighting stories that explore the meaning of living in two worlds, where women feel divided and yet present in each. The group then produced a photographic catalogue detailing the experiences of the migrant and Italian women who participated in the performances.

Elide La Vecchia of Vagamonde says that while all the women were confident their work together would be "an effective means for allowing each woman's capabilities and worth to emerge," some had questions about practical concerns, such as finding the time to dedicate to the project and the spaces where they could rehearse and perform, and others wondered just how far the participants' trust and openness could be taken. Looking back, La Vecchia deems the project a great achievement: "with some time having passed now, and after great effort and much joy, we of Vagamonde can affirm that the outcome of our theatrical laboratory was a happy outcome" (Associazione Vagamonde and Festina Lente Teatro 2004, 4). Given the success of *Voci invisibili*, Vagamonde held another laboratory/production in 2005 called *Scene madri*, based on the work of Virginia Woolf. *Scene madri* plays with the notion that even if not all women are mothers, all women have a mother, and mothers often serve as carriers of gender and cultural norms that shape their identities. In the production, it becomes evident that migrant mothers negotiate norms across national contexts and often determine degrees of integration for their families. They therefore hold power in a domestic context that may or may not translate in public space.

Vagamonde has been working with Festina Lente Teatro (FLT), a mixed-sex, multiethnic theatrical group active in Parma since 1997 that describes its work as "a 'difficult' theatre that makes dramaturgy with the stories of migrant women, with the poetic visions of the insane, with stories of indigene women, with their discomforts, with racism and discrimination" (*Festina Lente Teatro* 2018). FLT has described its laboratories as special moments guided by passion and freedom where different thoughts can be heard without always having to be expressed in proper grammar, a practice that has allowed a more poetic language to develop and enabled non-native Italian speakers to break free of the limitations of having to speak correct Italian. FLT has also brought formal plays to the stage.[3]

Multiethnic cooking is another area in which intercultural women's centers have made significant progress building new feminist practices. Several women's centers in Emilia-Romagna, such as Trama di Terre, Vagamonde, Agorà dei Mondi, Associazione Migrazione, and Associazione che la festa continui, have offered cooking classes or opened internal cafés featuring the many culinary traditions of the women who frequent their centers. A member of the Bologna-based Associazione Mondo Donna Onlus explains, "The kitchen has always been a place for sharing, for meetings among cultures, as such it reveals itself in our center as a strength, often as a starting point, to communicate one's way of being, of thinking, albeit in a foreign and difficult context like the one on which our guests live" (Associazone Mondo Donna Onlus 2018). Inside the centers, Italian and migrant women have the opportunity to cook for fun, rather than to feed their families, while learning about the flavors and traditions of many cultures. In a strong food culture like that of Emilia-Romagna, known for its specialties such as pasta Bolognese, pumpkin tortellini, prosciutto, and parmigiano reggiano, cooking is valued for its connections to local history and identity. For migrant women, cooking is often one important means of maintaining connections to the home country and passing them along to the next generation (Pető 2007; Gabaccia 2000). In these multiethnic spaces, many women report being able to talk about food easily; this then can lead them to discuss other aspects of their lives. Women in Trama di Terre in Imola, for example, have used the socialization that takes place in its *cucina abitata*, a multiethnic café inside the intercultural center, as an impetus for events programming and even political action. The easiness of mealtime conversation allows ideas to flourish and turn into new insights and opportunities for the women participants.

As is also the case with the theater, however, multiethnic cooking has left the confines of the walls of the women's associations and become an integrative activity for the broader community. Several women's associations have started offering multiethnic catering services that offer reciprocal benefits for migrant women and locals. Associazione Mondo Donna Onlus, for example, has extended its work with women who live in its temporary housing facilities by offering them positions in the catering service. Women chosen for this work undergo several training courses, including not only cooking but also business courses that build skills in accounting, public relations, and event organization. The women who staff the catering service explain that it has given them a chance to find purpose and personal fulfillment while the association's leaders note that the Bolognese community has responded favorably to the opportunity to learn about other cultures. Over the course of just a few years, the women have already hosted more than one hundred events, including weddings, office parties, and gallery openings (http://www.mondodonna-onlus.it). Alida Guatri of Vagamonde explains that her association's catering service has also been very important in giving migrant women an opportunity to reinvent themselves. She states that it

> gives a voice to women who have professional qualifications in their countries but for whom Italy doesn't recognize their degrees, even college and masters . . . and they find themselves doing very humble jobs. However, we realized that with cooking, and with the possibility to participate in specialized training with recognized groups in our region, women succeed at climbing back up in the chair and finding new jobs that weren't theirs to start with but that are nevertheless dignified. (phone interview with author, November 17, 2010)

CONCLUSIONS

The examples above point to a great deal of potential to develop more mean-ingful relationships among women of different backgrounds, which could result in greater access to social services, employment, and education for all of them. More extensive creative intercultural exchanges could also assist in developing a newly energized feminist politics as well as expanded public support for the needs of growing immigrant communities. Provincial leaders such as Tiziana Mozzoni of Parma already recognize the numerous advan-tages of women's activism in a variety of creative endeavors:

> giving women the tools for carrying out activities and services (language and cooking courses, organizing dinners and cultural get-togethers, theatrical labs, to name just a few) useful to respond to social needs that are sometimes "invisible" but fundamental that you may encounter in a foreign city is an opportunity to experiment with the skills and professionalism of women out-side of a charitable approach and with a view to promoting a culture of under-standing that allows the migrant to be the protagonist and leader of her own path of integration. (Associazione Vagamonde and Festina Lente Teatro 2004, 1)

These more recent forms of cultural interaction are, in fact, giving more visibility to the experiences of migrant women and highlighting their capac-ity for integration and their desire to make their new cities and country their home, whether temporarily or permanently.

Migrant women who engage in creative practices as actresses on the stage or as caterers in a villa ballroom greeting party guests demonstrate their willingness to adapt to a new place by speaking Italian, learning new skills, and seeking a full life as members of the community. Alida Guatri points out what this means to Italian women who get to see migrant women as contribu-tors to their communities outside the limits of domestic spaces and to get to know them as individuals rather than as the needy or disorderly masses depicted in the news or berated by anti-immigrant politicians: "You can see [the migrant] in another role, not just a subject in need of the social services of this city, but also as someone who can give something to this society, therefore her voice, her experiences, her history, her specificity, also with respect to the country of origin that she puts in play" (phone interview with author, November 17, 2010). A visible presence in daily life grants access to becoming a regular, nonthreatening, and non-servile "citizen." Guatri says that Vagamonde is aware of the significance of its approach to cultural inte-grative practices that put migrants and Italians side by side: "What is most interesting to us is to enter into the social fabric with things that can seem normal—like theater or like cooking—but in fact we realized that precisely because they seem so normal they penetrate the most under the skin of our interlocutor" (phone interview with author, November 17, 2010). Creative intercultural activities have given Italian and migrant women new tools with which to explore their differences, recount hardships, share happy memories, and reach understandings that were difficult to achieve through other forms of interaction, especially those based primarily on an assistance model.

I am encouraged by the work of intercultural women's associations in Emilia-Romagna, but I do not want to overlook some of the challenges they continue to face. First, the possibility to transform identities is exciting and liberating, but when the performance is over or the party favors put away, women return to inhabiting their own identities, no matter how fractured they may be, and having to face the realities of their daily lives. Women are still judged each day by the identities they physically manifest or choose to put forward. Second, power imbalances continue to inform relationships and determine access to advancement. While it is a step forward that Italian feminists acknowledge the contributions of migrant women, equal opportunity is not a reality so long as integration stops short of the rights of citizenship and discrimination continues. Third, the problems of financing women's associations and their activities and finding volunteers and participants for them have worsened in the past several years as state, regional, and city governments have had to cut expenses. Women are especially hard hit by economic declines and political instability. Finding private funding sources is difficult and time-consuming and therefore detracts from other activities. Finally, there continues to be the challenge of location, scope, and scale. Intercultural women's associations are generally welcomed in Emilia-Romagna but have had less impact in other regions where the political climate is averse to migration or where financial burdens are felt even more. Such concerns keep the question of unity among migrant and native women an open one.

NOTES

1. I briefly discuss the histories of Italian and migrant women's associations before turning to an analysis of the creative practices used by several intercultural women's centers operating in the central Italian region of Emilia-Romagna. It is my contention that as the integration of migrants has advanced during the past twenty years, thereby overcoming some of the constraints that earlier characterized migrant women's lives, new opportunities have emerged to improve relationships between Italian and migrant women. Creative endeavors, such as theater, art, dance, and social activities, such as cooking and festivals, have provided new levels of engagement for women of diverse backgrounds. Improved communication is beginning to result in exciting feminist practices that are enabling Italian and migrant women to surpass some of the stopping points of their previous work together.

2. The association offers services, such as Italian language courses and afterschool programs, but also numerous cultural and artistic activities, such as multiethnic dinners and art exhibits. And in 2005, members published a book of migration stories entitled *Donne dell'altro mondo*. By confronting the difficulties faced by migrant women while also recognizing their

contributions to the cultural life of the community, associations like Che la festa continui are participating in a growing aspect of associational life.

3. In *Un posto dove stare* (La Vecchia 2005) the story of the migrant Ilda merges into the life of her Italian observer, Fausta. In the end, both women share the ups and downs of life, encountering obstacles and finding the courage to overcome them. The play stresses the complexities of human emotions and points out that whether migrant or native, all women experience pain and joy in their lives. Rather than reducing women's experiences to a singular characteristic, however, *Un posto dove stare*, like the other plays staged by the theater groups, shows how shared qualities of life are mutated by a multitude of events.

REFERENCES

Annassim. 2011. Accessed January 2011. www.flashgiovani.it/stranieribologna/pagina/212/279/.

Annassim: donne native delle due sponde del Mediterraneo. 2018. Facebook. Accessed August 8, 2018. https://www.facebook.com/donnediAnnassim/.

Andall, Jacqueline. 2000. *Gender, Migration and Domestic Service: The Politics of Black Women in Italy*. Hampshire: Ashgate.

Associazione Mondo Donna Onlus. Web site. http://www.mondodonna-onlus.it/storia.html. Last accessed August 8, 2018.

Associazione Vagamonde and Festina Lente Teatro. 2004. *Voci Invisibili*. Parma: Gruppo Cabiria.

Associazione Vagamonde. Accessed August 8, 2018. http://associazionevaga-monde.blogspot.com/.

Braidotti, Rosi. 1994. *Nomadic Subjects: Embodiment and Sexual Difference in Contemporary Feminist Theory*. New York: Columbia University Press.

Butler, Judith. 1990. *Gender Trouble: Feminism and the Subversion of Identity*. New York: Routledge.

Calavita, Kitty. 2004. "Italy: Economic Realities, Political Fictions, and Policy Failures." In *Controlling Immigration: A Global Perspective*. 2nd ed., edited by Wayne Cornelius, Takeyuki Tsuda, Philip L. Martin, and James Hollifield, 345–80. Stanford: Stanford University Press.

Case, Sue-Ellen. 2008. *Feminism and Theatre*. Reissued ed. New York: Palgrave Macmillan.

De Lauretis, Teresa, ed. 1987. *Sexual Difference: A Theory of Social-Symbolic Practice*. Bloomington: Indiana University Press.

Engroba Oberti, Valeria and Alessandra Cataneo. 2018. "Mappatura delle Associazioni di donne migranti e di donne native e migranti in Emilia-Romagna." Centro Stampa Regione Emilia-Romagna. Accessed August 8, 2018. http://sociale.regione.emilia-romagna.it/immi-grati-e-stranieri/approfondimenti/mappatura-delle-associazioni-di-donne-migranti-e-di-donne-native-e-migranti-in-emilia-romagna-anno-2017/view.

Festina Lente Teatro. Accessed August 8, 2018. http://teatrofestinalente.blogspot.com/.

Gabaccia, Donna. 2000. *We Are What We Eat: Ethnic Food and the Making of Americans*. Cambridge: Harvard University Press.

International Organization for Migration. 2018. "Migration Flows Europe." May 25, 2018. https://reliefweb.int/sites/reliefweb.int/files/resources/missingmigrants-iom-int-region-med-iterranean-pdf_4.pdf.

IRIDE, Associazione Interculturale di Donne Siena and Theatrikos, Laboratorio Teatro Donna Colle di Val d'Elsa. 2003. *La Signora del Labirinto: Diario di un viaggio collettivo alla ricerca di sé. Materiali, immagini e percorso del laboratorio teatrale interculturale Conosci il mio paese?* Poggibonsi: Progetto Lavoro.

La Vecchia, Elide. *Un posto dove stare*. 2005. Play directed by Andreina Garella. Festina Lenta Teatro.

Parati, Graziella, and Rebecca West, eds. 2002. *Italian Feminist Theory and Practice: Equality and Sexual Difference*. Madison, NJ: Farleigh Dickinson University Press.

Parreñas, Rhacel Salazar. 2001. *Servants of Globalization: Women, Migration and Domestic Work*. Stanford: Stanford University Press.

Pető, Andrea. 2007. "Food-talk: Markers of Identity and Imaginary Belongings." In *Women Migrants from East to West: Gender, Mobility and Belonging in Contemporary Europe*, edited by Luisa Passerini, Dawn Lyon, Enrica Capussotti, and Ioanna Laliotou, 152–64. New York: Berghahn Books.

Pojmann, Wendy. 2008. "'We're right here!" The Invisibility of Migrant Women in European Women's Movements—The Case of Italy." In *Migration and Activism in Europe since 1945*, edited by Wendy Pojmann, 193–208. New York: Palgrave Macmillan.

Tardi, Susanna. 2010. "The Changing Roles of Italian-American Women: Reality vs. Myth." In *Anti-Italianism: Essays on a Prejudice*, edited by William Connell and Fred Gardaphe, 95–106. New York: Palgrave Macmillan.

Zincone, G. 2001. *Secondo rapporto sull'integrazione degli immigrati in Italia*. Bologna: Il Mulino.

"Arriving Too Soon Is a Mistake"

Amnesia in the Postcolonial Archives:
The Antonaros Case

Fulvio Pezzarossa

In analyzing the concept of the birth of migration writing in Italy (Pezzarossa and Rossini 2011),[1] it is helpful to consider Giuliana Benvenuti's (2009) insight on the persistence of the "trace of a (neo)colonial glance under the cover of a fascination for places and cultures described as genuinely 'primitive,' 'poor,' 'distant,' 'abandoned'" (De Robertis 2014: 2), also underscored in Graham Huggan's work on the processes of a globalized literature and *marketing the margins* (2001). A narrative work with African roots, which some have privileged, is not always "an instrument of docile realization of programmes decided at discussions in university campuses [. . . that] always entails the risk of favouring the diffusion, and in fact also the creation, of works that are nothing other than the projection of ideological ambitions, of misunderstood good intentions, of pernicious distortions of reality" (Manai 2017, 224–25). Critical contributions aimed at intersectional reflections (Romeo 2018) should develop within the framework of a wider rehabilitation of figures and documents that redesign the history, objects, forms, and modes of migration and of postcolonial writing.

When I began as a student at the Univeristy of Bologna, I found a likeable classmate, Alfredo Taracchini, who was born in Addi-Cahieh in 1950 where he'd lived for several years, before arriving in the Romagna area via Egypt and France. Upon graduation, my friend started working in the cultural institutions of the Municipality and for decades was the Director—the youngest in Italy—of Imola, the theater in his city. He was also a journalist, a playwright, an author, an expert in cooking and tourism, and a prominent television personality.

His university period in Bologna, then the center of international attention for its political and cultural ferment, was a fundamental passage for his eclectic preparation and it was here that Taracchini became close to Roberto Roversi. His friendship with the great poet and bookseller Roversi, an intellectual of national and central prominence in the city, allowed Taracchini to focus on literary resources and objectives. The important publisher Rebellato (ATA 1970) had already printed "a collection of poems I wish I hadn't written" (ATA 1989, 30) by Taracchini. But Roversi found "among those pages, something good, ethical, civil, strong, interesting" (Roversi 19). In his famous Palmaverde bookshop, Roversi printed a hundred copies of Taracchini's mimeographed novel *Rapporti sperimentali* (Experimental Relationships).[2] The novel is marked by a strong political commitment and formal innovations, and which Taracchini later described as "a tale that I wrote in the years of the massacres and coup attempts in Italy. [. . .] It is a story written experimenting with the narrative use of everyday language" (ATA 1989, 29). The novel includes grotesque and unsettling passages and is innovative in its imaginative set-up. It includes peripheral and uneducated characters who develop a reactive conscience on a long journey through Italy, in which politics, society, and sexual mores are transforming. But the novel also violently challenges the optimistic narrative of the West (ATA 1989, 18).

One wonders whether the received wisdom that sketches the stages, moments, currents, themes, and figures of the elusive migration literature does not, in fact, overlook figures like Taracchini who, already in the 70s and 80s, was writing of exile and displacement. In 1984 Taracchini made his entrance into the institution of Italian letters by publishing *Ritorno a Carobèl* (Return to Carobèl) for Feltrinelli (ATA 1984). Years later he rewrote that fortunate parable in ironic terms in a text (*I Romagnoli: la tribù di Fellini*) dedicated to the Romagna regional identity which he had shared since adolescence, between the anxiety of setting up home and feeling not at home (ATA 1997b).[3] In the text, a simulated strangeness allows Taracchini detachment from one of his most representative myths, the Fellini of the subtitle, while he focuses on the contradictory melting pot originating from the tourism of the Riviera that masked racist tendencies towards the first African migrants who were collectively referred to by "the single term *Moroccans*" (*I forestieri* [The Foreigners]) (ATA 1997b, 28–30: 29),[4] and good-naturedly tolerated, as was *L'Autore* (The Author) (ATA 1997b, 91) himself, "one of the first African immigrants to have come to the Romagna region," ahead of time and forced to sell another trinket:

> He experienced for himself that arriving too soon is the same error as arriving too late: in that period—it was the mid-1950s—no-one from the Romagna

region would have wanted a sweater with a tacky green crocodile stuck on, even for free. And only petrol lighters were appreciated.

He then decided to devote himself to literature, writing novels, plays and poems. [. . .] He is not yet fully integrated but speaks the dialect fluently [. . .]. In this way he was able to know the natives from the inside, understand their customs and visit their villages [. . .]. So much so that, apart from *piadina*,[5] he is now convinced that Romagna and his native village on the Equator resemble each other in many things like two drops of water. (ATA 1997b, 91)[6]

The connection between the two worlds is made concrete in the official signature that admitted his multifaceted identity into the literary field: he used his maternal Greek surname, Antonaros, for his books.[7]

An editorial system already sensitive to signs of otherness contributed to this choice. As Alba Morino recalls, involved in a period of success at Feltrinelli (Briganti 2014): "We asked [him] to sign with his maternal name of Antonaros and we spoke with him for the first time of 'the deep rivers of the culture of the exile'" (ATA 2005, IV cover), placing him in the major series of The Narrators, following volumes by Saramago, Kafka, Blixen, Gordimer, and Yourcenar. The heteronym therefore takes on an arduous cohesive function in the diffidence of a protection that filters the anxieties of the split identity, also present on the professional side for Taracchini: "I needed something that kept the writer separate from the work I do" (ATA 1989, 30). This was a useful choice to exorcise "the burdensome comments of people on the brown and delicate skin of my mother" (Regazzoni 1989, 45), the condition of diversity that the narrator aspired to release through writing, to evoke an intricate migration itinerary, embodied by characters who face a difficult or impossible formation, stuck in a condition of youth unbalanced between several worlds. A reading today of a multifaceted and unstable text, placed in a social and cultural context in which the migratory theme was nonexistent, prompts us to ask about the method of discovery of the postcolonial *before* the postcolonial, which is traced not only in the content but also in the "epic, precipitous but guarded writing, full of accumulations, flashes, smells, noises, silences, boats, screams, blood and tenderness," which conquered Morino (ATA 2005, IV cover).

This is, even today, an unsettling and "surprising [. . .] hymn to the mixed race" (Tirinanzi De Medici 2018, 61) that crescendos when the narration leads into the mythic Eritrean place of Carobèl, the contradictory and tragic homeland that also emerges in the subsequent works, in which the protagonists of a long family saga arrive: a lineage of intrepid migrants who, leaving from Samarcanda, overcome Mediterranean crossings and shipwrecks. That maternal story uses imaginary hues to mediate the conflicting features of the epic, of the perpetually lurking horrors and violence, leading to setting aside

Every nostalgic-elegiac inclination, kept under control by the fictional en-
chantment of narration that seems a winning method to describe the life of the
emigrant, made of continuous movements and occasional encounters (hence
the functionality of the numerous characters just mentioned.) And instability is
the key element of the novel: the instability of a nomadic life, but also a
discursive instability, due to the continuous slips of the discourse [narrative]
that preferentially describe the open, unconventional situation of the emigrant.
(Tirinanzi De Medici 2018, 61)

The protagonist escapes the destruction of the mythical African city overwhelmed by internal violence, and to which it is impossible to return. However, the thousand troubles of the emigrant accompany him from Egypt to the
Marseilles *banlieue* of Edenville. There he impersonates his friend Ruet, who
sees the dreams of an illusory revolution prematurely fading. But the current
issues, in a world faced with desperate fugitives, reconverge in paranoid
interpretations of the clash of civilizations, as can be seen in the center of the
book:

"You are too aggressive. Too compliant. Too timid. Too harsh. You are always too much," Ruet said to me.
"You who?"
"You and your family. All of you emigrants. Difficulty in adapting, I
think."
"I didn't know what to say. He too was also 'too much' from many points
of view." (ATA 1984, 59)

Antonaros resonates very little with the methods widespread in Europe of
portraying the African world (Bandia 2008), since he "goes beyond the reach
of what could be [. . .] even a certain indulgence of the exotic" (Volponi
1989, 52) and turns the geocritical reference dimension (Westphal 2009) to a
wide Mediterranean horizon, in his works of narrative invention and numerous travel and adventure writings.

The Mediterranean horizon pervades the 1994 theatrical text *Balkanica*
(*Mediterraneo è* . . . [Mediterranean is . . .] ATA 1994a, 27–28). Based on a
rewriting of the original human condition, here "Eve drives Adam crazy and
he becomes a fierce enemy of Muslims after Eve meets Ammar, 'a beautiful
wounded Muslim.' Pity brings him to safety, but pity turns into love" (ATA
1994a, 11). It presents a brilliant paradox based on the belief that "humour is
a destructive and therefore *anti-conservative* force" (ATA 1994a, 14). The
central theme is obviously

War, militarism, intolerance.
The ex-Yugoslavia seen from both sides of the Mediterranean. But the
Mediterranean is the underlying theme, and also the true protagonist; it

emerges continuously with its scents, its music (Balkan, Maghrebine, Spanish, Neapolitan), with sheep (multiple symbol), wine, olive trees and bread.

The Mediterranean is so central to this story that, while telling scenes and stories of the Balkan war, every time we are in Beirut, in Palestine, in Algeria, in a disorganised Italian south. (ATA 1994a, 1)

Antonaros then returns to his African world with sounds, voices, colors, habits, landscapes, and places that reflect the memory of his native Eritrea, but aware of the temptations of an aesthetic and exotic evocation: "half of us [immigrants] show off their exotic originality, the whims of the south and just about manage to make folklore. And the other half [. . .] can only look back or be moved by their irremediable feelings of inferiority" (ATA 1987, 32). *Mahò. Storia di cinema e petrolio* is a reflection born in the heart of a novel focused on the image of the phantasmagoric and grotesque *Mahò*, a real Babylon (a term certainly not unknown to subsequent developments of the postcolonial romance),[8] an imaginary Eritrean resort on the Red Sea, where the grim dictatorship of a fierce albino, Almereida, becomes established at the opening of the twentieth century (the historical perspective allows greater critical penetration of the present). He appears to be entirely subjected to the Western exploitation of lethal oil fields, and is finally overthrown by the rebellion of the exploited natives. He is opposed by the narrative and artistic desire of Jacob Gisc who is overwhelmed by a passion for the newborn cinematic medium. The inclusion of the topos of the cinema has a metacritical function, alluding to the narrative structure of several novels of the 1980s, in which the "cinematographic references" articulate a diegetic proposal that precedes solutions of a dismantling, intertwining, "violation of realism and its codes" [*Modelli testuali postcoloniali* (Postcolonial textual models) by Silvia Albertazzi (2013, 82–104: 86)], and which coincides with "the choice of a fantastic narrative code" (Tirinanzi De Medici 2018, 42). At the time of the novel's writing there was much literary excitement around the magical realism of South America, understood as "a way to affirm the difference, fulfilling the ideological function of giving imaginative expression to autonomy, to independence, to freedom of expression and behaviour" (Albertazzi 2013, 87), which the protagonists of Antonaros's novel find in the assembly technique: "Now they could have constructed tales with intertwined plots, sudden appearances, or leave a speech in suspense, start another one, insert an effect scene, and resume the story shortly after" (ATA 1987, 115).[9]

Barilli (1989) detected a similarity between Autonaros's Mahò and Gabriel García Marquez's Macondo: "Mahò was up there, suspended in the sky, sprouting from an amba, with immense, deep roots" (*La torre di Babele*) (ATA 1987, 39). The Mahò story might also suggest to us Italo Calvino's *Citta invisibili* (Invisible Cities). And we might note that Marquez's novels arrived in Italy through Morino. Carlo Tirinanzi De Medici however, argues that the absurd Mahò is less isolated, archaic and immobile than Marquez's famous village (2018). It is still at the mercy of the first world needs that impose traffic and trade, which trample local needs. This reflects also the devastation suffered by Africa during its postcolonial phase. In the desolating image of an entire continent defeated, the text assumes an evident counter-narrative style, where "the distortion of the representation produced by melo-dramatic paradigms makes it possible to bring out more clearly [. . .] the economic relationships that devour individual lives" (Tirinanzi De Medici 2018, 62), demonstrating the alienating functionality of a magical-grotesque writing missing from other migratory texts.

It is impossible here to sketch the vastness of the journeys, writings, interests, and themes of an author who, by precocity, is perhaps a stranger to the postcolonial, but who is without a doubt Italian. This distinguishes him from certain contemporary writers intent on exhibiting their transnational, transcontinental, translinguistic, features, but who at the same time reject the reductive labels of *migrant writers* (most recently Scego [2018]), considered incongruous with the profile of new Italian intellectuals, who can loudly exclaim: "I write literature and that's enough!" without differentiating terri-torial and cultural extraction (Vlasta 2011); in short, a dialectic between *passing* and *posing* is sometimes entangled in choices and aspirations that are contradictory and uncertain in their aims.

Antonaros is an example of successful integration within the national cultural timeframe based on his ability to participate in the Italian world, facing its social, political, and cultural vicissitudes at a high level, naturally enhancing a broader and more contoured sensibility that is open to his African origin. This inspires in him the eagerness to travel, for instability, gathering the complex stimuli that derive equally from his experiences "in Italy, in the Mediterranean, in the south of Europe, in this uncertain geogra-phy that is at the north of the third world, and at the south of development" (ATA 1989, 16).

Unsettling notes of melancholy and instability have hampered neither Antonaros's inexhaustible high-quality output, nor his entry into the recent canon of Italian literature, as can be demonstrated by the paper "La torre di Babele" (The Tower of Babel) (ATA 1996). Its theme is "memory, which transforms a space into a "monument" [. . .] despite the feeling of loss, of absolute precariousness of today's world" (Casari 1996, 12). Certainly, this was well-received by the general society and its cultural institutions, which welcomed his work naturally, without the uncertain steps and uneven path-ways into which the works of migrant writers are forced today, within the more general process of marginalization of the other, also in the literary world itself (Pezzarossa 2018).

But we must ask ourselves how many migrant writers can exhibit a standard that is constant in large-scale narratives, that is continually varied in tone, and that moves from the fabulous heroic to the intimate, from the external focus to the inner focus on the characters; which stages the psychological tensions and the great dimensions of adventure, the dramatic and vital re-enactment of the past and the living suffering of contradictory tensions between revolution and destruction of the present. Antonaros's personal style shuts out editorial interferences, readily adapting to self-driven ends, such as the passionate denunciation of the Bologna massacre (ATA 1981), or to a successful universal history of wine (ATA 2006). Antonaros continually demonstrates a shrewd ability in overtaking, not trailing after, external markers, often anticipating great themes that orient successive moments in the social and cultural history of the nation.

Antonaros is therefore neither a relic of the splendid 1970s nor an unknown migrant writer: he clearly states that he is an "anomalous Italian: various, different cultures coexist in me" (ATA 1989, 30), and he disseminates references to his complex identity in his writings. A collection of short stories, published in *Enne Erre. Le nostre ragioni* (N. R. Our reasons), were dedicated to exile, the central theme of his existence. Of these, the epistolary dialogue with Maria Chiara Gnocchi stands out in "Le parole dell'esilio" (Words of Exile) (ATA 2005, 9–13):

> My exile [. . .] knows of the sea, the smoke of oil from the truck in which I left the mountains of the plateau, and for the first time, I went down to the coast. [. . .] That day my diaspora and the tangle of my ego began.
>
> The steamer and the sea remain archetypes of my imagination, the space of a pain and responsibility disproportionate to my strength: that of having to protect my mother from the adversary who awaited us on the other side.
>
> An enemy, my father, who had left a few years earlier, and who now reappeared. (ATA 2005, 5–6)

The prospect of family rift and and the suspension between cultures that marks mixed-race offspring provokes psychological wounds courageously declared within an original dialectic that welcomes the "tension between the *homeland* [. . .] and the *motherland*" (ATA 2005).[10] The writing that flows from it serves to overcome that intimate tangle:

> all of the sudden I realised that the problem was no longer the bread and the granary, the homeland or the "motherland," neither here nor elsewhere. Or, even less, the sublimation of the singularity of an experience, because it concerns everyone, indigenous and immigrants, whites and blacks [. . .].
>
> Today my exile is only the subplot of this effort. And the search for words to tell of this effort with which I try to *withdraw myself,* to *free myself* [. . .] reducing to the essential. [. . .] that also has an equivalent in the language,

rigidly avoiding those situations of perceived diversity "the alibi of having felt constantly misunderstood." (ATA 2005, 8–9)

These roots create the impossibility of projecting a myth onto the future and are expressed in the admission that "I tell of my discomfort, of not feeling in the right place, the need to go somewhere else and to look for strong bonds and firm roots somewhere" (ATA 1989, 22–23), in a setting of contradictions that make it obligatory to "non tornare a Carobèl" (not return to Carobèl) (ATA 2005, 11–16). In fact, he frees himself from that myth that has been simplified by mass tourism. Contrarily, reality reveals a hellish world in which "children are killed, women are gutted, towns and villages are burned. Carobèl is hell, the loss and destruction of the dream of a thing, the disappointed expectation of a happy oasis that does not exist. It is the death of those few African illusions that I had preserved." The narrator is thus forced to "accept to be alone, without roots, in an unpleasant yet tolerated isolation, and distant from a homeland-motherland unbearable because it is a failure and in any case unpleasant" (ATA 2005, 14), overwhelmed by the overflow of a globalizing flattening that makes of that native land also a "land of new slaves, new colonialism at home [. . .] neo-slavery of black immigrants in European cities" (ATA 1989, 16). These are statements made in 1985 that express a highly critical attitude towards neo-colonial politics. Antonaros decided not to content himself with the cover "of the babble of the interethnic, of the multicultural" (ATA 2005, 16). Instead of a linguistic intermixing, which has been called the result of "the individual and collective memory of those [. . .] 'emerging' peoples, of their millennial treasure [. . .] handed down from oral tradition and very recently from writing, of which he is a debtor but not imitator" (Amaya 10), Antonaros uses "effects borrowed from theatrical and cinematographic techniques" (ATA 1984, IV cover), which like the world of circuses and magazines allow nuances in a "grotesque and compassionate key" (Barilli 1989, 43). These nuances derive from an experience broader than that of other immigrants, telling of a world that limits the space for exoticism and otherness, in the urgency of building relational opportunities and cues:

> *Immigration*—with all its tragedies and pains—has at least the merit of having killed the charm of exoticism in the West, leaving, instead of contemplation, the perception of something not identical to itself and the "notion of the other." Some limit themselves to annoyance, conflict, and refusal. Others have been able to move things from glorification to awareness. Few to communication. For everyone the bare observation remains that it is no longer possible to find even in a foreign land everything that was believed impossible to find in their own. (ATA 1998, 140).

A narrow horizon, in which the natural exchange that animates the Mediterranean basin finds obstacles and stumbles, as described by the hallucinatory atmosphere of *La piattaforma* (The Platform) (ATA 1997a), a claustrophobic novel where the Oedipal tensions and isolation of a postmodern father without loved ones are consumed in the artificial insularity of that capitalistic structure from which the source of modernity springs, which now makes old routes, old modes of transits and crossings, and natural human relations impossible. This is also the meaning of *L'ultimo Grand Tour* (The Last Grand Tour), because it is impossible to relate the journey distorted by the superficial standardization of tourism, so that only "history and food can suggest new meanings to the experience of travel" (ATA 1994b, IV cover).[11]

While his literary education widened and varied the framework of his own interests, that education nevertheless projected Antonaros into a recognized role as an intellectual in whole parts remains the basic reference. This intellectual role is evident when rereading as an autobiographical mirror the touching pages dedicated to the memory of the "teacher and friend" (ATA 2013, 14). Roversi, who had pointed out to Antonaros simple and penetrating tools to examine the manifestations and passing of human history:

> Roversi was always aware enough to know well that the identity of each person is an indefinable object: that the roots of every man expand in the darkness and that, going deeper into the ground, the roots widen, and the more they widen, the more the plant is strong and solid [. . .]. And that no identity is built on nothing, but only in the comparison and exchange with different identities and other stories. And that the identity of each person is more solid when the capacity for comparison and exchange becomes strong. (ATA 2013, 16)

This is the declaration of a continuous faith in the power of literature as a foundation of civil life outside of ornamental strategies, and as capable of offering tools useful to the relationships between men over time, and more so the more it becomes the expression of a culturally broad and articulated narrative, and available in innovative forms (De Robertis 2007). "Thus giving back to writing the ability to look at reality. And to feel indignation for injustice, for the humiliation caused to the weakest, and at the same time, for those reading, the desire to really change things" (ATA 2013, 13).

This occasions reflection on the possibilities that await a literary sector that I believe is in crisis (Pezzarossa 2015) vis à vis its effective integration into the national canon (Fracassa 2012). Antonaros has avoided (not only for chronological reasons) the ambiguous labels of *migrant* and *postcolonial*, by offering the critics an enduring creative capacity that resists highlighting the differing brands of personal identity that force focus on the appearance of the author (Mengozzi 2013), and that delivers a continuity that is reactive and that participates in the cultural context of which the author has been a significant part, notwithstanding that "to date his books have been much less read and reviewed than they should be" (Regazzoni 1989, 46).

Therefore, if we can place him "in the group of the so-called Italian 'new novelists,' together with De Carlo and Busi, Tondelli and Del Giudice, Tabucchi and Pazzi" (Barilli 1989, 41), our task will be to verify the consistency of his writing given the dramatic present on the themes of diversity, convinced that

> Only very few works surpass what a historicist would call the test of time: if the critics cannot yet establish which ones, they can nevertheless put some writings back in circulation, because they are surprisingly modern (for example those of Alfredo Antonaros, who offers a reflection on roots, migration and diversity much more interesting today than when it was written thirty years ago.) (Tirinanzi De Medici 2018, 10)

NOTES

1. Mia Lecomte (2018) also stops the chronology for poetic works, referring to persons of a cosmopolitan vocation rather than of a strictly migratory experience.

2. I am grateful to Antonio Bagnoli, nephew of Roversi and director of Edizioni Pendragon, which has published numerous books by Taracchini, for offering me the valuable texts in electronic format.

3. *Imola* in (ATA 1994b, 51–52).

4. Antonaros suggests an interesting origin for the derogatory term *Moroccans*, connected to the experience of the fascist legionaries alongside the Francoist troops in the Spanish civil war.

5. *Piadina* is thin Italian flatbread typically prepared in the Romagna region.

6. The profile is missing in the re-edition (ATA 2011). But the reason for being ahead of time is often referred to, as in the important text *Il venditore d'ozio* (The Seller of Idleness).

7. Sometimes the accented spelling Antonàros is used, and in the essayist volumes "Antonaros" is accompanied or replaced by the paternal surname.

8. "The Africa of my stories is Babylon," with the subsequent articulated explanation (ATA 1989, 15–16).

9. See (ATA 1989, 18–20: 19): "After the cinema we will tell and listen in a completely different way."

10. See also (ATA 1998, 34): "Today, when the absence of homeland has become a common condition of almost everyone, the return is no longer to the land, to the space of origin (to the culture of possessing and heritage), but to private relationships, personal affections, the sense of belonging to a community." "In a word to the womb (to marriage as to the culture of receiving and welcoming): how good it would be perhaps to start calling it 'motherland.'" The debate on this term, made current by Scego (2018), does not take into account the early use, in a different sense, by Taracchini: see Silvia Contarini (2012) and the subsequent comment by Scego.

11. The volume contains the stated adhesion to the essential life and professional experience with the promotion of the *Gambero Rosso* (Red Shrimp) project, the first gastronomic-themed TV channel, at the end *Il venditore di ozio*.

REFERENCES

Albertazzi, Silvia. 2013. *La letteratura postcoloniale. Dall'Impero alla* World Literature. Roma: Carocci.

Antonaros, Alfredo Taracchini (ATA). 1970. *Di vetro, di terra. Padova: Rebellato*.

———. 1981. *Agosto è un pesce sventrato*. Bologna: Il Pesce Solubile.

———. 1984. *Tornare a Carobèl. Romanzo*. Milano: Feltrinelli.

———. 1987. *Mahò. Storia di cinema e petrolio*. Milano: Feltrinelli.

_____. 1989. *Il dibattito*, in *Alfredo Antonaros*: 15-31.

———. 1994a. *Balkanika*. Ancona: Ars books .

———. 1994b. *Moto a luogo. L'ultimo Grand Tour*. Bologna: Pendragon.

———. 1996. "La torre di Babele." *Testo letterario e immaginario architettonico*. Milano: Jaca Book: 43–53.

———. 1997a. *La piattaforma*. Milano: Jaca Book.

———. 1997b. *I Romagnoli, la tribù di Fellini*. Torino: Sonda.

———. 1998. *Viaggi. Saggio*. Theoria: Roma.

———. 2005. *Le parole dell'esilio*. Milano: EnneErre—Le nostre ragioni.

———. 2006. *Storia universale del vino*. Bologna: Pendragon.

———. 2011. *Romagnoli. Guida sentimentale a una terra e al suo popolo*. Bagnacavallo (RA): Discanti.

———. 2013. "Conoscere Roberto Roversi." In *La mia piccola Atene emiliana. Pieve di Cento, e altri luoghi*, Roberto Roversi. Bologna: Pendragon: 13–19.

Bandia, Paul F. 2008. *Translation as Reparation. Writing and Translation in Postcolonial Africa*. Manchester-Kinderhook: St. Jerome.

Barilli, Renato. 1989. "Antonàros e il viaggio al termine dell'espressione." In *Alfredo Antonaros*, Pesaro: Banca Popolare pesarese: 41–43.

Benvenuti, Giuliana. 2009. *Il viaggiatore come autore. L'India nella letteratura italiana del Novecento*. Bologna: il Mulino.

Biblioteca Comunale di Imola. 2010. *Alfredo Antònaros. Raccontare il mondo*. http:// bim.comune.imola.bo.it/documenti/9966/81/8311.

Briganti, Annarita. 2014. "Alba, la pasionaria dell'editoria 'I miei piccoli libri clandestini.'" *La Repubblica*, February 11, 2014. https://ricerca.repubblica.it/repubblica/archivio/repubblica/ 2014/02/11/alba-la-pasionaria-delleditoria-i-miei-piccoli.html.

Brugnettini, M. Annunziata and Adina Santini, eds. 1989. *Alfredo Antonaros*. Pesaro: Banca Popolare pesarese.

Carotti, Carlo. 2005. "L'Ufficio stampa della Feltrinelli. Il contributo di Alba Morino." *Fabbrica del Libro* 11, no. 2: 20–23. www.fondazionemondadori.it/cms/file_download/46/ carotti .pdf.

Casari, Rosanna, et al., eds. 1996. *Testo letterario e immaginario architettonico*. Milano: Jaca Book.

———. 1996. "Introduzione." In *Testo letterario e immaginario architettonico*. Milano: Jaca Book: 9–14.

Contarini, Silvia. 2012. "Matria, Patria, Dismatria." *Nazione Indiana*, August 23, 2012. https:// www.nazioneindiana.com/2012/08/23/matria-patria-dismatria/.

De Robertis, Roberto. 2007. "Insorgenze letterarie nella disseminazione delle migrazioni. Contesti, definizioni e politiche culturali delle scritture migranti." *Scritture Migranti* 1: 27–52.

———. 2014. "Da dove facciamo il postcoloniale? Appunti per una genealogia della ricezione degli studi postcoloniali nell'italianistica italiana." *Postcolonialitalia. Postcolonial Studies from the European South*, February 14, 2014. http://www.postcolonialitalia.it/in-dex.php?option=com_content&view=article&id=56:da-dove-facciamo-il-postcoloniale& catid=27:interventi&Itemid=101&lang=it.

Fracassa, Ugo. 2012. *Patria e lettere. Per una critica della letteratura postcoloniale e migrante in Italia*. Roma: G. Perrone.

Huggan, Graham. 2001. *The Postcolonial Exotic. Marketing the Margins*. London: Routledge.

Lecomte, Mia. 2018. *Di un poetico altrove. Poesia transnazionale italofona (1960–2016)*. Firenze: F. Cesati.

Manai, Franco. 2017. "Gli studi postcoloniali italiani fuori confine in due diversi approcci." *Narrativa* 38: Italia fuori Italia. Diffusione, canonizzazione, ricezione transnazionale della letteratura italiana degli anni Duemila: 215–225.

Mengozzi, Chiara. 2013. *Narrazioni contese. Vent'anni di scritture italiane della migrazione.* Roma: Carocci.

Pezzarossa, Fulvio. 2015. "Al finire di esigue narrazioni. Come evapora la letteratura migrante." *Between* 5, no. 10 (November): "L'immaginario politico. Impegno, resistenza, ideologia." (Eds. S. Albertazzi et al.): 1–31. http://ojs.unica.it/index.php/between/article/view/1964/1887.

———. 2018. "'Il meglio dell'umanità.' Un laboratorio di scrittura accogliente." In *"Aspettano di essere fatti eguali." Dialogare con l'altro*, edited by S. Giovanni, 3–26. Persiceto, Bologna: Eks&Tra. https://www.eksetra.net/wp-content/uploads/2018/11/Ebook13x20.pdf.

Pezzarossa, Fulvio and Ilaria Rossini, eds. 2011. *Leggere il testo e il mondo: Vent'anni di scritture della migrazione in Italia.* Bologna: CLUEB.

Regazzoni, Enrico. 1989. "Il magma della lontananza." In *Alfredo Antonaros*, Pesaro: Banca Popolare pesarese: 45–46.

Rodríguez Amaya, Fabio. 1989. *Antonàros, uomo e trovatore del melting pot*, in *Alfredo Antonaros*: 5–11.

Romeo, Caterina. 2018. *Riscrivere la nazione. Letteratura italiana postcoloniale.* Firenze: Le Monnier.

Scego, Igiaba. 2018. "Dietro la parola migrante." In *Parole oltre le frontiere. Dieci storie migranti*, 319–322. Milano: Terre di mezzo.

Tirinanzi De Medici, Carlo. 2018. *Il romanzo italiano contemporaneo. Dalla fine degli anni Settanta a oggi.* Roma: Carocci.

Vlasta, Sandra. 2011. "'Faccio letteratura e basta!' Letteratura della migrazione in Austria tra disapprovazione e riconoscimento." *Scritture Migranti* 5: 227–252.

Volponi, Paolo. 1989. "La sabbia rossa (a proposito di tornare a Carbèl)." in *Alfredo Antonaros*, Pesaro: Banca Popolare pesarese: 51–53.

Westphal, Bertrand. 2009. *Geocritica. Reale Finzione, Spazio.* Roma: Armando.

When Jacopo da Fiore Watched the Monkeys in the Treetops

Adrián N. Bravi / Translated by
Kevin Regan-Maglione

It was the first time that Jacopo da Fiore,[1] a short and tiny man with a long beard, found himself in the middle of a jungle in front of a dead monkey that was floating near the riverbank. He just realized that it was a monkey when a guy asked Jacopo what was so special that he stayed there all that time watching one of those beasts hopping around in the trees, "They drop down every day. . . . They come down from the branches and stay there, swinging around."

"I didn't know that; it's the first time I've seen a dead animal in the water."

"And if you pay attention, in a bit those fish will show up, the ones with jaws that will make it disappear in a second. Just wait and see."

There were other monkeys hanging by their paws on the branches of the trees. They were eating, screaming, and swinging around. The others were watching the dead one that floated lifelessly on the water's surface. They seemed happy, but they were actually sad. Jacopo da Fiore wondered if the monkeys were able to contemplate the sense of life and death. Jacopo got a branch to pull the body out of the water on the off chance that the other monkeys would want to be there for a last goodbye. It wasn't that easy bringing it to the riverbank because it was large and reluctant to be moved. Besides, touching the drowned body disgusted him. He'd also decided that there were entire armies of lice in that hirsute fur coat. To make it worse, when he moved the branch toward the animal's body, it stirred up a small cloud of insects that seemed to be crawling right at him. At the same time, however, he didn't want to leave the affair unresolved, so he went looking

129

for Sandoval the Indian, a half-naked savage covered in necklaces and painted skin, to ask him for a hand.

When the Indian arrived at the riverbank, he looked up toward the group of ten monkeys sitting on a branch, who were now observing him to try and figure out what his intentions were. Sandoval, however, didn't have any specific purpose. He first looked at Jacopo and then at the monkeys again up high and then at the dead one. He tried to make the foreigner understand, with a look up and then down, that at the beginning you're up in the trees and eventually you fall down.

"That's life," said Sandoval, using other words, well, hopefully anyway, that was the meaning.

Jacopo da Fiore tried to explain to him that in his country the dead, whether man or animal, are put in the ground and that it would be appropriate to do likewise for the monkey, "That is, if we can, clearly," he said. Then he added that if there were a Christian instead of a monkey, well then, in that case, he explained in his own way to Sandoval, you even put two or three rocks on top and a wooden cross, depending. Judging from the gestures, it seemed like the Indian thought it was a good idea, but he wasn't doing anything to follow through on it. Actually, it seemed like he wanted to go back into his hut and do whatever he was doing before. Jacopo da Fiore tried to hold him back and make him understand with gestures that it would be better to pull the monkey out of the water and then he himself, Jacopo, would handle putting it underground with rocks above it. The Indian didn't seem too enthused about having to grab the beast to bring it to the riverbank, "What kind of ideas are these?" he thought to himself. He wasn't used to pulling dead animals out of water. "What's going through this foreigner's mind?" Maybe it disgusted him too, the thought of grabbing that soggy body and bringing it out by its paw. And what if then, once it's on solid ground, the other monkeys decided to pounce on top of him? It can happen. Now, however, since Sandoval was in a hurry and didn't have time to waste on the oddities of that white man with a gray beard, he moved up to the riverbank. He pulled the monkey's body toward himself with a branch and, when it was within hand's reach, he grabbed it by a paw, lifting it up in the air, and threw it over to the ground like a sack of potatoes.

"Is it all right now?" Sandoval asked in his own language, "Is it fine or not?"

Jacopo da Fiore said yes, that it was fine, even though he would've liked to clarify that the deceased deserved a minimum amount of respect and consideration: "We can't really fling the dead in the air and throw them on the ground like that, what kind of practice is that? *Deus fit in omnibus omnia,*[2] so says Scotus Eriugena, understand Sandoval? This means that God becomes everything in every thing. . . . Even in this monkey God is here. . . . In all of nature *creata e non creante.* . . ."[3] But Sandoval stopped listening to him and went back into his hut where his wife, or one of his wives, was waiting for him; no one yet had managed to guess how many wives there were, or what they did with their lives, beyond staying holed up inside in the hut.

Now another group of ten monkeys had joined the original ten that were sitting on the tree trunk looking down. They seemed curious to know what that small man would do with their dead family member that had been in the river. Jacopo da Fiore, in the meanwhile, was digging a hole with a shovel he always kept within reach in front of his hut. When he got half a meter deep, he pushed the cadaver into the hole with another branch and then began to cover it with dirt. Some of the monkeys stood up on the trunk and began to shriek. They certainly took it as a complete madman's gesture, but he carried on with the affair undisturbed, "I came here to sort out a few things, just so you all know, you baboons." The monkeys looked at each other and then, slowly, disappeared amongst the tree branches.

If the Indian Sandoval had taken the time to heed Jacopo, he would've made him realize why he was doing this and, since he was there, he would've explained to him how the nature of the universe and all its creatures was made. He had spent many years of his life illuminating the abbey's manuscripts of Father Martini Della Quercia, an old abate who struggled to introduce printed texts into his library. This is despite the fact that almost a century had passed since everyone had begun to use movable type and typographies had shown up in every city in Europe.

While Jacopo da Fiore was finishing filling up the hole with that damp, black dirt that stuck to the shovel, the miniature manuscripts he had made in the abbey's *scriptorium* came to mind: Pliny's *Historia naturalis*, for example, with plant and animal drawings, a text on Saint Augustine's predestination, or another one on Albertus Magnus' prophecy. However, the one miniature that captured this jungle the most was the one that depicted a heavenly scene on an entire page, with the various hierarchies of all living things, from the angels on down; the scene found inside Scotus Eriugena's *Periphyseon* and was transcribed by Bernardo Cristofori da Volterra. The abate Martini Della Quercia held this text particularly dear to his heart and he read it and reread it, also annotating it and interleaving sheets of paper between one page and the next. That evening when Jacopo da Fiore had wound up outside of the Indian Sandoval's hut, who was sitting silently with a leafy branch in his mouth (apparently that's how you brushed your teeth here), he asked: "So, how's it going, Sandoval?"

The Indian stared at him and said nothing. He made a parabola shape with his hand as if he wanted to indicate all the heavens: "What are my troubles in comparison to all of the immensity that grows above us?" he seemed to wonder, or at least that's how Jacopo interpreted it because at that moment the sky began to fill up with stars. The sunset's silence, and that marine blue, almost indigo, provoked them to reflect on space and time.

"You know something, Sandoval?" asked Jacopo da Fiore. "Our world is spangled with hierarchies...And this jungle and those monkeys, or these parrots that fly around, even that small branch you have in your mouth that you clean your teeth with, are all an expression of this great heavenly design."

"Oh yeah?" asked the Indian.

"Of course . . . I'll tell you something more. All of nature is divided into four different species," and so as to avoid any misunderstandings, Jacopo touched his hand with four fingers from the other. "First there's God, or rather, a nature that was not created but creates everything which unfortunately we men are not able to know because it's eternal and so forth. . . . Then there's a created nature and it creates at its own time: angels, the word, and everything that has to do with divine thought and the four causes,[4] do you understand? The third is the created nature that does not create, which is all real material set in space and in time; I don't know, this jungle, for example, or that monkey that I put in the earth, even the ones that are above the trees . . ." Jacopo pointed at everything so that Sandoval could compare all the worldly objects that surrounded him. "And finally, there's a nature that is not created that does not create, which is God himself, which all things reach toward, all thoughts; in this case, however, God coincides with absolute nothingness, which I'm adding in here . . ."

"I understand," said Sandoval, moving his head to the side.

"I illustrated the book that talks about these four divisions and before departing I went into the abate Martini Della Quercia's room and I took it with me. . . . I couldn't leave without that manuscript. . . . That manuscript is a part of me. . . . If you wait here, I'll show you. Don't move." Jacopo da Fiore made a sign to Sandoval and went into his hut, which was adjacent to the Indian's. Shortly after he returned with the manuscript wrapped in a thick cotton fabric. He opened to the page with the drawing of that heavenly scene and tried to explain to the Indian that everything there was a part of creation, where all of nature was determined by space and time: animals, leaves, rivers, winds. Sandoval looked curiously at the drawing. He opened his eyes, he furrowed them, then he opened them again. At a certain point he grabbed the manuscript with his hand and he first turned it to one side and then the next, even upside down and from its side.

However, since Sandoval had grabbed it as if it were a piece of wood, Jacopo felt obligated to scold him: "Hold on, don't mistreat it like that. Are you insane? You need to be a bit careful with these things. . . . Technically, you should wash your hands before touching it. . . . Who knows where you've put your dirty hands."

Sandoval got up and said something like: "Excuse me for one second," and went toward his hut with the manuscript in his hands. At that point, Jacopo da Fiore tried to hold him back by grabbing him by the arm, but the Indian shook free with a tug and went into his hut. Jacopo himself would've liked to go inside as well so he could understand what he wanted to do with that book: "Sandoval, Sandoval," he called from outside, "You need to be careful with that manuscript, Sandoval. It's the first book of Scotus Eriugena's *Periphyseon*, transcribed by Bernardo Cristofori da Volterra. . . . It's not just any old book, the entire universe is in there. And I have to bring that book back because Father Martini Della Quercia will certainly be looking for it. . . . Sandoval, do you hear me?" Jacopo da Fiore said again, pulling the tent flap to the side. He looked inside the hut so he could see what Sandoval was doing and he saw the Indian lying down on the ground while leafing through the manuscript. There were five other people next to him who were curiously observing the pages: three women, a little girl, and an adolescent boy. After a bit, they started to laugh uncontrollably, while slapping the ground.

"Sorry, Sandoval, I'll show them the pages, what do you all find so funny?" He moved closer to the group but no one turned toward the monk. "What's going on, laughing like this, Sandoval?" Jacopo da Fiore asked again. No one answered him, as if they weren't listening to him or if the question were a part of some other conversation. "I don't understand," he added, while he was taking a few steps forward to reach the group. When he was behind the three women, he lifted up his head and saw that the Indian was pointing out a particular miniature with his finger. "Excuse me, Sandoval, that drawing up top represents the four causes, whereas these are the creatures[5] of air, fire, water, and earth. That over there is a cherub and there in the background is God which everything goes back to."

They kept on with their sidesplitting laugher and when Jacopo bent over enough to pick up the manuscript (he couldn't conceive how those drawings could elicit such a reaction), one of the women, who was laughing more obscenely than the others, pushed him so hard that he fell on the ground. At that moment, the teenager that was next to her started to jump on top of the monk's body, either as a game or to keep on laughing and then a little girl joined him. So Sandoval, who was perhaps fed up with all the racket, grabbed the monk by his arm (as he had done with the monkey) and dragged him out, making Jacopo crawl on the ground. He threw in a few words, maybe to justify his reaction.

When Jacopo da Fiore was outside of the hut, he tried to dust off his tunic with his hands and he said out loud, "If you want to die, you pagan, go ahead. You know, I don't give a damn about your soul, I couldn't care less. You think that I came here, in the middle of this cursed jungle to convert savages like you with your leaf loincloths, or those tattoos and those pierced lips? It was the abbot that sent me here, to punish me, so who do you think you are? I'm going back as soon as I can. I was just fine there in the abbot, drawing all day. It was the grappa that did me in. . . . I'd laid up a stash of grappa that Brother Modesto had made and the abate, with his pimply belly sent me to the other side of the ocean as a punishment. Do you get it, Sandoval, or not?"

When they stopped laughing, Sandoval came out of his hut and pointed to the treetops and said something that was maybe referring to the winds or the leaves. Anyway, it was something that had nothing to do with what Jacopo had just told him, let alone with the manuscript. So that's why the monk grabbed the Indian by his shoulders and screamed at him with all of his might, making his words ring out in all the jungle:

"You're a savage. . . . How can you laugh about these kinds of things, with those crooked teeth of yours?"

Sandoval looked at him right in the eyes, he smiled, revealing once again a legion of gigantic incisors. The Indian did the very same thing to Jacopo and screamed an unintelligible phrase in his language that could've meant, "I know, I know, and what's the problem?"

Once they fell quiet, they all sat down on a kind of bench in front of the hut: "Do you think you'll give me back the *Periphyseon* or do you want to keep it so you can keep on laughing about it? You know, I don't know if Scotus Eriugena would've been pleased to know that a savage like yourself would crack up over of his book on the nature of things." Sandoval shrugged and pointed out a spot on a branch with nothing there.

The next morning the Indian presented himself in front of Jacopo da Fiore's hut with a dead tapir, riddled with arrows. He and a few other Indians who were barely covered with a loincloth had carried it to the monk. They seemed happy and pleased with the Saint Sebastian they brought him: "Do you like tapir or not?" The Indian asked. Jacopo congratulated everyone there, and said that he had never seen a tapir up close. He said that the tapir seemed to be a boar with an overhanging nose, but no one understood him. He then made the sign of the cross and went back into his hut. After a few hours, one of the laughing women came in to inform him that the tapir was ready to be eaten. The monk reluctantly got up and joined his dining companions who were waiting for him sitting around the animal that had been cooked over the fire. When they finished eating, Sandoval grabbed the monk's arm and brought him to a place behind the hut where there was a clearing with a large smooth stone. There was a young boy sitting on top of the stone and he was drawing on some large dried leaves with a little pen that he had taken from the monk's bag. They were quick but efficient sketches in their variety of subjects they represented. Sandoval randomly picked up a leaf that had a drawing of a monkey hanging on a branch and he showed it to the monk: "Look, look how well my son draws," he said to everyone around and then he cracked up. He grabbed another leaf that had a drawing of a little man with an arrow and a tapir next to him and he said more or less the same thing: that his young son manages to draw well. He then grabbed another leaf but to understand its meaning he had to consult the boy because it wasn't clear what momentary whim he had followed. He explained to his father that it was about a starry sky and that there was a bird with open wings in the middle. There were also other abstract drawings that represented the surface of water. Only Sandoval was laughing because the small boy seemed very concentrated when he had the little pen in his hand. "Come on, why don't you make a drawing of this guy here," Sandoval suggested to his son, meaning the monk. So, he grabbed a large dry leaf and made a sketch of another small man with a long beard. Sandoval couldn't hold himself back from how much he was laughing. Who knows why the drawings made him laugh like this? When they finished looking at all of the leaves (in the meantime the little boy kept on drawing without stopping, like someone obsessed), the Indian grabbed the monk's hand and brought him into his hut. He grabbed Scotus Eriugena's manuscript and returned it to him accompanied with a long speech of thanks. A speech that, amongst other things, he wanted it to convey to Jacopo that both he, Sandoval and the boy, had realized that everything can be represented, all you need is a little pen in your hand. One thing, however, Sandoval hadn't understood, and he tried in his way to ask the monk: what about all of those pages, with all the same kind of writings that looked like ants lined up one after another, what did they mean?

Jacopo da Fiore thought about it for a bit and then he tried to explain to Sandoval that those weren't drawings, but words, and that words were a voice: "In this case, they are Scotus Eriugena's voice that explains how the universe is made."

The Indian looked at him, curious, without understanding: "Words?" he asked.

"Yes, Sandoval, words. . . . When you use words you make a thought visible," but the Indian wasn't able to understand this, not even when the monk tried to write a few random words on a piece of paper. "You see, this, for example, is the word *monkey*," he said while he was writing down the word *monkey*, "this other one is the word *tree*," and the monk also wrote the word *tree*, "and both of them mean different things, one's an animal, that one up here, and the other one is a plant. You can draw things, like your son does, but if you want you can write down the concept that represents the idea."

Sandoval looked at him without understanding: "Concept?" he asked again. "What concept?"

"Yes, well, concept, or a specific and detailed thought, depending on however you want to call it."

The Indian, without listening to further explanations that didn't line up with his worldviews, went back to his son who had in the meantime kept on drawing like mad. Sandoval patted his head and grabbed a small pile of ten leaves that had just been finished. He looked at them, one at a time, turning them over between his hands. While he was laughing, he thought how this boy with that small little pen that moved here and there so smoothly, in his innocence, was introducing something new to the jungle. Something that Sandoval still didn't have a name for.

NOTES

1. Jacopo da Fiore (Joachim of Fiore, ca. 1135–1202), belonged to the Cistercian monastery in Corazzo, Italy and left to establish a new order of Florensian monks in 1196 in Fiore, Calabria. A controversial figure in the Catholic Church, Jacopo insisted upon the sanctity of the Holy Trinity and its motif and he therefore divided history into three stages: the Father being the Old Testament, the Son is the New Testament. He postulated that the final and third moment, based upon the Holy Spirit, was to be ushered in by reading Scripture and using his own key to the puzzle, *Libre de concordia* (*Book of Concord*).

2. *Translator's note*: This Latin phrase means, "In all respects God happens in everything," which is similar to Jacopo's paraphrase. Thanks to Elizabeth Figlio for her translation assistance.

3. *Translator's note*: *la natura creata e non creante*, literally "Nature created but not creating." This a reference to the third of four categories outlined by John Scotus Eriugena (Giovanni Scoto Eriugena) in his *Periphyseon* (the Latin title *De Divisione Naturae* [*Concerning the Nature of Things*]), written ca. 877 CE, a work which attempts to reconcile the creation of all visible nature into a four-fold system or classification. The third category refers to the visible, material world. The four categories are: 1. La natura creante e non creata, nature that creates but is not created; 2. La natura creante e creata, nature that creates and is created; 3. La natura non creante e creata, nature that does not create and is created; and 4. La natura non creante e non creata, nature that does not create and is not created.

4. *Translator's note*: This is a reference to a four-part Aristotelian answer to the question of "why?" It is divided into material cause, formal cause, efficient cause, and final cause. For example, a chair: its material cause is wood, its formal cause is the chair's design, its efficient cause is the carpenter, and its final cause is for sitting.

5. *Creature* is a reference to Saint Francis Assisi's *Cantico delle creature*, or *Canticle of the Sun*, in which St. Francis praises God for all of his creatures, including the four elements.

Part 2

Diversity in Diversity

Le Mandorle Amare / The Bitter Almonds

Basir Ahang
Translated by Ashna Ali

IDENTITÀ / IDENTITY

Milano è silenziosa	Milan is silent
avvinghiata a ventole d'aria	grasping at gusts of air
e crine d'alberi in fiore	and fibers of trees in bloom
inghiottita dal caldo	swallowed by heat
di un'estate oziosa	of an idle summer
qua e là solo qualche bambino	children here and there
resiste al torpore d'agosto	resist the torpor of August
mentre lentamente il loro canto si diffonde	while their song spreads slowly
nell'ossigeno umido di questa città	into this city's humid oxygen
Mi siedo sulla sedia del balcone	I sit on the balcony chair
e un fuoco mi accende la sigaretta	and a fire lights my cigarette
aneliti di fumo volteggiano nell'aria	life-breaths of smoke swirl in the air

il silenzio ha rubato per un attimo

the silence has for a moment stolen

ogni significato recondito o
manifesto

every meaning hidden or made
manifest

il mio sguardo fugge verso il cielo

my gaze escapes toward the sky

piccoli pezzi di nuvole girano in
tondo

small pieces of cloud turn circles

come colombe in cerca di rifugio

like doves in search of refuge

assieme a loro, vola il mio pensiero

with them flies my thought

verso un passato remoto

toward a remote past

fatto di dolcezza e serenità

made of sweet serenity

sorvola gli alberi e poi ancora i
grattacieli

flies over the trees and beyond to
skyscrapers

e giunge fino a dove

reaches the point where

per la prima volta

for the first time

i miei piedi hanno toccato la terra

my feet touched the earth

la mia lingua un nome

my tongue touched a name

e le mie braccia una donna

and my arms touched a woman

la sigaretta è bruciata fino alla fine

the cigarette has burned to its end

e come un desiderio inespresso

Like an unexpressed wish

il suo fuoco mi brucia ora le dita

its fire now burns my fingers

Torno al mio balcone

I return to my balcony

e a questa città ingrigita

and this greyed city

dove il ritmo della vita scorre più
veloce

where the rhythms of life flow faster

than the pulsations of my heart

la testa si fa pesante

the head makes itself heavy

mentre una domanda aleggia imperterrita nella mente:	while a placid question lurks in the mind:
chi sei tu?	who are you?

un pezzo di nuvole	a piece of cloud
un albero sradicato perduto nel cuore del mondo	a tree uprooted and lost in the heart of the world

INCONTRO / RENDEZVOUS

le rotaie stridevano	the wheels screeched
mentre foglie autunnali si riversavano dal treno	as the autumnal leaves poured out from the train
sui binari bagnati	onto train tracks wet
e anneriti dal tempo	and blackened by time

. . .

punto d'incontro	rendezvous point
delle mandorle amare	of the sour almonds
la libreria centrale della città	the city's central library

durante quel nostro appuntamento	during that meeting of ours
a Vienna	in Vienna
la luna sembrava tagliata a metà	the moon looked sliced in half

. . .

sulle spalle portavi	you carried with you
il freddo delle montagne	the cold of the mountains
e un cuore addolorato	and a heart anguished
per l'esilio	from exile

e con esso ogni singolo pezzo della tua esistenza	and with it, every single piece of your existence

. . .

flusso d'orgoglio ed ebbrezza infelice	flush of pride and unhappy inebriation
un Do-baytī [1] ti spronava ad agire	a Do-baytī spurred you to act
un Dambura[2]	a Dambura
legava i fili del tempo	braided the threads of time
a tutto ciò che eravamo stati	to all we had ever been
nostra intera esistenza	our entire existence

MEMORIA / MEMORY

le lancette della memoria	the arrows of memory
scorrono all'indietro	run backward
per percorsi aggrovigliati	across tangled routes
di luoghi antichi ove per la prima volta	of the antique places where
i tuoi piedi iniziarono il viaggio	your feet began their journey
	for the first time

frammenti di vita	fragments of life
si fondono in forme d'argilla	fuse into clay forms
avvolgendo i pendii delle montagne	curling up the inclines up mountains
in un manto d'amarezza	of a blanket of bitterness
che nemmeno il sole è ormai più in grado di sciogliere	that by now not even the sun is able to melt

eppure quel luogo ti amava	and yet that place loved you
e tu ricambiavi	and you loved in kind
memore della prima volta in cui	mindful of the first time
milioni di particelle di luce	millions of particles of light
ti baciarono il viso	kissed your face

e come un pianto di fronte alla storia	and like a cry in the face of history
ti eri elevato	you rose
senza sapere dove posarti	not knowing where to settle
come foglia sparsa dal vento	like leaves scattered
ad ottobre	by October wind
accarezzi le rughe della tua fronte	you caress the furrow of your brow
e raccogliendo i piedi dalla strada	and picking yourself back up
ti consegni al vento	you deliver yourself to the wind
sapendo che in fondo	knowing that ultimately
la patria non è altro che un luogo in cui sentirsi al sicuro	homeland is nothing but a place where you feel safe

LO SPECCHIO / THE MIRROR

Io non sono un negro, sono un uomo	I am not your negro, I am a man
disse Sir Baldwin alla telecamera	said Sir Baldwin into the camera
Io non sono un ebreo, sono un uomo	I am not a Jew, I am a man
disse Albert al ligio funzionario che lo stava interrogando	said Albert to the loyal official who was interrogating him
Io non sono un clandestino, sono un uomo	I am not an illegal migrant, I am a man
disse il passante quando qualcuno lo colpì per sbaglio dal balcone con una carabina	said the passerby when someone shot him from a balcony by mistake
Io non sono la norma e tu non sei l'eccezione	I am not the norm and you are not the exception
disse chi aveva capito	said he who understood

e se nella radice vi è chi vede la gramigna

and if in the root there are those who see a weed

non è nella lente che va ricercata l'imperfezione

it is not through the lens that the imperfection sought

ma nello specchio che riflette l'immagine

but in the mirror that reflects one's own image

RONDINI / SWALLOWS

Osservo le nuvole cariche di pioggia

I see clouds thick with rain

nembi oscuri si dirigono verso est

obscured nimbuses heading east

verso il luogo che per primo mi vide al mondo

toward the first place in the world that saw me

e così fa la tempesta

and so makes a storm

una radio accesa porta con sé cattive notizie

a radio brings bad news

dicono che dove son nato

they say that in the place where I was born

Il cielo è stato inghiottito

The sky has been swallowed

le rondini

the swallows

profeti di primavera

prophets of Spring

sono fuggite via

have all escaped

e sono arrivate fin qui

and come all the way here

senza più ali

with neither wings left

né un cielo in cui volare

nor a sky in which to fly

Mi rifugio su una collina abbracciata dalle alpi

I find refuge on a hill embraced by the Alps

e perdendomi tra i glicini in fiore	and lose myself amongst the flowering wisteria
Penso a quelle rondini senz'ali	I think of those wing-less swallows
e se anch'io come loro non trovassi più la strada?	what if like them I lost my way?
come si può ritornare?	how does one return?
come si può vivere in una città senza cielo?	how does one live in a city without sky?
oggi qui è la prima mattina di primavera	this is the first morning of Spring
se solo le rondini non mi avessero svegliato	if only the swallows hadn't awakened me
se solo	if only
se solo	if only
se solo	if only

NOTES

1. Do-bayti è una forma poetica persiana basate in quartine cantate.
2. Dambura è un liuto a collo lungo.

Defying the Chromatic Norm

Strategies of Invisibility and
Italian Transdiasporic Blackness

Caterina Romeo

In the openings of the two memoirs *The Skin Between Us* (2006) and *La mia casa è dove sono* (2010, My Home is Where I Am), both African Italian American writer Kym Ragusa and Italian author of Somali origin Igiaba Scego interrogate the intersection between their blackness and Italianness, although from different standpoints:[1]

> *What are you?*
> Black and Italian. African American, Italian American, American.
> Other. Biracial, Interracial. Mixed-Blood, Half-Breed, High-Yellow, Redbone, Mulatta. Nigger, Dago, Guinea. (Ragusa 2006, 25)

> What am I? Who am I?
> I am black and Italian.
> But I am also Somalian and black.
> Then am I African Italian? Italian African? Second generation? Uncertain generation? *Meel kale*? A nuisance? A black Saracen? A dirty n*****?[2]
> (Scego 2010, 31)

The first intersection in which both authors recognize themselves is the one between their blackness and Italianness ("Black and Italian," writes Ragusa, "Sono nera e italiana" [I am black and Italian], writes Scego), which creates an ideal relationship of continuity between the (hi)stories of mobility of the two authors and of their families. They are both black, and their families are part of the Italian diaspora, whether Italy is their point of departure or arrival. The intersection of blackness and Italianness is considered undesirable for

147

the two communities in which Ragusa grew up (African American and Italian American in New York City) and for US society at large; this is also the case for the Italian society in which Scego was born and raised (Rome). Read as a continuum, the racial history of transdiasporic Italy that the two stories recount differs from the narrative of a hegemonic Italian whiteness. Such narrative constitutes the principle based on which black Italians who do not conform to the Italian chromatic norm[3] are generally perceived as foreigners and the children of migrants are denied citizenship and kept outside of the national body considered homogeneously white. As Ragusa contends, however, this presumed whiteness was not considered such in the United States, where the color of Italian Americans was a symbol of subalternity and where the intersection of her Italianness and blackness was rejected—although for different reasons—by her Italian American and African American sides of the family. Both Ragusa and Scego denounce the social pressure through which they have constantly been kept at the margins of their communities and societies and show how the hypervisibility of their blackness—and the sense that no positive trait was ever associated with it—had induced them to adopt complex strategies of invisibility.

Kym Ragusa's memoir revolves around the ambivalent way in which the author, African American on her mother's side and Italian American on her father's side, is perceived in the United States from a racial point of view, both in her two communities of origin and in the broader context of the dominant US culture. In her blood, as the author herself claims, two ethnic groups converged that were never meant to come together, although they occupied contiguous spaces in New York City (Black Harlem and Italian Harlem), a few blocks apart from one another. When she was born, her father had not revealed her existence to his family, fearing their rejection. If her father's Italian American family discriminates against her because of her blackness—which, the author contends, her paternal grandmother manages to forget only by availing herself of "an almost acrobatic capacity" (Ragusa 2006, 223; Romeo 2008)—her mother's African American family, who had a very active social role in Harlem's African American community and was very light-skinned, considers Kym's Italian American side of the family to be "white trash" (Ragusa 2006, 29). Even though the color assigned to Italians in the United States was white by law,[4] their whiteness was not considered equal to Anglo-Saxon whiteness, but rather a whiteness "of a different color" (Jacobson 1998), characterized by a dark complexion (DeSalvo 2003).[5] Such processes of racialization enacted by the mainstream culture both towards the African American and the Italian American community—although in different ways—most of the times did not generate solidarity and collaboration between them. Italian immigrants, considered "white ethnics," had made a "possessive investment in [their] whiteness" (Lipsitz 2018)[6] and had distanced themselves from communities occupying lower social positions such as the African American, Hispanic, and Asian ones.

Ragusa explores her own complex sense of not belonging—white among blacks, black among whites—which is dependent on the constant conflict between her two communities of origin and also on their both being kept at the margins of the dominant culture. For Kym—as is evident also in the list of adjectives that she uses to define herself at the beginning of her memoir—her own difference is not inscribed within a reductive white/black dichotomy, but color and race constantly intersect with other categories, such as gender, ethnicity, and social class (primarily), but also sexuality, beauty, religion, and level of education. In the complexity of her context of origin, telling one's story solely from a racial point of view can lead to dangerous essentializations. Race and color, however, are central in the ways her two families and communities perceive her and each other. African American children at school call Kym "whitey" and urge her to return to the land of the whites (Ragusa 2006, 156). However, when she plays with Italian American children, she is called the derogatory "n" word by a girl, who is quickly reassured by Marie that Kym is not a n***** but rather her cousin—indicating the impossibility of her being both—and that she only seems black because it is almost dark outside (Ragusa 2006, 179).

If Ragusa's blackness must be erased in order for her to be able to claim her Italian origins, Igiaba Scego shows how blackness and Italianness are considered as mutually exclusive also in contemporary Italy. In a previous text, the short story "Salsicce" (Sausages), Scego's female protagonist had expressed her deep disorientation in observing hordes of people lining up in front of the police station to leave their fingerprints, which the newly passed Bossi-Fini law had made a mandatory step for the obtainment of a stay permit (Scego 2005). Her physical resemblance to the migrants standing in line makes her wonder if she should be lining up also, in spite of her Italian citizenship. In *La mia casa* the doubt runs deeper and becomes more Hamletic: the author examines her own subjectivity construction process, growing up as a black person in Rome, and shows how her blackness has always prevented her from acquiring a state of full Italianness. Igiaba Scego's awareness that her difference constitutes a disvalue and the social rejection she is subject to due to her blackness begin to take shape at school in her interaction with other children. The author is constantly othered, marginalized, and compared to Kunta Kinte, the protagonist of the television mini-series *Roots*, based on Alex Haley's novel, which in 1978 had brought the history of US slavery into the homes of Italians for the first time:[7] "You're like Kunta Kinte, a dirty n*****—we're going to whip you. You were born to be a slave" (Scego 2010, 151–52).[8]

To avoid being insulted, Scego tries to make herself invisible, and since her color does not allow her to get lost in the crowd, she chooses the strategy of silence. She utterly rejects the Somalian language and speaks in Italian as little as possible: "You don't talk; you make monkey calls. We can't understand anything . . . you're weird. You guys are like gorillas" (Scego 2010, 150). Trying to attain invisibility through inaudibility is a strategy also used by Rwandese Italian writer and activist Espérance Ripanti, who claims: "I had deceived myself [. . .] into thinking that if I didn't make too much noise, I could have been invisible, too" (Ripanti 2019, 10). Both Scego and Ripanti enact a synesthetic process of de-racialization: since their skin color does not allow them to neutralize people's sense of sight, they try to disappear by neutralizing people's sense of hearing through remaining silent. Whether inherited by parents and/or imposed by society, silence leaves indelible scars, as Burkinabe Italian writer Leaticia Ouedraogo points out in her Fanonian short memoir "Nassan Tenga": "We were emotionally illiterate. Unable to speak about ourselves, not able to verbalize our feelings. Our pain" (Ouedraogo 2019, 112).

Nigerian Irish author Emma Dabiri (following Byrd and Tharps 2014) contends that the true marker of blackness is not skin color but rather hair texture and that tightly coiled Afro hair identifies people as black (as is the case for African albinos) more than dark skin (as is the case for East Asians and South Asians, who are not considered black even though they are darker than Africans and much darker than African Americans) (Dabiri 2019, 12–16). In Ragusa's *Skin* prologue, the author on a ferry from Calabria to Sicily (her family's regions of origin) knows that her olive skin is hardly visible in Southern Italy, where people mostly have a similar skin color. Her tightly coiled "Afro" hair, however, is tied back to avoid prying eyes, a camouflage tactic deployed by Ragusa since she was a child in order to make herself invisible (Giunta 2003). Kym's hair has often constituted a battlefield and taken on a symbolic meaning precisely because it is the distinctive trait that most reveals her African origins. Yet, as her light-skinned African American maternal grandmother Miriam contends, those thick, intricate curls were inherited from her father ("those damned Sicilians with their African blood") (Ragusa 2006, 56), and they are a sign of her Sicilianness rather than of her Africanness. A couple she meets in Palermo at a later point, however, observe that Kym's Sicilianness also reconnects her to her Africanness, if in longer and more articulated ways: "Palermo is like your Harlem—we are the blacks of Italy" (Ragusa 2006, 235).[9] And yet, Ragusa's numerous references to her maternal side of the family's history of slavery underline the uniquely traumatic heritage of most people of African descent in the United States. In the same scene with the Palermitan couple—where an African prostitute appears who has powdered her face white in order "to make herself more beautiful to Sicilian men" (Ragusa 2006, 236)—readers are reminded that Southern Italian and African "Africanness" imply very different processes of racialization and have historically traced very different trajectories.

Even if Kym's hair texture was indeed inherited from the Italian American side of her family, as Miriam claims, it is in any case a trait that she shares with the black community in Harlem. In preparing for combing her hair once a week, Aunt Gladys would assemble on the table "all the objects of a ritual that has been passed on from black women to black girl children across the generations, across centuries, across the weeping Atlantic" (Ragusa 2006, 57). The "taming" of the hair is considered a transhistorical, trans-national ritual that connects Kym to the other black girls in the neighborhood through their common inheritance of abduction, violence, and slavery. This connection to African diasporic women creates a sort of Black Atlantic of aesthetic practices through the rituals of everyday life. Such rituals, shared with those same girls who would otherwise consider her too light-skinned to belong, contribute to structure Kym's identity construction process, although the effect they produce is only provisional: "My hair would be tamed momentarily just as my identity would be fixed momentarily. In that mirror I would be a six-year-old black girl-child who lived in Harlem. It would be enough, for a time, to hold all the contradictions and questions at bay" (Ragusa 2006, 58).

In a later text, the author reveals that the powerfulness of her hair as a race signifier becomes more evident to her once she grows up. She performs visual experiments by repeatedly going to a photo booth to take pictures of the back of her head and of her hair: "From the time that I wore my hair, as now, in a few lopsided braids, to the time I cut it short and bleached it until it glowed a sickly orange, to the time I shaved it off completely. After that, I recorded the patterns and shadows the stubble made on the back of my head" (Ragusa 2008b, 59–60). Ragusa had been inspired by Lorna Simpson's photographs, in which black women had their backs turned to the camera as if in an ostensible refusal of the gaze (Ragusa 2008b, 60). To this gaze, which historically had exoticized, objectified, and violated black women's bodies and beauty, Ragusa offers a sequence of images that shift from a recognizable hair style (lopsided braids), to an unrecognizable one (very short and bleached hair), to an annihilation of her hair—and femininity—(shaved head) reminiscent of the shaving of slaves' heads by the slave traders before they were boarded into slave ships (Byrd and Tharps 2014, 10).

Wearing untamed Afro hair for Ragusa comes at the end of a long process of self-awareness and self-fashioning. Her natural hair powerfully appears in her memoiristic documentary *fuori/outside*, in which the writer and director employs "the narrative techniques of storytelling and the imagery of personal memory" in order to revisit "a past that is broadly historical yet anchored in the intimate relationships between a granddaughter and her [grandmother]" (Tenzer 2002, 213). The documentary is Ragusa's attempt "to cross the lines of time, memory, and color" (Ragusa 1997, 01:05) and is framed as a letter to her paternal grandmother, who had exerted the strongest resistance in accepting Kym as blood of her blood. Ragusa's relationship with the paternal side of her family is one of exclusion, but also of an inclusion that demands the erasure of a part of her heritage and then her complicity in the stigmatization of the African American community (concerned about the imminent arrival of new neighbors, Kym's Italian American grandmother Gilda had said to her black granddaughter, "I hope they're white") (Ragusa 2006, 223).

In *fuori/outside*, Ragusa is no longer hiding: she appears with her Afro hair loose while conversing with her paternal grandmother, walking with her around the neighborhood, or filming inside and outside of her house. The image on the cover of *La pelle che ci separa*, the Italian translation of *The Skin Between Us*, is a still frame from the documentary *fuori/outside*: the author's face, partially hidden by the camera, is surrounded by her untamed, tightly coiled hair, finally left free, in an affirmation and acceptance of her cultural heritage always perceived as conflictive by both sides of the family and by society at large, even though the destiny of her people from both sides had been historically connected. (Kym's extradiegetic voice says to her grandmother: "You grew up in a time when Southern Italian immigrants were lynched along with African Americans"; Ragusa 1999, 09:39).

Claiming the right to wear one's natural hair signals a process of construction of individual and collective identities and the quest for an aesthetic that does not mimetically reproduce the canons of whiteness. In her article "Capelli di libertà" (Freedom Hair), Igiaba Scego scrutinizes the processes of skin whitening and hair straightening with chemical products as camouflage practices and encourages black Italian women to adhere instead to an aesthetic aimed at rediscovering the natural beauty of their bodies rather than being bound by Western and Eurocentric canons (Scego 2016). In the article, Scego discusses the Nappytalia website (which started as the Facebook page Afro-Italian Nappy Girls), established in 2014 by Ghanaian Italian Evelyne Sarah Afaawua. On the website, Afro-Italian Nappy Girls is defined as "the first *Italian* community born for girls who have decided to wear their natural Afro-curly hair, with advice, vocabulary, stories and role models" (Nappytalia website, my emphasis). This website is specifically intended for African Italian women (and men) "with Afro hair, daughters and sons of mixed couples, a new generation of Italians who do not want to forget their origins, who want to claim their forgotten identities" (http://www.nappytalia.it/afro-italian-nappy-girls/). [10] As Evelyne Afaawua observes in the short documentary *Nappy Girls*, African Italian women like her have interiorized Italy's negative perception of their bodies and, as a consequence, have learned to discipline their hair (through relaxation, extensions) so as to be able to pass, at least in part (Coppola). [11] Their desire to claim their African descent emerges from a process of self-awareness, acceptance, and empowerment and produces aesthetic contra-canons through which these historically racialized bodies demand that their presence in the physical and symbolic space of the nation be legitimized, thus rewriting their history of oppression as well as the history of Italy.

Examining the Nappytalia blog and the Hijab elegante Facebook page (created in 2012 by twenty-one-year-old Moroccan Italian K. N.), Annalisa Frisina and Camilla Hawthorne claim that race is constantly reconstructed through "readings" of hair, body shape, and specific pieces of clothing and that practices of self-representation such as the way women wear their hair and how they dress (including the "veil") reproduce and consolidate (or, conversely, call into question) the privilege of whiteness and Catholicism in Italy (Frisina and Hawthorne 2015, 2018). Disseminating representations of counter-canonical Italianness through the internet has played a crucial role in re-creating diasporic connections across Europe (and beyond) and in enacting counter-hegemonic practices (Frisina and Hawthorne 2018, 727). These are acts of daily anti-racism (Makaping 2001, 86),[12] which counteract "everyday racism" (Essed 1990). The resignification of daily aesthetic practices "is a process of unlearning and breaking free from internalized regimes of normativity and oppression, which construe afro-textured hair as 'bad,' 'ugly,' and 'inferior' compared to long, straight, Caucasian hair" (Lukate 2019, 123). Such process contributes to redefining the very concept of the "somatic norm" (Puwar 2004), to establish which bodies have the right to occupy what spaces and in what function and to assert which bodies can be considered as belonging to the nation and which bodies instead should be excluded or differentially included. Far from being a superficial matter, the creation of new aesthetic canons contributes to constructing new transnational imaginaries and to establishing new practices of inclusion based on the physical characteristics of (re)subjectified bodies.

* * *

Reading the reflections of Igiaba Scego (but also of other African Italian writers, intellectuals, activists, and entrepreneurs such as Leaticia Ouedraogo, Esperance Ripanti, and Evelyne Sarah Afaawua) in continuity with those of Kym Ragusa emphasizes how their blackness deeply questions and opposes the construction of the Italian national body as white from a transnational and transdiasporic trajectory. The diasporic continuum of which these authors are part shows that the racial history of Italy—as well as Italian national identity and culture at large—has been shaped both inside and outside national borders. These authors' performances of invisibility—at earlier stages in their lives—constitute their attempt to deflect attention from physical features, such as skin color and tightly coiled hair, which are markers of racial categories and of a difference from the white norm socialized as undesirable. Through counter-hegemonic aesthetic practices that connect African American, African Italian, and other African diasporic women,[13] they question and redefine hegemonic national aesthetic canons in ways that do not allow the systematic erasure of blackness and that instead demand its inclusion into the process of shaping Italian and European identities. This process sets the notion of Italianness apart from an obsolete, racist conception derived from biologism and links it to daily lives, education, cultural practices, and the individual and collective desire to belong and to imagine national and transnational communities as encompassing subjects whose diverging characteristics from the (presumed) national norm radically challenge the very existence of a (presumed) national homogeneity (Lombardi-Diop and Romeo 2012), thus enabling new ways of participation.

NOTES

1. Kym Ragusa and Igiaba Scego met in Rome in August 2009 while Ragusa was in Italy to receive the John Fante Prize, awarded to her for the Italian translation of *The Skin Between Us*, titled *La pelle che ci separa*, translated by Clara Antonucci and Caterina Romeo (see Ragusa 2008a).

2. All translations are my own unless otherwise noted. As the "n" word is not part of my heritage and my family history, in this article I have chosen not to spell it out only unless I am quoting from Ragusa's memoir. In my own translations and when I refer to the actual use of the word in Ragusa's texts, the word will be written n*****, as is the case here.

3. The expression "chromatic norm," which I have coined in a previous book chapter (Romeo 2012), is based on Nirmal Puwar's notion of "somatic norm" (Puwar 2004), but it also differs from it. If Puwar's "somatic norm" takes into account the differences in race and gender, my notion of "chromatic norm" is instead centered on the intersection of race and color and therefore on the higher visibility of certain bodies as compared to others. I find this notion can be very useful in analyzing the construction of space as white through the systematic erasure of non-white bodies.

4. See, among others, Thomas Guglielmo 2003.

5. In the essay titled "Color: White / Complexion: Dark," Italian American writer and intellectual Louise DeSalvo analyzes her grandmother's immigration documents and examines how they indicated both the color assigned to her grandmother (white) and her perceived complexion (dark). DeSalvo's reflection is articulated around the fact that her grandmother's skin was not, in fact, dark, but rather light. Italians were considered white by law, as were other Europeans, because Europeanness (associated with the origin of the Western culture and civilization) could not be marked by blackness. However, the construction of the Italian complexion as "dark"—whether it was in fact phenotypically dark or not—suggested the undesirability of Italian migrants to the United States, associated with rural and poor Southern Italy.

6. For an analysis of the structural advantages that "white" Americans have historically derived from their presumed whiteness, see Lipsitz 2018. For an analysis of the racial status of Italian immigrants in the United States, some seminal texts are as follows: Roediger 1991; Orsi 1992; Vecoli 1995; Luconi 2001; Guglielmo and Salerno 2003; Guglielmo 2003; Caiazza 2018.

7. As Scego notes, for Italian children the Kunta Kinte character left none of the deep sense of freedom that enlivened him, but only the fact that he was a slave. This ended up legitimizing the equation "black = slave" in children's eyes. See Scego 2010, 151–52.

8. The same kind of insult is directed at Daniel, the narrator of Jadelin Mabiala Gangbo's novel *Due volte* [Two times]. He is called "lurido schiavo" (filthy slave) by the other children of the religious institute where he lives with his twin brother, David. See Gangbo 2009.

9. Expressions such as "Calafrican" ("calabrese" and "African") are meant to assimilate Calabria, and by extension Southern Italy, to the subaltern position of the African continent and to attribute to the South an (almost) colonial status vis-à-vis Northern Italy. Such subalternity rests on a number of factors, mainly a racial difference and a lack of civilization and culture.

Writer and anthropologist Geneviève Makaping, however, who is originally from Cameroon and has lived and worked in Calabria for over three decades, has remarked how being African and Calabrian in Calabria grants access to very different social positions and levels of privilege. See Makaping 2001.

10. For the origins and development of Nappytalia and Afro-Italian Nappy Girls, see the Nappytalia website and Hawthorne in Frisina and Hawthorne 2015 and 2018.

11. In spite of the documentary's intention to show the existence of African Italian women and valorize Afaawua's process of self-awareness and determination to create a community of African Italian women, I find the ways in which this short documentary stereotypically essentializes, sensualizes, and sexualizes black female bodies very problematic. At the beginning of the narrative Evelyne introduces herself, discusses her origins, and is represented in her daily routine. Later the narrative transitions from her individual story to the community of black women she has created, within which they discuss their African Italian identity. For unexplained reasons, the main narrative is cross-cut with scenes of woman after woman dancing sensually in what appears to be a dark empty disco. Their bodies are intermittently illuminated in different colors for the pleasure of the (presumably white and male) beholder. In the main narrative, the discussion these women hold on their heritage and identity, again for unexplained reasons, takes place in a public restroom—presumably the one in the disco. This confers to these black female bodies a seedy nuance, while the intrusion of the white, male director in this highly gendered space is perceived like a violation of the female black body. The bathroom location further suggests the private nature of a conversation, which instead should be public and invest society at large. When the narrative transitions from the individual black subject (Evelyne) to the black community, one of the women sings to the excitement and enjoyment of the others. In this scene, as well as in the dance scenes, the association of black women with music and rhythm is enforced and marks their absence from other symbolic and physical spaces. For instance, while Evelyne introduces herself at the beginning of the documentary, the other women do not tell their names, nor do they discuss their background or reveal their origins. This produces the perception that they have no identity or history of their own, that this group is an amorphous body that exists only as part of the community that Evelyne has created, and that they are only an extension of her story. Thus the narrative of the documentary singles out one exceptional individual black woman and authorizes—at least in part—her upward mobility, while in turn it still represents the larger community of black women in Italy as mute, inarticulate, musical, and sexualized. The colonial imaginary of the Black Venus deployed in the documentary is in stark contrast with the self-representation of Afaawua's website, where African Italian women are portrayed as resourceful, independent, intelligent, and endowed with self-awareness and agency.

12. This is a paraphrasis of Geneviève Makaping's "little acts of daily racism."

13. I am not claiming here that African American, African Italian, and other African diasporic women perform the same aesthetic practices, nor am I claiming that hair must necessarily constitute for them a symbol of their "Africanness" or that it constitutes such a symbol for all of them in the same way. I am claiming that counter-aesthetics (here connected to natural hair) has the potential to create powerful counter-narratives and that this practice has been performed—often in different ways—by African American, African Italian, and other African diasporic women. On the complex ways through which Afroeuropeans construct narratives that are different from both a white European and an African American paradigm, see, among others, Scarabello and de Witte 2019.

REFERENCES

Byrd, Ayana D., and Lori L. Tharps . 2014. *Hair Story: Untangling the Roots of Black Hair in America* (revised edition). New York: St. Martin's Press.

Caiazza, Tommaso. 2018. "Are Italians White? The Perspective from the Pacific." *California Italian Studies* 8.2: 1–15.

Coppola, Massimo, dir. *Nappy Girls*. 25 September 2014. *Corriere della Sera*. Accessed June 1, 2020. Video. https://video.corriere.it/nappy-girls/5291ec12-4416-11e4-bbc2-282fa2f68a02.

Dabiri, Emma. 2019. *Don't Touch My Hair*. London: Allen Lane.

DeSalvo, Louise. 2003. "Color: White / Complexion: Dark." In *Are Italians White? How Race Is Made in America*, edited by Jennifer Guglielmo and Salvatore Salerno. New York and London: Routledge. 17–28.

Essed, Philomena. 1990. *Everyday Racism: Reports from Women of Two Cultures*. Alameda, CA: Hunter House.

Frisina, Annalisa, and Camilla Hawthorne. 2015. "Sulle pratiche estetiche antirazziste delle figlie delle migrazioni." *Il colore della nazione*, edited by Gaia Giuliani. Firenze: Le Monnier Mondadori.

———. 2018. "Italians with Veils and Afros: Gender, Beauty, and the Everyday Anti-Racism of the Daughters of Immigrants in Italy." *Journal of Ethnic and Migration Studies* 44.5: 718–35.

Gangbo, Jadelin Mabiala. 2009. *Due volte*. Roma: Edizioni e/o.

Giunta, Edvige. 2003. "Figuring Race." *Are Italians White? How Race Is Made in America*, edited by Jennifer Guglielmo and Salvatore Salerno, 224–33. New York and London: Routledge.

Guglielmo, Jennifer, and Salvatore Salerno, eds. 2003. *Are Italians White? How Race Is Made in America*. New York and London: Routledge.

Guglielmo, Thomas. 2003. *White on Arrival: Italians, Race, Color, and Power in Chicago 1890–1945*. New York: Oxford University Press.

Hijab Elegante. n. d. Accessed June 1, 2020. https://www.facebook.com/Hijab-elegante-146442872150423/.

Jacobson, Matthew F. 1998. *Whiteness of a Different Color: European Immigrants and the Alchemy of Race*. Cambridge, MA: Harvard University Press.

Lipsitz, George. 2018. *The Possessive Investment in Whiteness: How White People Profit from Identity Politics*. Twentieth Anniversary Edition. Philadelphia: Temple University Press.

Lombardi-Diop, Cristina, and Caterina Romeo, eds. 2012. *Postcolonial Italy: Challenging National Homogeneity*. New York: Palgrave Macmillan.

Luconi, Stefano. 2001. *From* Paesani *to White Ethnics: The Italian Experience in Philadelphia*. Albany: State University of New York Press.

Lukate, Melissa Johanna. 2019. "'Blackness Disrupts My Germanness.' On Embodiment and Questions of Identity and Belonging Among Women of Color in Germany." *To Exist Is To Resist. Black Feminism in Europe*, edited by Akwugu Emejulu and Francesca Sobande, 116–28. London: Pluto Press.

Makaping, Geneviève. 2001. *Traiettorie di sguardi. E se gli 'altri' foste voi?* Soveria Mannelli: Rubbettino.

Nappytalia. n. d. Accessed June 1, 2020. http://www.nappytalia.it/afro-italian-nappy-girls/.

Orsi, Robert. 1992. "The Religious Boundaries of an In-between People: Street Feste and the Problem of the Dark-Skinned Other in Italian Harlem, 1920–1990." *American Quarterly* 44.3: 313–47.

Ouedraogo, Leaticia. 2019. "Nassan Tenga." *Future. Il domani narrato dalle voci di oggi*, edited by Igiaba Scego, 97–124. Firenze: Effequ.

Puwar, Nirmal. 2004. *Space Invaders: Race, Gender and Bodies Out of Place*. Oxford–New York: Berg.

Ragusa, Kym, dir. 1997. *fuori/outside*. Video: Ibla Production.

———. 2006. *The Skin Between Us: A Memoir of Race, Beauty, and Belonging*. New York: Norton.

———. 2008a. *La pelle che ci separa*. Roma: Nutrimenti. Translated by Clara Antonucci and Caterina Romeo. Afterword by Caterina Romeo.

———. 2008b. "Three Women, Three Photographs." *About Face. Women Write of What They See When They Look in the Mirror*, edited by Anne Burt and Christina Baker Kline, 55–61. Berkeley, CA: Seal Press.

Ripanti, Espérance Hakuzwimana. 2019. *E poi basta. Manifesto di una donna nera italiana.* Gallarate: People.

Roediger, David R. 1991. *The Wages of Whiteness: Race and the Making of the American Working Class.* New York: Verso.

Romeo, Caterina. 2008. "Una capacità quasi acrobatica." Afterword to Kym Ragusa's *La pelle che ci separa*, 249–70. Roma: Nutrimenti.

———. 2012. "Racial Evaporations. Representing Blackness in African Italian Postcolonial Literature." *Postcolonial Italy. Challenging National Homogeneity*, edited by Cristina Lombardi-Diop and Caterina Romeo, 221–36. New York: Palgrave Macmillan.

Scarabello, Serena, and Marleen de Witte. 2019. "Afroeuropean Modes of Self-Making: Afro-Dutch and Afro-Italian Projects Compared." *Open Cultural Studies* 2: 317–31.

Scego, Igiaba. 2005a. "Salsicce." *Pecore Nere*, edited by Flavia Capitani and Emanuele Coen, 23–36. Roma-Bari: Laterza.

———. 2005b. "Sausages." *Metamorphoses: The Journal of the Five College Faculty Seminar on Literary Translation* 13.2: 214–25.

———. 2010. *La mia casa è dove sono.* Milano: Rizzoli.

———. 2016. "Capelli di libertà." *L'Espresso* 42.1: 34–36.

———, ed. 2019. *Future. Il domani narrato dalle voci di oggi.* Firenze: Effequ.

Tenzer, Livia. 2002. "Documenting Race and Gender: Kym Ragusa Discusses 'Passing' and 'Fuori/Outside.'" *Looking Across the Lens: Women's Studies and Film*, double issue of *Women's Studies Quarterly* 30.1–2: 213–20.

Vecoli, Rudolph. 1995. "Are Italians Just White Folks?" *Italian Americana* 13: 149–65.

Reconfiguring "la donna del Sud"

Trans-Mediterranean Narratives

Marta Cariello

SUBALTERNITY, HISTORY, AND THE SOUTH

This essay proposes an exploration into the figure of "the southern woman," with reference to the geo-cultural cartographies of southern Italy and of the Mediterranean area, looking into the ways in which such a figure is rewritten, complicated, and possibly subverted in trans-Mediterranean narratives of Italy, with a specific reading of two works by Italian-Somali writer Igiaba Scego.

"La donna del Sud" is a trope within the wider trope of the Italian woman. The poetic image drawn by Canadian-Italian poet Gianna Patriarca rings like a painful yet affectionate claim to distance herself (and perhaps the reader) from "Italian women":

> These are the women
> who were born to give birth
>
> . . .
>
> (Patriarca, 1994, "Italian women," 9)

We may presume that the women Gianna Patriarca has in mind are those from the central region of Italy where she was born; however, she deliberately speaks of a comprehensive, collective "Italian Women," as the title of her poetry collection makes evident: *Italian Women and Other Tragedies*. Patriarca's poetics are deeply connected to her own condition as Canadian-Italian, and the women of the opening poem in this collection speak to and among women of different generations and diverse locations inside material and cultural practices of Italy, Canada, and the space (and time) between. Indeed, the image of devout women who are "born to give birth," sacrificing—as Patriarca writes—their own breath, voice, and blood for their kin, certainly recurs specifically in the discourse (and also in the reality, as discourse shapes and is shaped by reality) of the southern Italian woman. The figure of the *mater dolorosa* is at the root of a Catholic culture that has inexorably tied not only womanhood to reproduction but also reproduction to suffering and sacrifice.

Notably, the female figure has been tied to fertility and its icon thus worshipped in southern Italy since ancient times, as, for example, the Matres Matutae found in the area of Capua testify.[1] However, the idea of the woman as dignified only as a "suffering mother" and through the expulsion of any element of pleasure attached to the reproduction and mothering process is embedded most powerfully in Western society—and specifically in southern Italy, for what concerns this study—in the figure of the Madonna. The particular intensity of the cult of the Virgin Mary in southern Italy and in Spain has long been the object of anthropological and psychoanalytical studies (Carroll 1986, Tentori 1982, among others). In particular, Nancy Frey Breuner (1992) takes an interesting feminist psychoanalytic perspective on the theme, analyzing Michael Carroll's Freudian study *The Cult of the Virgin Mary* (1986) and critiquing the male-centered perspective it adopts. A number of elements would seem to be involved in the rootedness and intensity of the Marian cult in southern Italy and Spain, among which are the historically rural character of these areas and the strong incidence of patron-client relationships, two elements that appear to concur respectively to the development of goddess cults and to the recourse to supernatural mediators (Leach 1966; Carroll 1986, 29–31, 38; Lazzarich 2019, 153–7). More complex theories, postulated by Carroll and critiqued by Breuer, involve Freudian analyses of machismo (Carroll 1986), as well as male and female devotion, and the empowering character of the figure of the Madonna and her independence from man (Breuer 1992). The reasons behind the intensity of the cult in these geographical areas are clearly many and too complex to analyze in the space of this essay; however, what is worth underlining with reference to the discourse on and around "the southern woman" is that the element of locality plays a fundamental role, and, as emerges from the texts analyzed below, the shift in the figure implies a redrawing of the grounds inside which "local" categories and power relations are rooted.

The trope of virginity and the close association of women with family and motherhood are, indeed, Christian-rooted elements of so-called southern culture. However, a more nuanced reading of the geo-historical interconnections shows a more complex picture. The entanglements of trans-Mediterranean encounters emerge here in a commonality of cultural and religious traits and in the uninterrupted use of such traits in the exercise of both patriarchal power and what Anibal Quijano (2000) first called "the coloniality of power," or the construction of "the other" as subaltern in the scale of Western (Northern?) modernity.

The particular positioning of the southern Italian woman within a network that stretches across the geo-cultural space of the Mediterranean makes her a particularly charged figure of subalternity. She is seen as sharing, among other things, sartorial practices with Muslim women, and is also considered as signifying the measure of modernity (in the same manner as women in Muslim countries in today's Western "humanitarian wars" and "democracy exports") and whose body is, evermore today in Italy, destroyed by the exercise of patriarchal power.[2]

In a 1981 article in the review *Man*, published by the Royal Anthropological Institute of Great Britain and Ireland, scholar Maureen Giovannini (1981) analyzed the results of a study she had conducted on the symbolic and cultural signifiers assigned to the women—and their bodies—in a Sicilian village she called "Garre." In the context of this study, the female figure emerges as a symbol of the family, as multiple vehicles of metonymies and metaphors of nurturing, protection from the outside world, and, at the same time, penetrability. The need to protect the precincts of the family, so crucial in a context that was essentially rural (*latifondista*), took the form of defence—and parallel control—of the female body, a defence that in turn served as cohesive factor for the family unit.[3]

Ernesto De Martino's well-known ethno-anthropological studies of southern Italy and magic depict a dimension somewhat related to Giovannini's study, in which, again, the female body is bearer of potential evil forces yet at the same time custodian of the key to the elimination of such evil (De Martino 1961). This woman is central, for example, in the phenomenon of *tarantismo* in Salento, as well as in ritual weeping in Lucania (De Martino 1958, 1961).[4] She carries on her body not only social disorder but also the possibility of claiming and taming such disorder. The southern woman embodies an intimidating form of power and a territory that must be controlled.

Such ethnographic and anthropological observations, certainly coming from different scholarly perspectives, show an image of the "southern woman" that is not surprising. It is indeed a cultural construction that still persists today and that becomes even more compelling when read in relation to the wider interconnections of the Mediterranean geo-cultural space and within the dynamics of North-South power relations. Within this network of relations, "the North" is here intended as the hegemonic discourse that has construed not only "the South" (or better yet, "il Meridione," in the specific case of Italy) but also "the Orient": a South on the border, but also intertwined, with the "alterity" of the Arab world, with reference here to Edward Said's (1978) fundamental theorization of Orientalism. The system of knowledge production and power relations that has "othered" the non-European has also produced the discourse of subalternity that informs the idea of southern Europe first theorized as "meridionism" by Manfred Pfister (1996; see also Cazzato 2017). Within this theoretical framework, the idea and discourse of "the South" of Italy and of Europe will be used in this essay as sometimes coinciding with, or as part of, the wider geo-cultural formation of the Mediterranean.

An "archaeological" approach to the discourse on women and on the female body in the Mediterranean region points to the multiplicity of its roots, which do not belong to just one side of the Mediterranean or just to one cultural-religious formation. It bears underscoring that the three monotheistic religions are situated inside a common history of the elaboration of such discourse, which in turn is rooted in a deeply misogynistic Hellenistic culture. Furthermore, a deeper reading unearths the almost-erasure from history of the position of women in some pre-monotheistic Mediterranean societies, in which they appear to have had prominent social or public roles (such as ancient Egypt, for example; Vercoutter 1965). The claim on the part of Christian European culture to roots in Greek antiquity and the parallel negation by Islamic culture of any type of continuity with and descent from the *jahiliyya* (pre-Islamic period) have produced a discourse that distances Europe from the (eastern or southern) "Islamic periphery," thus virtually erasing any common root (Ahmed 1992).

This narrative is a fundamental part of the process through which modernity, invariably embodied in a "liberated and emancipated" woman, is distanced from its (colonial) other and from the instrumental idea of "backwardness," symbolized by a covered, prisoner, dependent woman. The "southern (Italian) woman" is located at a threshold within and without modernity, on the edge of the Mediterranean and therefore in an area where archetypes of power and weakness, heroism and oppression co-inhabit, where the linearity of "modern" time meets its crisis.

The symbolism linked to the southern woman tells not only of a specific semiotic web in which we still dwell today but also has, as with any other cultural element, a precise genealogy that tells another story. It tells the story of a Mediterranean in which the women from Garre can be the protagonists and take center stage, tracing a cartography of misogyny through the Hellenistic domination, up to the advent of the monotheisms, the narratives of European "progress," and those of Islam. The history of misogyny as well as the commonality of roots and the various narratives of resistance are all pieces of another history of the Mediterranean.

The idea of "another history" is summoned here as an invitation to think outside the acquired linearity of Western modernity. It is not, however, a reformulation of history somehow "outside time," dead on its track, so to speak; rather, it is a critique of that sole track upon which Western humanism has been laid. The short-circuit appears therefore to be not in the time line but in the episteme itself. The voices coming from "elsewhere," though undoubtedly immersed in the all-encompassing dynamics of the late-capitalist global market, have introduced languages (artistic and linguistic) that challenge the very basis of Western humanism. It is not only a question of including "the other side" of history but rather of attempting to read, for example, the historical-cultural formation of the Mediterranean (or, of the South), inside the sartorial practices of Algerian women, to see therein the navigations and the power relations between the shores and along the centuries of this specific "South." To read, in other words, the history book inscribed in those practices. Or, for example, to register the connections among the women poets of the pre-Islamic period and the erasure of the female voices in the Mediterranean space over the centuries or, also, the links between the gestures and bodies of the *tarantolate* and of the women in the centuries after the affirmation of the monotheisms in the region. This network of multiple narratives, in which different and juxtaposed languages and temporalities are at work, is one of the stories and histories of the Mediterranean, or of "the South."

The short-circuit engendered by the interruption in the Mediterranean narrative has inevitably and deeply touched also the Italian episteme and national narrative (despite the staunch resistance even within the academia). New languages and new voices have been speaking and remapping the grounds for at least three decades. Interestingly, these new voices have been predominantly women's (Basili and Limm, n.d.), and their female characters have shifted the grounds and borders of discourses of womanhood and southernness. Igiaba Scego, among others, re-writes the space and the body politics of women in and from "the South," in a particularly interesting game of juxtapositions, substitutions, and semantic slippages involving stereotypes and archetypes of Italian women, of African women, and of "the South" in general.

SHIFTING (NARRATIVE) GROUNDS AND THE NEED FOR INTERSECTIONS

In Igiaba Scego's 2015 novel, *Adua*, the protagonist is a Somali woman who immigrates to Italy in the 1970s in search of a life of success and glamour in the film industry. She instead appears in only one film, a soft-porn B-movie in which her black skin is the main attraction of the blatant exoticism of the time.[5] Forty years later, Adua significantly tells her story to a piece of Rome, so to speak: she chooses Bernini's statue of the elephant that supports the obelisk in piazza Santa Maria sopra Minerva to recount her life story, while her voice is interspersed with a third-person narrative of her father's life as a slave and as an interpreter for the Italians during the Fascist regime.[6] Adua's negotiations with Italy, with her own story, and with her body become intertwined also with the present-day arrival of the new immigrants, crossing the Mediterranean after long and horrifying journeys from different parts of Africa. She tells the elephant/Rome/the (Italian) reader about her marriage to a young Somali man, whom she helps, and perhaps also loves in some way; he eventually goes on to a better destination in Europe to chase his own dreams farther away from the Mediterranean. Adua lives in Rome, which functions as a specific threshold in Italy between North and South, "the center" of Italy, but also a doorway to the Meridione and the Mediterranean. Adua looks no further north than Rome, unlike her young husband. Instead she looks south, way south: to Somalia and the idea of returning "home." Adua also looks *like* the south. She embodies a fundamental shift in the imaginary and the discourse of the South: Adua was oversexualized as a young and beautiful girl and later as a woman; she is discarded by the (white) Italian society as an older woman. However, she carries a past that is only apparently erasable; she bears the name of the first battle won against the Italians, as her father tells her:

"I named you after the first African victory against imperialism. I, your father, was on the right side. And you must never believe the opposite. [. . .] Inside your name there's a battle, my battle. . . ." (Scego 2017, 41)

She is also a bearer, therefore, through her very existence, of the former colonial nation and its resistance, as well as her father's agonized battle with his own conscience and with colonialism. In a form of continuation of the conflicts that she was born into, Adua is the victim of sexual violence when she arrives in Italy; it is her first confrontation with the new country and the illusion she had nurtured all her life through the movie theatre that the Italians had built in her hometown in Somalia. The physical violence is prolonged through the violence inflicted upon her by the public display of her exploitation in the film and the broken promises it contains.

When Adua's young husband sees her film, we learn of the squalor and delusion that it brought into her life:

> He saw me running naked on the golden sand at Capocotta, he saw when Aldo de Luigi put his hands on my butt, he saw me making out with Nick Tonno in a 1953 Chrysler and he also saw what my privates looked like then. Yes, he saw everything. [. . .] he too was sucked into my headlong expressions of love dubbed at the Via Margutta studio. They gave me a languid, honeyed voice for the movie. "Yours is too harsh," the director told me. Then he added, "If it's dubbed, your sacred body will get the drawl it needs to make every man in the world go head over heels." (Scego 2017, 82)

The fact that her voice is dubbed over (a rather common practice at the time) functions symbolically for the loss of agency that Adua undergoes, epitomized by the replacement of her "harsh" voice, deemed an unfit match for the audience's implied fantasies.

Adua sees herself at the time of her film also through the eyes of her best friend, Lul, who is also Somali. Lul has already moved back to the country and is pushing Adua to move back as well. Adua imagines what her life would have been like if she had known Lul back when she first arrived in Italy:

> If Lul had been there she would have checked the press every day to see what came out about the movie and about me. She would have spared me the pain of headlines like "Burning Hot Black Hole" or "Steamy Kiss from the Abyssinian Abyss." She would have demanded a title for me that was certainly more dignified than "black Venus. . . ." (Scego 2017, 153)

In the first passage, we read of Adua's movie through the awkwardly positioned eyes of her young Somali husband, filtered through Adua's confession to the elephant. In the second passage, the narration again develops on three levels. Adua tells the elephant her own story; she does so, however, through what she imagines Lul's eyes would have seen. Finally, the (Italian) reader is positioned at the end of this double passage as not only a third receiver of the narrative but also as the "original" audience of those films and only once-removed facilitator and beneficiary of that exploitation. By speaking "today" of herself (and of Italy) in the 1970s, by choosing a material—and monumental—piece of the Italian capital to do so, and, furthermore, by having to distance herself in order to actually see who and what she was through the eyes of her husband or her friend, Adua brings a highly problematic legacy to the Italian reader, who is faced with the evidence of a past that simply does not pass. Each narrative level shows the evidence of historical removal and of the racial and colonial unconscious of the Italian national narrative.

Adua is the incarnation of the dream of domination of white European—and Italian—patriarchy, the incarnation of a body devoid of the moral bounds of kin or family: a body that no longer symbolizes (also) the perimeter of the family and its protection but only penetrability from the outside. The white Italian man, and Italian society as a whole—as significantly symbolized by the film producer's wife, who orchestrates Adua's exploitation—is now "the outside," thus no longer protecting, but attacking, penetrating, violating. A (further) South is there to be conquered and colonized. Adua's exploitation, it is important to note, takes place well after direct colonialism is over; the backlash of Italian racial unconscious takes the form of visible difference, something that was much more difficult to name among the North-South axis of "internal" discrimination and hegemony.

In an earlier short story titled "Identità" which is included in the collection *Amori Bicolori* (2008), Igiaba Scego construes a very direct and bitterly ironic (or perhaps scarily realistic) picture of the shift in sexualized body politics along the racial lines of today's Italy. Immigrant women have become the direct receptacles of the "evil-bearer" projection as well as the hypersexualized and dangerous imaginary that had been assigned to southern women along with the parallel and complementary role of custodians of the family and of morality. Notably, the latter role has not been extended to the new subaltern, immigrant subject, especially if she bears dark skin and comes from an "African" South. Indeed, the realm of both sexual pleasure and sin has been assigned to the immigrant woman along color lines. This shifting ground has created a mirror effect in which the dynamics of domination are much clearer than before. In "Identità," Scego depicts a young interracial couple living in Rome: Fatou, who is an Italian of Somali descent, and Valerio, who is a white Italian. The inner dynamics of the couple, and their intercultural encounter, are posed against an increasingly pressing system of social projections and expectations. The climax of this pressure, and the trigger to the burgeoning conflicts between the two, is an article by an obnoxiously flirtatious and racist woman journalist, who interviews them for her article "La calata delle barbare . . . quando il matrimonio si fa straniero" ("The Invasion of the Barbarian Women . . . when marriage becomes a stranger" [my translation]). The title is telling in itself, and the words the journalist uses to describe Fatou and the couple's life reek with exoticism and stereotypes, distorting or outright making up what they say or how they look:

> "Italian women no longer know how to seduce their men, of course they choose us," says Fatou, a very tall, young black woman. Fatou has a neck like a giraffe's and Bambi eyes that easily win over Italian men, but Fatou (oh, and she knows!) is not a helpless creature, she has claws and teeth that can hurt. (Scego 2008, 8 [my translation])

Fatou is construed by the journalist as apparently weak and defenceless, but actually fierce and dangerous for Italian men, and therefore potentially destabilizing for Italian society in general. The article is focused solely on the sexualization of immigrant women in the Italian imaginary. The description of Fatou and more generally the sexualization of women of color, it is important to underline, are closely connected to the Italian racial unconscious embedded, among other things, in the practice of *madamato* during colonialism. Indeed, Scego includes explicit and implicit references to such practices in her short story.[7]

The commonplace idea that immigrant women "steal" Italian men is highlighted in the article on Fatou and Valerio. It has indeed been a recurring theme in the past two decades in Italian media, culminating in a talk show on national public television, aired in March 2017, in which a list was read and discussed on the reasons to "Choose a Girlfriend from the East," which inferred that women from eastern European countries "are all mothers, but after having given birth, their bodies go back to being rock-hard," that they "forgive cheating," and that they "don't fuss, are not needy, and don't sulk," among other things. The list caused indignation and the program was subsequently shut down, but the fact itself that the authors and presenters had deemed it acceptable and perhaps laughable to present such a list is indeed quite telling and is only one particularly visible act of a more subtle cultural construction circulating in the nation's "common sense," in Gramsci's sense of the term.[8]

The same "dangers" posed by immigrant women to the stability of the Italian family are traced in the current hegemonic discourse in the Italian public sphere, as already mentioned, through a subtle but significant differentiation along a very specific color line: for example, eastern European women are "more liberated," "stronger," and "rational," and they cleverly appear obedient but actually dominate Italian men (especially elderly men), with the sole aim of taking their money. This reaction to the specific presence of women from eastern European countries reveals an anxiety in Italian society, which has a massive problem with caring for the growing elderly population; most of the caregivers are women from eastern Europe who are in many cases very well educated and clearly overqualified for the jobs they take, often holding degrees equal to if not higher than their Italian employers. Whereas the "dangers of eastern women" apparently lie mainly in their cleverness and dominant character, women from Africa are deemed dangerously "animal-like," therefore associated with an uncontrollable sexuality (and possible irrationality). The Italian imaginary, again digging deep into its colonial roots and becoming explicit in the uses of the black body in the erotic film industry of the "liberating" 1970s, is unable to de-eroticize the African female body, a body that is now inhabiting the Italian territory and is becoming an-other southern woman.[9]

Returning to Scego's short story "Identità," it is clear that, responding to the colonial imaginary (which has evidently not been erased nor eradicated) and in line with the type of domination fantasies that Adua's film conveys, Fatou too is sexualized as aggressive and potentially dangerous and as not adapting to her surroundings. The journalist describes the couple's home as follows: "Their home is decorated in a sober style, deeply on the primitive, ancestral side. Fatou has imposed her style on Valerio. . . ." (Scego 2008, 8 [my translation]).

We later find out that Valerio was actually born in Mogadishu, since his parents worked for an NGO, and that most of the "African" furniture—actually an "African corner" of their apartment—was his. Fatou, on the other hand, was born in Rome, has hardly ever been in Africa, and sometimes asks Valerio, "Tell me about Africa" (Scego 2008, 23). Through this inversion and confusion of identities, narratives, and histories, Scego undoes and opens up the space of the Italian nation. Her "southern women" bring in a new subject, perhaps another "unexpected subject," to echo Carla Lonzi (1970), that of the immigrant woman from a trans-Mediterranean route from a deeper kind of south. The dynamics of hegemony and subalternity then shift, but the multiplication of subjectivity also confuses and subverts orders and significations. The shift takes place again, crucially, along the lines of race. In this sense, Cristina Lombardi-Diop and Caterina Romeo's call for intersectionality appears fundamental when, in their Introduction to *Postcolonial Italy: Challenging National Homogeneity*, they claim the need

> not only for an understanding of how immigrant women de-center the "grand narratives" of Italian feminism, but also for an exploration of the intersecting ways in which these women are racialized, sexualized, and marginalized based on a number of factors, including religion, sexual orientation, social class, and citizenship (or the lack thereof). (Lombardi-Diop and Romeo 2012, 15)

The "uninvited guest" (Curti 2007) on Italian ground, the immigrant woman, has opened up a conversation that most crucially interrogates the coordinates of the centuries-long hegemonic discourse on southern women (and those "Italian women" Patriarca engages with) but it also works on and around the edges of Italian nationhood and its narrative. The uninvited guest rewrites the locations of "the South" and positions herself in trans-Mediterranean localities of destabilization, border sabotage, and resistance.

NOTES

1. Matres Matutae are votive statues from the area of Capua (in Campania, southern Italy) dating between the seventh and first centuries BCE. They are dedicated to the Dea Matuta, the local divinity of fertility and motherhood; they are usually sculpted out of tufa stone and hold babies in their arms. See Nava 2015.

2. Statistics when writing this article indicate that in Italy a woman is killed every seventy-two hours and that over half of such murders are committed by male partners or ex-partners; one-third of the female population between sixteen and seventy years of age declares to have experienced physical and/or sexual violence. These statistics are controversial and the official data have been contested by feminist collectives and research groups. See, among others, Senato della Repubblica Italiana 2018; Weil, Corradi, and Naudi 2018.

3. This observation, as well as the theoretical elaboration on "la donna del Sud" in the geo-cultural formation of the Mediterranean, are included in Chambers and Cariello 2019.

4. Tarantismo is the cathartic ritual dance performed in Salento (Puglia) by those bitten by a tarantula (*tarantolati/e*). It is also tied to the worship of Saint Paul to whom a chapel is dedicated in Galatina (Puglia), and the *tarantolate* are said to become brides to Saint Paul. The complex phenomenon was famously studied by De Martino. See De Martino 1961; see also Daboo 2010. Ritual weeping refers to the particular part of the cultural process of resolution of the crisis of mourning in Lucania, practiced until the advent of Christianity.

5. The reference is explicitly to a series of 1970s soft-porn Italian films that reintroduced the trope of the "black Venus." See Giuliani Caponetto 2012 and Ponzanesi 2005.

6. For a study of the affective relevance of cityscapes in Italian literature of migration, and in particular of the urban resignification in Scego's (2010) *La mia casa è dove sono* (*My Home Is Where I Am*), see Parati 2017.

7. Colonial concubinage, or *madamato*, was practiced and encouraged by Italians in North Eastern Africa, until the Fascist Racial Laws prohibited mixed-race marriage. See Trento 2012; Volpato 2009.

8. See, among others, Ansa 2017; Stanco 2017.

9. The discourse on immigrant women and the process of stereotyping according to ethnicities and racial divides is impossible to tackle in the space of this essay. A general overview and references to the different ethnic groups present in Italy today can be found, among others, in Giorgi 2012.

REFERENCES

Ahmed, Laila. 1992. *Women and Gender in Islam: Historical Roots of a Modern Debate*. New Haven: Yale University Press.

Ansa. 2017. "Scoppia caso Paola Perego, Dg Rai: 'Parliamone sabato' chiude. Bufera dopo grafica su donne est." March, 22, 2019. http://www.ansa.it/sito/notizie/politica/2017/03/20/scoppia-caso-perego-maggioni-errore-folle-mi-scuso-2_c104fa0d-79e7-46ae-bb92-24016f1a7af0.html.

Basili and Limm. Banca dati degli Scrittori Immigrati in Lingua Italiana e della Letteratura Italiana della Migrazione Mondiale. http://basili-limm.el-ghibli.it/.

Breuner, Nancy Frey. 1992. "The Cult of the Virgin Mary in Southern Italy and Spain." *Ethos Journal of the Society for Psychological Anthropology*. 20, 1: 66-95.

Carroll, Michael. 1986. *The Cult of the Virgin Mary*. Princeton: Princeton University Press.

Cazzato, Luigi. 2017. *Sguardo inglese e Mediterraneo italiano. Alle radici del meridionismo*. Milano: Mimesis.

Chambers, Iain, and Marta Cariello. 2019. *La questione mediterranea*. Milano: Mondadori.

Curti, Lidia. 2007. "Female Literature of Migration in Italy." *Feminist Review* 87: 60–75.

Daboo, Jerri. 2010. *Ritual, Rapture and Remorse. A Study of Tarantism and Pizzica in Salento*. Bern: Peter Lang.

De Martino, Ernesto. 1958. *Morte e pianto rituale*. Torino: Biblioteca di cultura scientifica.

De Martino, Ernesto. 1961. *Sud e magia. La terra del rimorso*. Milano: Il Saggiatore.

Giorgi, Alberta. 2012. "The Cultural Construction of Migrant Women in the Italian Press." *e-cadernos ces* 16: 66–91.

Giovannini, Maureen J. 1981. "Woman: A Dominant Symbol within the Cultural System of a Sicilian Town." *Man*, New Series 16, no. 3: 408–26.

Giuliani Caponetto, Rosetta. 2012. "Blaxploitation Italian Style: Exhuming and Consuming the Colonial Black Venus in 1970s Cinema in Italy." In *Postcolonial Italy: Challenging National Homogeneity*, edited by C. Lombardi-Diop and C. Romeo, 191-203, New York: Palgrave.

Lazzarich, Diego. 2019. *Gratitudine politica I. Dall'età classica al medioevo*. Milan: Mimesis.

Leach, Edmund. 1966. "Virgin Birth." *Proceedings of the Royal Anthropological Institute of Great Britain and Ireland*, no. 1966: 39–49.

Lombardi-Diop, Cristina, and Caterina Romeo, eds. 2012. *Postcolonial Italy. Challenging National Homogeneity*. New York: Palgrave.

Lonzi, Carla. 1970. *Sputiamo su Hegel*. Roma: Editoriale grafica.

Nava, Maria Luisa. 2015. "Le Matres Matutae di Capua." In *Catalogo mostra* Mater, Parma, Palazzo del Governatore. Milano: Feltrinelli.

Parati, Graziella. 2017. *Migrant Writers and Urban Space in Italy: Proximities and Affect in Literature and Film*. New York: Palgrave.

Patriarca, Gianna. 1994. *Italian Women and Other Tragedies*. Toronto: Guernica.

Pfister, Manfred. 1996. *The Fatal Gift of Beauty: The Italies of British Travellers*. Amsterdam: Rodopi.

Ponzanesi, Sandra. 2005. "Beyond the Black Venus: Colonial Sexual Politics and Contemporary Visual Practices." In *Italian Colonialism. Legacies and Memories*, edited by J. Andall and D. Duncan, 165–89. Oxford: Peter Lang.

Quijano, Anibal. 2000. "Coloniality of Power, Eurocentrism and Latin America." *Nepantla* 1, no. 3: 533–80.

Said, Edward W. 1978. *Orientalism*. New York: Pantheon.

Scego, Igiaba. 2008. "Identità." In *Amori bicolori*, edited by Flavia Capitani and Emanuele Coen, 5-33. Roma-Bari: Laterza.

———. 2010. *La mia casa è dove sono*. Milano: Rizzoli.

———. 2015. *Adua*. Firenze: Giunti. Translated by Jamie Richards as *Adua* (New York: New Vessel Press, 2017).

Senato della Repubblica Italiana. 2018. *Femicide The Final Report of the First Italian Joint Committee of Inquiry. Data and Statistics*. https://www.senato.it/application/xmanager/projects/leg18/English_Focus_Femicide_1.pdf.

Stanco, Renato. 2017. "Rai, lo scivolone sulle donne dell'Est costa il posto a Paola Perego." March 20, 2019. https://www.lettera43.it/it/articoli/media/2017/03/20/rai-lo-scivolone-sulle-donne-dellest-costa-il-posto-a-paola-perego/209368/.

Tentori, Tullio. 1982. "An Italian Religious Feast: The Fujenti Rites of the Madonna dell'Arco, Naples." In *Mother Worship: Themes and Variations*, edited by James J. Preston, 95–122. Chapel Hill: University of North Carolina Press.

Vercoutter, Jean. 1965. "La Femme en Egypte ancienne." In *Histoire mondiale de la femme*, vol. 1, edited by Pierre Grimal, 63–152. Paris: Nouvelle Libraire de France.

Volpato, Chiara. 2009. "La violenza contro le donne nelle colonie italiane." *DEP Deportate Esuli Profughe*, 10: 110–131.

Weil, Shalva, Consuelo Corradi, and Marceline Naudi, eds. 2018. *Femicide across Europe: Theory, Research and Prevention*. Bristol: Policy Press.

The Guest

Shirin Ramzanali Fazel

I was born in a corner house at the end of an alley. Far from the noise of the bumpy roads, busy with rusted pick-ups spitting black smoke, and from the market jammed with people. It is an old stone building with two entrances. One door leads to the storeroom, where my father keeps his stock. The other opens onto a large barren garden: two tall palm trees and a bushy jasmine with tiny white flowers. This space becomes an open kitchen during festivities. Relatives from my mother's side gather with their noisy children and bring life to our home.

The house once belonged to a man from the Far East, Chinese or Malay. He never went back home and never got married. He was in his late fifties when he arrived, a successful merchant, an honest man who kept to himself. Some say he fled persecution, or that he was exiled from his village. My father became his trusted business partner and when the old man died, he left the house to him. It is a big house with many rooms and small windows. Most of the time we keep the shutters half open, so the noon heat stays out. Two rooms we never use are piled with old furniture and boxes of the previous owner's belongings: embroidered jackets and hats, a silver sword, books, lacquer trays, porcelain cups, and a couple of paintings. My father is reluctant to get rid of things that belonged to a man who treated him like a son. He too came from a far land, from Kimbarawe.

A steep staircase took you to the roof terrace and a large sunny room. We used this room to store rice, beans, dates, sugar, and cooking oil. I used to hide and play there during my childhood, when the house was crowded with boisterous friends.

Once a year, my father's relatives visited. The mood in our house changed when they came. He was quiet and Mum seemed sad and nervous and would not allow me to sit by my father. I wished these men would disappear. I never received a pat on the head or a smile from them. I felt strange in their presence. It was the way they looked at me—those black eyes staring at me like dark storm clouds, as if I'd done something wrong. I could not run away, I could only stand there, hypnotized.

Once they left, my father was cheerful again. He would play with me on the carpet. He would hug me and tickle me. I loved playing with my father. He let my fingers explore his hair—it was soft and silky like the feathers of a crow. I wished I had his hair. I got mine from my mother.

Mum was obsessed with my hair when I was a child, always pulling at my curls with a plastic comb or scooping Vaseline from a big jar to tame the rebellious strands. When I screamed from the pain and I felt the comb stick, she would remind me in a sing-song tone: "Ayah, I prayed so deeply to have you. We waited for many years. I gave so much in charity. I had so much *sabr*. Remember, Allah rewards patience. *Alhamdullilah*. We are so happy to have you in our life."

When I was growing up, I would hear people gossiping and looking at me in an odd way,

"Ayah is the miracle child."

"Her parents never lost hope."

I would hear women whispering about the several miscarriages Mum had had.

"She has her mother's complexion."

"They have the same hair too!"

My parents were very strict about my education. I attended a secondary school for girls and only wanted to play soccer. My girlfriends called me a tomboy. I did not care about looks while they wanted to whiten their complexions like the models in magazines. My hairdresser wanted me to straighten my hair, but I knew my father would be disappointed. As a child, I told him how much I wanted his smooth hair. He always said: "Ayah, you have beautiful hair, a forest filled with trees where bright birds sing." He would chirp and make me laugh.

My father came from a conservative family. The youngest child, he left his village to discover new lands. When he came to Kimbarawe, he met people from different cultures. He felt free from the burden of his community's rigid way of thinking. I never met the women of his family, never saw photos of them. When I was born, my father named me "Ayah," after his mother.

My father used to tell me stories of his childhood: how his mother defended him against his brothers. She taught him to tell the truth, to go against the tide if it was right. When he decided to travel, she let him go. But when he got married, his family was outraged. His brothers tried to force him to divorce my mother and marry within the family. That was their tradition. But he was unshakable, even when they said: "She won't be able to bear children."

My father fell in love with my mother the first moment he saw her. The daughter of a barber, she was not of the same class or background. Though he knew his family would cut him off, he made his choice and asked the barber if he could marry his daughter. The barber was embarrassed, but after clearing his throat, he said: "Ali, you are a good, hard-working man. I am honoured. Promise me that you will not leave my Salwa."

In a firm voice, my father said: "I promise. I will never abandon her."

For a number of years, my uncles stopped coming to our house. My father never told me why they stopped coming, but I could hear Mum saying: "Ali, I am so sorry. They never forgave you for marrying me." He kissed Mum's hand softly and whispered: "You are the love of my life."

One day we found out that Hilal, my father's nephew, his sister's youngest son, was coming to visit after all these years. The news came as a surprise and thrilled my parents. They saw it as a gesture of reconciliation.

In the evening, sipping spiced tea under a sky full of stars, my father said: "Things are changing. Young people are more open minded. My mother raised Hilal." Mum's eyes were full of hope. She said the whole house would be spotless, even the charcoal stove in the kitchen.

It was my job to prepare the guest room. I dragged the mattress into the sun. I removed baskets of cashews, heavy jars of oil, and sacks of beans, rice, and sugar. I cleared long hanging spider webs, scrubbed mold from the walls. I opened the windows to allow fresh sea air to blow through.

My cousin arrived on a rainy day. Mum's sisters and relatives gathered in our house. We perspired from the humidity and from the heat of the kitchen. A goat was slaughtered, crates of Coca-Cola and Fanta piled up. Trays of coconut and banana cakes were stacked high. It looked like a festival day. Everybody was curious to meet Hilal, who arrived carrying a rucksack and a beautiful stringed instrument he called an "oud." He was tall and slim. His skin glowed like the moon. Hilal was the perfect name for him. It meant "the slender crescent moon." His light ginger-colored beard contrasted with his pitch-black hair. His large eyes shone.

Raising his hand, he saluted us and said, "*Assalamualeikum!*"

"*Waaleikum salam!*" we replied in chorus.

Mum, showing her gold teeth, said, "*Marhaban!*"

My father patted Hilal on the shoulder and with a toothy smile ordered, "*Yalla, Yalla.* Let Hilal freshen up and then you will all have a chance to meet him. He has had a long journey."

Then both of them headed for the staircase as the women started gossiping.

"He is a bachelor."

"He is the first cousin from Ali's family to visit."

"He is Leila's youngest."

"He looks different from his uncles."

"His face is like a full moon."

"He is the spitting image of Ali."

Mum shushed them. She did not like gossip.

* * *

After a few days of chatter and neighbors popping in, the house became quiet again. Hilal went out with my father in the mornings, introducing him to friends, giving him advice on business opportunities. They had lunch together late in the afternoons, where the very best dishes were served. But Hilal was not a big eater. He nibbled at every plate before complimenting his host. "Blessed be the hands that cooked the food. Delicious."

Mum was happy to have him as a guest, unlike my father's brothers. Smiling, she told me, "Your cousin is gentle. He would be a good husband." I, too, was intrigued by him even though we had exchanged few words. He was not like the boys who tried to get my attention on the way to school, racing their cars with the windows open, reggae music playing loud.

Hilal told me, after his afternoon nap, that he often went on walks by himself, passing stalls where second-hand clothes from the rich countries are sold; ladies mini-dresses, T-shirts, jeans, men's shirts, children's clothes, knickers, pants. He was not interested in the local bars selling cold soft drinks and warm beer, and stalls with charcoal grills serving barbecued chicken wings and bony goat meat.

Passers-by greeted him with genuine warmth. Young girls pretended not to look at him. Bored shopkeepers in white *jallabia*—robes—invited him to have a cup of coffee with them. He declined gently with a shake of the head, raised his arm and waved his long slim hand. He told me he walked slowly, but his thoughts were always elsewhere. Curious children ran after him; they have not seen a man with long hair before. He left behind him the cramped houses, suspicious stray cats, and busy alleys and headed for the sea.

Big waves splashed on the rocks. Standing still, he contemplated the angry sea trying to tame his own confusion, which had been growing since he was a child. His grandmother used to talk about her son, Ali. He always wanted to meet his lost uncle. When she used to bathe him, she would say: "These are the same breadstick legs that Ali has, and his straight black hair." She would go on: "The way you blink your eyes and fold your arms when you are embarrassed. You are so clever, like Ali. You ask questions all the time, you want to discover the world just like him." This ghost of an uncle robbed him of his grandmother's love. His childhood innocence they erased. The belief that a grandmother will always love "her boys" equally. When she passed away, surrounded by her family, her last whispered words were, "Where is Ali?"

Hilal told me that for years he heard his mother and his aunties cursing angrily: "What we did for Mother was never enough, she always missed Ali."

"A curse on him, he never came back."

"How could he fall in love with that ugly creature?"

"They told us she is black as coal."

"She controls him with the devil's help."

"Even his daughter does not resemble him."

"Poor Ali. Curse the day he met that evil woman."

"He never came back to his mother."

Hilal wanted to meet this man his grandmother loved. The man he hated as a child, the man who forced him into the shadows making him a nobody. Finally, when he announced he was going to see his uncle Ali, his family was against it. His mother cried, "You will not come back, you will end up like my brother."

When he first met his uncle, Ali, he said he was cold, his emotions tied up in a cage, while Ali, this middle-aged man, hugged him with tears in his eyes: "Hilal, welcome, I am so happy to see you. You have honored us by coming." Spending time with his uncle he found a roller-coaster of thoughts rushing into his mind.

Hilal often stayed outside until the sun sank out of sight and darkness covered the sky. With quick lone-wolf steps he returned to his room, accompanied by the full moon.

Mum insisted that Hilal have supper, but she could not persuade him to eat. In the end, they compromised. He would take a thermos of tea and a basket of fresh fruit. He would not eat bananas or papayas. He preferred guavas, oranges, and passion fruit, just like me. Before his return, I prepared the tray and carried it to the terrace.

The room was so tidy. His blue jeans, his T-shirt—everything was folded neatly. Even the bed was made. I stretched out the white bed sheet with the palm of my hand to smooth the tiny creases left by his body. I found myself sniffing his pillow. The smell made me dizzy. Never had I felt like this. In a corner sat that beautiful oud of his. Like a sleeping baby. That night, I could hear the languid sound of the oud, the soft music it made. On silent feet, as if in a trance, I followed the notes upstairs.

I huddled in a corner and watched Hilal play and sing, his voice melancholy. The electric light bulb hanging from the ceiling was off and his face was lit by the moon. Our eyes met for the first time. He invited me to sit next to him as he continued to play and sing long verses. I could feel each note like a raindrop flowing over my body, and then his arm was around me. It was the first time a boy had touched me. He was my cousin.

Hilal said, "Ayah, your name makes me think of my grandmother. You are so beautiful." He stroked my face with his hand and touched my thick braids until I moved away, embarrassed.

I said, "Your hair is beautiful, like my father's."

Hilal laughed. "My grandmother used to say I had the same hair and eyes as your father. I was jealous of him growing up. Almost hated him."

"My father suffered, not being able to see his family."

"I am here now, Ayah."

"Mum and my father are happy you came."

He moved close to me again put his arm around me. I lay my head on his shoulder.

* * *

At school word of our guest spread. My friends said, "Ayah, your cousin is so handsome. What is he like?"

"I saw him at the market. He doesn't look at girls."

"Is he here to propose to you?"

"You would be lucky to become his bride."

Trying not to show my emotions, I said, "He is very reserved and doesn't talk much."

I longed for the night to come. I yearned for his songs. Silently I tip-toed up the stairs. We talked a lot.

"Ayah," he asked, "What are your secret dreams?"

I felt safe with him: I whispered, "I want to become a soccer player."

He was not surprised and didn't tease me.

"You can become anything you want."

"And you Hilal? What are your dreams?"

"I want to be a famous musician. Travel all over the world. Ayah, you are my soul mate."

My head went hazy. Every inch of my body was alive. I forgot to be embarrassed about being alone with a boy.

In the morning, this magic dissolved. Hilal was distant, not a muscle in his face revealing emotion. I wasn't sure what was real. A remorseful voice whispered, *"Ayah, what will your parents think? What if people come to know?"*

I longed for the night, hoping Hilal would be there waiting for me, reassuring me with his tenderness. He made me feel beautiful and cherished. We became lovers.

He breathed sweetly in my ear: "Ayah, you will be my bride."

"Will you tell your family? Will they accept me?"

He did not answer.

"When are you going to tell *Baba*?"

"I have to find the right moment."

At home, I stayed in my room pretending to study to avoid conversations with Mum. I remembered how she said, "Allah rewards patience."

I woke up to hear my father's voice, asking my mother, who was frying *mandazi* for breakfast. "Where is Hilal? Why is he not up?"

Mother's voice was shrill: "Ali, go to his room and see if the boy is well."

In my room, I worried, hoping and praying he was alive. It seemed ages before father came down. I could only hear a feeble voice: "Hilal has gone."

My heart sank. My hands trembled. I was blind to my surroundings. Voices grew muffled and I couldn't grasp what they said. He left in the night like a thief.

I became detached. Our house became silent as a graveyard. People gossiped.

"What a shame! Ali's nephew left without saying good-bye."

"I wonder what happened. What are they hiding?"

"We thought he came to propose to his cousin Ayah."

My father's shoulders fell, as if carrying a heavy load. His head sunk between his shoulders, like a wounded bird. He did not invite his customers to sit and chat over a *khahawa*. They respected his grief.

My friends at school pitied me with their eyes. I wanted to disappear from the world.

"Why did your cousin leave?" some asked.

I didn't know what to answer.

I didn't want to be at school. I felt sick.

At home, the smell of frying onions and garlic made me vomit. Each morning, I felt sick. Mum watched me, but said nothing. Her eyes terrified me. It was as though she could read my mind. I wanted to escape, to hide away in a far country. I don't know what was happening to me. I had dark circles beneath my eyes. I stayed in bed, crying. I could not sleep. Hilal's voice whirled in my brain, like a Dervish under the moon.

* * *

I had never felt so lonely in my own home. My mother was so distant and did not embrace me in the morning, did not place a hand on my shoulder. She did not smile. I was cut off from her. I was disappearing like a ghost.

Mother asked me: "Ayah, don't lie to me. Have you missed your period?"

I confessed.

"Ayah, you are pregnant."

I was silent.

"Did he force you?"

I burst into tears.

Mum was shocked. Her suspicions were true. How could her own daughter have done such a thing? She was to blame. She was not a good mother. She did not teach her daughter how to be respectable. What was she to do now? She had heard of girls getting pregnant, running away from home. She wished I had never been born.

Mum confined me to the guest room. I was a prisoner. That place, once so fantastical, was gloomy now. I could hear *jinn* teasing me, see fish-shaped yellow eyes laughing at me. I opened my eyes searching for them. They dissolved in the air.

Mum told everyone I was not well, that I needed rest. Food poisoning, she said. I was not to be disturbed. I felt guilty, worthless. I had done something terribly wrong. I should have been punished for my sin. The shame on my family.

I had betrayed my father. *H*e always trusted me. He was always proud to take me places where only boys were allowed: night safaris, sleeping in tents. To the beach where men chanted on *Moulid*, the birthday of the Prophet.

My father came to my room. "Ayah, my child, how are you feeling? Do you need a doctor?"

"No," I said, "I will soon be better; it is my tummy, something I ate. The fish at the market was not fresh." I didn't cry.

"Rest, my dear." He stroked my head, murmured a prayer, and left the room.

Mum was in the kitchen. I smelled boiled henna root and herbs, and listened as she filled bottles. She forced me to drink the disgusting liquid. Her hands were shaking. I swallowed the dense bitter potion to the last drop. I was terrified, not knowing what to expect.

I was alone in my room, shut away. I thought I would throw up. I felt painful contractions, like the worst menstrual pain. I sweated. I fell asleep between bouts of pain. I lost a sense of time.

At daybreak, sunlight fills the room. A sharp pain in my back wakes me. I am wet between the legs. I wish the sun would sink back, that it had never risen, and that darkness still covered the earth.

Questions of Authoriality and Literary *Meticciato* in *Scrivere di Islam: Raccontare la diaspora*

Simone Brioni

Shirin Ramzanali Fazel's short story "The Guest," included in this collection, can be seen as representative of the author's body of work for at least four reasons. First, it does not spectacularize the Eastern African reality; it references a commonplace episode.[1] Secondly, it problematizes racism, discussing East African prejudice against people with darker skin color (in this case, the family of a young woman, Ayah); in her previous literary works, *Lontano da Mogadiscio* (Far from Mogadishu, 1994) and *Nuvole sull'equatore. Gli italiani dimenticati* (Clouds over the Equator: The Forgotten Italians, 2010), Fazel addressed the subject of racism in Italy and in the Italian colonies. Thirdly, "The Guest" portrays Muslims who do not follow the norms of their religion, namely to follow through on a promise of marriage. Hilal's desertion of Ayah can be seen as either an act of vengeance, or an act committed by a man who is truly in love with Ayah, but feared his family would have disowned him had he followed through in marrying her. Having discussed, in other contexts, the importance of Islam in her life, Fazel aims to show the contradictions in the ways in which people practice religion or fail to follow its tenets. Lastly, "The Guest" tackles the sensitive topic of abortion rights— often under threat by religious and political authorities—reconfiguring abortion as an act done to maintain the family's honor. There is a strong link between Salwa and her daughter Ayah: if a mother fails to educate her daughter about the consequences of sex, she is blamed by the community. Ayah gets pregnant and her mother, Salwa, decides she must abort the child and assists her in doing so. Ayah complies because she feels dazed, confused, and ashamed of having dishonored her family. Although presenting some of

179

the features that characterize her literary works—such as the theme of *metic-ciato* (miscegenation), the complex relationship between a mother and a daughter—this short story expands the East African geographic territory her previous works depicted. Indeed, "The Guest" is set in a village in Tanzania rather than in Somalia, where Fazel's previous novels take place. A recent biographic and bibliographic note compiled by Chiara Giuliani indicates that Shirin Ramzanali Fazel has caught the attention of many scholars working on literature about emigration (2020), suggesting that her oeuvre occupies an important role in this field.

This article analyzes Fazel's literary work with a particular emphasis on *Scrivere di Islam: Raccontare la diaspora* (Writing about Islam: Narrating a Diaspora). It delineates a critical and historical context within which this text can be read, and its attempt to reverse the colonial paradigm within which an Italian critic interprets work written by an African writer, suggesting that collaboration might be a way to rethink scholarly activity in a more inclusive and diverse way. The use of the Italian term *meticciato* in the title of this article aims to emphasize its significance in the history of Italian colonialism in Somalia, Fazel's home country. Somalia was an Italian protectorate from 1885 to 1905; it then became a colony, and it was part of the Italian Empire from 1935 until the end of the Second World War. The Italian Empire in Africa included Libya, Eritrea, and Ethiopia (Del Boca 1976–1984; Labanca 2002). In 1934, when Libya became a unified Italian colony, Mussolini decided to assume the title of "Protector of Islam" in order to create alliances against France and the United Kingdom, despite the fact that he had signed the Lateran Treaty with the Catholic Church in 1929. John Wright argues that this decision sprang from political opportunism:

> The rapid conquest of the Ethiopian empire in 1935–1936 had brought many more Muslims under Italian rule: those of Eritrea, Somalia, Libya, and Ethiopia were by 1936 estimated at about nine million. Italy had thus become a leading "Muslim" power, conscious that her imperial record provided a means of enhancing or damaging her standing in Islamic opinion everywhere, but most particularly in the increasingly nationalistic Arab world. (Wright 2010, 125)

I believe that this point is significant, as Italian neofascist parties often discriminate against Muslim immigrants by referring to Europe's alleged "Christianity," thereby concealing this rather unknown, yet fundamental part of Italian history. It is equally important to point out that Italians committed the biggest mass murder of Christians in Africa, namely the 1937 "Yekatit 12" extermination. "Yekatit 12" coincides with February 19 on the Gregorian calendar. On this day, almost 20% of Addis Ababa's entire population—19,200 people—were killed in Debre Libanos, Ethiopia, in retaliation for the failed assassination attempt on a Fascist official, General Rodolfo Graziani (Campbell 2017).

Despite the numerous crimes committed by Italians in their colonies, from 1950 to 1960 the United Nations entrusted the management of Somalia (Amministrazione Fiduciaria Italiana della Somalia, AFIS) to the former colonizers, a unique case in the process of decolonization (Morone 2011; Tripodi 1999, 106–137). AFIS was a *de facto* continuation of colonial rule, during which time the Italian government questionably gave the former Fascist administration the duty of guiding this African country to independence and democracy.

The decision to give Italy this political responsibility is surprising, given that during colonialism Italians implemented a form of apartheid in their colonies, thanks to law 1019 of 1936, which denied mixed-race people the rights of citizenship, and to law 880 of 1937, which penalized interracial relationships with a five-year prison sentence (Giuliani 2018, 65–108). Italy also implemented systematic segregation measures, thanks to the 1938 racial laws. Discrimination against mixed-race individuals in colonial society had long-lasting effects both in the former colonies (Morone 2018, 167–92) and in the Italian collective imagery (Comberiati 2018, 193–215).

The term *meticcio/meticcia* (mixed-race) was employed, in a derogatory way, during colonial times, and especially during Fascism, to denote those who were not recognized as belonging to the "superior Italian race" (Giuliani Caponetto 2015). Recently, however, the term has been reappropriated to indicate collaborative, intercultural practices with an anti-racist aim. For instance, this term is used in the title of Wu Ming 2 and Antar Mohamed's *Timira. Romanzo Meticcio* (Timira. A *Meticcio* Novel). The novel recounts the story of the Somali Italian actress Isabella Marincola, and aids in the understanding of the colonial legacy in both Italy and Somalia. A passage from the book reads: "Stories belong to everybody—they emerge from a community and are returned to a community—even when they take the form of autobiography and seem to belong to an individual" (Wu Ming 2 and Antar Mohamed 2012, 503). Regarding this quote, I claimed elsewhere that "'meticcio' collaborations [. . .] are a mediation between different perspectives on History, and they can help redefining the concept of national belonging and reclaiming rights for those people who would like to be considered Italians regardless of the color of their skin" (Brioni 2014, 114). The narration of personal stories that contributes to the emergence of collective narratives and memories is at the core of my collaboration with Fazel in *Scrivere di Islam: Raccontare la diaspora*.

SHIRIN RAMZANALI FAZEL'S LIFE AND WORK

Shirin Ramzanali Fazel is an Italian writer of Somali and Pakistani origin. She was born in Mogadishu, in 1953, during Somalia's Italian trusteeship, and as a child she attended Italian schools in the Somali capital city. She moved to Italy in 1971, where she lived for periods until 1996—in Novara from 1971 to 1976 and in the Vicenza area from 1985 to 1986 and again from 1989 to 1996. She also resided in Lusaka (Zambia, 1976–78), Jeddah (Saudi Arabia, 1978–84), and New York (United States, 1986–89). From 1996 to 2004, Fazel lived in Kenya, before returning to Italy, and then moving to Birmingham, England, in 2010. Although Fazel now lives in the United Kingdom, she has maintained strong ties with Italy and goes often to Carmignano di Brenta, a village in the province of Padua, where she lived from 2005 to 2010, and where one of her daughters currently resides.

Fazel's first novel, *Lontano da Mogadiscio*, describes the author's experience of migration and the legacy of Italian colonialism in her country of origin. I emphasize elsewhere this novel's contribution to "decolonizing the Italian collective memory, testifying to a Black person's experience in Italy from the seventies to the nineties [. . .], and [to preserving] the memory of [. . .] Mogadishu [before its destruction during] a devastating civil war beginning in 1991" (Brioni 2013b, n.p.).[2] Literary works by Somali authors are published in multiple languages; Somalia did not have an official alphabet until 1972, when the Latin alphabet was introduced and recognized.[3] Fazel is a native Somali speaker, but as she moved to Italy before 1972, her written Italian is better than her written Somali. *Lontano da Mogadiscio* became a landmark text in Italian postcolonial and migration literature, and was reprinted by Datanews three times, in 1994, in 1997, and in 1999. The novel's fourth edition, *Lontano da Mogadiscio/Far from Mo g adishu,* was published in 2013 by Laurana in e-book format and in an expanded, revised, bilingual version (Italian and English, translated by the author). This edition offers new reflections on the Somali diaspora, on dislocation, on the loss of identity, and on the search for a reconciliation between past and present.[4] These ideas also emerge through her participation in Asha Siad's short film *Memories of Mogadishu* (2018), which compiles the memories of those living in the city before the outbreak of the civil war in 1991.

Fazel's second novel, *Nuvole sull'equatore. Gli italiani dimenticati* is set during the Italian trusteeship in Somalia. The novel explores the main character Amina's emancipation from male authority, and the discrimination her daughter, Giulia, faces for being a *meticcia* young woman (Burns 2013, 57). The expanded version in English *Nuvole sull'equatore: Clouds over the Equator: The Forgotten Italians* was published in 2017 (Fazel 2017a). In 2018, the author's first collection of poems in English, *Wings,* was published. The collection was subsequently published in Italian. One of these poems,

"Mare Nostrum," inspired Elizabeth Bossero's composition for the flute "Silentium Nostrum" (2018).

Fazel's intellectual and public activity is not limited to her writing; it also encompasses her research and presentations at cultural institutes and universities (Brioni 2020, 18–19). For example, from 2013 to 2016 the author was on the advisory committee for "Transnationalizing Modern Languages," a research project aiming not only at creating innovative methods for teaching modern languages and cultures in universities, but also at developing research practices that could impact culture and society beyond academia. Fazel's appointment recognizes the relevance of her creative work to postcolonial and decolonial studies in the Italian context. Fazel also conducted two creative writing workshops: "I Write with More Than One Voice" and "Writing across Languages and Cultures," which included writers from Nigeria, Sudan, Somalia, Croatia, France, Bulgaria, and Poland, who had emigrated to the United Kingdom. The workshop's composition mirrored the cultural diversity in Birmingham; people from different cultures who do not often have the opportunity to meet and express their multilingual identity in English. The project's website emphasizes that interdisciplinary activities facilitate "a better understanding and communication between and across diverse cultures," inviting workshop participants to examine the "role of translation, understood in its broadest sense, in the transmission, interpretation, and sharing of languages, values, beliefs, histories, and narratives." Moreover, these transnational and participative research practices offered new resources and theoretical tools to answer a key question in a globalized society: "How do people respond creatively to living in a bilingual or multilingual environment and to identifying themselves as mobile individuals or communities?"

ISLAM AND ME

Fazel developed the core of "Io e l'Islam" (Islam and Me) in 2007. The first draft was completed in 2009 and is a poetic account of the discrimination Muslims experience in Italy. In 2018, Fazel rewrote it using the poetic draft as its impetus and source material. In its current form, "Io e l'Islam" is an autobiographical account that develops into a critique of the media's erroneous connection between Islam and extremism.[5] At the same time, "Io e l'Islam" testifies to the undeniable impact this representation has on many Italian Muslims, who are subjected to verbal and physical abuse in a suffocating atmosphere of hostility and hatred. According to recent research, "many Italians see [. . .] Muslims as a threat to national safety: four out of ten disagree with the claim that Islam is a peaceful religion" (Dixon et al. 2018, 104).

This perception of Muslims in Italy has greatly influenced the internal political debate. For instance, the xenophobic political party "Lega" (The League)—which has played a significant role in recent Italian history and has been part of four government coalitions (1994; 1999–2003; 2008–2011; 2018–2019)—tried to prevent Muslim communities from building mosques in Italy, a right that is granted by article 19 of the Italian Constitution. "Io e l'Islam," as the title suggests, narrates the personal experiences of a European citizen who is considered to be "different" due to her skin color and the wearing of the *hijab*. Fazel recounts a story familiar to other Muslim women in Europe and which counteracts a uniform and homogenizing account of Muslim culture.[6]

"Io e l'Islam" is divided into five chapters. The personal dimension suggested by the title invites the reader to appreciate the ways in which individuals interact with collective identities, be those religious or national. The first chapter, "Cara Italia" (Dear Italy), recounts several episodes the writer experienced while she was living in Italy, and shows the change in the social perception of African immigrants from the 1970s to the present. "Cara Italia" speaks of the ambivalent relationship that many Italians of the diaspora have with Italy, summarized in the last sentence of the section, "Con gli occhi di chi ci vive" (From the Locals' Perspective): "To look at Italy from within and from abroad, is an exercise I could happily do without. This is my country, too" (Fazel 2020, 21).

The second chapter, "Il mio Islam quotidiano" (My Daily Islam, Fazel 2020, 58–69), narrates her relationship to her faith and her daily spiritual practice. This chapter includes prayers and a subjective explanation of the precepts of Islam in daily practice. Fazel features other Muslim women's accounts, sometimes using the third person singular, sometimes the first person singular, as if to underscore her proximity to the stories she is telling. Although this section describes a personal spiritual journey, it is possible to read it in relation to other places in the text where Fazel discusses Islamophobia and the inability of Italian institutions to respect religious freedom—a reading which sheds light on the political dimensions of private experiences: religion may offer shelter and protection from a society that is often hostile. Moreover, the account of Fazel's private religious experience has political implications because Muslims are often depicted as a collective subject, rather than as a group of individuals who experience their spirituality in different ways. Muslims comprise 2% of Italy's population today. They are mostly Sunni, but come from different countries, including Morocco, Albania, Tunisia, Senegal, Egypt, Bangladesh, and Pakistan. It is perhaps because of this heterogeneity that Italian Muslims have not been able to reply cohesively to the attacks they have received to date.

The third chapter, "Birmingham, UK" (Fazel 2020, 70–81), compares Fazel's life in the United Kingdom to her past experience living in Italy. In

Lontano da Mogadiscio, Fazel rediscovered Somalia through Italy; in "Io e l'Islam," the author looks at Italy from the perspective of life in the United Kingdom. In this chapter, as well as in other parts of the text, the author uses the first-person plural pronoun to refer to, in different contexts, either women or Birmingham residents, Italians, Somalis, or Muslims, exposing the author's fluid identity and a sense of belonging that is constantly renegotiated. The section "Small Heath Park" has a special role in the chapter, as it describes the neighborhood in South-East Birmingham where the Ghamkol Sharif Mosque is situated. This is one of the biggest mosques in the United Kingdom, and a point of reference for Muslims and Somali people in Britain. The documentary *Africa Is You: The Somali-Dutch Community in Birmingham, UK* (2016) by Linde Luijnenburg, Ahmed Magare, Dennis Mulder, and Anna van Winden was filmed in this neighborhood, which testifies to its centrality in the affective geography of Somali migrants in the Midlands.

In the fourth chapter, "Islamofobia" (Islamophobia, Fazel 2020, 81–86), Fazel documents the accounts of many women and men who have been subjected to racism because they were Muslim. As Laura Mahalingappa, Terri Rodriguez, and Nihat Polat point out, religious discrimination has psychological, emotional, and social implications, thus it is important to safeguard any religious belief in its diversity (2017, 4–6). The stories that are gathered in this chapter remind us that for too long Catholicism has been presented as an invisible norm in Italian identity.

The last chapter, "Contraddizioni" (Contradictions, Fazel 2020, 86–92), presents Fazel's critiques to the *umma*, the community of Muslim worshippers. Fazel's inability to connect with some of interpretations of Islam's precepts inspired my relationship with the subject of this study. I am not a Muslim, and my interest in this religion is a way to promote not only religious diversity in Italy, but also secularism. In a country where the word "cristiano" (Christian) is still used as a synonym for "person," to understand different religions is of primary importance in the protection of civil rights.[7]

One could see *Scrivere di Islam. Raccontare la diaspora* as stemming from the critical reflection Charles Burdett initiated in *Italy, Islam and the Islamic World: Representations and Reflections, from 9/11 to the Arab Uprisings* (2016), albeit from a different angle. Burdett advocates a reexamination of Italian Studies, one which stresses the presence of new subjects and new identities as a result of migration. The most complete study of representations of Islam in Italy to date, *Italy, Islam and the Islamic World* analyzes various "cultural practices of signification" (Burdett 2016, 7), including novels on Muslim migrants in Italy, texts on the Arab Spring, travel books on Iran and Afghanistan, and sociological essays on Muslim communities in Italy. Burdett also focuses on journalist Oriana Fallaci's racist texts and conspiracy theories, which present Islam as intending to destroy the Western world (Fallaci 2001; Fallaci 2004a; Fallaci 2004b).[8]

In addition to the subject matter, Burdett's text inspired the creation of *Scrivere di Islam: Raccontare la diaspora* because it is written in a manner that attracts the general public, despite being targeted at an academic audience. Moreover, *Italy, Islam and the Islamic World* demonstrates that "though it may be tempting to think of Italian culture as in some way self-contained, separate and distinctive from other cultures [...] it is continually defined and redefined by its interactions with social and economic phenomena from across the globe" (Burdett 2016, 15).

By applying a transnational dimension to the study of a national culture, Burdett poses questions that are vital to understanding the postcolonial, multicultural, and multireligious identity of contemporary Italy:

> What is the nature of the Italy that we study? What is the meaning of the nation state in a transnational world? How can we think beyond territorially bounded notions of Italian culture? Are our methodologies adequate to address a social, cultural, and *religious* reality that is, under the pressure of globalization, changing at an extremely rapid pace? (Burdett 2016, 198)

In an attempt to address some of these questions, *Scrivere di Islam: Raccontare la diaspora* features a section, "A quattro mani: Note collaborative sull'industria culturale, sulla scrittura diasporica e sulla pratica decoloniale" (Notes on Collaboration in Cultural Industries, on Diasporic Writing, and Decolonizing Practices, Brioni and Fazel 2020b, 93–116), written by Fazel and myself, that explores the collaborative process leading to the publication of the print editions and English translations of *Lontano da Mogadiscio/Far from Mogadishu* (2013) and *Clouds over the Equator: The Forgotten Italians* (2017a) / *Nuvole sull'equatore. Gli italiani dimenticati* (2017d).[9] "A quattro mani" is written in the form of a dialogue and discusses the opportunities for people belonging to minorities to express themselves. This conversation preceded our decision to write *Scrivere di Islam: Raccontare la diaspora* collaboratively, in a hybrid form, and through an open-access publication platform. If "minor" literature invites us to overcome the conceptual barriers of nation-states and to reconsider ideas of identity and alterity, literary criticism needs to follow this example and find new strategies for discussing the content, context, and experiences of authors. We believe that collaborative writing—intended both as a methodology and as a research trajectory—can be one of these strategies.

The hybrid dialogue between Fazel and myself focuses on five main themes—memories, belonging, points of view, translation, and the market—and concludes that although literature written by authors who immigrated to Italy is still considered "minor," it has transformed Italian culture, introducing new questions, themes, and ways of communicating in the critical debate. In this sense, Fazel's career is representative of the experience of many authors who immigrated to Italy and attempted to contradict the dominant narrative about immigration—which casts it as a problem—despite an unwelcoming publishing environment. In particular, we discuss the possibilities new technologies offer writers belonging to subaltern groups. This collaborative text aims at providing suggestions for how the Humanities can be conceptualized, including its relationship to a practical problem, namely the urgency of listening to the voices of immigrant artists and intellectuals in Italy.

ITALIAN POSTCOLONIAL LITERATURE AND THE CULTURAL MARKET

Scrivere di Islam: Raccontare la diaspora is a development—and, partly, a translation—of the collaborative essay "*Lontano da Mogadiscio* and *Nuvole sull'equatore*: Memory, Points of View, Belonging, Language, and the Market," that was commissioned for a forthcoming academic volume on "minority" cultures in Europe. Although Fazel's ideas are appealing to an academic audience, finding a general interest publisher for her work proved particularly difficult. Indeed, both *Far from Mogadishu* and *Clouds over the Equator* have been published via the Amazon self-publishing service CreateSpace. This paradox is a constant element of Fazel's publishing history: while her work has circulated in academic journals, edited volumes, and websites specializing in migration literature like *El Ghibli. Rivista di Letteratura della Migrazione* (El Ghibli. Journal of Migration Literature), she has often struggled to reach a general audience.

Our collaborative process leading to the publication of the English translations of *Lontano da Mogadiscio* and *Nuvole sull'equatore*, and to a subsequent new Italian edition, differed from the traditional relationship that exists between a writer and a literary critic. My contribution to the publication of *Lontano da Mogadiscio/Far from Mogadishu* was not limited to the writing of the introduction. I took charge of the editing and proofreading, communicating with the publishers, and marketing the book. I had a very similar role in the publication of *Nuvole sull'equatore* and *Clouds over the Equator* in 2017. For *Scrivere di Islam: Raccontare la diaspora*, I wrote the preface and coauthored a text with Fazel that was subsequently translated into Italian by her. I was editor and curator of Fazel's "Io e l'Islam," where I suggested potential stylistic and formal amendments. My contribution to the text itself was limited to proposing bibliographical references and posing questions to Fazel. In return, Fazel offered suggestions on the introduction, and reviewed the final version. Moreover, our dialogue was fundamental to the writing of my monograph, *The Somali Within*, both from a linguistic and a cultural standpoint.

Collaboration is not unusual in migration literature; indeed, it is constitutive of this specific literary genre. Since the 1990s, Italian migration literature has featured innovative authorial models, which differed from those of "canonical" literature. Texts like Pap Khouma's *Io venditore di elefanti* (I Was an Elephant Salesman: Adventures Between Dakar, Paris, and Milan, 1990, edited by Oreste Pivetta); Carla De Girolamo, Daniele Miccione, and Mohamed Bouchane's *Chiamatemi Alì* (Call Me Alì, 1990); Mario Fortunato and Salah Methnani's *Immigrato* (Immigrant, 1990); and Alessandro Micheletti and Saidou Moussa Ba's *La promessa di Hamadi* (Hamadi's Promise, 1991) have involved extensive collaboration between multiple parties. Analyzing twelve collaborative works written between 1991 and 1997, Daniele Comberiati and Bieke Van Camp underscore how Italian coauthors took on various roles, including "coauthors [. . .] curators [. . .] or author[s] of the introduction [. . .], maintaining an active role in the ideation and writing of the text" (Comberiati and Van Camp 2018, 93–94). Comberiati and Van Camp also highlight the influence of the Italian coauthor's profession in determining the type of text that was produced:

> the works by a coauthor who is a journalist feature socioeconomic considerations, and the narrative plot functions to highlight this aspect; when the coauthor is a writer, the style remains similar to that of the Italian writer's previous and consecutive literary works; lastly, when the text is coauthored by an academic, footnotes and bibliography become fundamental elements. (2018, 93)

As a result, these interactions have produced texts that are extremely difficult to categorize. For example, Comberiati and Van Camp show that *Io venditore di elefanti* is not only a literary work, but offers insight into the study of Italy's changing social reality (2018, 100).

Collaborative works addressed the "political urgency of telling stories concerning migrants'" life and aspirations that are different from those recounted by [. . .] the media (Burns 2007, 136).[10] Sometimes, these collaborations resulted in misappropriations and disagreements (Burns 2003; Parati 2005, 99–100). Often, Italian coauthors were seen as responsible for the text's narrative style, while the migrant's, or more recently, the "second generation"[11] writer's personal experience legitimized the story's authenticity. As Comberiati and Van Camp demonstrate, this vision implies that the "foreign author" is presented as a "witness rather than a writer," and overlooks the fact that the migrant coauthors were intellectuals and writers in their own countries and "had intellectual profiles that could definitely manage the autonomous production of a text" (Comberiati and Van Camp 2018, 94).

I would like to emphasize two further aspects of the collaborative writing experience. First, these collaborations attempt to fill in the Italian author's cultural and experiential gap regarding migration. Secondly, they are inspired by oral communication, therefore they focus on a dialogical dimension, in which translation processes and intercultural communication strategies assume a fundamental role. In this sense, there is a continuity between the collaborative experiences of the 1990s and more recent examples. I am thinking, for instance, of the narrative community that emerged in the documentaries I codirected with Graziano Chiscuzzu and Ermanno Guida *La quarta via. Mogadiscio, Italia* (The Fourth Road: Mogadishu, Italy, 2012) and *Aulò. Roma Postcoloniale* (Aulò: Postcolonial Rome, 2012), and which I cowrote with Kaha Mohamed Aden and Ribka Sibhatu, respectively. In the documentaries, Aden and Sibhatu tell the story of their native countries, Somalia and Eritrea, while at the same time retracing the legacy of Italian colonialism in the cities they live in, namely Pavia and Rome.

Aden describes the documentary's creative process as a "collective space, open to debate," in which Mogadishu came back to life, thanks to a "narrative community, made up of those who created the paratextual apparatuses of the documentary: translations, soundtrack, editing, photography, and those who shared with us opinions and feedback, balconies for filming, or trucks for transporting materials. This community offered their competence and their resources in order for the story to take a new form and be shared further" (Brioni 2013a, 96–97). This type of authoriality is unusual because, as Lorenzo Mari points out, "the coauthoring relationship [is] reversed: Ribka Sibhatu and Kaha Mohamed Aden are the guarantors of the documentary's validity, rather than the native Italian-speaking directors and screenwriters" (2013, 131). As a result, these documentaries are hybrid products, both autobiographical accounts and visual essays, that reference historiography and cultural theory, and were realized through collaboration with historians, translators, writers (including Fazel), literary critics, and musicians (Brioni 2013a). For this reason, *Aulò. Roma postcoloniale* and *La quarta via. Mogadiscio, Italia* were distributed with print volumes by an independent publisher and film producer in Rome: Kimerafilm.

Another interesting example of participation and hybridization in cultural works addressing colonialism in Italy is *Timira. Romanzo Meticcio* (2012), by Wu Ming 2 (Giovanni Cattabriga) and Antar Mohamed. The adjective *meticcio* in the title not only refers to the collaboration between authors of different ethnicities, it also describes the combination of texts, including primary sources, letters, and photographs. For this reason, *Timira* can either be seen as a creative nonfiction book, or a fictional book based on historical sources and on Isabella Marincola's direct testimony. This mosaic of genres is a constitutive trait of the collective of writers in Wu Ming's cultural production. Indeed, their novels feature a list of the primary sources consulted, which include historical essays, and they often comment on the narrative techniques they utilize. Wu Ming 1 (Roberto Bui)'s *New Italian Epic 2.0*

(2008) uses the essay form to problematize the dichotomy between criticism and artistic practice in contemporary literature. According to this text, theoretical reflection on the act of writing is constitutive of Italian literature from 1993 to 2008. This aspect is also present in *Timira*, which features four letters in which Wu Ming 2 interrogates his role in the collective writing process of the novel. In this sense, *Timira* successfully combines the linguistic experimentations of a writer belonging to one of the most successful writer collectives in Italy and the narrative methods of a "minor" literary genre such as migration literature. Indeed, *Timira* references some short stories and novels by Somali Italian authors, such as "Dismatria" (Exmatriates, 2005) by Igiaba Scego, in which Isabella calls Somalia her "matria" (mother country, Wu Ming 2 and Antar Mohamed 2012, 282), and *Nuvole sull'equatore* (Wu Ming 2 and Antar Mohamed 2012, 516). Reflections on collaboration, such as those appearing in *Timira,* do not feature in collaborative works of the early 1990s, and they demonstrate the coauthors' increasing awareness of and respect for the cultural process that they are experiencing.

However, I believe that attempts to consider collaborative works of the 1990s as completely different (and overall qualitatively inferior) than more recent texts, or to see an evolution from coauthored texts inspired by the writer's biography to single-authored novels with seemingly more articulated narrative structures, might overlook the fact that the first texts published by migrant authors in Italian have presented new authorial subjects and experimental and collective forms of narration. In other words, to describe this process as an "evolution" might undermine the impact of literary works that displayed not only "new possibilities [. . .] for conceiving of human identity, but also suggest[ed] new ways of creating a text" (Bond 2018, 101). I do not want to underestimate the importance of migrant writers' self-representation, but the critical emphasis on single-authored models in migrant writing can be seen as a "normalization" of the authorial figure and the role that the "author" embodies in Western culture and in the commercial marketplace.

It is equally important to point out that the texts have undergone a creative process that has increased their reach and longevity. I already referred to the cases of *Lontano da Mogadiscio,* originally published in 1994, which became a bilingual text with additional reflections from Fazel about her migration to the United Kingdom in 2010, and of Ribka Sibhatu's *Aulò. Canto-Poesia dell'Eritrea* (Aulò. Song-Poetry from Eritrea), a children's book published in 1993 that became a documentary in 2009 (Brioni 2014). One could also mention Fernanda Farias De Albuquerque and Maurizio Iannelli's *Princesa. Dal Nordest a Rebibbia: Storia di una vita ai margini* (1994), a text that was transformed into an interactive project edited by Ugo Fracassa and Anna Proto Pisani in 2013.

Hybridity and dialogism are the two main features of the volume Fazel and I coauthored, and they appear throughout Fazel's entire literary career, although she was the first migrant writer to write about Italian colonialism without the help of a coauthor. Many academic articles emphasize *Lontano da Mogadiscio*'s hybrid nature, given that this text is at the same time a travelogue, an autobiographically inspired story, an account of life in a city devastated by the civil war, and a journalistic essay that has been introduced to the Italian audience by a journalist, Alessandra Atti di Sarro (1994, 8–10). For this reason, Rhiannon Noel Welch defines the narrative voice in *Lontano da Mogadiscio* as "autobiographical and anthropological" (2010, 217), and Burns claims that this text is "at once familiar (autobiography, testimony, narrative) and perplexing (all and none of these)" (2006, 177). Loredana Polezzi describes *Lontano da Mogadiscio* as "a patchwork of passages, often less than a page long, which take a multitude of forms: from the poem to the mini-historical essay to the etymological gloss, the anecdote, the list, or the intimate diary entry. [. . .] the fragmented structure of the [text] is also symptomatic of the fractured personal and collective histories with which [the author identifies]" (2006, 219). In other words, *Lontano da Mogadiscio*'s narrative form mirrors its subject matter, and its description of a diasporic experience cannot be reduced to a specific genre.[12]

After the publication of *Lontano da Mogadiscio,* Fazel gave several interviews to discuss the book and its main themes that were published in academic volumes.[13] These interviews suggest that research on the diaspora requires contributions from diasporic subjects to understand the narration of migration in all its complexity. These participative texts not only testify to academic interest in Fazel's work, they also suggest their authors' intention to overcome the limits of a Eurocentric Humanities education and to better understand the multicultural reality of contemporary Italy. As I wrote in a blog post with Cecilia Brioni on collaborative practices, there is still a tendency to view lecturers and professors in the Humanities as elitist, solitary figures, whose approach to understanding modernity originates from their innate individual qualities and their studies rather than from their experiences in the world (Pease 1995). Collaboration helps to break the boundaries between disciplines, enriching textual analysis, and above all situating research practices in a social and cultural context: "To show that knowledge originates from a dialogue locates the researchers' activity within a set of power relationships broader than just those expressed by the omniscient figure of the 'genius' or the one-way relationship between a single author and a 'text' to analyze" (Cecilia Brioni and Simone Brioni 2018).[14]

An influential essay by Roberto Derobertis on the subject argues for the importance of positioning and situating one's own research: "When we talk about postcoloniality, where do we situate ourselves, namely those who are discussing postcoloniality in Italy? [. . .] This 'starting from myself' comes from the need to question [. . .] the 'position' from where we are making

Italian postcoloniality, and the stories, languages, maps, places, issues of gender, race and class" (Derobertis 2014, n.p.).

My collaboration with Fazel in *Scrivere di Islam: Raccontare la diaspora* enabled me to question the role of cultural workers through my own personal experience, starting from the assumption that academia is not an impartial space of knowledge production, but rather a context that needs to be constantly reinvented, because it is troubled by social, economic, and historical tensions. As I wrote elsewhere, the Italian literary canon is a clear example of the production of patriarchal, classist, white, Catholic, and heteronormative privilege: to put it into question means to rethink what defines Italianness and who is excluded from this "imagined community" and from the rights that belonging to it entails (Brioni 2015, 145–55). Migration literature completely changed my perception of what we consider "Italian literature" and suggested new questions and priorities for scholars working in the field of Italian Studies. In my personal experience, it interrogated the ways in which my research practices either allow or contest the perpetuation of this privilege.

The dialogical dimension of *Scrivere di Islam: Raccontare la diaspora* also tried to expand the academic debate and to facilitate dialogue between different subjects and disciplines, between the study of cultural artifacts and artistic practices. To find a synergy between those who create artistic works and those who analyze them can produce a social transformation, offering engaging and inclusive fruition opportunities. If critical thinking and interpretation are fundamental to the creation of an artwork, art offers critical thinking practices the chance to develop a pleasurable aesthetic experience which could facilitate civic education (Sommer 2014). The Humanities' engagement with social issues could break those institutional barriers, excluding certain subjects from the academic context. In an age characterized by the massive presence of fake news (O'Connor and Weatherall 2019; Zimdars and McLeod 2020), the Humanities should be rigorous in finding new ways of conveying different perspectives in order to overcome a unilateral and Eurocentric vision, especially when it comes to narrations around Muslims in Italy that are toxic, if not overtly racist.

The application of a scientific method to the disciplines connected to the Humanities has led to increasing selectiveness in the publication process, which often requires external review. In commercial publishing too, texts are reviewed by an editor collaborating with the author to create a work that is stylistically and formally acceptable, and above all palatable to the cultural industry (Gross 1962). It would therefore be shortsighted not to include these professional figures' contribution to the text that is published. Even though *Scrivere di Islam: Raccontare la diaspora* is neither an academic essay nor an autobiographical account, its revision process conforms to the contemporary textual production process, where numerous professional figures collaborate on the creation of the literary work. The text also aims to problematize the idea that literary criticism can interpret a literary work better than the author can. This concept is reminiscent of a colonial model, especially when it refers to postcolonial or migration literature in Italian. Indeed, our collaboration went against the model of white literary critic having the last word on a writer of African origin's work.

Contemporary Italian culture cannot be limited to national borders. Its analysis requires a redefinition of disciplinary fields, a promotion of intersectionality (Camilotti and Crivelli 2017), and above all, a welcoming cultural space that mirrors today's multicultural, multireligious, and multiethnic Italian society. I believe it is fundamental to interrogate Italian Studies' role in enabling the exclusion and ghettoization of foreign or minority subjects, in terms of gender, religion, race, and class. We need to develop a model that respects pluralism, intercultural translation, differences, and the complex transnational geographies that constitute every person's story. The issues surrounding the marketing and publication of *Lontano da Mogadiscio* and *Nuvole sull'equatore* inevitably had us facing questions about the uneven relationship between who controls the production of knowledge and who is subjected to it: this collaborative text is an answer to these considerations. To examine the practices through which knowledge is produced is not new to certain members of the academic community, especially those with an activist orientation (Gustavsen 2003). For example, the ideas behind the collective *Decolonize the Media* (Mirzoeff and Halberstam 2018, 213), or those stated in *Decolonize the University* (Bhambra, Gebrial, and Nisancioglu 2018), are similar to those we adopt in our project.

Traditionally, the Humanities have long privileged individual achievements over collective efforts, and they have prioritized theoretical research that had little connection to practical matters. Although a theoretical approach to culture might be useful to better appreciate practices aimed at social change, the urgency of discussing the discrimination of Muslims in Europe led Fazel and myself to develop a *meticcio*, a collaborative, hybrid text, that we hope will inspire new participative practices. If today the decolonization of Italian Studies is a priority, we wish for an increasing number of artists, activists, and researchers to put their talents and skills into practice to develop new forms of understanding between people of different cultures. These experiments would bring about methodological enrichment, the development of new theoretical standpoints, a better ethical and cultural awareness, and a new attention to the needs expressed in diaspora and postcolonial literature, so that academic research and public engagement can successfully contribute to the pursuit of social justice.

NOTES

1. An earlier version of this text was previously published in the introduction to the volume *Scrivere di Islam: Raccontare la diaspora* (Brioni and Fazel 2020, 13–36). I would like to sincerely thank Cecilia Brioni for translating the adapted text from Italian into English, and Jessica Lott for her careful linguistic revision of this article.

2. In this study, I discussed *Lontano da Mogadiscio*'s major reviews and analyzed Fazel's short stories. As I have written about her literary works in other contexts, some of the ideas in the present study reference articles I have published elsewhere. The list of publications can be found in the "Bibliography" (Brioni 2013b; Brioni 2015; Brioni 2017a; Brioni 2017b).

3. On Somali postcolonial literature, see Brioni 2015, Gerrand 2016, Lori 2013. On the literature produced in the Horn of Africa, see Ranzini, Proto Pisani, and Favier, 2016, Comberiati and Luffin 2018.

4. Starting in 2017, this publication became available in print, both in English (Fazel 2017b) and in Italian (Fazel 2017c).

5. On the Italian media's representation of migrants, see Bond, Bonsaver, and Faloppa 2015, 29–200. Among the Italian writers who have discussed Islamophobia in biographical texts, with a particular attention to the role of media, see Takoua Ben Mohamed's comics and Sumaya Abdel Qader's novel *Quello che abbiamo in testa* (What We Have in Mind, 2019).

6. On women and gender in Islam, see Salih 1998 and Ahmed 1992.

7. On the concept of "person" in relation to debates about immigration, see Lago 2001.

8. Other texts about Islamophobia in Italy include Proglio 2020, Massari 2006, Sciortino 2002, Frisina 2007.

9. Shirin and I have further expanded these reflections in the article "Scrivere di Islam: A Collaborative Project." See Brioni and Fazel 2020a.

10. For an analysis of collaborative texts, see Burns 2003, Burns 2007, Meneghelli 2006, Mengozzi 2013, Parati 2005, Romeo 2018, Wood 2006.

11. I use the term "second generation" for the sake of convenience and clarity. For a more thorough discussion of the controversial usage of this term, see Thomassen 2010.

12. This feature is quite common in postcolonial and migration literature in Italian. For instance, Geneviéve Makaping's *Traiettorie di sguardi. E se gli altri foste voi?* (Trajectories of Gaze. What If You Were the Others? 2001), a text inspired by the author's biography, is at the same time an anthropological inquiry into the relationship between Italians and the Other and with Blackness. Another example is Rino Bianchi and Igiaba Scego's *Roma Negata. Percorsi postcoloniali nella città* (Negated Rome. Postcolonial Paths in the City, 2014), a collaborative work made up of an essay by Scego and a collection of photographs by Bianchi, which testifies to the traces of colonialism in Rome.

13. See Brioni 2012, Brioni 2017b, Pesarini 2018, Venturini 2010. Literary criticism on migration literature includes *La quarta sponda* (The Fourth Shore, 2009), an influential collection of interviews with some of the main women writers on the subject, who discuss Italian colonialism and its legacy with Daniele Comberiati.

14. On the importance of locating research and of collaborative practices in transcultural research, see Wells et al. 2019, and Wall and Wells 2020.

REFERENCES

Abdel Qader, Sumaya. 2019. *Quello che abbiamo in testa*. Milano: Mondadori.

Ahmed, Leila. 1992. *Women and Gender in Islam: Historical Roots of a Modern Debate*. New Haven: Yale University Press.

Atti Di Sarro, Alessandra. 1994. "Introduzione." In Shirin Ramzanali Fazel, *Lontano da Mogadiscio*, 8–10. Roma: Datanews.

Bhambra, Gurminder K., Dalia Gebrial and Kerem Nisancioglu. 2018. *Decolonising the University*. London: Pluto.

Bianchi, Rino and Igiaba Scego. 2014. *Roma Negata. Percorsi postcoloniali nella città*. Roma: Ediesse.

Bond, Emma. 2018. *Writing Migration Through the Body*. New York: Palgrave Macmillan.

Bond, Emma, Guido Bonsaver and Federico Faloppa. eds. 2015. *Destination Italy. Representing Migration in Contemporary Media and Narrative*. Oxford: Peter Lang.

Brioni, Cecilia and Simone Brioni. 2018. "Interdisciplinarity and Collaborative Writing in the Humanities: Lara Saint Paul and the Performativity of Race." In *Interdisciplinary Italy*, May 22. Accessed June 19, 2020. http://www.interdisciplinaryi-taly.org/interdisciplinarity-collaborative-writing-huma-nities-lara-saint-paul-performativity-race/.

Brioni, Simone. 2012. "Orientalism and Former Italian Colonies: An Interview with Shirin Ramzanali Fazel." In *Orientalismi italiani: vol. 1*, edited by Gabriele Proglio, 215–25. Torino: Antares.

———. 2013a. "Pratiche 'meticce': Narrare il colonialismo italiano 'a più mani'." In *Postcoloniale italiano: Tra letteratura e storia*, edited by Franca Sinopoli. 89-119. Latina: Novalogos.

———. 2013b. "'A Dialogue That Knows No Border Between Nationality, Race or Culture': Themes, Impact and the Critical Reception of *Far from Mogadishu*." In Shirin Ramzanali Fazel, *Lontano da Mogadiscio / Far from Mogadishu*, s. p. [ebook]. Milano: Laurana.

———. 2014. "Across Languages, Cultures and Nations: Ribka Sibhatu's Aulò." In *Italian Women Writers, 1800–2000: Boundaries, Borders and Transgression*, edited by Patrizia Sambuco, 123–42. Madison: Fairleigh Dickinson University Press.

———. 2015. *The Somali Within. Language, Race and Belonging in 'Minor' Italian Literature*. Cambridge: Legenda.

———. 2017a. "Gli italiani dimenticati: 'meticciato' e l'eredità del colonialismo in Nuvole sull'equatore," translated by Cecilia Brioni. In Shirin Ramzanali Fazel, Ramzanali Fazel, *Nuvole sull'equatore. Gli italiani dimenticati. Una storia*, 207–16. Scotts Valley (CA): CreateSpace Independent Publishing Platform.

———. 2017b. "Letteratura oltre i confini. Clouds over the Equator: A Forgotten History e Wings di Shirin Ramzanali Fazel." In *Nazione Indiana*, July 19. Accessed June 19, 2020. https://www.nazioneindiana.com/2017/07/19/letteratura-oltre-confini-clouds-over-the-equator-forgotten-history-wings-shirin-ramzanali-fazel/.

———. 2020. "Scritture Meticce – Narrazioni Diasporiche." In Simone Brioni and Shirin Ramzanali Fazel. *Scrivere di Islam: Raccontare la diaspora*, 13-36. Venezia: Cà Foscari Edizioni.

Brioni, Simone and Shirin Ramzanali Fazel. 2020a. "'Scrivere di Islam': A Collaborative Project", *gender/sexuality/Italy* 7. Accessed February 23, 2021. https://www.gendersexualityitaly.com/1-scrivere-di-islam/

———. 2020b. *Scrivere di Islam: Raccontare la diaspora*, Venezia: Cà Foscari Edizioni.

Burdett, Charles. 2016. *Italy, Islam and the Islamic World. Representations and Reflections, from 9/11 to the Arab Uprisings*. Oxford: Peter Lang.

Burns, Jennifer. 2003. "Frontiere nel testo. Autori, collaborazioni e mediazioni nella scrittura italofona della migrazione." In *Borderlines. Migrazioni e identità nel Novecento*, edited by Jennifer Burns and Loredana Polezzi, 203–12. Isernia: Cosmo Iannone Editore.

———. 2007. "Outside Voices Within: Immigration Literature in Italian." In *Trends in Contemporary Italian Narrative 1980-2007*, edited by Ania Gillian and Ann Hallamore Caesar, 136–54. Newcastle: Cambridge Scholars.

———. 2013. *Migrant Imaginaries. Figures in Italian Migration Literature*. Oxford: Peter Lang.

Camilotti, Silvia and Tatiana Crivelli. 2017. *Che razza di letteratura è? Intersezioni di diversità nella letteratura italiana contemporanea*. Venezia: Edizioni Ca' Foscari.

Campbell, Ian. 2017. *The Addis Ababa Massacre. Italy's National Shame*. New York: Hurst.

Comberiati, Daniele. 2009. *La quarta sponda. Scrittici in viaggio dell'Africa coloniale all'Italia di oggi*. Roma: Caravan.

———. 2018. "Decolonization: Representing the Trusteeship Administration in Somalia." In *The Horn of Africa and Italy. Colonial, Postcolonial and Transnational Cultural Encounters*, edited by Simone Brioni and Shimelis Bonsa Gulema, 193-215. Oxford: Peter Lang.

Comberiati, Daniele and Xavier Luffin. eds. 2018. *Italy and the literatures from the Horn of Africa (Ethiopia, Eritrea, Somalia, Djibouti)*. Roma: Aracne.

Comberiati, Daniele and Bieke Van Camp. 2018. "La figura del coautore nelle letterature testimoniali in Italia." *Incontri. Rivista europea di studi italiani* 33, n. 1: 89–104.

De Girolamo, Carla, Mohamed Bouchane and Daniele Miccione. 1990. *Chiamatemi Alì*. Milano: Leonardo.

Del Boca, Angelo. 1976–84. *Gli italiani in Africa orientale*. 4 vol. Roma-Bari: Laterza.

Derobertis, Roberto. 2014. "Da dove facciamo il postcoloniale? Appunti per una genealogia della ricezione degli studi postcoloniali nell'italianistica italiana." Postcolonialitalia. In *Postcolonial Studies from the European South*, February 17. Accessed June 19, 2020. http://www.postcolonialitalia.it/index.php?option=com_content&view=article&id=56:da-dove-facciamo-il-postcolo-niale&catid=27:interventi&Itemid=101&lang=it

Dixon, Tom et al. 2018. "Un'Italia frammentata: atteggiamenti verso identità nazionale, immigrazione e rifugiati in Italia." In *The Social Change Initiative*. Accessed June 19, 2020. https://www.ipsos.com/sites/default/files/ct/publication/documents/2018-08/italyitfinal_digital.pdf

Fallaci, Driana. 2001. *La rabbia e l'orgoglio*. Milano: Rizzoli.

———. 2004a. *La forza della ragione*. Milano: Rizzoli.

———. 2004b. *Oriana Fallaci intervista sé stessa*. L'Apocalisse. Milano: Rizzoli.

Farìas De Albuquerque, Fernanda and Maurizio Jannelli. 1994. *Princesa. Dal Nordest a Rebibbia: Storia di una vita ai margini*. Roma: Sensibili alle Foglie.

———. 2013. *Princesa 20*. Edited by Ugo Fracassa and Anna Proto Pisani. Accessed June 19, 2020.http://www.princesa20.it/

Fazel, Shirin Ramzanali. 1994. *Lontano da Mogadiscio*. Roma: Datanews.

———. 2010. *Nuvole sull'equatore. Gli italiani dimenticati. Una storia*. Cuneo: Nerosubianco.

———. 2013. *Lontano da Mogadiscio / Far from Mogadishu* [ebook]. Milano: Laurana.

———. 2017a. *Clouds Over the Equator. The Forgotten Italians*. Scotts Valley (CA): CreateSpace Independent Publishing Platform.

———. 2017b. *Far from Mogadishu*. Scotts Valley (CA): CreateSpace Independent Publishing Platform.

———. 2017c. *Lontano da Mogadiscio*. Scotts Valley (CA): CreateSpace Independent Publishing Platform

———. 2017d. *Nuvole sull'equatore. Gli italiani dimenticati. Una storia*. Scotts Valley (CA): CreateSpace Independent Publishing Platform.

, and Simone Brioni. 2020. "Io e l'Islam." In *Scrivere di Islam. Raccontare la Diaspora*, 37–92. Venezia: Cà Foscari Edizioni.

Fortunato, Mario and Methnani Salah. 1990. *Immigrato*. Roma: Theoria.

Frisina, Annalisa. 2007. *Giovani musulmani d'Italia*. Roma: Carocci.

Gerrand, Vivian. 2016. *Possible Spaces of Somali Belonging*. Melbourne: Melbourne University Publishing.

Giuliani, Chiara. 2020. *Shirin Ramzanali Fazel*. Forthcoming. https://modernlanguages.sas.ac.uk/research-centres/centre-study-contemporary-womens-writing/ccww-languages/italian

Giuliani, Gaia. 2018. *Race, Nation and Gender in Modern Italy: Intersectional Representations in Visual Culture*. New York: Routledge.

Giuliani Caponetto, Rosetta. 2015. *Fascist Hybridities. Representations of Racial Mixing and Diaspora Cultures Under Mussolini*. New York: Palgrave.

Gross, Gerald. ed. 1962. *Editors on Editing. What Writers Need to Know About What Editors Do*. New York: Grove Press.

Gustavsen, Bjørn. 2003. "New Forms of Knowledge Production and the Role of Action Research." *Action Research* 1, vol. 2: 153–64.

Khouma, Pap. 2010. *I Was an Elephant Salesman: Adventures Between Dakar, Paris, and Milan*, translated by Rebecca Hopkins. Bloomington: Indiana University Press.

Labanca, Nicola. 2002. *Oltremare. Storia dell'espansione coloniale italiana*. Bologna: il Mulino.

Lori, Laura. 2013. *Inchiostro d'Africa. La letteratura postcoloniale somala fra diaspora e identità*. Verona: Ombre Corte.

Mahalingappa, Laura, Terri Rodriguez and Polat Nihat. 2017. *Supporting Muslim Students. A Guide to Understanding the Diverse Issues of Today's Classrooms*. Lanham: Rowman and Littlefield.

Makaping, Geneviéve. 2001. *Traiettorie di sguardi. E se gli 'altri' foste voi?* Soveria Manelli: Rubbettino.

Mari, Lorenzo. 2013. "Simone Brioni (a cura di), Somalitalia. Quattro Vie per Mogadiscio. Somalitalia: Four Roads to Mogadishu; Ribka Sibhatu, Aulò!Aulò!Aulò! Poesie di nostalgia, d'esilio e d'amore. Aulò! Aulò! Aulò! Po-ems of Nostalgia, Exile and Love." *La Libellula. Rivista di Italianistica* 5: 130–32.

Massari, Monica. 2006. *Islamofobia: la paura e l'islam*. Roma: Laterza.

Meneghelli, Donata. 2006. "Finzioni dell'io nella letteratura italiana della migrazione." *Narrativa* 28: 39–51.

Mengozzi, Chiara. 2013. *Narrazioni contese. Vent'anni di scritture italiane della migrazione*. Roma: Carocci.

Micheletti, Alessandro and Saidou Moussa Ba. 1991. *La promessa di Hamadi*. Novara: De Agostini.

Mirzoeff, Nicholas and Jack Halberstam. 2018. "Decolonize Media. Tactics, Manifestos, Histories." *Cinema Journal* 57, vol. 4: 120–23.

Morone, Antonio Maria. 2011. *L'ultima colonia. Come l'Italia è ritornata in Somalia, 1950–1960*. Bari-Roma: Laterza.

———. Antonio Maria. 2018. "Racism: Meticci on the Eve of Colonial Down-fall." In *The Horn of Africa and Italy. Colonial, Postcolonial and Transnational Cultural Encounters*, edited by Simone Brioni and Shimelis Bonsa Gulema, 167–92. Oxford: Peter Lang.

O'Connor, Caitlin and James Owen Weatherall. 2019. *The Misinformation Age: How False Beliefs Spread*. New Haven; London: Yale University Press.

Parati, Graziella. 2005. *Migration Italy. The Art of Talking Back in a Destination Culture*. Toronto: University of Toronto Press

.

Pease, Donald. 1995. "Author." In *Critical Term for Literary Studies*, edited by Frank Lentricchia and Thomas McLaughlin, 105–17. Chicago: Chicago University Press.

Pesarini, Angelica. 2018. "Dinamiche neocoloniali di genere, 'razza' e migrazione. L'universo femminile di Shirin Ramzanali Fazel in Nuvole sull'equatore'." In *Donne e Sud. Percorsi nella letteratura italiana contemporanea*, edited by Ramona Onnis and Manuela Spinelli, 127–35. Firenze: Franco Cesati.

Polezzi, Loredana. 2006. "Mixing Mother Tongues: Language, Narrative and the Spaces of Memory in Postcolonial Works by Italian Women Writers (part 2)." *Romance Studies* 24, vol. 3: 215–25.

Proglio, Gabriele. 2020. *Islamofobia e razzismo. Media, discorsi pubblici e immaginario nella decostruzione dell'altro*. Torino: Edizioni SEB27.

Ranzini, Paola, Anna Proto Pisani and Olivier Favier. eds. 2016. *Les littératures de la Corne de l'Afrique. Regards croisés*. Paris: Karthala.

Romeo, Caterina. 2018. *Riscrivere la nazione. La letteratura italiana postcoloniale*. Milano: Mondadori.

Salih, Ruba. 1998. *Musulmane Rivelate. Donne, Islam, Modernità*. Roma: Carocci.

Scego, Igiaba. 2005. "Dismatria." In *Pecore nere*, edited by Flavia Capitani and Emanuele Coen, 5–21. Roma-Bari: Laterza.

Sciortino, Giuseppe. 2002. "Islamofobia all'italiana." *Polis* 16, vol. 1: 103–123.

Sibhatu, Ribka. 1993. *Aulò. Canto-Poesia dell'Eritrea*. Roma: Sinnos.

———. 2012. *Aulò! Aulò! Aulò! Poesie di nostalgia, d'esilio e d'amore / Aulò! Aulò! Aulò! Poems of Nostalgia, Exile and Love*. Edited by Simone Brioni, translated by André Naffis-Sahely. Roma: Kimerafilm.

Sommer, Doris. 2014. *The Work of Art in the World. Civic Agency and Public Humanities*. Durham: Duke University Press.

Thomassen, Bjørn. 2010. "'Second Generation Immigrants' or 'Italians with Immigrant Parents'? Italian and European Perspectives on Immigrants and Their Children." *Bulletin of Italian Politics* 2: 21–44.

Tripodi, Paolo. 1999. *The Colonial Legacy in Somalia. Rome and Mogadishu: from Colonial Administration to Operation Restore Hope*. London: Palgrave Macmillan.

Venturini, Monica. 2010. "Incontro con Shirin Ramzanali Fazel: tra Italia e Somalia." In *Controcànone—Per una cartografia della scrittura coloniale e post-coloniale italiana*, 137–46. Roma: Aracne.

Wall, Georgia and Naomi Wells. 2020. "Emplaced and Embodied Encounters: Methodological Reflections on Transcultural Research in Contexts of Italian Migration." In *Modern Italy* 25, vol. 2: 113–129.

Welch, Rhiannon Noel. 2010. "Intimate Truth and (Post)colonial Knowledge in Shirin Ramzanali Fazel's Lontano da Mogadiscio." In *National Belongings. Hybridity in Italian Colonial and Postcolonial Studies*, edited by Jaqueline Andall and Derek Duncan, 215–33. Oxford: Peter Lang.

Wells, Naomi et al. 2019. "Ethnography and Modern Languages." *Modern Languages Open* 1, vol. 1. Accessed June 19, 2020. http://doi.org/10.3828/mlo.v0i0.242

Wood, Sharon. 2006. "A 'Quattro Mani': Collaboration in Italian Immigrant Literature." In *Collaboration in the Arts from the Middle Ages to the Present*, edited by Sara Bigliazzi and Sharon Wood, 151–62. Aldershot: Ashgate.

Wright , John. 2010. "Mussolini, Libya and the Sword of Islam." In *Italian Colonialism*, edited by Ruth Ben Ghiat and Mia Fuller, 121–30. New York: Palgrave Macmillan.

Wu Ming 1. 2008. "New Italian Epic 2.0. Memorandum 1993–2008. Letteratura, sguardo obliquo, ritorno al futuro." *Wu Ming Foundation Website*. Accessed June 19, 2020.https://www.wumingfoundation.com/italiano/WM1_saggio_sul_new_italian_epic.pdf

Wu Ming 2 and Antar Mohamed. 2012. *Timira. Romanzo meticcio*. Torino: Einaudi.

Zimdars, Melissa and Kembrew McLeod. (2020). *Fake News: Understanding Media and Misinformation in the Digital Age*. Cambridge (MA); London: MIT Press.

Albania Mon Amour

*Tales of Female Love and Duty in the Italian Writings
of Vorpsi, Dones, and Ibrahimi*

Lidia Radi

"I went abroad and Albania seemed a distant planet to me." Thus did Bessa Myftiu defend her decision to write in French about her Albanian experience after emigrating to Switzerland in the early 1990s (Vizion Plus TV 2014).[1] Similarly, Ornela Vorpsi, an Albanian writer living in France,[2] declared it impossible to narrate her childhood stories in her native language. Accordingly, she embraced a foreign language both as a survival tool that distanced her from the past and as a literary device that avoided a pathetic or melodramatic style (Bond, Burns, and Mauceri 2013, 211–12). Anilda Ibrahimi, an Albanian emigré to Rome who composes her novels in Italian, further underscores the fraught correlation between language and identity by claiming that in the postmodern world, all identities are contaminated since they are in constant movement (Pedrazzi 2018). She is able to tell old Albanian stories and narrate her own past because the "reenactment of [her] memories and impressions has happened elsewhere, in a neutral space, strengthened by a distinct distance, both geographical and linguistic" (Pedrazzi 2018).

In these accounts, Albania, despite its close geographical proximity to the Western world—coastal Italy is only forty-five miles away—is perceived even by its own intelligentsia as a far-away country, a distant planet even, whose remote reality cannot be represented by its own language. It has to be narrated in a kind of trans-literation through the lenses of another mentality and by means of a foreign tongue. Albania, this small country of approximately 28,000 km^2 has remained mysterious to Western scrutiny due to its history of almost five hundred years of Ottoman domination and five decades of ruthless communism. These two somber historical chapters were connected by a short-lived declaration of independence proclaimed on November 28, 1912, and subsequent short foreign invasions until 1945 (Halili 2013, 47). Post-communist Albania[3] developed a variegated political and cultural landscape, juggling between modern democracy, corruption, and the ghosts of a recent communist past. In the summer of 1990, thousands of Albanians entered foreign embassies seeking better lives abroad. A few months later, many others escaped by boat towards the coasts of Italy or hiked across the border to Greece. It is estimated that between 1990 and 2002, almost half a million Albanians left their country to migrate elsewhere (King-Mai 2011, 68–70).

The three women writers whose works are examined in this article are likewise migrants from Albania. Elvira Dones left communist Albania and her family in 1988. During a professional trip to Italy, she fled to Switzerland where she reunited with her now-husband following a dramatic sequence of events masterfully described in her first autobiographical work, *Dashuri e Huaj* (*Senza Bagagli* [No Baggage]). She is now a renowned writer, documentarist, and journalist who lives and works between Switzerland, Albania, Italy, and the United States (Radi 2018). Both Vorpsi and Ibrahimi left Albania in the early 1990s, after the fall of communism, and have lived in other countries for various periods of time. Vorpsi arrived in Italy in 1991. After completing her studies at the Accademia di Brera, she moved to Paris in 1997, where she still resides, having become a naturalized citizen (Vorpsi 2010). Ibrahimi lived in Switzerland between 1994 and 1997 and then permanently established herself in Rome (Hein 2010, 300).

These three writers are the most well-known, celebrated, and award-winning Albanian female writers in Italian transnational literature (Romeo 2018, 24–27), and their first works in Italian[4] —the principal focus of this analysis—came out within a few years of each other. Vorpsi's *Il paese dove non si muore mai* (The Country Where No One Ever Dies) first appeared in 2005, Dones's *Vergine giurata* (Sworn Virgin) in 2007, and Ibrahimi's *Rosso come una sposa* (Red Like a Bride, my translation) in 2008. All three books explore Albania's complex, painful, and at times surreal past, as well as its more recent encounters with the Western world. All three novels trace the main protagonists' migratory path toward Western contexts, and since all three were originally published in Italian, they were also first intended for a Western audience. While Dones utilizes Italian to write a story that connects Albania to the United States, Vorpsi and Ibrahimi connect the language of narration (Italian) to the country where their protagonists ultimately settle. All three works offer meaningful perspectives on the interface between two cultures, two mentalities, and two languages. On the one hand, these writers create stark depictions of life in a bunkered Albania that are mediated by their Western experience; on the other hand, they contaminate both the Italian language and Italian mentality with "Albaneisms." They force upon the Italian language Albanian expressions that are untranslatable, expressions that Italian or Western readers must make an effort to understand. Moreover, as these writers navigate the complex, difficult lives of women in an Albanian patriarchal context, they also subtly comment on Western customs and traditions, leading their readers to reevaluate their perceptions of the role of women in these so-called developed countries.

This article will examine these depictions of women in order to demonstrate how these works provide a nuanced set of perspectives on Albania and the West that resist easy contrasts between "retrograde" and "progressive," "Western" and "non-Western."

ALBANIAN "PROVINCIAL" LIFE IN *SWORN VIRGIN* AND *ROSSO COME UNA SPOSA*

Dones's *Sworn Virgin* and Ibrahimi's *Rosso come una sposa* are set in two villages in the northern and southern mountains of Albania respectively, and trace most of the historical events taking place in these locales in the course of the twentieth and early twenty-first centuries. Both villages are anchored in the *Kanun*, the most important customary Albanian oral legal tradition, which dates back to the mid-fifteenth century (Resta 1996, 15). These laws and customs have for many centuries regulated the social life of these local communities, defying the power of foreign governments and challenging "modern" reforms imposed by communism.

The descriptions of these two villages evoke the reality of their geographical isolation and their inhabitants' deference to tradition as a survival mechanism. Dones tells us that the northern mountains are considered "cursed," but Hana, the main protagonist, has more ambivalent feelings about them:

> Bjeshket e Namuna, the "cursed mountains." The name was too definitive; it left so little room for hope. And yet, close up the mountains were tame, you just needed to know how to take them. You just needed to learn to sleep there without thinking of the name, a name made up by an outsider, some traveler who knew nothing about the place. There's no curse, just caution and silence. If you don't attack them, the mountains, they'll leave you alone. (Dones 2014, 28)

The reader is immediately confronted with the dual nature of these mountains. They are described as cursed and hopeless, but only by the untrained eye of random travelers. Hana understands that the real curse comes from rebelling against the mountains. This depiction powerfully captures the main female character's life journey. As a woman, Hana knows the unforgiving rules of the *Kanun*, with which the mountains are identified. She is fully aware of the merciless power of the societal boundaries in her own community and that only by taming herself and not rebelling will she survive. This becomes the cautionary tale for the rest of the story: just as one cannot prevail over the savage forces of nature, a woman must quickly learn to suspend her will and not challenge society. According to the norms of the *Kanun*, a woman had no rights; she was exclusively at the mercy of her father, brothers, or husband (Resta 1996, 15, 41–42). Even in the context of the absolutist centrality of communist power that penetrated every corner of Albanian life, this tradition persisted.

Hana, orphaned of both parents, is raised by her uncle Gjergj and her aunt Katrina. She is a dutiful adoptive daughter who helps the household run smoothly after Katrina dies, all the while conducting her studies at the University of Tirana. When Gjergj becomes very ill, she cannot inherit the house unless she gets married, an option she forcefully rejects. Gjergj asserts: "A woman who is not married is worth nothing. [. . .] Women are made to serve men and have children" (Dones 2014, 133). Hana quickly retorts: "I don't want to be married and submit to the orders of a man, wash his feet, even. I will not be a slave. [. . .] Women are the same as men" (132–33).

On November 6, 1986, Hana becomes a *burrneshë*, a "sworn virgin." She "scratches the date on the wall of the guest room. It takes her a good hour to do it properly" (144). The precision of the date and the permanent wall incision hint at the solemnity and the irrevocability of her act. While the English translation, "sworn virgin," focuses on her sacred promise to remain a virgin, the Albanian word suggests the radical transformation from being a woman to being a man, acquiring all the rights, privileges, and freedoms that the *Kanun* gives to a man. She renames herself Mark Doda: "Now you're a man. You're a man. A man!" (145). When her uncle dies, Hana/Mark is indeed a respectable man in his community: "Men and women show him equal respect" (148). By focusing in this tradition of the *Kanun*, Dones seems to suggest that it contradicts the very difference that it wants to affirm. If masculinity boils down to a change of dress and of habits, then how can it possibly be imagined as intrinsically superior to femininity? Dones implies that her protagonist's life choice undermines the oppressive moral and social norms that regulated women's lives within her community for centuries.

Indeed, Hana's overnight transformation implicitly challenges the village's devotion to masculinity, just as the sudden respect the villagers show her illustrates their foolish blindness to reality. Who really is this Mark, the man that everyone now reveres? A woman in man's clothes, a *burrneshë*, a brave he-she whose fluid identity undermines, both in Albania and in the Western world, all of our perceptions, prejudices, and stereotypes about gender differences: "When she observes people, Hana does not see a woman or a man. She tries to penetrate the unique spirit of the individual, [. . .] to imagine the thoughts hiding behind those eyes" (158).

Thus amid these mountains that have protected and overwhelmed her (145) Hana develops a non-binary way of thinking, asserting her independence in a strict patriarchal society. Dones hints at her protagonist's autonomy by giving her the symbolic name of Hana, the Moon. In standard Albanian, *hëna* is the moon, but in the Northern Albanian dialect, *hëna* becomes *hana*. Hana's name possibly alludes to Artemis/Diana, the virgin goddess of the moon and of the hunt. Whether at her feet or adorning her head, Diana's half-moon, so often depicted in paintings,[5] is the distinct sign of a death sentence she quickly throws back at Acteon's undesirable gaze (Ovid 2009, Book III). Diana's bows and arrows are Hana's rifle that her uncle hands down to her as she walks downstairs as a *burrneshë*: "He passes her his rifle. [. . .] It has belonged to six generations of Doda clansmen. Gjergj has kept it oiled for thirty-six years" (Dones 2014, 144). Hana/Mark Doda will now become the sole defender of her/his own house. Her gaze will not kill, but the gaze will reflect back the absurdity of her village's mentality.

Ibrahimi's *Rosso come una sposa* is also set in a mountainous village, this time in the southern part of Albania. Kaltra, the village,

> was hidden among high mountains. It seemed not to be in touch with anything or anyone, except with time. [. . .] The mountains rose toward the sky like well sharpened knives. As if they wanted to cut these existences out of the world. [. . .] Yet no one in Kaltra felt isolated. They felt powerful like tombstones that, unaware, enjoy eternity. The past was the only certainty and clinging to it ensured survival. [. . .] The white houses were hidden by trees and dense vegetation, but they stood next to each other, the opposite of what one might imagine in scattered places like these. (Ibrahimi 2008, 17–18, my translation)

While Dones modifies the "cursed" nature of Hana's mountains by suggesting that this qualifier originates in a superficial understanding of them, Ibrahimi's depiction of Kaltra conveys a harsh reality that no one can escape. The village is lost amid these sharp cutting peaks that allow no way out to their human inhabitants. However, the robust white stony houses are closely connected to each other, despite what outsiders' minds might imagine. Hana's solution to the indomitable nature of the mountains and its inhabitants was to adopt "caution and silence" all the while, as Dones implies, she dissents through her absurd self-transformation. Kaltra women appear to acquiesce to the severe majesty of their mountains and the unquestionable authority of their men. They formally consent to the authority of the *Kanun*. They remain women and do not take on men's roles. But, as we quickly learn, they are in reality the absolute rulers, the peacemakers, and the diplomatic mediators in their communities. They are the main, sometimes the sole, protagonists of Ibrahimi's stories. They watch over centuries-old traditions with care and wisdom, transform their burdens into legends, and hand down their knowledge to new generations of women. Their tough, astute femininity is a subtle, indestructible thread that connects them all.

At the beginning of the story, we learn that the unforgiving laws of the *Kanun* have, in the early twentieth century during the reign of King Zog, damaged the Buronja family. Dora's great-grandfather Habib hit and accidentally killed his son's friend while the two teenagers were engaged in a trivial fight over a girl. According to the strict rule of the *Kanun*, one should "pay blood with blood" (Resta 1996, 132), but Habib's wife, Meliha, is a "wise woman." Not only does she concede to the boy's family half of their lands, she arranges and seals a peace between the two families by marrying her daughter Sultana to Omer, the brother of the killed boy. Later, another tragedy hits the family: Sultana dies in childbirth, and this time it is Omer's mother who asks Meliha to marry her fifteen-year-old daughter Saba to Omer. Saba is young but smart and wise. She is the bride covered in red clothes that opens the novel, and is presented to the readers "as a human sacrifice offered to the gods to propitiate rain" (Ibrahimi 2008, 5). In the novel, red is a symbol of life, death, and of the loss of virginity. Red is the color of the bridal dress and the maternal house roof (Carotenuto 2014, 287). Being in a loveless marriage with a man who is still in love with his dead first wife, Saba tries "not to provoke her husband's hate" in any way. Consequently, she never seeks his opinion about anything nor does she involve him in any family matters. By doing so, she makes him feel like a completely useless and ineffective man, and Omer, with his childish, primitive, and unsophisticated manners, cannot reverse Saba's behavior towards him. Overwhelmed by emotions that he is incapable of handling rationally, Omer turns to drinking *raki*. Ibrahimi purposefully retains the Albanian word to underscore the symbolic status this liquor has in Albanian culture: a solution to men's problems. After all, the lone bar of the village was for men only, where they went to drink Turkish coffee and *raki*. Men sire children, but almost never act as fathers. Omer cannot even remember his children's names just as his daughters cannot recognize his face: "His daughters are unsure of their father's face when they are out, and he doesn't even remember their names" (Ibrahimi 2008, 34).

The advent of communism introduces some emancipatory changes for women,[6] and although these changes seem to be more in form than in substance, women in Kaltra take full advantage of them as they accuse their men of patriarchalism, return to their studies, take jobs, and openly disobey their marital vows. Unlike Hana, whose story seems suspended in time, Saba keeps up with the times, as she holds Omer accountable for his patriarchal behavior by threatening to talk to the party secretary: "'Tomorrow I am going to have a chat with the secretary of the party,' said Saba. And her husband became a little lamb. One might say that she was blackmailing him. But in reality, the women of his village had been blackmailing him his whole life" (Ibrahimi 2008, 48). This exposes the truth about men's power even in the darkest times in these remote patriarchal villages. In this southern mountain village, as in those of the north, reality and its perception do not match. Ibrahimi's stories[7] give voice to women who become both the storymakers and the storytellers, the teachers of other women. They narrate about men, men who seem mostly absent or irrelevant, are consumed by alcohol, huddled alone with other men or absent from home for work. As the fragility of patriarchal authority in Kaltra is gradually revealed—in part through the stimulus of Communist ideology—Saba reaches a point where she understands that "things simply were the way they seemed to be" (Ibrahimi 2008, 49).

Dora, Saba's granddaughter, has been nourished by stories of the women of her family and village, she is part of the thread of this community of strong-willed women. In this novel, she plays a pivotal role, as she is the connection between the women of the past, her grandmother and other Kaltra women, and the future, her own children born and raised in Western countries. She carries the weight of memory, of keeping these stories alive, but she also bears the burden of change, of switching paths.

The death of the dictator Enver Hoxha in 1985 brought some mild political changes and a lessening of authoritarianism and isolation in Albania. Dora, as her grandmother Saba had done in her Kaltra village, takes advantage of this opportunity. She wants to taste some independence and she makes a solemn decision to spend the rest of her life in a capital city: "I couldn't really choose as I wished. For example, London or Paris were capitalist capitals. Only one came to mind that wasn't: Tirana" (155). Even "the air there seemed different from the rest of Albania" (155).

Tirana is idealized by both young female protagonists in Dones's and Ibrahimi's novels. During her college years in Tirana, and before her transformation into a *burrneshë*, Hana gets close to her classmate Ben. When he tries to convince her to date him, she says: "Things are different up there, the world doesn't work like you people in Tirana think it should" (Dones 2014, 127). The gap between the province and the capital is evident in Ibrahimi's book as well. Dora recalls her cousin Greta, who lives in Tirana, telling her friends: "my cousin Dora is here, the one from the province! Guys, she is Dora, yes, the one who lives in the province, I've talked to you about her, remember?" (Ibrahimi 2008, 156). Progress seems to be a natural characteristic of Tirana, and despite Hana's and Dora's complaints about the unfriendliness or even lack of compassion of its inhabitants, life in the city is described with some admiration for its open-mindedness.

Ornela Vorpsi, however, depicts the capital in a different manner, as she introduces to the reader the most vulnerable category of all: fatherless or divorced women who are single. They are a perceived threat to the "moral" order within the community. Women, outside of "progressive" Tirana, would gain independence by either becoming *burrnesha* or by forging solidarity with other married women. Vorpsi shows us that in the capital these options were not available to women who were not attached to men, and they were therefore subject to the judgmental gaze of the community.

"PROGRESSIVE" TIRANA IN *THE COUNTRY WHERE NO ONE EVER DIES*

In her first work in Italian, *Il Paese dove non si muore mai*[8] Vorpsi depicts the disruption to community life through short stories that describe her, her mother, and other beautiful, lonely women of Tirana. From the very first pages of her work, Vorpsi describes her life as *"marked"* by "stains" (2009, 6, 10) like the ones "that marked those wedding photos. The stains infected me. I can still see the brown one covering my mother's right eye and temple. Now she doesn't even try to hide her unhappiness" (Vorpsi 2009, 14). The wedding she is referring to is that of her parents' now broken marriage. Her father, a political prisoner during the communist regime, suddenly disappears from their lives at the hands of the government, causing her mother to become a lone woman, to "look sick and depressed" (13), to become "a bundle of nerves" (19), and to be affected by *"nervosa gravis"* (32), thereby marking Vorpsi's life forever. This heartbreaking beginning unleashes a succession of short stories, often unrelated to each other, but all somehow connected to the protagonist.[9] Above all, these stories serve as cautionary tales for the author herself and for others to witness: "The teenager described by Ornela Vorpsi exposes the fact that in Albanian society a woman cannot move freely, for the streets are dominated by the male gaze which undresses, penetrates, judges, and where every 'pretty girl is a slut'" (Barbarulli 2010, 132). Fatherless young Ornela is forewarned by these tragic stories that describe the unhappy fates of beautiful and lonely women living in Tirana.

The judgmental community gaze is evident from the first story in which Vorpsi describes the prejudice of the community towards her beautiful mother. After walking her audience through every step of her mother's beauty routine in preparation for her evening visits to her grandmother, Vorpsi describes "the eager eyes of our men and the jealous glances of our women following her every step down the road. I could see the envy in their eyes. There was something very bitter in them, corrosive like an acid eating through their veins and intestines. One small dose would have been enough to destroy a castle, a whole town. If they could have, they would have torn the flesh off her bones and eaten her alive . . . or thrown her to the dogs" (Vorpsi 2009, 12).

The vividness of this description conveys the fatal power that others' judgements have over lone women. The beauty of Vorpsi's mother, along with her forced solitude (she was the wife of a political prisoner), are seen as an instigation to male desire. She is quickly judged as disruptive, and is punished by the collective gaze. This community of men and women expels those who seem to create a distraction from the orderly, structured world of the *patria* (the fatherland). In the Albanian culture depicted in these short stories, displayed female beauty outside the context of a marriage becomes a community affair insofar as it blurs boundaries of desire that the regime cannot control.

The social environment depicted in this work is grim, and the solitude of these women absolute. The absence of a nurturing community is a result of the prejudices that women face whenever they are perceived to defy the rules of patriarchy. These women are repeatedly assaulted, often verbally in the streets and physically or sexually in private spaces.

They are always alone when violence happens, when they face the tragic consequences of "the insisting, penetrating, and controlling gaze that [. . .] people direct at others—especially women" (Alù 2015, 258).

In Dones's and Ibrahimi's stories, progress seems to be a distinct characteristic of the capital, just as urban spaces are routinely perceived as politically and culturally progressive, especially in the West. Vorpsi, however, gives us a more nuanced image of the city: "progress and freedom" are a reality only insofar as societal rules are not broken. The community is not there to protect the individual, but instead to keep the communal order by "repeatedly star[ing] at and gaz[ing] into other people's lives, their tragedies, and their bodies" (Alù 2015, 258).

RETURNING THE WESTERN GAZE
IN VORPSI, DONES, AND IBRAHIMI

The implicit or explicit judgment of the community is crucial to all three texts. Whether women conform, adapt, or rebel against societal rules, these rules determine most of their life choices. The migratory movements experienced by all three writers and their characters do not free them from this critical gaze—from judgments about identity and behavior that, after all, have been internalized over the centuries. Instead, they find in their cultures of destination the stimulus to re-examine their native traditions, values, and biases; to see these from a more nuanced vantage point. This does not mean simply rejecting one's origins, it means having the opportunity to perceive more fully the complexities of one's native culture. The West has often dismissed Albania as a primitive and backward country. These three writers complicate such a stereotypical narrative by helping their readers understand that even a small country like Albania embodies a multifaceted reality. In addition, in their passage between countries, they also openly and honestly turn their own critical gaze onto the Western world.

Dones's *Sworn Virgin* is structured as a journal with many scenes that switch back and forth between Hana's migratory journey to the United States and her previous life in a tiny northern village in Albania,[10] thus creating a kind of dialogue between the two cultures. Many of the entries in this atypical journal are presented as dialogues between various characters. We first meet Hana on a plane on her way to Washington as she engages in a conversation with her traveling companion Patrick. This physical journey between two places powerfully parallels Hana's complex life story: she is between two cultures, two languages (three if you include the language of narration[11]), two countries, and most importantly, two genders. Hana became a man in Albania by simply putting on men's clothes. Now she is dressed as a woman. While her clumsiness in starting to wear a skirt echoes her inexperience wearing men's clothes fifteen years earlier, her quest to find out what it means to be a woman creates more anxieties: "She is excited and lost at the same time. On the outside she looks almost like a woman. What's missing is her vision, the point of view from which she is supposed to read the world" (Dones 2014, 158). Hana's challenge is double, because she is trying to learn "femininity" in a Western context, using the English language: "She started feeling the presence of her breasts a year ago, as soon as she got her green card and decided to emigrate to America" (12). "She thought everything would be easier. When she had become Mark she had had no real experience of femininity" (158).

Her Albanian cousin Lila, who had migrated earlier to the United States, tries to help her transition between genders and countries, although she seems oblivious to Hana's anxieties: "All you're trying to do is to become a woman, not a PhD or whatever it's called" (159). Lila's impatient remark is striking in its implicit suggestion that from her perspective as an Albanian, to be a woman is easy—not even close to getting a PhD. Perhaps Dones points here to a further difficulty for Hana. Lila's inherited "Albanian" femininity is not available to her, since she must take on the task of re-acquiring her gender in the solitude of a Western context. Of course, Hana's linguistic barrier makes such a transition even more complex. The break with Albania is double: not only does Hana break her *besa*, her promise to be a sworn virgin according to the *Kanun* law, but she is also forced to do so in a foreign language and country. Interestingly the virginity of the female protagonist is key in both countries, as it determines her gender transitions. In both cases, Dones opts for a technical resolution: in Albania she becomes a sworn virgin while in the United States she goes to a gynecologist to free herself from virginity in order to align her body with Western socio-sexual values.

Ibrahimi's main character Dora faces a similar linguistic and cultural dilemma. On the one hand, what it means to be a woman happens in Italian, and it is through the lens of Western culture and language that patriarchal Albania is narrated. On the other hand, it is Italian that puts a halt to the very tradition of passing on female identity, as we have seen it throughout *Rosso come una sposa*. In a sense, Italian is the language of rebirth, of a new life outside patriarchal Albania, but her grandmother Saba would not have been able to speak or understand this new language, let alone its mentality. Dora sees herself as between "two worlds: the West and the East," (Ibrahimi 2008, 138) and decides to adopt Italian as the language of communication with her children: "I wrote to her [Saba] in the language that I speak with my children" (261). With these words, placed on the final page of her novel, Ibrahimi leaves her readers wondering whether and how the transmission of womanhood will take place now that Dora is in the West.

We are also left wondering about the lives of Eva (Vorpsi's alter-ego) and her mother in *The Promised Land*, the epilogue to *The Country Where No One Ever Dies*, after their flight from Albania to Italy. In these final pages, Vorpsi summarizes with concision and sharpness her first impressions of Italian women. The differences between real-life Italian women and those depicted on TV ads is shocking to Eva. Once in contact with Italian reality, Eva wonders "where were all those diligent housewives with perfect figures, despite having given birth to hordes of children? The women who knew how to keep their husbands happy while hanging out their family's gleaming laundry—washed with Dash detergent—to dry in the sun?" (Vorpsi 2009, 107). It is important to note here that during the period of communist rule, Italian television was the only access Albanians had to the Western world (Bond and Comberiati 2013a, 67). In this passage between countries, and in the encounter with Western reality, Vorpsi realizes that "the idealized body of Italian women is revealed to be a mediatic illusion, and migration embodies the moment in which foreign corporeality is rewritten according to a new set of standards" (Pinzi 2013, 183).

Vorpsi is asking her Western readers a fundamental question: Who determines canons of female beauty, honor, and family life in the West? The answer lies in a small but fundamental detail that only attentive eyes can decipher. Throughout her short stories, Vorpsi shows that men shaped much of women's fates in Albania. In the final pages of this work, following her encounter with the realities of Italian culture, she reveals that it is in the glossy scenery of commercials and advertisements—the famous brand of detergent that appears between dashes in Vorpsi's question—that one ought to look for standards of female beauty, family values, and women's roles in modern Western culture.

At the end of her book, Vorpsi *talks back* (Parati 2005) to her new country by drawing an interesting parallel between her native country (Albania) and the Western reality she has just embraced. She describes the random encounter that her mother (a lone woman with a suitcase) has with an Italian passerby at a bus stop: "'What's going on?' asked Eva. Blushing nervously, her mother replies: 'I think he wanted to carry my suitcase for me.' 'What did he say?' She tried to remember. He said: 'A quanto scopi?'"[12] (Vorpsi 2009, 108). Indeed, upon arrival in Italy, the female Albanian body was often literally commercialized (Pinzi 2013, 183), but of course, none of "the songs she'd [Ornela] learned by heart from the Italian hit parade" (Vorpsi 2009, 109) or of the TV adds would ever depict it.

CONCLUSION

The experience of migration, as a passage from one language to another, from one culture to another, from one world perspective to another, is at the core of these texts. This journey is not a mere geographical displacement, but a complex, nuanced movement in which the lines between departure and arrival are blurred. If the term *migrant writer* is firmly and rightly rejected by all three writers because of the restrictive category it represents, it is the very act of migration itself that allows these writers and their characters to free themselves from the societal constraints of their country of origin and allows them to evaluate Western culture without the filters automatically assumed by local intellectual and cultural traditions. The many passages involved in the migration process establish a real permeability of ideas, customs, traditions, and behaviors between the two or more countries involved in these works. Our writers' *Art of Talking Back* (Parati 2005) and their characters' outlook on their destination countries encourage fresh perspectives on the often-unquestioned norms of the "native" community. Readers are invited to embrace the freedom of a fluid mentality, one that enriches rather than isolates.

The use of a foreign language, the discomfort of the migratory process, and an introspective analysis of what it means to be a woman in patriarchal Albania and in the "free" West are inextricably linked in the three texts that this essay has examined. The familiarity of the mother tongue cannot explain or describe the abuses of the *patria*, the place of the father, and only the foreign language provides a tool for writers to express freely their femininity. However, this foreign medium is not idealized, and the freedom of the West is revealed to be, at least in part, a myth.

The complexity of these literary works that masterfully exemplify the "border and frontier conditions" (Bhabha 1994, 11) challenges the simplistic and easy etiquettes of a literature outside the "canon." These writers have torn down the barriers of what one might call monoisms, as they live, think, and write between different countries, languages, and mentalities. What they offer to their Western readers is a kind of in-between thinking. They provide thought-provoking, nuanced narratives that shake prejudice and destabilize social constructs. They invite their readers to rethink their assumptions about the countries and people they "fear," and also to examine their own assumptions from a multicultural perspective. These writers reveal and undermine the closed mentalities of both countries of origin and destination and suggest that by staying in a monocultural and monolingual context, one risks becoming blind, confusing shadows on the wall for real people.

NOTES

1. Bessa Myftiu has extensively explained her position on using a foreign language—French, in her case—to tell stories about Albania. In the preface of the Albanian version of *Confessions des lieux disparus*, Myftiu states, "This novel was originally written and published in French. Expressing myself in the language of Molière gave me an unlimited freedom. Since I write in a foreign language, this allows me to treat with a comic tone events that would otherwise be difficult to digest" (Myftiu 2010, 7, my translation).

2. In a final note to the 2018 edition of *Il paese dove non si muore mai*, Ornela Vorpsi explains the process of choosing Italian rather than her native tongue: "Albanian language would reawaken demons in me," but Italian is "a language acquired past childhood. And since it is void of childhood memories, I could shape it, formulate it, manipulate it, I could narrate what I could have not otherwise narrated, aided also by a certain recklessness that came from not possessing this language" (Vorpsi 2018, final author's note, my translation).

3. For a well-informed and thorough panorama of the dramatic years that led to the fall of communism, and mass migration to neighboring countries, please see Ervin and Ron Kubati 1991.

4. For both Vorpsi and Ibrahimi, these works are their first texts written in Italian. Dones has published other works, but they were translated from Albanian. *Vergine Giurata (Sworn Virgin)* is Dones's first Italian novel.

5. See Titian, *Diana and Actaeon*. 1556–59. The National Gallery of London.

6. Among many economic, agricultural, and industrial reforms, Enver Hoxha took pride in the advancement of women's conditions during communism. In 1976 the Communist party transformed gender equality into law. "*Articles 40 and 41* of the 1976 Constitution of the People's Socialist Republic of Albania deal specifically with women's rights. Article 40 declares: All citizens are equal before the law. No restriction or privilege is recognized on the rights and duties of citizens on account of sex . . ." (O'Donnell 1999, 100). Although there were discrepancies between the law and the actual lives of women, Ibrahimi tells us that Kaltra women took full advantage of these changes.

7. "The women who narrate others and themselves all move in this direction, writing and *taking a stand* also for those who cannot afford it, giving them their voice back, and *answering* to internalized constructs and images" (Camilotti 2009, 7). These words refer to Parati's *Migration Italy. The Art of Talking Back in a Destination Culture* (2005).

8. Comberiati notes that this novel was first published in a French translation, which is more of a rewrite (Comberiati 2010, 226).

9. "Although Vorpsi moves away from confessional 'ego-documents' [. . .] by exploring a more sophisticated way of writing, her texts are unquestionably autobiographical" (Alù 2015, 256).

10. "We are presented with a sort of journal, constantly and purposefully fragmented by the internal shifts of the protagonist: a back and forth in time and in space that reflects Hana's mood changes, with frequent use of flash-backs, as revealed by the titles of the chapters, [...] which determine fluctuations between the present and the past" (Pellegrini 2013, 153–54, my translation).

11. Hana is trying to learn English as she moves to the United States. *Sworn Virgin* is Dones' first work in Italian.

12. "How much for a fuck?" This translation is mine, since the English translation leaves the question in Italian. Just as Eva's mother didn't understand, so English-language readers who do not understand Italian are left wondering.

REFERENCES

Alù, Giorgia. 2015. "Looking through Coloured Shards: Words and Images in Ornela Vorpsi's Works." In *Enlightening Encounters: Photography in Italian Literature*, edited by Giorgia Alù and Nancy Pedri, 254–78. Toronto: University of Toronto Press.

Barbarulli, Clotilde. 2010. *Scrittrici migranti. La lingua, il caos, una stella*. Pisa: Edizioni ETS.

Bhabha, Homi. 1994. *The Location of Culture*. London: Routledge.

Bond, Emma, and Daniele Comberiati, eds. 2013a. *Il confine liquido: rapporti letterari e interculturali fra Italia e Albania*. Lecce: Salento books.

———, eds. 2013b. *Narrare il colonialismo e il postcolonialismo italiano*. Lecce: Salento Books.

Bond, Emma, Jennifer Burns, and Cristina Mauceri. 2013. "Intervista a Ornela Vorpsi presso l'Università di Oxford il 24 novembre 2009." In *Il confine liquido: rapporti letterari e interculturali fra Italia e Albania*, edited by Emma Bond and Daniele Comberiati, 203–20. Lecce: Salento books.

Camilotti, Silvia. 2009. *Roba da donne. Emancipazione e scrittura nei percorsi di autrici dal mondo*. Roma: Mangrovie Edizioni.

Carotenuto, Carla. 2014. "Figure di donna in 'Rosso come una sposa' e 'Non c'è dolcezza' di Anilda Ibrahimi." In *Tra innovazione e tradizione Un itinerario possibile*, edited by Maria Luisa Caldognetto and Laura Campanale, 283–298. Luxembourg: Edizioni Convivium.

Comberiati, Daniele. 2010. *Scrivere nella lingua dell'altro. La letteratura degli immigrati in Italia (1989–2007)*. Bern: Peter Lang.

Dones, Elvira. 2007. *Vergine Giurata*, Milano: Feltrinelli.

———. 2014. *Sworn Virgin*. Translated by Clarissa Botsford. London: And Other Stories.

Halili, Rigels. 2013. "Uno Sguardo all'altra sponda dell'Adriatico: Italia e Albania." In *Il confine liquido: rapporti letterari e interculturali fra Italia e Albania*, edited by Emma Bond and Daniele Comberiati, 31–71. Lecce: Salento books.

Hein, Christopher. 2010. *Rifugiati: vent'anni di storia del diritto d'asilo in Italia*. Roma: Donzelli editore.

Homer, *Illiad*. Translated by Robert Fagles. Penguin Classics, 1999.

Ibrahimi, Anilda. 2008. *Rosso come una sposa*. Torino: Einaudi.

King-Mai. 2011. *Out of Albania. From crisis migration to social inclusion in Italy*. New York-Oxford: Berghahn Books.

Kubati, Ervin and Ron. 1991. *Erëra lirie dhe rënkime dhimbjesh. Venti di libertà e gemiti di dolore*. Bari: ED Insieme.

Luciani, Serena. 2013. "I rapporti fra Albania e Italia subito dopo la caduta del regime." In *Il confine liquido: rapporti letterari e interculturali fra Italia e Albania*, edited by Emma Bond and Daniele Comberiati, 85–97. Lecce: Salento books.

Myftiu, Bessa. 2010. *Rrëfime nga vëndet e harruara*. Tiranë: Marin Barleti.

O'Donnell, James S. 1999. *A coming of age. Albania under Enver Hoxha*. New York: Columbia University Press.

Ovid. 2009. *Metamorphoses*. Translated by A. D. Melville. Oxford University Press.

Parati, Graziella. 2005. *Migration Italy. The Art of Talking Back in a Destination Culture*. Toronto: University of Toronto Press.

———. 2017. *Migrant writers and urban space in Italy*. Palgrave Macmillan.

Pedrazzi, Nicola. 2018. "Anilda Ibrahimi: il percorso solitario di una scrittrice." Interview by Anilda Ibrahimi. *Osservatorio Balcani e Caucaso*, May 31. https://www.balcanicaucaso.org/aree/Albania/Anilda-Ibrahimi-il-percorso-solitario-di-una-scrittrice-188089.

Pellegrini, Franca. 2013. "Traslazioni narrative: strategie di mediazione in Vergine Giurata di Elvira Dones e Rosso come una sposa di Anilda Ibrahimi." In *Il confine liquido: rapporti letterari e interculturali fra Italia e Albania*, edited by Emma Bond and Daniele Comberiati, 149–66. Lecce: Salento books.

Pinzi, Anita. 2013. "Corpi-cerniera: corpi di donna in *Il paese dove non si muore mai* di Ornela Vorpsi." In *Il confine liquido: rapporti letterari e interculturali fra Italia e Albania*, edited by Emma Bond and Daniele Comberiati, 167–84. Lecce: Salento books.

Radi, Lidia. 2018. "Scrittori senza frontiere: Il caso di Elvira Dones." *Critical Multilingualism Studies* 6, no. 1: 74–94.

Resta, Patrizia. 1996. *Il Kanun di Lek Dugajini. Le Basi Morali e Giuridiche della Società Albanese*. Lecce: Besa Editrice.

Romeo, Caterina. 2018. *Riscrivere la nazione. La letteratura italiana postcoloniale*. Milan: Le Monnier Università.

Vizion Plus TV. 2014. "Dita Ime—Besa Myftiu—20 Janar 2014—Show—Vizion Plus." YouTube, January 20. https://www.youtube.com/watch?v=4ZNTgvQL_mU.

Vorpsi, Ornela. 2005. *Il paese dove non si muore mai*. Turin: Einaudi. (2018. Roma: Minimum Fax)

———. 2009. *The Country Where No One Ever Dies*. Translated by Robert Elsie and Janice Mathie-Heck. Champaign: Dalkey Archive Press.

———. 2010. *Bevete Cacao Van Hooten*. Turin: L'arcipelago Einaudi.

Chiodi dell'esilio /
The Nails of Exile

Gëzim Hajdari / Translated by James Walker

La mia stirpe muore di venerdì.	My people die on Fridays.
Venerdì, gli antichi romani usavano eseguir le condanne a morte.	On Fridays, the Romans carried out their executions.
Di venerdì è morto anche Gesù.	Jesus died on Friday.
Mio padre Rizà, una mattina di venerdì chiamò mia madre	My father Rizà, one Friday morning, called my mother
e le disse:	and said:
"Oggi morirò!	"Today I will die!
Chiama Agìm, voglio dargli ultimo saluto!" Così è di abitudine in Darsìa.	Call Agìm, to receive my last instructions!"—the custom in Darsìa.
Agìm è il mio fratello più grande.	Agìm, my eldest brother.
In punto di morte gli disse:	On his deathbed, he told him:
"Io sto per morire, *amanèt*[1] vostra madre Nur,	"I'm about to die, *amanèt*,[2] your mother Nur
è senza pensione e malata;	is penniless and sick;
la casetta è umida e l'acqua piovana gocciola dal tetto;	this little house is dank and the rain comes in;

215

amanèt anche Gëzim in esilio, è
solo e lontano,

amanèt, Gëzim, too, in his lonely
exile,

oltre il mare negro dell'Europa,
vecchia puttana viziata!"

is far away across the dark, dark sea
of Europe, the rotten old whore!"

Poi, guardando dalla finestra
spalancata, aggiunse ancora:

Then, looking out the open window,
he added again

"Lavatemi il corpo con l'acqua
fresca del pozzo all'ombra del gelso
rosso,

"Wash my body with well-water in
the shade of the red mulberry,

e fatemi seppellire nella tomba di
mia madre,

bury me in my mother's crypt

morì lasciandomi orfano a sei mesi.

who left me, at six months, an orphan.

Lascio questa penna di sambuco
come ricordo

I bequeath this elder pen

per vostro fratello

to your brother

che scelse la strada del poeta,

who chose the path of the poet,

strada maledetta!"

cursed path!"

Chiese la *besa*[3] ad Agim che
avrebbe pagato il debito al
panettiere

He made Agìm pledge to settle the
baker's bill,

del quartiere, salutò Nur,

bid Nur farewell,

e si spense.

and died.

Era la penna con la quale scrisse il
diario della sua vita

It was the pen he used to chronicle his
days

durante gli anni di terrore,

during the years of terror,

quando tornava dalla campagna
come pastore dei buoi,

when he returned from the
countryside, a poor oxherder.

strappato poi da mia madre per
paura di essere sequestrato dal
Sigurimi.[4]

My mother later shredded the diary
for fear of discovery by the *Sigurimi*.[5]

Con i fogli del suo diario lei
accendeva il fuoco per riscaldare
noi bambini

With its pages she kindled the fire to
warm us children

nelle notti fredde d'inverno intorno
al focolare, nella casetta

in the cold winter nights by the
hearth, in the little flint house,

di pietra focaia, in cima alla collina
buia, in Darsìa.[6]

on the dark hill, in Darsìa.[7]

Rizà era lo scrivano del villaggio,

Rizà was the village scribe;

durante le domeniche,

on Sundays,

scriveva le lettere per i figli dei
contadini che facevano il militare.

he wrote the letters to farmer's sons
off in the army.

Da quando confiscarono i nostri
beni di famiglia durante il
comunismo,

From the time the communists
confiscated everything,

noi siamo nati e cresciuti nelle
casette semiterrate, umide e fredde,

we've been born and raised in cold,
wet cellars,

la povertà non ci si è mai tolta di
dosso.

poverty our constant companion.

Di venerdì è morto mio nonno
paterno Velì,

On Friday my grandfather Velì died,

rappresentante dei *bektashi* in
provincia,

regional *bektashi* representative.

I suoi avi provenivano dalle
Bjeshkët e Nëmuna,[8]

His ancestors from Bjeshkët and
Nëmuna[9]

trasferitosi in Darsìa per motivi di
vendetta

came to Darsìa seeking revenge

previsto dal Kanun[10] delle
Montagne.

as commanded by the Code of the
Mountains.

Velì aveva sposato in seconda
nozze Zyrà,

Velì's second wife, Zyrà,

guaritrice di morsi di serpenti
velenosi,

healer of venomous snake bites,

molto più giovane di lui.

Lei chiamava il suo marito: "Mio signore,"

anche Zyra morì di venerdì

in una giornata di fulmini e pioggia

di fronte alla collina di Harbor.

Di venerdì è morto Zybèr, cugino di Velì,

fu investito da un tronco di salice alla riva del torrente di Capok.

Ho visto con i miei occhi questa scena terribile,

avevo sei anni, mi portava spesso con sé,

piangevo disperato chiedendo aiuto ai passanti per strada.

Di venerdì è morta sua moglie Mynevèr,

donna giunonica e veggente.

Aveva occhi a mandorla,

sapeva leggere i pensieri dei contadini del villaggio.

Mynever era anche una sciamana, comunicava con *kecka*[11] e gli *xhin*.[12]

annientava le fatture che gli xhin facevano ai contadini,

facendo una controfattura.

Di venerdì è morto Osman, il fratello di Zyber,

è stato ucciso da *hasmi*[15] durante la notte delle nozze, sul letto matrimoniale:

much younger than him,

called her husband, "My lord."

Zyrà too died on a Friday

on a day of lightning and rain

near Harbor Hill.

On Friday Zybèr, Velì's cousin died,

felled by a willow trunk on the bank of the River Capok.

I witnessed this horrific scene;

at six years old, I was his frequent companion,

I wailed at passersby for help.

On Friday his wife Mynevèr died,

tall, shapely and clairvoyant.

She had almond eyes.

She could read the minds of village farmers.

Mynevèr was a shaman, in communication with *kecka*[13] and *xhin*.[14]

She canceled men's debts to the spirit world,

marking them paid.

On Friday Zyber's brother died, Osman,

killed for revenge, on his wedding night, in his wedding bed:

hasmi entrò nella sua stanza matrimoniale dal tetto della casa.

the avenger entering the wedding chamber from above.

Quella notte i familiari non fecero sapere nulla dell'accaduto

The guests were never told

gli ospiti festeggiavano, bevevano e ballavano allegri.

as they happily partied, drank and danced.

L'indomani il padre di Osman si rivolse agli ospiti:

When morning came, Osman's father cried:

"Illustri ospiti, ieri abbiamo festeggiato il matrimonio di mio figlio,

"Honored guests, you gathered yesterday for my son's wedding;

oggi vorrei che celebrassimo insieme il suo funerale!"

I call you together today for his funeral!"

Di venerdì è morta Meje,

On Friday Meje died,

sorella più grande di Velì,

Velì's oldest sister;

si svegliava di notte, si vestiva di bianco, e andava al fiume del villaggio

she awoke in the night, dressed in white, and glided to the village stream

a parlare con le spose notturne.

to speak with the night brides.

Di venerdì è morta Lidia, l'altra sorella di Velì,

On Friday Lidia died, Velì's second sister,

sposata lontana, oltre sette monti e sette fiumi.

wed away, across seven mountains and seven rivers.

Tra mio nonno e lei non scorreva buon sangue.

Between her and my grandfather no love was lost.

Si diceva che aveva calpestato all'una di notte gli *xhin*.

They say she stepped on a *xhin* in the night.

Di venerdì è morto Sabrì, nella città di Lushnje,

On Friday Sabrì died, in Lushnje,

fratello maggior di mio padre,

my father's older brother,

condannato a centouno anni dal regime di Enver Hoxha

sentenced to a hundred and one years by Enver Hoxha's regime

per aver combattuto durante la guerra nelle file	for having fought during the war in the ranks
del Partito Fronte Nazionale Albanese.	of the Albanian National Front Party.

Chiese di essere portato nel villaggio natale	He asked to see his village,
per vedere per l'ultima volta la collina, gli ulivi,	to see for the last time the hill, the olive trees,
baciare la terra d'origine, prima di scendere nella fossa.	to kiss the ground of his birthplace before descending to the grave.

Quando vide la lepre selvatica correre tra i cespugli,	When he saw the wild hare running among the bushes,
gli uccelli neri sui rami incurvati degli ulivi	the black birds on the arching olive branches,
e l'erba selvatica cresciuta al muro della vecchia casa,	the wild grass grown on the old house walls,
pianse a nenia come un bambino.	he wailed like a baby.

Di venerdì è morto Mustafà, il fratellastro maggiore di Riza,	On Friday Mustafà died, step-brother to my father.
menò sua moglie Hurmà nel cortile di casa.	He beat his wife Hurmà in their courtyard.
perché dopo aver partorito sette femmine, voleva che nascesse un maschio.	Because after seven girls he wanted a boy.

Di venerdì è morto Hysein, ubriaco di grappa, fratello di Mustafà,	On Friday Hysein died, Mustafà's brother, drunk on grappa.
quel giorno aveva litigato con mia madre	That day he'd fought with my mother
per futili motivi,	over something small;
fu travolto da una macchina sul boulevard della città.	he was struck by a car on the city boulevard.

Anche Hakì, il fratello di Hysen e Mustafa è morto di venerdì,

bevendo *rakì*[16] e discutendo del Diritto Romano,

sperava che lo Stato postcomunista avrebbe restituito

una piccola parte dei beni rubati dal Partito del Proletariato

alla nostra famiglia.

Di venerdì è morto anche Fatimè,

l'unica sorellastra di mio padre,

impazzita.

Di venerdì morirò anch'io,

crocifisso mani e piedi con i chiodi dell'esilio

sulle spalle il peso di tutti i venerdì mortali

di una stirpe severa.

Hakì, too, Hysein and Mustafà's brother, died on Friday,

drinking rakì[17] and talking about Roman Law;

he hoped the post-Communist government would pay back

some small part of what the Proletariat Party had stolen

from us.

On Friday Fatimè died too,

my father's only step-sister,

gone mad.

One Friday I too will die,

nailed hand and foot to the cross of exile,

on my back the weight of all the deathly Fridays

of my hard people.

NOTES

1. *Amanèt*: mi raccomando.
2. *Amanèt*: mind my (dying) word/wish.
3. *Besa*: la parola data per gli albanesi.
4. *Sigiurimi*: polizia politica segreta del regime comunista di Enver Hoxha.
5. *Sigurimi*: communist secret police under Enver Hoxha's regime.
6. Darsìa: la provincia della città di Lushnje, Albania, dove è nato il poeta.
7. Darsìa: the region surrounding Lushnje, Albania, where the poet was born.
8. Bjeshkëve ë Nëmuna: Le Montagne Maledette dove ha regnato per cinquecento anni il *Kanùn*, (Codice Giuridico Orale albanese) e la *besa* (la parola data, la promessa per gli albanesi).
9. Bjeshkëve and Nëmuna: the "Cursed Mountains" where the *Kanùn* (ancient Albanian oral law, or Code of the Mountains) and *besa* (word of honor) ruled for 500 years.
10. Kanun: il Codice d'Onore Albanese, nato tra 1300-1400; è il complesso del diritto consuetudine formato nel corso di 500 anni e tramandato oralmente di generazione in generazione, uno dei pochi diritti consuetudinari conservatisi in Europa.
11. *Kecka*: belle spose danzatrici vestite di bianco che apparivano di notte alla riva dei torrenti.

12. *Xhin (djinn):* anime malvagie che escono di notte e hanno una potenza soprannaturale sugli uomini e sulle cose. Il mito appartiene alle fiabe albanesi di Darsìa.

13. *Kecka*: beautiful brides in white who appeared by night, dancing along the banks of rivers.

14. *Xhin* (genie/jinn): evil spirits who come out at night, with supernatural powers over men and objects. An element of the Albanian folktales of Darsìa.

15. *Hasmi*: la persona in vendetta di sangue a causa di un omicidio.

16. Raki: Grappa albanese.

17. Rakì: Albanian grappa.

Beyond the Canon

Women's Italian Writings of Migration

Lidia Curti

BORDERS, DOORS, THRESHOLDS

Intervals allow a rupture with mere reflections and present the perception of space as breaks. They constitute interruptions and irruptions in a uniform series of surface; they designate a temporary hiatus, an intermission, a distance, a pause, a lapse between different states; and they are what comes up at the threshold of representation and communication—what often appears in the doorway . . . there where the aperture is also the spacing-out of disappearance. (Minh-ha 1999, xii)

"Canons are the condition of institutions and the effect of institutions. Canons secure institutions as institutions secure canons" (Spivak 1993, 270). As soon as the word "canon" is heard, a limit is drawn, marking the border between itself and its own transgression. This extra-textual signal is like "a guardian at the door who like Cerberus stays on the threshold."[1] This Cerberus has hidden and silenced other voices, marginalizing what exceeds the narratives authorized by the dominant language, the fatherland, the patriarchal legitimation, or the colonial regime marginalizing what is impure, anomalous, or monstrous. Disciplinary barriers are a form of violence linked to national formations and resulting in practices of exclusion; in the case of literature, these barriers are directed towards eccentric and minority writings and are connected to sexual, ethnic, and social differences. A counter-literature is required to break through those barriers and counter that form of violence.

The relation between female writings and the institutional canon has been an object of discussion within feminist criticism. Rather than falling into a pattern of assimilation or opposition, feminist critics have suggested a net of connections in contrast with the linearity of the canon and its fixed geographical and disciplinary boundaries. The boundary between criticism and fiction, philosophy and poetry, as discussed by Jacques Derrida in *Parages* (2010), has been undone by Luce Irigaray and Hélène Cixous, among others. In their language, genre differences are evoked and erased at the same time. Commenting on the meeting of philosophy and poetry in Cixous' writings, Monica Fiorini speaks of an open non-genre, where the frontiers are crossed and re-crossed ceaselessly as they cannot be simply erased (2003, 142).[2]

In her introduction to *Oltrecanone*, Annamaria Crispino describes the essays in the book as suggesting a new cartography external to canonical hierarchies, designing "a reticular and interconnected" structure (2003, 10). For Laura Fortini it is not a question of quantitative extensions—of adding a name here or there to Bloom's authoritative, and authoritarian list—or of entering an agonistic relationship with the Western canon. She underlines the dangers of an inclusion tending to domesticate "Elsa Morante's thoughtful melancholic narrative, Anna Maria Ortese's visionary art, together with all those who took their writing beyond the wall of the canon" (Fortini 2003, 29; my translation). In *Il romanzo del divenire* (The Novel of Becoming), Adriana Chemello speaks of "a tale of relations" for the female *Bildungsroman* and of the construction of social, intellectual, symbolic, and affective links as a way to gather strength from that female continuum (2007, 21).[3] This collection of essays reconstructs a critical genealogy of the female narrative alternative to the canonical *Bildungsroman*, pointing out that female stories of formations are not the result of a linear and conclusive process but one of a "becoming" (Bono and Fortini 2007, 11). For these heroines, happiness coincides with being in the world starting from the self. For them, the conflict between norm and rebellion ends in the incompleteness and openings that mark the female novel of formation.

Recourse to different and partial genealogies would be more useful than opposing female literature as a block to the Bloomian macro-category. Rather than a sequential development, the labyrinth and weaving provide another route leading to a net of interconnected traditions within a female symbolic order, "a place that is rootedness and home," as Adriana Cavarero says (2009, 26). In these articulations, female subjectivities emerge, opting to initiate from the self to say what and who they are.

MIGRANT SUBJECTIVITIES

Memory creates the chain of tradition which passes a happening on from generation to generation. It starts the web which all stories together form in the end. One ties on to the next, as the great story tellers, particularly the Oriental ones, have already readily shown. In each of them there is a Scheherazade who thinks of a fresh story whenever her tale comes to a stop. (Benjamin 1973, 98)

The construction of alternative traditions seems particularly relevant to me as the multiplicity of identities and cultures, in opposition to the canonical "one," moves from difference to differences in the perspectives of exchange and intersectionality. Diasporic narratives offer a good example, moving among different cultures, languages, and histories; in the interstices between one and the other—on the threshold, or at the door—between appearance and disappearance (Trinh 1999, xii–xiii; see epigraph). The postcolonial condition lives in a space of indistinction, in which identities are mobile and fluid, never fixed once and for all. If it is difficult to assign these writings to a specific national canon, the confrontation with the western literary canon, whether directly or indirectly, is unavoidable.

In *Culture and Imperialism*, Edward Said produces what we could call anti-imperialist counter-texts of some fundamental works in the British canon. He describes overlapping territories and intertwining histories in culture, literature, and the visual arts, quoting authors ranging from Dickens and Kipling to Conrad and Forster. He emphasizes that in these writings, such crossings are represented as false dualities. In her work *In Other Worlds* (1987), Gayatri Spivak has reexamined the British "great tradition" "in search of feminist readings" in Coleridge, Wordsworth, Yeats, Bronte, and, above all, Virginia Woolf's *To the Lighthouse*, only to find them missing— as also the anti-imperialist readings. In a later text on "the teaching machine" at an occidental university, with its failed response to female and ethnic marginality, she emphasizes that all literary canons have a political and authoritarian function (1993, 270, see epigraph). It is not to be forgotten that the British canon was always doubled: one for the mother country and another for the colonial territories. In the latter case, any work with an anticolonial potentiality had to be expunged.[4]

Female and feminist literatures occupy a space with their own specificities. Women's alterity can be linked to colonial subalternity, as the subaltern condition generally recalls colonial rule and oppression, even though it rarely presented as such. Diasporic writers live, or have lived, in the condition of suspension of an exile, either chosen or imposed. Such writers include westernized Asians, Africans, and Latinos; migrants and descendants of migrants in European countries; and members of oppressed or suppressed minorities such as Native Americans, Afro-Americans, and Chicano peoples. The fluctuations of identity recurring in women's writings is consistent with the impossibility of linguistic or cultural homogeneity. The link between these writings and a canonical tradition is neither visible nor transparent, nor easily traced; their belonging to a single culture was never really established. These writings recall material conditions and symbolic aspects of migration and exile, which interrupt the linearity and rationality of canonical genres.

It might be useful to go back to Benjamin's famous essay "The Storyteller" (1973), which allows us to establish a link between these writings and the anti-canonical genres described above. He makes a distinction between the novel, as an individual psychological narrative, and storytelling, such as Native American or African myths and folklore, linked to the memory of collective history, in a diffused, fragmented perspective.[5]

Here I would like to refer particularly to the voices of a minor literature of women writers of Africa and African descent in Italy, who, alongside those travelling from Eastern shores, are all part of a transversal Mediterranean phenomenon. They register a presence in fields as diverse as novels, poetry, visual art, journalism, media, and music. They choose to write in a minor language but still renew its modes and moods by placing themselves outside the forms of institutional literary tradition and by breaking boundaries between genres, disciplines, and cultures. Even within the same national border, they inhabit a hybrid space, both inside and outside; they are "inside out."

Most of these writers, and especially those from the Horn of Africa, reveal another view of Italian colonialism. They fill a void in official records by recalling the massacres, concentration camps, indiscriminate warfare and the racial laws of the Italian colonial regime, along with the brutal banalities of authoritarian rule. They thereby contribute to the knowledge of the Italian colonial past, a forgotten chapter in our culture, and rupture the vision of a homogeneous, white Italy, more European than Mediterranean, offering a scrutinization of ourselves and posing the question of how to shape our identity as Italians after colonialism.

They offer a narrative that goes beyond what has been permitted and promoted by the national and linguistic purity of the canon.[6] Here autobiography is a telling of the self as a becoming, an itinerary, and a movement back and forward in time and space along the migration routes.

OF FLOWERS AND PEARLS

In this literature, it is possible to discern the ghost of the Italian literary canon. A direct reference is offered by Gabriella Ghermandi's revisitation of Ennio Flaiano's *Tempo di uccidere* (A Time to Kill) in her novel *Regina di fiori e di perle* (A Queen of Flowers and Pearls). This ghosting is openly acknowledged by the author.[7] As in other writings by Italian authors of African descent, it is possible here to find a denunciation of the silence on the colonial past in Italian culture and history and the insistence on the necessity of entering this empty space via a counter-history of the Italian "conquest" of Ethiopia, with its iniquity and violence (Ghermandi 2007).

The heroine Mahlet is given the task to pass on the memory of Ethiopian colonial history and become her people's *griotte*. The memories of the anti-Italian resistance (1934–1941), related by different narrators, are interspersed with the tale of her growing up in the period of Menghistu's dictatorship. Among the many historical events of the Italian occupation, the use of gas bombing in 1935 is frequently recalled. In this remembering, the city of Addis Ababa becomes the emblem of an emotional geography, either in the estrangement caused by the presence of the Italians: "They were everywhere, so many that our city looked like the capital of their country, not of ours" (Ghermandi 2015, 191); or when covered with corpses, after the massacre ordered by Graziani in 1936, in retaliation for the attempt on his life: "For the next three days Addis Ababa went through hell" (Ghermandi 2015, 196); or even, by contrast, in the happy moments of the liberation.

Here the importance of the trace created by women's writings along the path of memory emerges in all its force, accompanied by the difficulty of its necessary telling; it is an impossible tale to tell because of its atrocity, but as Toni Morrison implies with one powerful phrase—"a tale not to pass on"—it must be told (Morrison 1987, 397). It is also a painful reminder for those of us who forget or ignore that part of our collective history.

Ghermandi's book has a polyphonic structure. It encompasses different genres: fantasy, history, fiction, and autobiography. It confronts the Italian canon through the coexistence of different voices and tales within its narrative frame. The intrusion into Italian of Amharic terms and words, describing tissues, clothes, food, perfumes, religious rites, and festivities, evokes a culture with a different sense of time and place. The insistent metaphor of weaving stands for the tenacious threads of friendship and collective ties crossing the plot as well as the events of individual and official stories.[8] The poetical epigraph at the beginning of the book says: "I gather flowers and pearls from the enchanted garden of my land": they are flowers and pearls of different contrasting colors, of every type and genre, hidden and visible at the same time.

Many of the stories speak of women "patriots" active in guerrilla warfare, but "The Turtle Lady's Story" is entirely dedicated to female participation in the armed resistance, particularly to the participation of Kebedech Seyoum, a warrior who, between myth and reality, was one of the female leaders in the movement.[9] The turtle lady relates the tale of her mother, who joins the resistance becoming *arbegnà* (as the resistance partisans were called) after fleeing from the horrendous scene of Addis Ababa in ruins. This is her description of Seyoum: "There is something unique in women who are born to be warriors, something that cannot be explained, that is mysterious and that erupts from the depth of the earth with unparalleled force, mixed with the essence and sweetness of a mother. This is what I thought when I heard her voice" (Ghermandi 2015, 199). It is Seyoum herself who insists on learning how to shoot, thus making it possible for her to save lives in a scene inspired by Flaiano's novel. That scene, in which she kills two unarmed Italian soldiers, is a reversal of the event narrated in Flaiano's novel. Two texts are juxtaposed here, one filling the silences and the empty spaces of the other. [10]

Both texts include a naked female body, a magnet for the eyes of the *talian sollato* and a trap for him in spite of the complete reversal of subjectivity. The gaze of Flaiano's Italian officer, who is weighed down by solitude and lost in the forest—and in the desert of motivation and purpose common to the occupation troops—rests on that body: "The woman did not see me. She was naked and was washing herself at one of the pools, crouching as a good domestic animal [. . .] she raised her hands lazily to throw the water on her breasts and let it fall for the pleasure of feeling it splashing on her skin, in unison with the slow passing of time'" (1973, 19 [my translation]). He lingers, lazily observing her and noting her animal-like position and her timeless, slow gestures, which reflect his own melancholy as in a mirror, in a kind of premonition of what is going to happen. In the slumber following the violation of her body, he mistakes her for an animal and shoots her, after which he finishes her off while covering her face—as it is impossible for him to face the look of this "other"—benumbed by his fatalistic solipsism.

In Ghermandi's text, there is in the woman's specular and reversed gaze, a sense of purpose: the determination to act for and with a collectivity, and the strength of resistance to oppression and evil. Here Seyoum's first-person account begins with the description of the bathing of a female body: "Baring my chest I began to splash water on my neck, my face, and my breasts. More and more water, like a blessing. I washed off the sweat and the dust of the long march, splashing myself with abundant water. I cupped my hands to collect it and threw it on my body. It was cold, refreshing, transparent, sweet in my mouth that was dry from exhaustion. I wanted to go on forever; I was mesmerized by the sheer pleasure of it" (204).

Here, a woman puts her body in the forefront, reversing the mode of narration. She speaks with her naked body, transforming it from object to subject, from passive to active, from victim to weapon. [11] The first scene has a slow pace, finding its tragic denouement after many pages; the second is abrupt and sudden: "I took aim, and the eyes of the Italian soldier expressed confusion. He was not armed, I hesitated [. . .] I thought of our dead on Yekatit. Something inside me screamed: 'Out of our land!' I took aim as they had taught me, closed my eyes, and shot" (204).

Here and there in the novel, traces of the author's biography emerge as in, for example, Mahlet's departure from Ethiopia and her successive periods of study in Italy. [12] In Perugia, where Mahlet spends her first year learning

Italian, she observes migrating birds for whom arrival and departure are the same thing: "An hourglass scanned out their time, and when the sand had run out on one side and the hourglass was turned over, the place of arrival became the place of departure" (122). Nostalgia paves the way to dark thoughts: "surrounded by those medieval stones, I lived, experiencing only the things that were absent" (123). It is worse in Bologna, where she faces the disease of the West: solitude and individualism. Here, the movement becomes an interior journey leading to self-awareness and knowledge of her culture alongside the culture she finds herself confronting.

These overtones, common to many other stories of exile, are echoed further on in the book in the final narrative by Woizero Bekelech, who has migrated to Italy only to return home because, as she says, "I don't want to live with my heart split in two" (216). The critical look at Italy, the description of the conditions of exploitation and debasement of foreign domestic work, occupy much of her experience: "I spent two years in an arid desert, with no human warmth" (235).

Nostalgia permeates the descriptions of the places and of the natural beauty of the distant country; it shows in the notation of differences in smells, food, and language: "Language tells us about the people who speak it. And Amharic! Ah! Amharic, Bekeleh. Certain words fill your mouth like the pulp of the papaya, of the avocado" (Ghermandi 2015, 238). By contrast, in Italian houses the lingering smell of time is "a young odor very short-lived [. . .] of spices, of roasted coffee and incense. Not of anything that has built up over the years" (232–33).

We find these same accents in Cristina Ubah Ali Farah's *Madre Piccola* (Little Mother), which tells of the many places of the Somali diaspora in the world. Those wanderings are defined as "an interior movement" from one house to another. "You could be anywhere . . . wherever we took our sound, our smell" (2007, 112; my translation). Similarly, in Igiaba Scego's memoir *La mia casa è dove sono* (My Home is Where I Am), the Mogadishu map she reconstructs from memory emits the aroma of coffee with ginger and of the dishes of *beer iyo muufo*, as well as unpleasant smells like sewage or camel carcasses abandoned by the road, but also the remembered scent of the essences women put on at night, thus resurrecting "that lost Mogadishu" (2010, 34). The language of the new world is traversed by the presence of the original words referring to material objects, food, smells, tastes, trees, plants, forests—the flowers and the pearls of writing.

SPEAKING NEAR-BY, OR "A PEU PRÈS"

One cannot pretend to "speak for," or worse, to "speak about," but only can speak beside . . . [Ne pas prêtendre "parler pour," ou pis, "parler sur," à peine parler près de . . .] (Djebar 9)

"I do not intend to speak about/ Just speak near-by" (Trinh 96). Some of these themes find a correspondence in Italian narratives. As if in a mirror, some Italian novels (could we call them postcolonial?) have started interrogating the memory of our colonialism. They do not intend to speak for or to speak about, but rather, as Trinh (1992) and Djebar (1980) suggest, to speak beside—"on the side of" postcolonial voices, I would say. They also recall a mourning for a loss that Italian history and culture have not addressed. The Italians are not alone in not having addressed this. A similar amnesia is common to all forms of occidental colonialism, as Paul Gilroy has argued for British imperialism and Toni Morrison for slavery in American society.

One interesting example of "speaking beside" is Francesca Melandri's *Sangue giusto* (Right Blood, 2017), a long novel about the Italian occupation of Ethiopia. It narrates the same events we find in Ghermandi's novel and follows a similar itinerary, though from a different angle, namely that of an Italian woman of today. As a sort of signal, the novel starts with the perfume of exotic spices and food from far-off oriental countries that the heroine Ilaria smells while ascending the many steps to her sixth-floor flat.

Coming back from work, she finds a black youth waiting on the landing. His documents give his name as Shimeta Iegmeta Attilaprofeti. Here, we immediately have a reference to the title of the book: the question suspended to the end is whether Shimeta has the "right blood" to get citizenship in this country. More generally, the title refers to the *ius sanguinis*, the right of blood, the only basis Italian law accepts for belonging. The failure to extend the law to include *ius soli*, the right to stay on the basis of birth, marked the end of the center-left governments. The present one, which followed, is fiercely opposed to any immigration.

Shimeta's arrival unravels a story of Italian colonialism in Ethiopia and establishes a tie between a group of Addis Ababa natives and an Italian family that has lived through Fascism and the successive post-liberation governments, profiting first from the colonial regime and then from the political corruption before and during Berlusconi times. There is one man linking the two groups, the patriarch Attilio Profeti, father of four children from two different mothers. The black newcomer who bears his Italian grandsire's name, alongside his African names, is the child of one of these children. [13]

Ilaria, accompanied by her half-brother Attilio (yet another Attilio!), will slowly discover the hard truth about her father, whose favorite child she was, and will thus provide the reader a look at Italy's brutal colonial history from the inside. Attilio Profeti was a half-hearted fascist, assisted by luck and good looks, without a real allegiance or faith except to his own narcissistic drives, but no less guilty for all that. He had voluntarily enrolled in the occupying army and, assigned as he was to organization functions, exploited the colonial enterprise in Ethiopia, coming in contact with a crowd of profiteers, including Lidio Cipriani, an anthropologist not too ideologically distant from Cesare Lombroso.

One of the most interesting parts of the novel is dedicated to Cipriani, perhaps best known as the co-author of the notorious Racial Laws issued by the Mussolini government in 1938. It is largely ignored that these laws had been preceded by a 1937 version that was directed at the colonies. The premise on which Cipriani conducted his doubtful research on racial facial features in the Italian colonies was that of the superiority of the white "race," which had therefore to be safeguarded from contamination. In the novel, while working as Cipriani's assistant in Ethiopia, Profeti meets young Aba-ba, whom he rescues, so to say, from his pseudo-scientific investigations, and lives with her, for a while avoiding the rigour of the law. After he leaves, she gives birth to a son he will meet briefly only years later when called back to rescue him from Menghistu's jails. It is Ababa's grandson who turns up on Ilaria's steps, leading to her discovery of the Ethiopian part of her family.

Through Ababa's eyes, *Sangue giusto* exposes the racism and the moral evil of the Italian occupation and the wickedness and corruption of the subsequent native regimes, showing that the lesson of the Italians has been learnt and imitated. This legacy is presented mainly through the vicissitudes of her son, the half-blood bastard forgotten by his Italian father, and then those of her grandson. The grim present of the new millennium when "immigration is equated with criminality" follows from the not-too-distant colonial past. The hazards and dangers of the crossing from the ex-colonial countries to the Italian coast are portrayed at length through Shimeta's hardships during the passage and after, in the atrocious Libyan jails. For him, the experience of migration is like having a wonderful dream while perched on the branches of a tree. "But you must urgently wake up, though. As you must not fall in order to keep your dream alive. This is what migrating means" (Melandri 2017; my translation).

The intersection of two women's points of view makes Melandri's book a very timely and important one, throwing light on Italy's indulgence in its colonial past and thus its complicity in current crises. It provides a pitiless, fierce picture that could also be the foundation of a shared future. Ilaria resumes her life under the colonial lens, posing the question of "how we have become what we are" and opening herself up to the possibility of being Italian in a different way.[14]

Even before knowing about her family's colonial involvement, Ilaria suffers all the indignities of the failed acceptance of the *stranieri* (foreigners) and is very critical of the society she lives in.[15] The ethnic mélange of certain areas of Rome, such as where Ilaria lives, between Stazione Termini and the famous Piazza Vittorio, is described as a positive feature and a strength of a postcolonial society in its complexity. However, there is the regret that these areas are becoming fashionable objects of media attention while the basic needs of their inhabitants are neglected by the institutions, continuing the condition of injustice and inequality.

Pagine nascoste by Sabrina Varani (Hidden Pages 2017) is a documentary film inspired by *Sangue giusto*. Varani and Melandri went together to Ethiopia to trace the past, and Melandri was filmed while researching in archives and libraries or talking to people in some of the places the novel describes. It is difficult to say who, or what, came before and after, as the novel and the film partly developed together, reciprocally influencing one another. We see a double web of relations, Varani the director using Melandri the novelist to look at her subject matter in the same way as Melandri uses Ilaria: two women involved with a reciprocal itinerary.

Melandri bravely speaks in public meetings of the autobiographical aspects of her novel, stepping out of her role as a writer. Above all, she speaks about her own father, Franco Melandri, who unlike Attilio Profeti never went to Ethiopia. However, Franco resembled Attilo Profeti in that he remained a fascist till the end of his life, like the majority of Italians of his times. As the film shows by interviewing a *partigiano*, there were other Italians who made different choices. Like Ilaria when she discovers her father's colonial dealings, Francesca Melandri knew of her father's past fascist allegiance, but was shocked when she found an article during her research that he wrote in 1945 in "difesa della razza" (Defence of Race).

Timira. Romanzo meticcio (Wu Ming 2 and Mohamed 2012) also examines both sides of Italian colonialism. The title itself, apart from the more obvious ethnic implications with hybridity and metissage, refers to the book's mixed authorship. At the center of the book is an Italian Somali woman of mixed parenthood, Isabella Marincola, also called Timira, whose memories are recorded or reconstructed by a writer from the Wu Ming 2 collective in collaboration with her son Antal Mohamed Marincola.[16]

Timira first comes to Italy when she is two, as an illegitimate child, "una bastardella" (68), that her Italian father has recognized and taken back to Italy to live with his lawful family and a reluctant stepmother. She travels between Somalia and Italy, between past and present, here and there, and is personally involved in Somali historical events, mainly in the postcolonial period, as well as in post-war Italian life, commencing with her participation in the film *Riso Amaro*, in which she appears as one of the "mondine" alongside Silvana Mangano.

Timira. Romanzo meticcio tells the story of a woman's material and interior formation within a framework and a context that recalls the female postcolonial works discussed above, in particular those by Ali Farah and Scego. Most of the book is dedicated to the web of relationships Timira creates and carefully cultivates with her son (who leaves his native Mogadishu in 1983 to study in Italy) and, above all, with her Somali community, both at home and in Italy. The book creates a narration across two countries through the analysis of her relationship with her Somali community and with the Italian writer who has the task of assembling the pieces of her life in a book.

OF WRITING AND SONGS

There are two conclusions to Ghermandi's book. One is given by the fulfilment of Malhet's promise. After Mahlet has gathered all the stories and faced the pain of memory, she will cross the sea and carry them to the land of the Italians to destroy their possibility of forgetting: "that is why I am telling you this story. That is also mine. But now, yours as well" (Ghermandi 2015, 270). Once the convulsed and tormented pilgrimage is over, she still finds it difficult to move from word to narration, or as Benjamin would say, from the collective and fragmentary storytelling to the introspective novel based on an individual subjectivity. The denouement of the tale happens through the verses and the song recited by Aron the *azmari*, an old storyteller and musician, to remind us of the continuity of cultural memory through a diversity of languages and forms; in this case, music is connecting the intellectual purpose back to the collective emotions in a virtuous circle. [17] The *azmari* recites the verses evoking the time of the Italians, accompanied by his violin: "I'm counting on you, child. Don't lose the story" (260). Once she remembers, she knows what she has to do: "All you have to do is write," her mother tells her (265). "I opened the window and sat down. In a corner of the desk there was a box full of pens. They had thought absolutely of everything. I took one, opened the big notebook, and began to write" (267).

The second conclusion opens on the landscape surrounding her native home, as befits the beginning of any autobiography, but in a total reversal of time and place: "I was born in the town of Debre Zeit, thirty miles from Addis Ababa. There are five lakes, some surrounded by houses and some at the edge of town. At sunset flamingos fly cross the sky, going from one lake to the other, and the deep pink of their wings blends with the color of the setting sun. [. . .] Debra Zeit is the city of dust, of flowers that, once faded, fall from the plants and swirl around, carried by whirlwinds" (Ibid, 268).

The recollection continues, from reconstructing details of the family house to narrating the many members of the extended family, starting with the three elders. Once the thread of collective memory has been restored, she is reminded of the promise she made to become the storyteller, and the storywriter, of the terrible events of colonization, and to remember on behalf of two groups, both Africans and Italians. Her story telling is meant to remind us of a history we have forgotten but also to declare that her writing is now part of our culture and memory, if not our official canon.

The exilic condition, the sense of being "inside out," becomes here the condition of life and thought, the foundation of a poetical vision. The exile from the canon of female writing may follow the same route and make these writings a part of our literature, in consonance or dissonance with it. The crossing of borders—from prose to poetry, from words to music, from ethics to aesthetics—puts the authority of the canonical language and tradition under siege.

These epics of nostalgia, of melancholy, of displacement, and of the memory of terror are building a tradition and a counter-genealogy with an additional force added by the perspectives suggested above. This different perspective puts in question the foundations of the canon, which had been based on national, cultural, and linguistic boundaries, through suggestively breaking the vision of Italy as an independent national entity. As narratives by women about women, these works create a female *Bildungsroman* within a postcolonial perspective that intercedes the construction of the self as female, with the opening towards other worlds, and a different genealogy within a "female continuum."

The necessity of a painful memory and its mourning opens a series of questions, including: "Where is a nation headed that denies the right to migration, builds walls, and deprives people of the right to citizenship?" It is a question that leads to few certainties.

NOTES

1. This was the metaphor Jacques Derrida used to mark the line of demarcation for canonical genres that were not to be crossed (2000, 302). He was also referring to the impossibility of distinguishing essay writing from poetry as they are always in reciprocal "vicinity." (*Parages* is the title of the book.)

2. The fluctuation of literary genres is often linked to sexual difference in Cixous's writing, to the sense of instability and multiplicity of sexual roles and identities. The movement from one language to another—prose, poetry, music, visual arts—links these languages in an inscription of traces.

3. "The female *Bildung* [. . .] is accomplished in acquiring the awareness of the self, of one's own strength and will. An introspective journey, an interior search, a 'becoming woman' enabling to think of herself 'as grand' and master of her own destiny" (Chemello 2007, 23 [my translation]).

4. Both Shakespeare and Romantic literature were considered dangerous but, ironically, became favorite choices in postcolonial Indian narratives, where they appeared in a complex love-hate knot. Interesting examples are Anita Desai's *Clear Light of Day* (1980) and Coetzee's *Disgrace* (2000). In V. S. Naipaul's *Half a Life* (2001), the bitter portrait of the teacher who pronounced Wordsworth's name only by its initial, "W did this, W said that" (2001, 11), is emblematic of the alienating effect of the canon.

5. See epigraph (Benjamin 1973, 98). Benjamin mentions Scheherazade but does not seem to consider a female specificity as he concludes his essay with "the righteous man" encountering himself in storytelling.

6. Two major examples are given by Ali Farah's *Madre Piccola* (2007), with the vision of a shared motherhood and the formation of a woman in symbiosis with another woman and with the author in symbiosis with them. The same happens in Igiaba Scego's *Oltre Babilonia* (2008), with the events of two women's lives relating across continents.

7. See *Acknowledgements* in the Italian edition, *Regina di fiori e di perle*: "from that novel, in fact, came the idea of this one" (Ghermandi 2007, 301, my translation). See also Cristina Lombardi Diop's post-faction in that edition.

8. This narrative jigsaw is the result of careful research conducted on historical sources, archival documents, and oral accounts, which are listed in the acknowledgements: "I have only been the one who has gathered the voices" (2007, 301).

9. After her husband's death in Hailè Selassié's army in 1935, Seyoum takes the command of his troops, moving from the lost war to guerrilla warfare in the mountains. The author has traced this figure, which is mostly absent in historical documents, in the Ethiopian patriots archives in Addis Ababa.

10. When interviewed by Clotilde Barbarulli, Ghermandi acknowledged Flaiano as the only writer dealing with this subject in the Italian literary canon. "Flaiano had seen and decided not to keep silent" (Barbarulli 2013; my translation). Flaiano's novel effectively renders the anguish in the soul of the occupants themselves, a colonial "melancholy" stemming from a sense of guilt and the foreboding of an impending loss. This complex postcolonial feature is effectively analyzed in Ranjana Khanna's *Dark Continents* (2003) and Paul Gilroy's *Postcolonial Melancholia* (2005).

11. Such female warriors are described in other tales of war and resistance: for example, Assia Djebar (1980) tells of women's role in the Algerian revolution, and Mahasweta Devi (1978) writes of a woman involved in the Naxalites revolt in her short story "Draupadi." After being captured and fiercely tortured, Draupadi uses her own mutilated body as an instrument of attack; by refusing to cover it, she transforms it from a powerless target to a weapon.

12. The feelings of distance and nostalgia recall Ghermandi's own experience, divided between two cultures, an Italian father and an Ethiopian-Eritrean mother, on each side missing the other.

13. The child is named Attilio because of his father's love of Verdi's opera *Attila*. The irony of the child's name alluding to the leader of the Huns lies in his status as a victim of colonial conquest rather than becoming a conqueror.

14. Within the historical novel genre, Melandri's novel could be linked to Anna Banti's *Noi credevamo* (1967), for the look on a past involving her forerunners and on the resulting situation of inequality and oppression in Southern Italy after unification. Or the novel could be linked to *Itinerario di Paolina* (1937) and *Artemisia* (1947), both depicting a journey of personal awareness and knowledge, in which the author, in reconstructing the figures of women in the past, puts herself in question.

15. She is not a one-dimensional character; she is Attilio Profeti's daughter, but she is also a mother, a stepmother, and a sister of three (now four) different brothers. She reacts very differently to the post-fascist era and is in love with a man with opposite political commitments; they have a lasting relationship in spite of contradictions and breakups.

16. The latter is not too far from the Italian migration literature in its beginnings, a collaboration of sorts between first-generation migrants assisted by an indigenous writer or journalist. In *Mediterranean Crossroads*, Graziella Parati (1999) points out limits and shadows of this phenomenon. See also Sandra Ponzanesi and Daniela Merolla (2005) and Lidia Curti (2018). This case is different, as it belongs to a later period in terms of generations and culture, with no linguistic difficulties involved (both Timira and Antal are bilingual). In this case, the Italian partner is Wu Ming 2, a collective that hardly ever mentions individual contributions and, interestingly, follows anti-canonical ways of writing and publishing.

17. The crossing of different artistic languages is a recurring element in these tales of exiles. These tales often contain echoes of syntax, images, and sounds from ancestral poems and songs, as in the last part of Ali Farah's *Madre Piccola*. In Ghermandi, the passage from writing to music and song is also extra-textual, as she has founded the *Atse Tewodros Project* (2013), which is intended to recover Ethiopian history through an encounter between Italian and Ethiopian musicians. The songs, written and sung by Ghermandi herself, are mostly resistance songs, traditional lullabies, and descriptions of the beauty and richness of diversity ("people of so many colors") in an embittered world; sometimes the question is asked: "Why do we love this migration / divesting us of all respect?"

REFERENCES

Ali Farah, Cristina Ubah. 2007. *Madre Piccola*. Milano: Frassinelli.

Barbarulli, Clotilde. 2013. "In Etiopia condividiamo le narrazioni." *Letterate Magazine* (April 30): 50.

Benjamin, Walter. 1973. "The Storyteller." In *Illuminations: Essays and Reflections*, edited by Hannah Arendt, translated by H. Zohn. London: Collins-Fontana, 83-110.

Bono, Paola, and Laura Fortini. 2007. *Il romanzo del divenire. Un bildungsroman delle donne?* Roma: Iacobelli.

Cavarero, Adriana. 1990. *Nonostante Platone*. (Second edition 2009). Verona: ombre corte.

Chemello, Adriana. 2003. "Oltre il recinto." In *Oltrecanone: Per una cartografia della scrittura femminile*, edited by Annamaria Crispino. Roma: manifestolibri, 34-50.

———. 2007. "Una *Bildung* senza roman. Donne in divenire." In *Il romanzo del divenire. Un bildungsroman delle donne?* edited by Paola Bono and Laura Fortini. Roma: Iacobelli, 14–33.

Crispino, Annamaria. 2003. *Oltrecanone. Per una cartografia della scrittura femminile*, Rome: manifestolibri.

———. 2014. *Oltrecanone. Generi, genealogie, tradizioni.* Rome: Iaco bellieditore.

Curti, Lidia. 2018. *La voce dell'altra. Scritture ibride tra femminismo e postcoloniale*. Roma: Meltemi.

Derrida, Jacques. [1986] 2010. *Parages*. Stanford: Stanford University Press.

———. 2000. *Paraggi. Studi su Maurice Blanchot*. Milano: Jaca Book.

Devi, Mahasweta. 1978. "Draupadi." In *Agnigarbha*, translated by Gayatri Spivak, 187–96.

Djebar, Assia. 1980. *Femme d'Alger dans leur appartement*. Paris: Éditions des Femmes.

Fiorini, Monica. 2003. *H.C. Libera viaggiatrice dei margini*. Florence: Alinea Editrice.

Flaiano, Ennio. 1973. *Tempo di uccidere*. Milan: Rizzoli Libri.

Fortini, Laura. 2003. "Segni." In *Oltrecanone*, edited by Annamaria Crispino. Rome: manifestolibri, 11–32.

Ghermandi, Gabriella. 2007. *Regina di fiori e di perle*. Postfazione di Cristina Lombardi Diop. Roma: Donzelli.

———. 2013. *Atse Tewodros Project*. Addis Abeba. CD-ROM.

———. 2015. *Queen of Flowers and Pearls*. Translated by Giovanna Bellesia-Contuzzi and Victoria Offredi Poletto. Bloomington: University of Indiana Press.

Gilroy, Paul. 2005. *Postcolonial Melancholia*. New York: Columbia University Press.

Khanna, Ranjana. 2003. *Dark Continents. Psychoanalysis and Colonialism*. Durham: Duke University Press.

Melandri, Francesca. 2017. *Sangue giusto*. Milano: Rizzoli. Kindle.

Morrison, Toni. 1987. *Beloved*. Waterville, ME: Thorndike Press.

Naipaul, V. S. 2001. *Half a Life*. New York: Vintage.

Parati, Graziella. 1999. *Mediterranean Crossroads. Migration literature in Italy*. London: Associated University Presses.

Ponzanesi, Sandra, and Daniela Merolla. 2005. *Migrant Cartographies. New Cultural and Literary Spaces in Post-Colonial Europe*. Lanham-Oxford: Lexington Books.

Said, Edward. 1993. *Culture and Imperialism*. London: Vintage.

———. 1998. *Cultura e imperialismo. Letteratura e consenso nel progetto coloniale dell'Occidente*. Roma: Gamberetti.

Scego, Igiaba. 2010. *La mia casa è dove sono*. Milano: Rizzoli.

Spivak, Gayatri Chakraworty. 1987. *In Other Worlds. Essays in Cultural Politics*. New York: Methuen.

———. 1993. *Outside in the Teaching Machine*. New York: Routledge.

Trinh, T. Minh-ha. 1992. *Framer Framed*. London: Routledge.

———. 1999. *Cinema Intervals*. London: Routledge.

Varani, Sabrina. 2017. *Pagine nascoste*. Istituto Luce Cinecittà.

Wu Ming 2 and Antar Mohamed. 2012. *Timira. Romanzo meticcio*. Torino: Einaudi.

Kinships

Relations of Care and Experiences of Locality
in Transnational Italian Narrative

Jennifer Burns

The notion of kinship, core to anthropological studies, has been recuperated and rethought in recent decades through the lens of feminist theory and inquiry into the posthuman (Butler 2000; Haraway 1991). That kinship is dependent upon family ties—traditionally blood ties—has been revealed as a construct, a naturalizing of human and cultural values (largely associated with the "West") rather than a "natural" phenomenon (Riggs and Peel 2016). The core unit of the family which has inhabited the heart or hearth of the European novel from the nineteenth century to the present is thus displaced by new forms of relations between individuals and within social groups, which may well draw upon biological matches or mixings but also on different lineages of care, memory, shared experience, and recognition. This more inclusive and expansive form of intimate and social relations is compellingly visible in migrant and diasporic communities, where the very experience of distanciated relations with "home" is predicated, on the one hand, upon deep bonds with a place of "origin," often represented as extended family and shared memory, and on the other hand, upon the potentiality (and the risks) of forging different relations with and through the new and unfamiliar. Compelling too is the centrality of space to this revisioning of bonds: the anthropological notion of kinship as defining a group in a given locality is lent new significance by the focus on the local and topographical that emerges in experiences of migration, both as a counterweight to the global trajectories of mobility and as an everyday necessity. Whilst more inclusive and anti-heteronormative definitions of family, parenting, and community are emerging and thriving widely in societies across the globe, it is therefore worth considering what transmigrant and transnational subjects and the bonds that they form and re-form in new spaces can tell about how we might rethink human (and nonhuman) relationality in the present. Put crudely, if kinship is culture, is a transcultural individual or community a particularly prolific case study for observing how kinship might be reconfigured? And are narratives and fictions of transcultural experience a particularly promising mode of reimagining individual and collective relations for the present and future?

This essay intends to test these questions by examining in detail the work of Italian writer and visual artist Gabriella Kuruvilla, before situating her work briefly in relation to that of Amara Lakhous, a writer of Italian novels who migrated to Italy from Algeria in 1995. Kuruvilla is an Italian citizen of mixed Italian and Indian parentage who was born and raised in Milan and still resides there. Stephen Clingman notes that "transnational fiction [. . .] does not necessarily come from writers who travel or books that do; on the other hand, it can be undertaken by a writer who never leaves home" (Clingman 2009, 10), offering a helpful reminder that the transnational in this context is a matter of "disposition," as he identifies it, rather than necessarily a first-hand experience of mobility.[1] In the novel *Milano, fin qui tutto bene* [Milan, So Far So Good] (2012), I would suggest that Kuruvilla deploys her mixed Italian and Indian heritage alongside her "indigenous" knowledge of Milan, combined with an inclusive creative "disposition," to speak through her narrative fictions as at once an insider and an outsider, an informed ethnographic observer and vocalizer of the diverse forms of relationality experienced in a multicultural Italian city. The analysis to follow will focus on the elements and qualities of contemporary kinship that she describes in order to expose what is distinctive about the impact of transmigration in Italy on more conventional values and practices of kin and community. I will then turn more briefly to Lakhous's novel *Scontro di civiltà per un ascensore a piazza Vittorio* [Clash of Civilizations over an Elevator in Piazza Vittorio] (2006) in order to frame these distinctive qualities differently, particularly in terms of migration and narrative form.

Kuruvilla's novel explores a flexible network of friendships, maternal and filial bonds, loving and sexual relationships, casual or intermittent connections, favors, housing arrangements, and commercial, entertainment, and service-based relations, all of which intersect and perpetuate each other because of their formative co-dependence with the specific streets, intersections, and material histories of Milan. As the title suggests, the locality not only of Milan but of specific areas of Milan close to the center and increasingly identified since the 1990s for their ethnic mix are the substance of the novel. The territory of Milan in fact provides the structure of the novel, which is divided into four sections identified with four interconnecting zones of Milan (via Padova, viale Monza, Sarpi, and Corvetto.) Each section is narrated in the first person by a different subject: two Milanese women, an Egyptian man, and a man who is a Neapolitan migrant to Milan. The focus, then, is locality and the way that the local "folds together" (Amin 2004, 34) plural nationalities, ethnicities, cultures, languages, behaviors, and human relations. Interestingly, Kuruvilla's fictional practice is also to "fold together" the stories of individuals in these urban zones who may not "know" each other but who come to know each other in specific and often quite meaningful ways—becoming characters in each other's stories, in effect—because of the interfaces produced in such a circumscribed but internally mobile physical environment. Individual subjectivities and stories, bearing the cultural histories that subtend them, bump into each other in *Milano, fin qui tutto bene*.

Relations of care are uncovered in the novel in their diversity, disrupting more rigid structures of caring associated with the heteronormative family, and positing instead (or in addition) less formalized and more expansive, sometimes momentary, affects and expressions of care for others. In three of the four sections of the novel, conventional family and marital relationships are absent or broken: Anita Patel, narrator and subject of "via Padova," lost her Italian mother and Indian father in a car accident at the age of eighteen and lives with her infant son whose biological father is absent; Samir, who narrates "viale Monza," migrated away from his family in Egypt and also has an infant son whom he rarely sees and with whose Italian mother he has contact but not a sustained relationship; Stefania, in "Sarpi" separated from her husband on the basis of his accusations of infidelity against her, which she denies. Only Tony, narrator in "Corvetto," lives within his extended family and has a relatively long-term heterosexual partner, but the narrative explores both the affection and the constraints of these bonds and tells of his negotiations to extract himself from their conventional forms and seek a more agile ecology of caring.

In all sections of the novel, other relations take the place of these missing or compromised forms of conventional kinship and offer reciprocal care in ways that are interestingly contingent, reflecting again the mobility of relations as well as of populations in globalized society. In the first section of the novel, Anita has a "best friend," Gioia, whom she has known since school days and clearly knows well. It is Gioia who collects Anita from hospital after she has given birth, unaccompanied, to her son Fabio. Gioia and Anita meet fairly frequently to catch up as friends, their conversation unfiltered, direct, and animated by an intelligence that reflects both their shared experience of success in school and the more complex mutual understanding of what matters to and what hurts the other. In short, this is a solid and genuine friendship, but the two women inhabit starkly different worlds: Gioia lives in a smart loft apartment in Brera, and her presence is always signaled by the arrival of her brand-new Bentley Continental GT, whilst Anita lives in via Clitumno, off via Padova, in cheap housing and with no luxury goods. This difference marked by urban localities and the lifestyles that they index is not only superficial: there is a critical distance that separates the two and a level of frustration that each one expresses towards the other and her lifestyle. Whilst this level of intimacy with the other is a mark of their bond, it also creates pain. For example, Anita describes—with full and somewhat ironic self-awareness—how an encounter with Gioia is marked by envy, "from the frustration of not having what I want and not being what others want. Gioia, on the other hand, has everything she wants and is everything that others want" (Kuruvilla 2012, 44–45). The depth of this painful difference from her friend is alluded to in the racializing comment that follows: "Gioia is also the prototype of beauty in the West today. [. . .] Tall, thin and blonde: perfectly designed for this place and this time, unlike me, who is always out of place and out of sync" (Kuruvilla 2012, 45). The strong relation of care celebrated in idealized notions of modern friendship is thus confirmed by Anita's lasting and honest relationship with Gioia as narrated here, but its tensions and threats to individual wellbeing are also exposed. Gioia proves herself to be "always there" for Anita when needed but at the same time is never there in the same place as Anita. This somewhat polluted relation of care is one that seems to fit the dynamic and unsettled environment of contemporary urban sociality.

Empathy surfaces in more incidental circumstances in Anita's narrative and elsewhere in the novel to produce attachments of care that may have little longevity but profound effect, in terms both of individual sense of self and place in the world and of activating new forms of kinship. The novel is peppered with these affective epiphanies, which articulate both the potential for surprise fostered within localities characterized by cultural diversity and the less visible presence of a robust infrastructure of human care. One example, constructed over time and yet fleeting and minimal in the actual occurrences that generate it, is the relationship between Anita and Julius, the South American proprietor of a grocery shop where she regularly buys tinned beans and powdered milk. Anita reflects: "I go to Julius' shop because I don't want to shut myself away at home and I want to live the street. Because I like him and I like his shop and I like his customers and I like feeling a bit ill-at-ease too. [. . .] I don't much like tinned beans and my son doesn't much like powdered milk, but for Julius they're a cover and for me they're an excuse, to help me feel like I'm participating actively in this world that is via Padova" (Kuruvilla 2012, 21).

The simple pleasure of a repeated mutual connection is underlined by the repetition of the verb "to like," and this connection is focused on a human individual, Julius, but at the same time used to expand outwards to the material location he inhabits and the wider community he engages with. This is a form of kinship in action: shared spaces, shared demands, shared supply, and shared everyday practices produce shared feeling. Julius' empathy is articulated specifically, as with Gioia, in terms of some productive critical estrangement or "unease." The goods Anita buys are themselves not liked or wanted, but they produce a human as well as commercial transaction that rewards both parties. The self-conscious performance of a routine exchange enables a more capillary and far-reaching connectivity to be nurtured.

A more sustained episode within the "via Padova" narrative explores the possibilities and the obstacles of a different and unexpected form of relationality. Anita is approached by a young Roma woman whilst eating in a restaurant, and the encounter produces immediate effects of both recognition and estrangement: "Then she gets up and comes towards us: kohl-lined eyes, pierced nose, plaited hair, bronzed skin, heavy jumper and flowery skirt. She reminds me of the women from Rajasthan who sell silver goods and fabrics for a few rupees on the beaches of Kovalam. I realize that there's a newborn baby curled up in the sling hanging across her chest. We're alike, I think: perhaps she's thinking the same" (Kuruvilla 2012, 32).

Anita's gaze here first identifies the woman according to a stereotype of ethnicity and gender, "othering" her according to how she looks. It then articulates a recognition that is both critical and self-critical: she reminds Anita of women vendors she encountered in India, which makes a connection in terms of Anita's own Indian heritage, but at the same time maintains a distance in that her act of recognition manifestly rests upon her being a tourist in India, inhabiting again a somewhat orientalizing position. Ultimately, that both women have infant children with them is what appears to instantiate a bond of some kind or at least a recognition of shared experience. Their respective care for their child creates the possibility of some kind of care for each other.

This possibility is realized, incrementally and with reservation, as Anita bends to the invitation of the young woman, Lejla, and to her own sense of guilt in rejecting and estranging Lejla, and accompanies Lejla to her home in a Roma camp. This episode, spanning several pages and fittingly interrupted by a digression to narrate an interconnected episode of encounter, sees Anita in the shops of via Padova and in a bar and then sees her following the river to the camp on the urban margins, talking quite intimately with Lejla along the way, meeting children in the camp, and listening to a detailed history of displacement from Lejla's mother before finally buying from Lejla an over-priced necklace that she does not like. This purchase is a tactic for taking her leave but is also a gesture of kindness: a means of giving by proxy to someone whose condition she empathizes with and whom she identifies with her own experience and feelings. Whilst cynical about what she partly narrates as her entrapment (the orchestrated process of familiarization that leads to her purchase), Anita comments also on the emotional impact of the connection made: "I've never worn necklaces. I put it on. I need to feel it on me. I feel lonely, suddenly, as I come out again into via Padova" (Kuruvilla 2012, 44).

No new and lasting friendship or family is forged in this encounter, and yet something happens from a chance encounter extended over an afternoon that establishes a form of strongly (but not exclusively) feminized sociality, an emotional and ethical recognition that creates a sense of kinship.

As indicated by the topography of the intraurban journey that Anita and Lejla take, these forms of contingent kinship in Kuruvilla's novel are predicated upon deep habitation of urban space. It is helpful here to recall Rosi Braidotti's theorization of nomadic thought, specifically her statement that "both the critique of ahistorical Eurocentrism and the quest for alternative genealogies of European universalism express a form of ethical and political accountability that requires adequate understandings of one's specific location, that is to say, one's embedded and embodied perspectives" (Braidotti 2011, 215). Principles of embeddedness and embodiment inform Kuruvilla's narrative and particularly the modes of interaction and relationality between individuals and groups.

Anita, in the first section, claims an ownership of her locality that is predicated upon her own lifetime of residence there (or thereabouts, since her family home was in a nearby but more middle-class neighborhood) and her knowledge of the modern social and cultural history of the city. She describes everyday urban features as her own ("il mio bar," [my bar] "la mia panchina" [my parkbench]) and knows the streets and those who routinely inhabit them intimately, albeit with a sense also of the capacity of the unexpected to emerge. Samir, in the second section, moves through the streets in a way that expresses his street knowledge (Piazzale Loreto is full of police, Porta Venezia of prostitutes) and also his familiarity with the places that a migrant can and cannot easily occupy, thus underscoring his experience as an outsider. Stefania, in the third section, similarly describes the everyday of via Sarpi in detail and with a sense of belonging, voiced in part through the analytical history she, like Anita, can offer of the presence of Chinese migrants and their families there, which in turn produces feelings of apparently unproblematic but conclusive distance: "I'm not frightened of the Chinese. Their world runs alongside mine: we follow two parallel tracks that will never meet, or only in infinity" (Kuruvilla 2012, 116). In the fourth section, Tony tells, again from the position of an informed insider-outsider, of decline in Corvetto and of the passage through the zone of different migrating communities from both within and outside Italian national territory, which itself measures a process of downward economic and social mobility. He articulates this in an image of bypassed and neglected Christian culture: "the patron of the area: 'El signurun,' a huge statue of Christ benedictory, the hand of his right arm broken and a wooden cross over his left, in effect a decaying divinity, positioned at the point of an angular terrace at the intersection with via San Dionigi" (Kuruvilla 2012, 160).

As the examples above demonstrate, embeddedness and embodied experience of locality bring—to return to Braidotti's formulation—genuinely "adequate understandings" of location, which are circumspect and critical, charting the exclusions and inequities to which "ahistorical Eurocentrism" has been blind, as well as valuing the plural relations produced by cultural diversity and socioeconomic change. As Braidotti further enjoins, "we need to think global but act local, in the situated here and now of our lived experience" (Braidotti 2011, 20). This situatedness is brought to life in Kuruvilla's novel by the consistent expression, in narratives voiced by different individuals, of the everyday and of the material. As illustrated already, this has much to do with presence in identifiable and empirically verifiable urban space, including specific streets, monuments, intersections, buildings, bars, and so forth. More specifically, the presence in the narratives of material objects that recur in different sections of the novel and create connections between them works to create a community of things. This at once lends material substance and purpose to human relations and also articulates an investment of the human in the material, or a material form of kinship that values the relationality of things not only as an adjunct or accessory to human relationality but as a means of forming bonds in itself.

This flow and exchange of things in *Milano, fin qui tutto bene* is light-touch and largely a vehicle of humor in the novel, and the way in which it activates encounters and the affects that attach to them is interesting. The most prominent example is the "letto a soppalco," (loft bed) which Anita wants to acquire so she and her son can sleep separately and more comfortably. Samir and his flatmates want to get rid of one; Tony at the end of the novel advertises his for collection, marking his transition to a new life ("a piece of the past taking its leave" (Kuruvilla 2012, 178)); Anita makes an appointment to claim it. Similarly, Stefania invests the money earned from selling one of her paintings in an expensive pair of boots, which she then accidentally leaves on the Metro. Tony finds them, and notes that, despite their value, "instead of selling them on I returned them to their owner" (Kuruvilla 2012, 145). The lost boots thus become the vehicle of an ethical interaction, a confirmation of community. Gioia's Bentley, as well as figuring as part of the representation of Gioia in Anita's story, appears as the vehicle used by Gioia's partner when he tries to have sex with Samir in the second section of the novel, and as the improbably glamorous vehicle driven by an improbably glamorous woman who turns up sporadically in Corvetto to buy cocaine, as noted by Tony in the final section. In this way, the mobility within a particular locality of objects, noted and recounted from the perspectives of different human agents through whose hands or vision they pass, enacts a sequence of relations that are both the reflection and the very substantiation of human relationality. As John Urry asserts, "individuals [. . .] exist beyond their private bodies, leaving traces of their selves in space" (Urry 2007, 15), noting that encounters between individuals, and the affects that those encounters produce, need not necessarily entail immediate personal propinquity but can be mobilized by the material (or digital, in Urry's argument) traces of themselves. In this way, Gioia and Tony, though never meeting each other, are related—as are Anita and Tony before they actually meet to exchange the loft bed. Material exchanges catalyze human curiosity and deliver mutual support and recognition along with the gratification of items that simply make everyday life better.

Language is also a striking vehicle of relations in Kuruvilla's novel, recording linguistic traces that create bonds within and, crucially, beyond the lived locality and the lived temporality in which the events of the narrative take place. The author's distinctive technique of folding together languages within the spoken narrative of any one narrator in the novel allows familial and cultural linguistic bonds, as well as imagined affiliations, to be expressed.

All sections of the novel incorporate one or more languages alongside the colloquial standard Italian that is the primary instrument of narration (Burns 2020). Anita blends into her discourse the idiomatic Italian of her mother, Samir brings Egyptian Arabic into the narrative, Stefania moves seamlessly between Milanese dialect and standard Italian, and Tony mixes both Neapolitan dialect and Rasta patois with the standard. As this description immediately signals, this technique of linguistic blending—or even of translanguaging[2] —enables bonds of conventional kinship to be brought into direct contact with the more diffuse forms of kinship that I have illustrated so far. For Anita, they bring her mother out of the past of her childhood and into the present of her adulthood and her own parenthood, in a different Milan from the one in which she was raised. They similarly bring Samir's heritage along with his present-tense sense of at once cultural distance and intercultural negotiation into his narrative of viale Monza. For Stefania, they articulate a form of "authentic" Milan of the past and enable her to voice the dialogue between this and the multicultural Sarpi of the present. For Tony, they both bespeak his heritage in another part of Italy and, in so doing, express the exclusion of this part of Italy from the dominant model of Italian economic success, thus giving accent to the very motivations for his family's migration. Rasta patois, on the other hand, is used by him as a lifestyle choice, the forward-facing expression of his musical and cultural preferences, as well as an oblique articulation of the subalternity of the Italian south historically. In mediating between these multiple languages, both "indigenous" to Italy and introduced through transmigration, the narrators in Kuruvilla's novel expand their kinship networks beyond the immediacy of the present in space and time, and voice in a very direct way, both audible and visible, the copresence of people, languages, cultures, and heritages in contemporary Milan.

Translation is used by Kuruvilla to bridge the potential divide of compre-hensibility between the languages with which the reader may be familiar and those used by the narrators. Translations are inserted fluidly into the narrative as an immediate, inclusive rephrasing of the "foreign"-language utterance, thus affording a translingual kinship in which recognition of otherwise un-known idioms enables bonds to be created between individuals who speak different languages. In its focus on mediation between languages and cul-tures, Kuruvilla's novel finds parallels with Amara Lakhous's *Scontro di civiltà per un ascensore a piazza Vittorio*, in which multiple languages are present, if not so immediately voiced in the narrative. Heteroglossic in simi-lar ways to *Milano, fin qui tutto bene*, Lakhous's novel also presents narra-tives spoken by a variety of speakers or witnesses, each voicing their opinion and experience of the narrator-protagonist at the center of the novel, Ahmed, known in Rome by most as Amedeo. Speakers also bring to the narrative their history, culture, heritage, and present experience of Rome's piazza Vit-torio zone, filtering their statements about Ahmed/Amedeo through the rela-tions they have established with the protagonist. Ahmed/Amedeo is thus placed at the fulcrum of an improvised kinship network, in which his rela-tionships, both intimate and incidental, become the material that connects individuals of diverse provenance, with diverse reasons for living in that part of Rome and diverse everyday practices, in the apartment building that they share. The focus on Ahmed/Amedeo enables connections to be articulated between both individuals and the cultural values by which they identify themselves and calibrate their experience.

The centrality of Ahmed/Amedeo also brings a distinctive perspective on the questions of conventional and reimagined kinships outlined at the start of this discussion. The core of the novel, in which the protagonist speaks for himself in eleven reflections narrated in the first person rather than being spoken of by others, is marked by a gradual loss of mastery of his narrative. The memory of his life in Algeria before migration, and particularly the severance of his relationship with his partner because of her violent death, becomes increasingly traumatic until it renders him speechless in his final interventions. The loss of relations of care established elsewhere in place and time and cemented by the act of migration—signaled also in the switch from Ahmed to Amedeo—appears here to be overwhelming, and the network of new relations established in the present locality of Rome appears not to be sufficiently substantive to sustain the protagonist. Ahmed/Amedeo in effect loses himself and his authority through the care and work he has dedicated to serving, nurturing, and speaking for others: he becomes the fictional charac-ter, "Amedeo," constructed and narrated in diverse and sometimes contradic-tory ways by others.

In this way, the multilingual and multicultural narrative of relationality in urban space in Lakhous's novel is somewhat different in its purposes and effects from that of Kuruvilla's novel. The form of the detective investigation in *Scontro di civiltà per un ascensore a piazza Vittorio* and the emphasis on migration install a greater emphasis on the authority of a single "successful" migrant who works towards full linguistic, cultural, and moral citizenship in the destination culture: it is in short a different kind of story.[3] Kuruvilla's more polycentric narrative, offering "thick description" (Geertz 1973) of events, practices, and relations in the heterotopic locality of Milan, bespeaks an anthropological and even ethnographic experience of kinship and enables the loose structures of contemporary relationality to be followed in their unexpected turns and intersections. Connections between individuals, and the ways in which these connections act upon individuals, prevail over the affirmation of discrete subject positions, recalling again Braidotti's "nomadic thought" (Braidotti 2011, 12) and its focus on forward and outward movement and becoming, which she aligns with "potential" (Braidotti 2011, 148).

In conclusion, I offer a long quotation from Braidotti that I reproduce in full because its detail seems to me closely to describe the work that Kuruvilla's novel performs:

> Figurations are forms of literal expression of the politics of location that bring into representation that which the dominant system had declared off-limits. They are situated practices that require the awareness of the limitations as well as the specificity of one's locations. A figuration renders our image of thought in terms of a decentered and multi-layered vision of the subject as a dynamic and changing entity; as such it can be taken as a dramatization of the processes of becoming. This process assumes that identity takes place in between nature/ technology, male/female, black/white, local/global, present/past- in the spaces that flow and connect such seeming binaries. We live in permanent processes of transition, hybridization, and nomadisation. And these in-between states and stages defy the established modes of theoretical representation precisely because they are zigzagging, not linear and process oriented, not concept driven. (Braidotti 2011, 217)

Milano, fin qui tutto bene may be comprehended as such a "figuration" of nomadic citizenship, the provisionality conjured by its title speaking of the emphasis on dynamism and process that Braidotti foregrounds. Telling of transnational subjects and multicultural spaces conventionally apprehended as "off-limits," the narratives within the novel are themselves "multi-layered" and dynamic, telling of the "becoming" of an interpersonal and social complex, predicated upon contingency, which may productively displace the normative familial and class structures that have historically underpinned the form of the novel. Kuruvilla's book immerses the reader in the "zigzagging" forms of relationality within the local that bring to life pluralized and newly empowering notions of kinship.

NOTES

1. Clingman discusses the navigation of boundaries as central to transnational fictions, defining navigation as follows: "It means *being prepared to be* in the space of crossing, in transition, in movement, in journey. It means accepting placement as *displacement*, position as *disposition*, not through coercion of others or by others of ourselves, but through 'disposition' as an affect of the self, as a kind of approach" (Clingman 2009, 24–25; italics in the original).

2. Translanguaging, as formulated by García and Wei, "considers the language practices of bilinguals not as two autonomous language systems as has been traditionally the case, but as one linguistic repertoire with features that have been societally constructed as belonging to two separate languages" (García and Wei 2014, 2).

3. On the construction of the migrant character who may "pass" as Italian, see Spackman.

REFERENCES

Amin, Ash. 2004. "Regions Unbound: Towards a New Politics of Place." *Geografiska Annaler. Series B. Human Geography* 86, no. 1: 33–44.

Braidotti, Rosi. 2011. *Nomadic Theory: The Portable Rosi Braidotti*. New York: Columbia University Press.

Burns, Jennifer. 2020. "Arabising Italian? Transnational Literature as Multilingual Transaction." *Journal of Multilingual and Multicultural Development*. DOI: https://doi.org/10.1080/01434632.2020.1720221

Butler, Judith. 2000. *Antigone's Claim: Kinship Between Life and Death*. New York: Columbia University Press.

Clingman, Stephen. 2009. *The Grammar of Identity: Transnational Fiction and the Nature of the Boundary*. Oxford: Oxford University Press.

García, Ofelia, and Li Wei. 2014. *Translanguaging: Language, Bilingualism and Education*. London: Palgrave Macmillan.

Geertz, Clifford. 1973. *The Interpretation of Culture: Selected Essays*. New York: Basic Books.

Haraway, Donna. 1991. *Simians, Cyborgs, and Women*. New York: Routledge.

Kuruvilla, Gabriella. 2012. *Milano, fin qui tutto bene*. Rome: Laterza.

Lakhous, Amara. 2006. *Scontro di civiltà per un ascensore a piazza Vittorio*. Rome: E/O.

Riggs, Damien W., and Elizabeth Peel. 2016. *Critical Kinship Studies. An Introduction to the Field*. London: Palgrave Macmillan.

Spackman, Barbara. 2012. "Italians DOC? Posing and Passing from Giovanni Finati to Amara Lakhous." *Postcolonial Italy: Challenging National Homogeneity*, ed. by Cristina Lombardi-Diop and Caterina Romeo. New York: Palgrave Macmillan: 125–38.

Urry, John. 2007. *Mobilities*. Cambridge: Polity.

The Two of Me

Gabriella Kuruvilla / Translated by Eleanor Paynter

The alarm rings. I need to change the ring. I can't stand this one. It sounds like an ambulance. Or something that signals danger, that makes you anxious.

All I need is more anxiety. No thanks, I'm doing just fine.

I place my open hands on Bear's ears. I cover them completely, but softly. Without applying pressure, without bothering him. It's a gesture of protection and care. Not aggressive, not invasive. A gesture I could use myself.

"It's nothing," I tell him. My voice quiet. "Stay asleep, little one," I add, without speaking, just moving my lips. But he understands. He can lip read. Really, with him there's no need to speak. Just another reason he's the best.

Then I smack the alarm clock to make it stop. The alarm, see, only understands harsh gestures. At last it's quiet again. I adore the silence. I'd live in silence, but there's the constant problem of communication. Trying to communicate with Kamala and Prabir only proves this point.

In the eyes of the law, Kamala and Prabir would be my parents. That conditional form is necessary. Not everything the law says is true. The law lies, but it's allowed to. The law legitimizes itself.

"Daughter, get up, it's seven o'clock."

Here she is, punctual as a Swiss watch.

Too bad she's a typical Indian woman: all wife, daughter-in-law, aunt, niece, sister, and, despite her venerable age, daughter. According to the law, she's also a mother. My mother. Except that, for me, she's not: and that's coming from the person with the most at stake in the matter. But this is in itself a controversial subject. The others aren't any better, but they don't concern me. Not really.

Kamala didn't do much to become a wife, daughter-in-law, aunt, niece, sister, and daughter. I mean, she hardly did anything to have those roles.

She's one of those people identities rained down on, but she carries them as if they were medals pinned to a uniform. As if she earned them on the battle-field.

As if she's done something in life. As if she was something in life.

"Daughter, get up, it's seven o'clock."

Maybe Kamala thinks she's an alarm clock, too.

It would be the only case in which the role she has is one she earned.

She's a wife and daughter-in-law thanks to her parents and Prabir's, who arranged their marriage when they were quite young and got them wed as soon as they were both eighteen.

She's a daughter, sister, niece, and aunt thanks to her relatives, who gave birth incessantly. Stringing children like pearls on an infinitely long neck-lace. And yet.

And yet she was the one who broke the chain, unable to bear children, despite all efforts. Disproving that where there's a will there's a way.

The truth is that when she tried to do something, whether on her own or with others, she never quite succeeded. Really, she didn't succeed at all.

Maybe it wasn't entirely her fault.

Maybe it was Prabir who couldn't make it happen. Or, as I suspect, they were both incapable. I think, in this case, it's actually the couple that didn't work. Not that in other cases everything goes smoothly. But I think this couple is really missing the basics. I mean, I can't imagine Kamala and Prabir having sex. I can't even picture them naked. But really, I thank God, who I believe in even though I'm not sure he exists, that I've never seen them having sex or naked. The first image would be a consequence of the second, I guess. And decidedly worse. Although both are creepy. But put them togeth-er and it's a hymn to chastity.

"Daughter, get up, it's seven o'clock."

But I can't thank the law, which I don't believe in even though I'm certain it exists.

It exists to the extent that it gave Kamala the right to call me "Daughter," using my life to protect her own. Or, at least, to protect her reputation. Because an Indian woman isn't exactly considered a woman if she's not also a mother. She's more like a mistake, a joke of nature.

Except that I'm not her daughter, not really. I'm more like a stopgap, or a band-aid stuck over an open wound. And everyone knows that when you put a band-aid over an open wound, it doesn't heal: it rots.

Despite all that, Kamala keeps calling me "Daughter." With the law on her side. But it's like putting a Louis Vuitton label on a purse that's not Louis Vuitton. And that makes me a fake. Illegal. Something hawked on the street. Something my real parents might sell, maybe. Actually, when I see immi-grant vendors around, men or women, I always look them in the eye, hoping to lose myself in their gaze: as if their eyes weren't a mirror but more like a door to their soul. Then, even if they don't open up to me, I always buy something: a book, usually. To establish even the smallest bond with them, even if it's just economic.

My room is full of books. Books about Africa, mostly. The words they contain are the only ones I seek. Because those words aren't forced on you by someone speaking but are available for whoever wants them. You can decide to read them or not. This is the freedom they offer.

"Daughter, get up, it's seven o'clock."

If I had the strength I'd get up, grab a book and settle in to read, to distract myself from the voice of Kamala, calling out. Calling me "Daughter." But I don't have the strength, not even to respond to her. To say, for instance, "I'm not your daughter." She should be grateful that I stay quiet.

I turn towards Bear. To him, I'm very grateful. For everything. He basically saved me. But that's not why I named him "Salvatore."

He is what he is, not just what he is for me. And not what I wish he was. Having expectations of others is a bit like placing a bag of stones on their shoulders, then getting upset if they don't carry it or, worse, if they leave it somewhere just to avoid scoliosis.

I look at Bear: his back is fine, mine less so. Less is an understatement.

"Daughter, get up, it's seven o'clock."

Kamala's gratitude towards me evidently doesn't include not waking me up.

But then I ask myself: "Why?" Why do other mothers, and even other dads, call their children "Amore," "Tesoro," "Micetto," "Topolino," "Pucci-pucci" or use other strange pet names, or even the child's own banal name, but Kamala and Prabir insist on calling me "Daughter"?

Why?

I'm full of questions like this, questions I try to avoid. But they come at me, attack me, enter my head, filling it, assaulting it. They bite. They kick and punch. They're quite violent. They really hurt.

And so I have to run away. But running from questions is difficult. Mostly because they're so much faster than me, and they always catch up in the end. The worst part is that sometimes, along with them, answers arrive. Those can be more painful than the questions. They often travel together, questions and answers. Like the cat and the fox. Or a criminal organization.

"Daughter, get up, it's seven o'clock."

I don't say anything, as usual. But once, I did say something, to both Kamala and Prabir.

"You know you should call me 'Laura,' not 'Daughter,'" I told them.

"Yes, Daughter," they replied in unison.

That's why I don't say anything. It's pointless.

And anyway, I know why they call me "Daughter." They probably honestly believe *in nomen omen*.[1] If one day they want a pear but get an apple, I worry they'll call it a pear, hoping—or, worse, certain—that it will become a pear. As if casting a spell.

To me, though, it seems like a kind of exploitation of naiveté. And by naive, I mean them, myself, and everyone else. Because it's the others they're trying to convince. For Kamala and Prabir, the opinions of others are incredibly important. But it's not their fault. It's the culture they come from. A culture in which appearance means everything.

"Daughter, get up, it's seven o'clock."

Calling me "Daughter" is an attempt to ignore appearances. Because appearance makes it clear that they're not my parents and I'm not their daughter. That actually, they're Indian and I'm African. So far, the only ones Kamala and Prabir have convinced are the others. You can tell that other people don't notice the difference between Indians and Africans. Or maybe they think two Indians can produce an African, like how a negative times a negative equals a positive. Maybe the math confuses them. But I hope that Kamala and Prabir haven't convinced themselves. They'll never convince me. Though I'd rather not be the exception here.

It's enough that I'm the only teenager whose best and only friend is Bear.

Though I'm sure that if other people could have Bear, they wouldn't want any other friends. He'd be their best and only friend, too. That's what he is. This is one certainty, at least for me.

Another, of course, is that I'm not Kamala and Prabir's daughter.

I have few certainties—but in this case, *melius est deficere quam abundare*.[2] Because certainties often crumble. They're probably made of the same stuff as hopes.

"Daughter, get up, it's seven o'clock."

I'm collapsing from exhaustion.

It must be the fact that she keeps calling me "Daughter" that glues me to the bed, preventing me from getting up. It's as if an enormous weight was crushing me. The weight of her need.

If we want to be honest, she's the one who behaves like a child. It's enough to hear her talking on the phone with her parents to understand she's never moved beyond inferiority and submission with them. And you don't understand it from *what* she says, considering I don't speak Malayalam. You understand it from how she says it. From the tone she uses, and the way she moves, pacing the house with shoulders hunched and head bowed, her phone glued to her ear. As soon as she hangs up, she straightens her spine, at least a bit. And she wipes the sweat from her brow. Even in winter, even if it's cold out. The nervous sweating with her parents is a problem. Or rather, it is a problem in itself. Because Kamala sweats with everyone, on every occasion. And in every season, no matter the temperature.

Actually, her inferiority complex is with the entire world, meaning even with Prabir. And, okay, there's the matter of roles, but she's like this with me, too, and in our case the roles should be reversed. But really, that's how she is with everyone. It's embarrassing to go shopping with her, for example, because it's a nonstop "Thank you," "Excuse me," "Sorry," "If I may," "If you don't mind," "If it's no trouble." I have a feeling those are the first Italian words she learned.

Back when I was still speaking to her I told her, "You're Fantozziana, Kamala."[3] She asked, "Couldn't you call me 'Mamma'?" and I replied "No" and so, maybe to change the subject, she asked, "Is Fantozziana a compliment?" And, whatever, I didn't feel like explaining it to her, that it wasn't exactly like she thought. I just said, "You should change outfits, what you're wearing is covered in sweat. Like you."

"Daughter, get up, it's seven o'clock."

Who knows what she's wearing now.

She changes her outfit like I change hairstyles—neither improves the situation at all. Each time we're back to where we started, if not worse.

Bear doesn't sweat. And he has beautiful hair. Always. I mean, it's not like when he wakes up in the morning, he stands in front of the mirror in a useless attempt to make his hair look acceptable. Not him. When he wakes up in the morning, he doesn't even look in the mirror. Because he knows he's just fine as-is. He doesn't need a mirror. Anyway, the mirror only tells you what's outside. Despite what Lombroso would say, convinced that our exterior reflects what's inside.[4] And so I hope, at least, that Lombroso was wrong. After all, everyone gets it wrong at least once in their life. Maybe this was his turn.

"Daughter, get up, it's seven o'clock."

She's still at it.

Kamala's always making mistakes. She herself is a mistake. Even her voice is wrong. It has an unbearable sound, even worse than the alarm clock.

Too bad that, unlike the alarm, I can't just whack her in the head to make her stop. Maybe then she'd stop calling me "Daughter" and start calling me "Laura."

It's true that in the past I called Kamala "Mamma" and Prabir "Papà." But I knew it wasn't right, that in fact the whole thing was wrong. That we were deceiving ourselves, or at least attempting to.

To tolerate the deception, I tried to view it as a game. A role-playing game. Harmless, mostly. Like the one where one kid says, "I'll be the doctor and you be the patient," and as they act it out they get that they're pretending. It's a performance that stops at a certain point. But we didn't stop and risked winding up like those actors who immerse themselves so deeply in a role that they're never able to step out of it again.

"Daughter, get up, it's seven o'clock."

A game is fun when it doesn't last long, they say.

That's not always true, but in this case it is.

Not that I ever considered it to be a fun game, this one.

It was probably in order to bring it to a close that, one day, out of nowhere, I asked Kamala and Prabir, "Was I adopted?"

"Daughter, what are you saying?" they replied in unison.

"Was I adopted?" I repeated, my voice beginning to shake.

"Daughter, what are you saying?" they replied again.

Sometimes I think Kamala and Prabir are one and the same person, I'm just seeing double. As if I were drunk. I've always wanted to drink. I abstain to keep Kamala and Prabir from multiplying infinitely.

"Was I adopted?" I asked a third time.

"Daughter, what are you saying?" they responded.

I felt my eyes fill with anger. In liquid form, as usual.

My body and mind were about to give in. Anger has this effect on me when it's about to peak. I was no longer able to move or think, except in a confused, chaotic, exaggerated way. Pathetically. I could have had seizures and screamed like I was possessed. The only way to avoid it was to leave. To lift the needle from the broken record of our dialogue.

I gathered what remained of my physical and psychological strength. What remained of me.

"I'm going out," I said.

"Daughter, where are you going?" they asked.

"Talk to me one at a time, first one and then the other, or one yes and the other no, or better yet, don't talk to me at all," I would have liked to respond.

Who knows how they managed to be so synchronized. Not even choirs get it right every time.

"I'm going to buy a notebook. I need it for school," I said.

In their minds, one shouldn't go out unless there's a practical reason.

"Daughter, come back soon."

"Daughter, get up, it's seven o'clock."

I could've decided not to come back at all.

Instead I'd come back, and early, because of an encounter—that is, *the* encounter. That event prompted me to make a choice—not to be alone.

What happened is that I'd gone outside and started running, probably to get as far as I could from Kamala and Prabir as quickly as possible. But I'd run right into a trashcan. I often bump into things, or people, when I run. I've thought of it as a kind of metaphor, like if life is an obstacle course, instead of jumping or scaling the obstacles, I run into them, and I stop and turn around. I had stopped, but I hadn't gone back. Not right away. I'd looked inside the trashcan, and there, surrounded by garbage, was Bear.

He stared at me, bewildered and sad. Like someone who doesn't understand why a thing has happened to him. He was out of place, it seemed. Or maybe not.

"Nothing grows from diamonds, but flowers grow from manure" is a saying I've always thought to be more poetic than true. In that case, though, it seemed like there was poetry in the truth.

I pulled him out of the trash, brushed him off, and looked him in the eye. I saw my reflection, and for the first time I wasn't judged. I was simply seen.

I took him in my arms and hugged him close. I felt better, even good.

I heard his heart beating, in sync with mine.

We were synchronized, like Kamala and Prabir. Except it wasn't our voices that were synchronized, but our feelings.

I said, "You're a bear and your name will be Bear."

"Oh, at last, someone who calls bread 'bread' and wine 'wine,'" he responded.

Or, at least, that's what I understood.

From that moment on I started calling Kamala "Kamala" and Prabir "Prabir" so as not to let Bear down. But also out of a sense of justice and revenge. My desire for revenge came from the betrayal of my sense of justice.

"Let's go back," I said to Bear.

I wanted to give him a home in a real house, not a street and certainly not a trashcan. The only house that I could call home, at least in form if not in content, was Kamala and Prabir's. And that's why I went back early. Plus, it's a super clean house. As a housekeeper, Kamala is truly perfect. More perfect than she is as an alarm clock, even.

"Daughter, get up, it's seven o'clock."

I often regret having come back early.

Still, I didn't come back alone, I came back with Bear: the two of me. Like there were two of them.

"Daughter, weren't you going to buy a notebook?" Kamala and Prabir asked when they saw me come back so early.

"This is Bear," I said.

"But it's not a notebook," they replied.

"Exactly, just like I'm not 'Daughter,'" I retorted.

"Daughter, enough of this nonsense," they finished.

"Daughter, get up, it's seven o'clock."

Who knows when they'll be done with it, with calling me "Daughter."

"You cut it out, stop calling me 'Daughter,'" I should have said.

Instead, I decided not to say anything.

I stopped speaking to them. But I couldn't stop hearing them, so I decided to pay attention to what they were saying and how they were saying it, noticing the difference between verbal language and body language. I noticed that Kamala would say "I'm happy" with a sad face, or that Prabir would say "I love you" while staring at the TV. He really does love the TV. So, in his own way, he was being honest.

There was still something strange in their "I'm happy" or "I love you." Not just because of how they said it, but for the very fact that they said it. Because Kamala and Prabir are Indian. And Indians hardly ever say these kinds of things in private. Much less in public.

In public they usually smile and swing their heads right to left, top to bottom, first toward one shoulder and then toward the other. As if they're doing a neck stretching exercise. I tried to do it in front of the mirror, to see how it worked. My head felt like an upside-down pendulum. I felt extremely silly, like them, and stopped immediately. It's not a wish of mine to look like Kamala and Prabir, especially when they act ridiculous.

Anyway, in public, other than smiling and shaking their heads from right to left, Kamala and Prabir don't say much.

So I concluded that, for them, saying "I'm happy" and "I love you" in front of me probably didn't equate to saying "I'm happy" and "I love you" in public, because in front of me, they don't feel like they're in public, but like they're with their daughter. Maybe they say "I'm happy" and "I love you" and "Daughter" because they believe that saying these things will make them come true.

They must trust in language, in spoken words, Kamala and Prabir.

It's almost endearing. But sweetness and pain look alike.

"Daughter, get up, it's seven o'clock."

"Shut up," I want to tell her.

But since I say almost nothing to her anymore, I don't tell her this.

Or maybe I could. This could be part of the almost.

Except I don't want to, because I know that even if I told her this, she'd keep at it, just like she keeps calling me "Daughter."

Anyway, I'm the one who shuts up, not her. Sometimes injustices are tolerated out of pure laziness.

Before, though, I never shut up. I'd say anything. In public or private. Not because I had faith in words. They simply came out of my mouth. Everyone called me "Broken Faucet." Everyone except for Kamala and Prabir, who never stopped calling me "Daughter." But now, even though I hardly say anything, not much has changed in my relationships with others or with Kamala and Prabir, which confirms that we can rely on words even less than we do.

The only one I still talk to is Bear. But I usually talk to him without speaking. I just think it. Sometimes I even say, "I'm happy" and "I love you" without speaking. I just think it with a happy expression and look him in the eyes. He hears me just the same.

The amazing thing is that he responds. Being responded to is in itself amazing. It's so amazing that sometimes I'm afraid he doesn't exist, that he's just a projection of my mind. A hallucination produced to satisfy some need of mine. The need to survive, perhaps. Some needs I don't understand. They originate in the gut but never pass through the brain. This is one of those.

I glance at him. I'd like to hug him, but I resist, so as not to wake him. He's probably still dreaming. He's smiling. Maybe he's having a premonition. Maybe he's dreaming about what we'll do when I come home from school, in which case he's right to smile. I smile, too, thinking about it.

"Daughter, get up, it's seven o'clock."

I should get up, so I can come home from school and do all the things Bear and I do when I'm back from school.

When I come home from school I go to our room, drop my bag on the floor, dive onto the bed, pull back the covers, take him in my arms, and play with him. If the weather is bad we stay in our room, but if it's nice out I take him to the playground.

We always go to the playground on the late side, when the others head home. I don't want the kids or their families or, even worse, their nannies, watching us. They usually give us strange or mean looks. The worst looks come from the nannies. Because kids play and parents are distracted, but the nannies are there to watch other people's children. And in my opinion, they're lonely and bored, and that combination makes a person stare too much. And in the end you'll always find something wrong, even if that something isn't really there. That's why the nannies give the worst looks, as if there were something strange or wrong in my playing with Bear.

They must be jealous. They'd like to be in my shoes, playing with Bear.

"Daughter, get up, it's seven o'clock."

Who knows what time it is in India. Who knows if there are playgrounds in India. Who knows if nannies would be jealous of Bear and me in India. I've never been to India. I'm not even sure I'd want to go. I don't have any ties with India. What I already know about it is enough. I haven't been to Africa, either, and that's a place I'd really like to go to. I don't know much about Africa, but I have a real connection with it, and I'd like to know all I can about it. What I've read in the books the vendors sell isn't enough.

Plus, it seems like it's impossible to know yourself if you don't know the place you come from. Even if, legally speaking, I'm from Italy. By that logic, I'm Italian. So sure, trust the law if you like. Ever since the law said that Kamala and Prabir are my parents, I've stopped trusting it. Other people must not trust it much, either, because other than the law, no one considers me to be Italian.

They all identify me by a color, more than a place. To them I'm black. And black, for them, isn't Italian. It's African, but it could be Indian, too. For them the south of the world is all one color.

"I'm not black," I'd like to say. "I'm African," I could explain, "and therefore I'm not Indian." But it wouldn't change a thing. They'd all keep thinking of me as black. Or, at most, as a person of color. Which, as far as descriptions go, has always seemed a bit general to me. Better to be called black, then.

Except that I'm not black. Kamala and Prabir aren't either.

We're truly different. We can't be joined by a color, which isn't even our color, anyway.

If we really want to go down the chromatic rabbit hole, I'd say that I'm very dark brown and that Kamala and Prabir are dark brown. It's a matter of gradation, but it's important, not something to disregard. Plus, there's the matter of our hair. Mine is curly and frizzy, but theirs is straight and soft. Kamala sleeps with rollers in, and when she takes them out, she has ringlets. Prabir, whose hair is actually white, dyes his. It's not really dye, which he says is artificial, but henna, which he says is natural. It turns his hair bright orange. As colors go, it seems even more artificial. And finally, there's the matter of features. Mine are more prominent, and theirs more subdued. We all have large eyes, noses, and mouths, but mine are really big and theirs are kind of big. Failed attempts at measuring up, somehow. Anyway, the truth that supersedes all others is that we're really different, them and me.

Except that none of us is black.

Bear and I are quite different, too. But this isn't a problem. In part because I never called him "Son," even though it would be fine if he called me "Daughter."

Thanks to him, I was reborn.

"Daughter, get up, it's seven o'clock."

I sit up in bed, slowly. From my waist up I'm vertical, and from my waist down I'm horizontal. I make an angle. I collapse back on the bed. Now I'm a straight line.

These rigid shapes have more to do with interior than exterior. My exterior is all curvy, unfortunately. I don't get why we humans can't sand ourselves down. I'd love to be a box, all angles, long and straight, like the popular models you see in magazines.

I roll onto one side, next to Bear, making myself into an S. A box could never do this.

"I really have to go now, see you later," I think. He understands.

The sun filters through the shutters. It makes lines of light on the wall, almost parallel and almost straight. It's the almost that bothers me. I wish they were perfectly parallel and perfectly straight. I wish there was something perfect in this world besides Bear. At least geometrically perfect.

I count the lines, almost parallel and almost straight, imperfect. I count them to myself, in my head, without making a sound, not a peep, not wanting to break the silence.

One, two, three, four, five.

"Daughter, get up, it's seven o'clock."

If only she'd said, "It's six."

I lose count, start over.

One, two, three.

"Daughter, get up, it's seven o'clock."

Of course, at this point, it's not seven anymore—it must be at least seven forty-two. If not later. Even Kamala must have lost count.

I get up, put a pair of pants over the camisole and underwear I slept in. I walk barefoot across the floor, reducing the sound I make to a minimum.

I stand before the mirror and look at myself. I should avoid this, I know from experience, but the only thing I've learned from experience is that we don't learn from experience.

I start running my hands through my hair: it's like putting them in an overgrown bush, full of brambles and thorns. I try to give them some kind of shape. An acceptable shape, I mean. Mission impossible.

There's a song that says that if you really want to achieve something, you will.

"You can get it if you really want," it says.

That song gets on my nerves, every time I hear it, because it's not true. The song tells a lie, like when Kamala calls me "Daughter."

Both of them are lying.

The singer of that song should be arrested for "creating hope that reality can't live up to" or, if the charge seems too long, for generating frustration. Frustration he passes on to others, washing his hands of it. Jimmy Cliff is his name. "Passing the Buck" or "Pontius Pilate" would be more fitting.

But then, he's got curly, frizzy hair, too. He almost always hides it under a hat. So, I guess I'll go out and buy myself a hat, too, to hide my hair. It's a little like sweeping dirt under a rug. This, too, is a lie.

"Daughter, get up, it's seven o'clock."

I open the door and see her. Actually, I see them. Kamala and Prabir are standing there, one next to the other, shoulder to shoulder. Like two statuettes or guards.

Prabir must have just shown up, otherwise I can't understand why he isn't saying, together with Kamala, "Daughter, get up, it's seven."

Or maybe he's become mute. So maybe it's true that "You can get it if you really want," every now and then.

I look at them, study them. I bow down. Stretch my arms out in front of me, placing one hand on top of the other, as if preparing to dive. I wedge myself between them. I move past them, separating them. The fact that I manage to physically separate them every so often gives me a sense of satisfaction. Who knows if they'd be harmless, if they were actually separated. As the saying goes, in unity is strength.

I think about Bear and already feel stronger. Too bad I can't bring him to school. The only time I did that I got in trouble. But that wasn't the problem, the problem was that all my classmates stared at me like the nannies at the playground. My friendship with Bear needs to stay far from the gaze of others.

I eat breakfast quickly, hoping that Kamala and Prabir don't sit down and try to chat.

Naturally, they sit down with me and try to chat. Together, of course.

So Prabir didn't become mute, after all.

I knew that "You can get it if you really want" is never true.

"Arrest Jimmy Cliff!" I shout.

That is, I think it intensely.

Bear hears me from the bedroom and nods his head up and down, a sign of approval.

I'm sorry if I woke him.

I inhale the milk and biscotti. I hope my stomach will chew them up, since my mouth doesn't have time. Because I don't have time. Because I don't want to spend any more time seated at this table with Kamala and Prabir talking to me. It feels like standing between two stereo speakers playing unbearable music. Fingernails on a chalkboard would be more pleasant.

I get up, grab my bag, and walk towards the door. The only reason I'm sorry to hear it close behind me is that I've left Bear and have to face school, eight hours that seem slower each day.

But even these hours will pass. Everything passes, in the end. The cemeteries testify to this.

And sure enough, they pass. I put my bag back on my shoulders and go once again to the door. The classroom door. Now I'm not leaving anything important behind me and I'm off to face the best part of the day. When I come home and play with Bear. Today it's sunny. That means we'll go to the playground later.

I pass by the playground. I always take this route when I go home. To check out the situation, see how crowded it is. I count the number of children, parents, and nannies. The nannies always outnumber the parents.

I never had a nanny. I had Kamala and Prabir. A nanny, though, would never have called me "Daughter," I think. That is, I hope.

I freeze. I see Kamala and Prabir there at the playground. I see them with Bear.

Kamala and Prabir are playing with Bear. They're holding his hands, one on one side and one on the other. They help him climb the castle steps, walk across the bridge, enter the tower, go down the slide and swing on the swing set. They do exactly what I do when I come to the playground with Bear.

I bend over and vomit. The words I didn't say, probably.

I wipe my mouth with the palm of my hand and wipe the palm of my hand on my pants. It's disgusting, the whole thing, but not as disgusting as what I've just seen.

Instinctively, I run. Faster than a Marine running to liberate a hostage.

"Take me, not him," I think.

I've always hated the idea of self-sacrifice, but we can't always be consistent. Especially with ourselves.

I trip, fall, get back up and run. If life is an obstacle course, I can't stop and turn back at every hurdle. Not now. I don't want to.

Where there's no will, there's no way, of course.

I'm so close to them, I can hear them. Kamala and Prabir call Bear, "Son."

"Mamma. Papà," I say.

I don't think it, but I say it.

Kamala and Prabir, at the same exact moment, turn away from Bear and look at me.

"Daughter," they say.

And it's okay.

"Thanks," says Bear.

I get the feeling that this time everyone heard him. Just not with their ears.

NOTES

1. In your name lies your destiny.

2. "Better too little than too much," a twist on the usual saying *Melius est abbundare quam deficere* (Better too much than too little).

3. Ugo Fantozzi is a fictional character, created by Paolo Villaggio for satirical stories and films of the same name. He is plagued by bad luck and submissive to those around him.

4. Cesare Lombroso was a nineteenth-century criminologist who developed a theory about associations between physical traits and propensity to criminal behavior.

Translingual Literature and Multi-Belonging

Ron Kubati

"How many times, since I left Lebanon in 1976 to live in France, have people asked me, with the best intention in the world, whether I felt 'more French' or 'more Lebanese?' And I always give the same answer: 'Both'" (Maalouf 2001, 1). There are several authors in Italian who write in more than one language or adopt self-translation. In fact, possessing more than one passport, citizenship, or residence permit is not a merely bureaucratic issue. Stateless person, illegal immigrant, uprooted, or non-belonger could equate dangerously to non-human as it emerges from Hannah Arendt's, Giorgio Agamben's, and Primo Levi's work.[1] It is no coincidence that the possession of two passports speaks of Italian-Americans, French-Germans, and so on. That legal hyphen is the thread of multi-belonging that is also a cultural issue. Multi-belonging can be seen as an inclusive solution, historically circumscribed, certainly transitory, the duration of which would in any case be difficult to anticipate. In this article I will focus mainly on the cultural strategies and other implications of Helga Schneider's *Mother, Let Me Go* (2001), Jhumpa Lahiri's *In Other Words* (2015), Gëzim Hajdari's "Corpo Presente" (Present Body, 1999), Milan Kundera's, *Ignorance* (2002), and Carmine Abate's, *La festa del ritorno* (The Homecoming Party, 2004).

MULTI-BELONGING IN LITERATURE

The protagonist of Schneider's autobiographical novel, *Mother, Let Me Go*, is the daughter of an SS functionary. She abandons her mother and her mother tongue, German, to write in Italian and build a new identity in Italy. Her identity arises from a denial: she does not want to be the daughter of a

Nazi; she does not want to be crushed by an unbearable collective and family trauma; she wants to be a new person. The burning need to overcome fears, poverty, and trauma evolves into a personal plan of redemption that springs from the self that craves the overcoming of those constraints. Helga's very complex relationship with her mother makes Helga want to recoup her German identity. Being the daughter of a German mother entails being a German, too. "She is so old, so fragile. Again, despite myself, I am touched. I am leaving, and I'm afraid I will not be able to break the bond that connects me to her. And to think that I have tried to do it a thousand times in a thousand different ways. Even denying my mother tongue" (Schneider 2001, 107). Despite her choice to live in Italy, despite her decision not to speak German, despite her willingness to condemn the horror, despite all this, a bond remains: she is still German, the daughter of her mother. That bond cannot be broken because of her history: her emotions, the imprinting of her beginnings, her pain, her first language. Helga no longer has only one single belonging. She has a bond, expressed by the hyphen (-), a sort of bridge that allows her and every multi-belonger to move from one belonging to another. When Helga cannot stand the pain of being the daughter of a woman who exterminated children in gas chambers, she escapes into the Italian language, speaking perhaps with a slight accent. And when her identity as a daughter makes it impossible for her to erase from her life the existence of her mother, who is now around ninety years old, Helga speaks German again, she turns German again, although a different kind of German, one who is more than a bit Italian, and not only in her attachment to coffee. [2]

Jhumpa Lahiri makes a similar choice in her memoir, *In altre parole* (In Other Words, 2015). Lahiri decided to learn Italian and moved to Rome, where she spent several years, as she explained in an interview published in *The Wall Street Journal:*

> Yes, I've been writing in Italian now for three years. I've written not just this book, but other things—diaries, short stories, things that are piling up with time. But it all feels like a dream; there is a kind of surreal element to it. I speak English. I grew up speaking Bengali. This is the normal, the known, the obvious composition of who I am. Then there's Italian, this strange, other component of me that I've just created. (Burnham Schwartz 2016)

After going back to New York, she started to experience a sense of nostalgia that was precious to her. "And so strangely the point of all this is that even though the nostalgia has been crushing at times in the past three months, I'm strangely proud of it. Because the fact of having it means I belong somewhere" (Burnham Schwartz 2016). The new language and the new belonging help her escape the pain of her past.

> English is loaded. In my search to become my own person, to define myself in some way and not be defined by others, English represented feelings of guilt. . . . That is why I learned Italian, because I wanted to feel at peace, and I wanted to be in a quiet room all by myself. When I opened that door, when I went into the Italian room, it was really quiet, and all of that dolore of the past—the confusion, the conflict, the feeling of what did it mean for me to be reading and writing vis-à-vis my parents and their world—it just went away. (Burnham Schwartz 2016)

When she was a child, she avoided speaking in Bengali in the presence of her friends, feeling the need to hide. A double sense of shame deriving from the need to hide her origins, coupled with the awareness of that need caused her deep pain. She felt that the use of the language and her relation with her parents were connected. "It was not possible to speak in English without feeling somewhat detached from my parents" (Lahiri 2015, 112). Inhabiting a third language, distant enough from the meanings and emotions of her main two languages, gives Lahiri a chance to explore the possibility of another new identity. She admits, however, the triangular relationship of the three languages, of the three belongings. Living for some time "in Italian," allows her some distance from the other two belongings. It is distance, not detachment. Being a prestigious American writer when she reaches Italy functions as a passport for Lahiri. Italy extends a welcome to her that it very rarely offers to migrants, who have to struggle to inhabit even its cultural margins.

"The shadow of a dog" (Hajdari 2011, 59) is how Gëzim Hajdari, an Italian-Albanian poet, describes his condition in both Albania and in Italy. The threshold of belonging and not belonging are themes brought by Hajdari to a new and even more evident level. The birth country is seen as feminine in his work as well. It is the mother/bad mother to be invoked, almost in the tradition of Leopardi. But, as if to underline the conceptual shift from "natural man" to "national man," now the bad mother/stepmother is not nature but the motherland. He emigrated to Italy in 1992.[3] The anguish of the individual bred in totalitarian collectivization of consciousness is, unfortunately, extended to the exile's condition of abandonment to such an extent that it is even uncertain whether Medea—perhaps the richest metaphor and theme of Hajdari's poetry—is related exclusively to the guilty motherland. "You will bow in front of me Medea/with guilt and you will find in the light steps scattered in the dark/my loneliness become love" (2001, 107). Due almost to a fluke of history, the "new man," Hajdari, fled to the West like so many other "new men" in search of a context in which the utopian, modern promise of redemption of the human condition through techno-scientific progress along with democracy, freedom, and prosperity was a reality. But the burden of the past –"We bring the list/of the dead in our pockets" (2011, 21)—is perpetuated in a condition that seems like a continuation more than anything: "Gëzim/The shadow of the dog will remain/wherever you go." Motherland as a bad mother/ stepmother, therefore; one remains tied to her, loving her, hating her, keeping her "in the pocket."

Hajdari, however, has an almost new mother country that is similar to the bad mother and that, given the migrant condition, does not quite replace it. The poet constructs his condition through bilingual poetry, always publishing his books simultaneously in Italian and Albanian, making it difficult for everyone to understand the language of the original draft.[4] Perhaps more than the writings of any other Italian poet born abroad, Hajdari's poetry lives in the condition between non belonging and multi-belonging. He knows that a precarious grip on multiple contexts is better, much better, than not belonging at all.[5] "Our fear/remaining without burial/in the West" (Hajdari 2001, 121.) The abyss of not belonging is black, dark, and fuels his poetry. "Where to stop my terror/the stones I threw upwind/opened an enormous abyss beneath me" (Hajdari 2001, 25). It is no coincidence that the status of those possessing two passports speaks of Italian-Americans, French-Germans, and so on. That legal hyphen is the thread of multi-belonging that, as we shall see, is also a very important cultural issue. The hyphen that marks multiple belongings has important cultural implications that in the contextualizing and re-contextualizing, the stripping and redressing, had already appeared in the Soviet Union. In this regard, Corrado Alvaro in his *Viaggio in Russia* (Journey to Russia 1985[1935]), provides important insight by showing how the nationality issue was addressed by the Bolsheviks:

> The Soviet man is new since he has obtained equal rights in front of the state without prejudice against race; the sons and grandsons of the old middle class are excepted from the equality, unless they have performed the necessary acts to deserve civil rights; public participation has been opened to the 200 races the Union is made up of; a new Latinized alphabet that puts all people in contact with culture and civilization has been bestowed on the Iacuti (the Samoyeds: the name was changed because Samoyeds means "those who eat each other"), on the Kirgizians, on the Uzbeks, on the Turkmen; culture and civilization is now something accomplished by the industrial bourgeoisie of the West, or those born under that sign. (75–76)

Our exclusive interest here is the effort that was made to bring together many ethnic groups within a new nation-state. "Precisely to the culture"—writes Alvaro—"the Russians entrust the task of cementing the many different nationalities and languages that make up the Union and the diffusion and the norm of their ideals of life" (46). Culture and civilization seem to be artistic, scientific, technological, and social knowledge borrowed from more developed contexts and, after passing through the ideological filters of the system, carried on in Russia itself. The Bolsheviks entrust to this knowledge not only the countrywide teaching of literacy, but also the construction of that form of cultural prosthesis that will become the characteristic trait of the "new man."

In addition to belonging to an original ethnic and cultural context, the "new man" has elements in common with the new citizens in terms of certain local universals, or rather Bolshevik universals.

The means for creating the "new man" were coercive, violent, and often criminal. Although the effort was immense and comparable to nothing that had come before, the belief that culture and knowledge were a means of emancipation from the mono-ethnic cultures held fast. Hand in hand with this solution, the Bolsheviks clothed their citizens in a unique legal mantle, that of the federation. Without it, and without the new common culture of the state, the abyss of non-humans that appeared in Europe between the world wars, would have been the same.[6] That is why today the legal bridge, the hyphen of multi-belonging, after having accompanied the complex and uncertain process of the building of the European state, preserves its fundamental importance throughout the world during the present time of high social mobility. In this historical phase, belonging to one, two, or more countries in a concrete, non-utopian way, though imperfectly, often remaining marginal, is much more realistic and much more pragmatic than directly claiming to be citizens of the world (or just human beings), although the latter remains the ideal horizon. But as Charles Taylor has pointed out, the multi-belonging requires multi-recognition: legal recognition, cultural recognition, more than one context recognition (1992). The nonrecognition or even the misrecognition, according to Taylor, "can inflict harm."[7] It remains unclear whether these groups of writers are recognized properly by their contexts or not. Every case is different, but since this condition is a very articulated one, they hardly are.

CULTURAL CAPITAL

Inclusion, belonging(s), and identities are part of an economic, political, and cultural process.[8] It is important to specify more fully here this process of the acquisition and the shaping of identity. From this point of view, Kwame Anthony Appiah's reply to Taylor on the themes of multiculturalism is illuminating: "Dialogue shapes the identity" (1994, 154). "I develop as I grow up, but the very material out of which I form it is provided, in part, by my society."[9] It is this material from the context "offered" (or imposed) to the individual to form their own identity that is important here. Individuals compose their identity with what is available in their own context. Becoming a multi-belonger means also to seek to expand the choices available and to form a combination—in an identity—that was not offered by any one of the individual contexts alone. Multi-belonging, then, means to expand the choices available in order to escape the limited offers of the single context. It is in this field of possibilities that the game of identity and of its source is played. It is the context that provides the raw material for the identities. If there is more than one context, the individual becomes the artist who with his or her own imagination, with a project, by investing a great deal of energy, creates his/her own identity. The first to take advantage of these spaces are the translingual writers who use multi-belonging by creating in their work additional cultural and anthropological values. Many other individuals use similar possibilities, finding employment, for example, as *cultural mediators* (Amara Lakhous's Amedeo/Ahmed of *Scontro di civiltá* is considered a cultural mediator by the critics for his ability to interpret different perspectives), which are professional figures created politically in the host context. Economists focus on the compared economy; lawyers seek customers with certain characteristics. It then becomes a creative way to use the context, but which, unfortunately, often produces poor results. Adding a new hyphen may to some extent help improve the combinatorial drawing from a larger number of opportunities.

The concept of *cultural capital*[10] and *habitus* proposed by Pierre Bourdieu (1980) can help to better articulate what different contexts can concretely offer these individuals. The changes of the *habitus* of all migrant groups can be slowed down by ethnic islands. When migrants organize with each other and exclude the outside influences as much as possible, the preservation of the original *habitus* is probable. Something changes with the "second generations" educated in Italy, and the 2017 proposal—that didn't make it in the Italian Parliament—for the new law of citizenship that is in part organized around the concept of *ius culturae* proves it.[11] The environment of school and work tends to prevail over that of the ethnic group, and the effort to strengthen a belonging goes somehow towards the culture of the previous generation since it is the weakest. But if the inclusion process fails, both economically and culturally, the need to recoup the origins of the previous generation becomes even stronger. The first generation of migrants, those with a different original cultural capital, who are able to use the language properly and have the most sophisticated cultural tools, come into conflict with the status quo either by radically changing part of their *habitus* or acquiring educational degrees and new cultural tools. They will eventually hybridize their cultural capital by building a vision and a profile that will exceed all context boundaries, including that of their origin. This surplus creates a form of alienation and externality with respect to all contexts, even with respect to new and potential ones. A complete identification tied to a national context is no longer possible. What is possible, however, or rather what is certain, is the feeling of relative belonging for specific historical intervals as well as for the sharing of the different experienced contexts. These belongings often require the hyphen to explain an experience of life and a cultural condition.[12] In Italy, there are many Italian-Romanians, Italian-Albanians, Italian-Algerians, and Italian-Americans (we put "Italian" at the beginning for reasons of linguistic convenience). There is also an increasing number of Italian-Albanian-French, Italian-Romanian-English, Italian-Bulgarian-Americans, and so on. If the hyphen enhances an intercultural or transcultural condition, the surplus in respect to all the contexts urges one to maintain a critical and vigilant point of view. "I am an exile exiled in exile," writes Hajdari (2001, 25). The exile in this case is the excess over all contexts, past and present. The individual who develops multi-belonging, always threatened by surplus and by externality, is an individual who frequently moves between different territories, an individual with several simultaneous territorial links who is increasingly deterritorialized.

The choice to write in two languages involves targeting two linguistic communities and demands the belonging, albeit problematic, critical, and marginal, to both cultural contexts. In regard to this aspect, it is important to stress the experience of two other writers *in Italian* who lived in a third country for several years. Ornela Vorpsi and Elvira Dones, both born Albanian, are now living in France and in the U.S., after a period spent respectively in Italy and Switzerland. Both continue to write and publish in Italian, at least until recently. Vorpsi, who was born in 1968, has now published her new novel in French. It is a complex phenomenon that could be partly explained by the notion of cultural and, specifically, linguistic capital. Vorpsi emerges as an Italian writer, while Dones, a journalist born in 1960, published first in Albanian. Of the three languages, both seemed to mainly favor the second language, Italian, presumably because the acquisition of a third language requires a fairly extended time interval. Indeed, Vorpsi has been living in France since 1997, and only in 2014 did she choose French for her writings. The length of the period one needs to be comfortable writing in another language, especially in a third one, is meaningful for the very concept of country/countries that I will approach in the next paragraph when talking about Kundera's *Ignorance*. However, with Vorpsi and Dones, the public and critical success (recognition) that some of their works have enjoyed in Italy plays an important role. The various awards and the attention received from the publishing industry and the public in Italy may be the equivalent of educational qualifications and therefore be somehow regarded as the cultural capital that can be used also from a distance. Certainly, it is a carefully cultivated form of cultural belonging. Hajdari too, who has spent recent years first in France and now in England, keeps writing bilingual poetry and spending time in Italy. For anagraphic reasons, he is not planning to use English for his writings.[13] A similar case is Lakhous, who has spent recent years in New York without losing his ties either with Italy or Algeria. The multi-belonging, if the abyss of not belonging is overcome, can become a great advantage and privilege. To achieve multi-belonging beyond the specific intercultural capital already mentioned, the individual needs economic resources and efficient and cheap transportation. The revolution wrought by the Internet in this regard is perhaps too obvious to mention. Multi-belonging is facilitated by the technological advantages of the twenty-first century. When it approaches acceptable levels, it becomes an enviable cultural condition that, ideally, the citizens of the West aim for as well.

IMPOSSIBLE RETURNS AND ORGANIZED RETURNS

The possibilities and modalities of multi-belonging vary depending on the components on either side of the hyphen(s) and depending, of course, on the historical period. Kundera's analysis in *Ignorance* with regard to the relationship that the émigré has with the old and the new country should be circumscribed to the historical period. This novel was published in 2000. Two decades of exile taken into consideration end together at the impassable border between the Czech Republic (Socialist Republic of Czechoslovakia at that time) and the rest of Europe. The frontier, the important differences between the two organizational systems, the barrier of police that divides two worlds has a profound impact so as to make possible the figure of an émigré.

> Europe's Communism burned out exactly two hundred years after the French Revolution took fire. For Irena's Parisian friend Sylvie, that was a coincidence loaded with meaning. But with what meaning? What name could be given to the triumphal arch spanning those two majestic dates? The Arch of the Two Greatest European Revolutions? Or The Arch Connecting the Greatest Revolution with the Final Restauration? For the sake of avoiding ideological argument, I propose that we adopt a more modest interpretation: the first date gave birth to a great European character, the Émigré (either the Great Traitor or the Great Victim, according to one's outlook); the second date took the Émigré off the set of The History of the Europeans . . . (2002, 30)

For Kundera, it was the barrier that separated two very distant political and economic systems, to make the return impossible and not even desired. The twenty years outside of Ithaca are those that count more than the return; they are the years that really count for Ulysses and for the protagonists, Josef and Irena. "For twenty years he had thought about nothing but his return. But once he was back, he was amazed to realize that his life, the very essence of his life, its center, its treasure, lay outside Ithaca, in the twenty years of his wanderings. And this treasure he had lost, and could retrieve only by telling about it" (Kundera 2002 34). When the Berlin wall comes down, when the Czech and Slovak Republics leave behind their communist past and become part of the EU, the figure of émigré probably disappears. "She had never disguised her views from him, so it was certainly possible for him to know her well, and yet he was seeing her exactly the way everyone else saw her: *a young woman in pain, banished from her country*. He himself comes from a Swedish town he wholeheartedly detests, and in which he refuses to set foot.

But in his case it's taken for granted. Because everyone applauds him *as a nice, very cosmopolitan Scandinavian who's already forgotten all about the place he comes from*" (Kundera 2002, 24).

The transformation of an émigré into a cosmopolitan also ends the question of return. There is no longer the barrier made by police, by obstacles, or by substantial differences of political organization or lifestyles. The years gone by have produced considerable changes.[14] There are no more nightmares that torment Irena, Josef, and all immigrants (a more appropriate term when it comes to overcoming geographic, economic, and political barriers because it concerns an extended multitude of people): the collective nightmares of return, the nightmares of remaining on the wrong side of the barrier.[15] It is clear that the hyphen is a bridge needed more when the distance between the two sides is important. If there is nothing to bridge, if one finds commonalities that help one to live in similar cities, as is the case with Kundera's character, there is no need to become a multi-belonger. As it is clear, the impossible return, the trauma of the removal of the original identity needs the hyphen, which is desired precisely because it is not there yet. In 2020 the émigré has not yet been fully expelled from the European scene, and the real border of Europe is now located in the South. The conditions that African and Asian migrants leave behind and the obstacles they must overcome to arrive in Europe are no less dramatic than those in the times of Eastern European communism. When the differences, the barriers, the walls, and the difficult circumstances remain, the impossibility of return remains a valid question. It remains equally valid to question the concept of country. "For the very notion of *homeland*, with all its emotional power, is bound up with the relative brevity of our life, which allows us too little time to become attached to some other country, to other countries, to other languages" (Kundera 2002, 121; italics mine).

The protagonists of Kundera's novel still fail in the process of returning, which turns into a goodbye to the first country not adequately said during the escape. The recalled past does not exist, and the future is in the countries where they have spent the last twenty years (France for Irena, Denmark for Josef). Their bond was transitional, their future impossible. And the concept of fatherland[16] (in the French edition, is used "patrie" [2000, 139–40]), precisely because it concerns periods of prolonged living elsewhere, changes, becoming less rigid and leaving space for something else. The circle of friends likewise changes, and with them the language of the inner voice; the language of friends, lovers, affections, readings, writing; and the language of work. Kundera himself wrote this novel and many others in French. The translation of the "fatherland" into "homeland" indicates clearly the need to adapt the concept of the country to different circumstances that reflect those of an increasing number of naturalized citizens. If the twenty years spent far from the "fatherland" by Kundera's characters increase because of their decision to continue living in the new "homeland," the time to become attached to another country is now sufficient and, in some cases, leaves room (time) for more than one country. There are new shared movie jokes, new songs to wake up to and new languages to teach to the children, to the new generation. All this, of course, requires better living conditions and better cultural and technological tools. All this has yet to come. All this is a reality still very imperfect. The mother tongue is the language of childhood, used when talking to the mother, to the parents, and to childhood friends ("It was the music of some unknown language. What had happened to Czech during those two sorry decades? Was it the stress that had changed?" [Kundera 2002, 54]), while the motherland of birth is, in the best of cases, the place where to spend holidays, Christmas, Easter, summer, where to take the kids and introducing them to relatives, cousins. For now, we can be imperfect multi-belongers who visit the past country/countries when the calendar of countries where we work allows us. Always at Christmas, sometimes at Easter, and maybe in the summer, as happens to the protagonist of Abate's novel, *The Homecoming Party*. Tulio, a young Calabrian (Arbëresh), goes to work in the French mines. After the loss of his first wife, and with a small daughter to take care of, he forms a family in the Calabrian village where he was born. Father and son tell perspectives of the same story around a bonfire, lit on Christmas during a feast for the emigrant's return. These are not the dynamics of return that Kundera talks about. In this case, the only barrier is economic. The periodic return is not in doubt. The two countries somehow divide the year. The times of the multi-belonging are clearly dictated by the organization of work. It is our context that provides, as said, the raw material for our identities. It is our current (political, technological, economic) context then that can decide to handle smoothly a new transnational and maybe transitory phase by supporting, both legally and culturally, multi-belonging dynamics.

NOTES

1. The extreme control dedicated to transforming the individual into merely a group of conditioned reactions in Auschwitz produced what Levi called the nonhuman, interpreted by Agamben (1998) as the subhuman. Agamben's term "simply man" recalls Arendt's conceptual and political analysis of the errors of the French Revolution that became apparent with the experiences of stateless persons during the early twentieth century (Arendt 1958, 1963). Their being "simply men" who were not legally protected by a political affiliation with a state opened the way to making the human being superfluous. Non-belonging in a world now organized according to the national model opened the abyss of non-humans. Agamben addresses this problem in an article published in *Le Monde*, where he focuses on the current phenomena of depoliticizing trends and increasing fear in contemporary France. Recalling Fascism and Nazism, Agamben points out: "It is in this context that we must think about the disturbing project of cancellation of citizenship for citizens with dual nationality, which recalls the fascist law of 1926 on the denationalization of 'citizens unworthy of Italian citizenship' and the Nazi laws on the denationalization of Jews. In November 2018, the Italian parliament passed a law that

makes possible the cancelation of naturalized citizenships for individuals who are condemned for specific felonies" (2016).

2. "It's amazing how you Italians are attached to your coffee," my cousin says, smiling. In her eyes, now, I am 'the Italian girl.' 'And you to your würstel,' I reply but without acrimony: I love Eva, despite the years spent apart; I feel as close to her as to a sister" (Schneider 2001: 20).

3. Mia Lecomte summarizes Hajdari's journey: "Winner of several awards, including the prestigious Montale in 1997 for unpublished works, thanks to this award the Albanian poet enjoys a period of a certain notoriety among the 'official' Italian critics, who over the years tend to forget more and more his poetic production, relegating it to the area of migrant writings, where on the contrary it will be increasingly studied and recognized by academics" (Lecomte 2018, 179).

4. According to Lecomte, who refers to Hajdari's interviews, the poet writes first in Italian and then translates into Albanian (2018, 178).

5. Lecomte observes, for instance, how Hajdari, after emphasizing with pain and anger the not belonging to his birth country, later recoups and re-elaborates his relation with it. "After having sung the demarcation of his poetic corpus, Hajdari recovers the history of his country, its very ancient cultural and popular tradition, and ethically re-establishes the profound meaning of a universal destiny of migrants" (Lecomte 2018, 185).

6. I refer here again to Arendt's analyses in *The Origin of Totalitarianism* (1958). The *en masse* appearance of stateless persons made it clear that loss of community was also transformed into a loss of rights. The distinctive new aggravating factor was that the loss of a country made a person unable to find a new one. It follows that stateless persons, who were no longer protected by a community, were expelled from humanity because they were *nothing but men*.

7. Taylor formulated the concept of recognition in the nineties, initiating a debate on multiculturalism that led to several publications involving many intellectuals, among them Habermas and Appiah. "The thesis is that our identity is partly shaped by recognition or its absence, often by the misrecognition of others, and so a person or a group of people can suffer real damage, real distortion, if the people or society around them mirror back to them a confining or demeaning or contemplatable picture of themselves. Non recognition or misrecognition can inflict harm, can be a form of oppression, imprisoning someone in a false, distorted, and reduced mode of being" (Taylor 1992, 25).

8. Zygmund Bauman analyzes the economic aspects of belonging versus not belonging. He maintains that the condition of the multi-belonging is available only to an international elite, while the majority, *the locals*, are denied that option. He examines the economic aspects of not belonging and how these translate into exclusion. Identity, in the conditions of modern liquidity, must be continuously renewed. Halting the process of identity construction results in the revocation of social status and class membership. Those who cannot maintain the process of building an identity end up among the ranks of the "sub-classes," among the ranks of the excluded. We should consider that among the excluded, the majority of members are stateless people, or undocumented migrants who are denied physical presence in the territory of a state and often end up living in "non-places." According to Marc Augé's intuition (1992), non-places include refugee camps. "Identity of a 'subclass' means absence of identity; the cancellation, or the negation of the individuality, of a 'face,' that object of ethical duty and of moral care. One finds himself out of that social space where the identity is sought, chosen, built, evaluated, confirmed or rejected" (Bauman 2003, 44). Absence from a social space where identity is a requirement means belonging neither to that social space nor any other. "It is the exclusion, and not the exploitation as it was hypothesized by Marx a century ago, that is today one of the main causes of the most visible cases of social polarization, of an inequality that becomes deeper and of increasing volumes of poverty, misery and human humiliation" (Bauman 2003, 46).

9. It is important to consider the context of this affirmation. A longer quotation helps to better understand Appiah's perspective: "It seems to me that this notion of authenticity has built into it a series of errors of philosophical anthropology. It is, first of all, wrong in failing to see what Taylor so clearly recognizes: the way in which the self is, as he says, dialogically constituted. The rhetoric of authenticity proposes not only that I have a way of being that is all

my own, but that in developing it I must fight against the family, organized religion, society, the school, the state—all the forces of convention. This is wrong, however, not only because it is in dialogue with other people's understandings of who I am that I develop a conception of my own identity (Taylor's point) but also because my identity is crucially constituted through concepts and practices made available to me by religion, society, school, and state, and mediated to varying degrees by the family. Dialogue shapes the identity I develop as I grow up, but the very material out of which I form it is provided, in part, by my society, by what Taylor calls its language in 'a broad sense'" (Appiah 1994, 154).

10. Cultural capital can exist in three forms in the incorporated state, that is, in the form of long-term provisions (*habitus*) associated with certain types of knowledge, ideas, values, skills, etc.; in the objectified state, in the form of cultural goods, paintings, books, dictionaries, tools, etc.; and in the institutionalized state, which is a form of objectification, as the different educational degrees (see Bourdieu 1980).

11. For a detailed explanation of this proposed law, see an unauthored editorial note of the daily Secolo d'Italia published on June 16, 2017: http://www.secoloditalia.it/2017/06/lo-ius-soli-spiegato-in-cinque-punti-come-cambia-la-legge-in-peggio

12. Anthony Julian Tamburri in his *To Hyphenate or Not to Hyphenate* (1991), suggest replacing or removing the hyphen in Italian-American adjective. The hyphen, in his view, signals the dominant group's resistance of accepting the new arrival (43) and it is even a colonizing sign (44). Tamburri's concern about the use of a hyphen is similar to the debate on the definition issue of Italian writers born elsewhere (any additional adjective to Italian, even *postcolonial*, could sadly be seen as a "colonizing sign"). Agreeing that a loose grip on the definition issue is a better choice, it is worth mentioning that these writers deal with heavier adjectives, in front (or after) the adjective Italian, than a "tiny" hyphen, which, however, in my article is invested with a different (legal, cultural, transnational) meaning closely related to the current historical context.

13. Gëzim Hajdari, email messages to author, June 2018.

14. "The gigantic invisible broom that transforms, disfigures, erases landscapes has been at the job for millennia now, but its movements, which used to be slow, just barely perceptible, have sped up so much that I wonder: Would an *Odyssey* even be conceivable today? Is the epic of the return still pertinent to our time?" (Kundera 2002, 54)

15. "Martin, her husband, was having the same dreams. Every morning they would talk about the horror of that return to their native land. Then, in the course of a conversation with a Polish friend, an émigré herself, Irena realized that all émigrés had those dreams, every one, without exception . . ." (Kundera 2002, 15).

16. Julius Kirshner, in his *Marriage, Dowry, and Citizenship in Late Medieval and Renaissance Italy*, traces the idea of Fatherland back to Roman Law and gender politics. "Justinians's *Corpus iuris* was the product of a vast empire, in which the status of a Roman citizen signified attachment to a common fatherland, not to a particular territorial community." Legitimate children acquired their father's *origo*, or place of origin; illegitimate children instead acquired their mother's place of origin. In Italian medieval communities, the legal capacities of women were again circumscribed. "The social reproduction of patrilineal regimes depended on sons succeeding their fathers as heads of the household and as masters of the family's patrimonial properties" (Kirshner 2015, 160).

REFERENCES

Abate, Carmine. 2004. *La festa del ritorno*. Milano: Mondadori.
Agamben, Giorgio. 1998. *Quel che resta di Auschwitz, L'archivio e il testimone*. Torino: Bollati Boringhieri.
———. 2016. "Zona grigie che preparano dittature." *Comune-info*, January 10. http://comune-info.net/2016/01/democrazia-dittature/.
Alvaro, Corrado. 1985. *I maestri del diluvio, Viaggio in Russia*. Massa: Memoranda edizioni.
Appiah, K. Anthony. 1994. "Identity, Authenticity, Survival." In *Multiculturalism, Examining the Politics of Recognition*, edited by Amy Gutmann. Princeton: Princeton University Press.

Arendt, Hannah. 1958. *The Origin of Totalitarianism*. 2nd ed. New York: Harcourt, Brace and Co.: World Publishing Company, Meridian Books.

———. 1963. *On Revolution*. New York: Viking Press.

Augé, Marc. 1992. *Non-Lieux, Introduction à une anthropologie de la surmodernité*. Seuil: Editions du Seuil.

Bauman, Zygmund. 2003. *Intervista Sull'Identità*. Edited by Benedetto Vecchi. Bari-Roma: Edizioni Laterza.

Bhabha, Homi. 2005. *The Location of Culture*. London & New York: Routledge.

Bourdieu, Pierre. 1980. *Le Sens pratique*. Paris: Minuit.

Burnham Schwartz, John. 2016. "How Jhumpa Lahiri Learned to Write Again." *Wall Street Journal*, 20 January. Online at: http://www.wsj.com/articles/how-jhumpa-lahiri-learned-to-write-again-1453305609 (accessed 28 November 2018).

Hajdari, Gëzim. 2001. *Stigmate*. Lecce: Besa.

———. *Corpo presente. Trup i pranishëm*. First edition: Tirana: Botimet Dritëro, 1999. New Edition: Lecce: Besa, 2011.

Harari, Yuval Noah. 2017. *Homo Deus: A Brief History of Tomorrow*. New York: Harper.

Jacoby, Rusell. 2000. *The End of Utopia*. New York: Basic Books.

Kundera, Milan. 2000. *L'ignorance*. Paris: Grand Livre du Mois.

———. 2002. *Ignorance*. Translated by Linda Asher. New York: HarperCollins Publishers.

Lahiri, Jhumpa. 2015. *In altre parole*. Parma: Guanda.

Lakhous, Amara. 2012. *Scontro di civiltà per un ascensore a Piazza Vittorio*. Roma: E/O.

Lecomte, Mia. 2018. *Di un poetico altrove. Poesia transnazionale italofona (1960–2016)*. Firenze: Franco Cesati.

Levi, Primo. 1958. *Se questo è un uomo*. Torino: Einaudi.

———. 1998. *This Is A Man,* Translated by Stuart Woolf. London: Vintage.

Maalouf Amin. 2001. *In the Name of Identity*. Translated by Barbara Bray. New York: Arcade Publishing.

Schneider, Helga. 2001. *Lasciami andare, madre*. Milano: Adelphi.

Secolo d'Italia (editorial board) published on June 16, 2017, http://www.secoloditalia.it/2017/06/lo-ius-soli-spiegato-in-cinque-punti-come-cambia-la-legge-in-peggio

Tamburri, Anthony Julian. 1991. *To Hyphenate or Not to Hyphenate*. Montreal: Guernica.

Taylor, Charles. 1992. "Multiculturalism and the Politics of Recognition." In *Multiculturalism, Examining the Politics of Recognition*, edited by Amy Gutmann. Princeton: Princeton University Press.

Index

99 Posse, 25

abortion, 179
activism. *See* hip-hop; discrimination; feminism; politics, Italy's; race
Adichie, Chimamanda Ngozi, 46
Afaawua, Evelyne Sarah, 152, 153, 155n11
Africa: colonialism in, 226, 227, 230; literature, 179–180, 226–227; migration from, 24, 26, 32–33, 118–119, 121; postcolonialism in, 122, 181, 182. *See also* hip-hop; migration; postcolonialism; race
Ajello, Nello, 48
Albania: gender roles in, 201–202, 203–205, 205–206, 206–207, 207–208, 211n6; geography, 199–200; history, 199–200; literature, 45, 47, 49, 50, 51, 199, 203, 205–206, 207; migration from, 200, 208–209. *See also* Dones, Elvira; Ibrahimi, Anilda; Kubati, Ron; Vorpsi, Ornela
Algeria, 55, 61
Ali Farah, Ubax Cristina, 5, 9, 95–101, 229, 232, 234n6, 235n17
Almamegretta, 25, 26
Alvaro, Corrado, 266
Anderson, Benedict, 78–80, 83, 90, 91n11
Arendt, Hanna, 263, 272n1, 273n5
antiracism, 153, 181. *See also* discrimination; race

apartheid. *See* segregation
Appiah, Kwame Anthony, 267, 273n7, 274n10
Austria, 1

Balotelli, Mario, 32
Bakthin, Mikhail, 5, 60, 64
belonging: in literature, 10, 118, 263–270, 271; migration causing lack of, 7, 27–28, 28, 29–30, 32, 37n6, 58, 124, 273n8; migration changing sense of, 185, 267–270, 270–272, 273n8; multiplicity of, 263–267, 267–270, 271–272, 273n8; and race, 149. *See also* identity
Berlusconi, Silvio, 25, 28, 230
Blank, David, 31

Childish Gambino. *See* Glover, Donald, Jr.
Christianity: beliefs of, 130, 132–134, 160, 168n; culture, 162; discrimination against Christians, 180; presence in Italy, 185. *See also* religion
Cixous, Hélène, 224, 234n2
colonialism: Italy defined by, 1–2, 165; Italy's rule in Africa, 163–164, 180–181, 226, 227, 230, 169n; writings on Italy's, 190–191, 226, 230, 231, 232. *See also* Austria; France; Spain; postcolonialism
Comitato, 25, 26

communism, 8, 200, 201, 204, 209, 211n3, 211n6, 270, 271. *See also* Hoxha, Enver

culture: cultural conflicts, 5, 65, 85, 123–124, 130, 132–134, 165–166; Mediterranean, 1, 159, 160, 162–163. *See also* culture, Italy's; religion

culture, Italy's: effects of migration on, 1, 3, 65, 186–187; gender roles, 5, 7, 159–163, 165–168; multiplicity of, 2, 8, 109; shift in, 1–2; Southern, 160–161. *See also* culture; Italy: Northern vs. Southern; religion

Derrida, Jacques, 224, 234n1

difference: and Italian literature, 3, 60, 74; and migration, 1, 58, 74; and race, 154n9. *See also* diversity; diversity, Italy's

discrimination: accusations against migrants, 25, 74, 81; fear of migrants, 53–54, 57, 58, 62, 82; hip-hop's engagement with, 4, 23–24, 24, 25, 26, 27, 28, 30; institutional discrimination against migrants, 25, 28, 58, 80–81, 105; against Muslims, 34–35, 54, 62–63, 183–184, 184, 185, 192, 193; based on race, 148, 149–150, 152, 154n7–155n10, 163, 165, 165–168, 181, 257–258, 169n; based on religion, 143–144, 180, 185; against second-generation migrants, 4, 30; stereotypes of migrants, 79, 83, 106, 143–144, 165–168, 231, 169n; systematic racism, 77–78; verbal abuse of migrants, 27, 55, 118, 126n4; violence against migrants, 54, 55, 62–63, 65n1, 105, 152; against women, 105–106, 113, 168n. *See also* antiracism; feminism; gender; migration; race; segregation

DiStefano, Antonio Dikele, 33, 35, 37n7

diversity, 1, 3, 185, 192, 193, 231. *See also* difference; discrimination; hip-hop; race

Dones, Elvira: on Albania, 201, 203, 205, 207, 208; biographical details, 45, 49, 50, 200, 269; feminist writings, 8, 201, 201–203, 203–205; use of languages, 200–201, 211n4, 211n11, 269; reception of, 44, 45–48, 49, 51

Eco, Umberto, 10, 75

Europe: comparison with Italy, 184–185; Italy's role in, 1; Northern vs. Southern, 1, 161–162. *See also* Austria; France; Italy; Spain

fascism, 126n4, 163, 180, 181, 230, 232, 272n1, 169n. *See also* Mussolini, Benito; Nazism

Fazel, Shirin Ramzanali: biographical details, 182, 183; feminist literature, 182; Islamic literature, 183–185; literature, 179–180, 181, 187, 194n2; migration literature, 182, 186, 190–191

feminism: abortion rights, 179; development in Italy, 104–108; in hip-hop, 35, 38n17; and kinship, 9, 237; multicultural, 6, 103–104, 105–106, 107–109, 110, 112, 168. *See also* discrimination; gender; literature, feminist; motherhood

Flaiano, Ennio, 226, 228, 235n10

Floyd, George, 31

Gaboriau, Émile, 82

gender: and Islam, 86–88, 161, 194n6; females in literature, 9, 81, 82–86, 95, 155n11, 163–168, 172; gender roles in Albania, 201–202, 203–205, 205–206, 206–207, 207–208, 211n6; gender roles in Italy, 5, 7, 108, 109, 110, 159–163, 165–168. *See also* discrimination; feminism; literature, feminist; motherhood

geography, Italy's, 1, 159. *See also* Italy, Northern vs. Southern

Germi, Pietro, 5, 64, 85, 90, 92n15

Ghali, 24, 33–35, 35, 36, 38n16

Ghermandi, Gabriella: biographical details, 228–229, 235n12; feminist writings, 227–228; literature, 227, 230, 233, 235n17; writings on Africa, 226–227

Giubre, Abdul, 54

Glover, Donald, Jr., 36

Hajdari, Gëzim, 265–266, 269, 273n3–273n5

Hall, Stuart, 4, 43, 44, 47, 51

hip-hop: and activism, 4, 23–24, 24, 25, 26, 27, 28, 30–31, 34, 35, 38n20; Black Italians' adoption of, 4, 23–24, 25–26; conversations about race through, 24, 27, 32, 33, 34, 35; evolution in Italy, 4, 23–27, 28, 29, 31, 33, 35–36, 37n1; evolution in the United States, 4, 23, 24, 26; global, 4, 23, 26, 35–37; migrants' adoption of, 28, 29, 30, 32; women in, 35, 38n17. *See also* 99 Posse; Almamegretta; Comitato; DiStefano, Dikele; Ghali; Glover, Donald, Jr.; Issaa, Amir; Kuti, Tommy; Mane, Gucci; Nuovi Briganti; Sangue Misto

Hoxha, Enver, 205, 211n6, 221n4–221n5

humanism, 162–163. *See also* posthumanism

Huntington, Samuel, 77, 78, 79, 91n7, 91n10

Ibrahimi, Anilda: biographical details, 200; feminist writings, 201, 208–209; use of languages, 199, 200–208, 208–209, 211n4; writings on Albania, 201, 203, 205, 207

iconography, 160, 161, 168n

immigration. *See* migration

Islam: and gender, 86–90, 161, 182, 194n6; beliefs, 184; community, 85, 86, 185; culture, 162, 179; discrimination against Muslims, 34–35, 54, 62–63, 183–184, 184, 185, 192, 193; presence in Italy, 180, 184, 185

Issaa, Amir, 4, 24, 28–31, 37n11

Italy: and postcolonialism, 6, 35, 191; national identity of, 2, 24, 25, 32, 184, 185, 186; Northern vs. Southern, 25, 26, 27, 79, 154n5, 159, 160, 161, 164, 165; stereotypes of, 1, 32, 79, 165–166. *See also* colonialism; culture, Italy's; diversity, Italy's; economy, Italy's; Europe; geography, Italy's; nationalism, Italy's; politics, Italy's; unification, Italy's

identity: balancing Black and Italian identities, 7, 32, 37n13, 147, 149, 153–154, 154n5, 154n9, 163–164; balancing migrant and Italian identities, 58, 69–72, 74, 79, 109, 119, 123,

163–164, 182; elements of, 86, 109–110, 125, 242, 270; Italy's national, 2, 24, 25, 32, 78, 184, 185, 186; in literature, 69–72, 74, 79, 86, 121, 139–141, 163–164; pride in racial identity, 24, 25–26, 30, 72, 79, 150–152; process of creating, 9, 125, 139–141, 267–268, 273n7–274n10; racial identity causing division, 9, 250–258; second-generation immigrants' struggle with, 24, 30; transformation of migrants' identities, 5, 109, 112–113, 185, 208. *See also* belonging

Jelloun, Tahar Ben, 46

Kadaré, Ismail, 49

kinship: and feminism, 9, 237; in literature, 238–242, 244; and migration, 237, 242, 245–246; and posthumanism, 9, 237

Kubati, Ron, 4, 10, 211n3; biographical details, 49, 50; reception of, 44, 49–51

Kundera, Milan, 263, 269, 270–271, 274n14–274n15

Kuruvilla, Gabriella: biographical details, 238; use of languages in writings, 244–245; literary themes, 238–239; use of location in writings, 242–243; kinship in literary works, 239–242, 244, 246

Kuti, Tommy, 4, 24, 32, 35

Lahiri, Jhumpa, 263, 264–265

Lakhous, Amara, 268, 269; biographical details, 55–56, 238; use of dialogue, 64, 65n3; use of gender, 81–90; migration literature, 60–64, 65, 69–74, 75–81, 90, 163, 245

League Party, 31, 32, 34, 54, 184. *See also* Salvini, Matteo

literature: African, 226–227; Albanian, 45, 47, 49, 50, 51, 199, 200–202, 203, 205–206, 207, 207–208; belonging in, 10, 118, 263–270, 271; changes in Italian, 3, 46–47, 75, 117; circulation of, 43–44; difference in, 3, 60, 74, 80–81; emotion in, 58–59, 60, 61–62, 63; engagement with race in, 51, 62–63,

77, 77–78, 87, 165, 179, 230; female
    authors, 9, 45, 160, 223–224, 227;
    females in, 9, 81, 82–86, 95, 155n11,
    163–168, 172, 224; identity in, 69–72,
    74, 79, 86, 121, 139–141, 163–164;
    kinship in, 238–242, 244, 245–246;
    translation, 45, 47, 48–49, 50, 75;
    translingual authors, 4, 45, 47–48, 56,
    64, 65n3, 183, 199, 211n1–211n2,
    244–245, 247n2, 263–265, 266, 269,
    271–272. *See also* literature, feminist;
    literature, migration; literature,
    postcolonial
literature, feminist: and Albanian culture,
    202–205, 206–207; authors, 163,
    211n7; and colonialism, 182; and
    Islamic culture, 86–90, 182; and
    migration, 163–168, 225; and war, 47,
    48, 227–228, 235n11; and Western
    culture, 201, 209–210. *See also*
    feminism; literature
literature, migration: activism through, 5,
    47, 59, 65, 76, 78–81, 83–85, 165–168,
    182; circulation and reception of,
    43–44, 49–50, 186–187, 193, 225;
    collaboration on, 188, 188–190, 192,
    235n16; examples of, 60–61, 62–64,
    77–78, 95–101, 163–165, 200,
    208–209, 238, 245–246; genre, 2–3, 9,
    69–74, 75–76, 118–122, 125, 126,
    194n12, 210–211, 238, 247n1; use of
    language in, 199, 208, 210, 224–229,
    245, 247n2. *See also* literature;
    migration
literature, postcolonial, 194n3, 194n12,
    234n4; decolonization through, 7, 182,
    193, 230–231; definition of, 6, 119,
    125, 191, 225. *See also* literature;
    postcolonialism
LoPorto, Tiziano, 48

Mane, Gucci, 36
Marxism, 78
MC Deda, 28. *See also* Sangue Misto
MC Neffa, 27–28. *See also* Sangue Misto
Mediterranean: culture of, 1, 159, 160,
    162–163; politics of, 120–121
Melandri, Francesca, 9, 230–232, 235n14

migration: from Africa, 24, 26, 118–119,
    121, 184; from Albania, 200, 208–209;
    alleviation of fear of migrants, 5, 53,
    55, 61–62, 65; effects of, 1, 24; to Italy,
    1, 24, 26; and kinship, 237, 242, 245;
    migrants' fears, 53, 57, 58, 61, 62–64;
    natives' fear of migrants, 5, 27, 53–55,
    58, 61, 62, 74, 124, 166–167, 184,
    194n5; and race, 25–26, 27, 30–31, 62,
    147; struggles of migrants, 3, 7, 25,
    27–28, 37n8, 57, 105–106, 113,
    122–124, 208–209. *See also*
    discrimination; literature, migration
Morrison, Toni, 227, 230
motherhood, 160, 161. *See also* abortion;
    feminism; gender
Mussolini, Benito, 180, 231. *See also*
    fascism
Myftiu, Bessa, 199, 211n1

nationalism, Italy's, 2, 78–79, 81, 82
Nazism, 8, 10, 49, 51, 263–264, 272n1. *See
    also* fascism
Nuovi Briganti, 25, 26

Orientalism, 161, 241
Ouedraogo, Leaticia, 64, 150, 153

Patriarca, Gianna, 159–160, 168
politics, Italy's: activism in Italy, 24, 25,
    27, 28, 30–31, 34, 35, 37n8, 38n20;
    effects of migration on, 1, 28, 104;
    influence of other countries on, 1, 47.
    See also colonialism; feminism; League
    party; Mediterranean: politics;
    migration; nationalism, Italy's;
    populism; postcolonialism; race;
    Salvini, Marxism; Matteo; unification,
    Italy's; xenophobia
postcolonialism: in Africa, 122, 181, 182,
    194n3; in Italy, 6, 35, 191; politics, 124.
    See also colonialism; literature,
    postcolonial
posthumanism, 9, 237. *See also* humanism

race: antiracism, 153, 181; and belonging,
    149; engagement with in literature, 51,
    62–63, 77, 77–78, 87, 143–144, 165,
    179, 230; and migration, 25, 32, 147,

149; racialization in Italy, 1, 25, 53, 148, 154n5, 165, 167. *See also* discrimination; colonialism; hip-hop; identity; migration

Ragusa, Kym, 7, 147, 147–149, 150–152, 153, 154n1–154n2

religion: differences in, 130, 132–134, 162; discrimination based on, 143–144; as divisive, 74; iconography, 160, 161, 168n; in the Mediterranean, 162; religious diversity, 185. *See also* Christianity; Islam

Ripanti, Esperance, 150, 153

Roversi, Roberto, 118, 125, 126n2

Russia, 266–267

Salvini, Matteo, 33, 34, 54, 55, 65n1. *See also* League Party

Saviano, Roberto, 35, 38n16, 46, 48

Sangue Misto, 24, 26–28, 30, 37n6–37n7

Scego, Igiaba, 7, 9, 37n13, 122; biographical details, 154n1; feminist literature, 163–166, 167–168, 168n; literature, 154n7, 159, 163; racial

identity, 147–148, 149–150, 152, 153, 190, 194n12, 229, 232, 235n7

Sciorra, Joseph, 36

segregation, 181. *See also* colonialism; discrimination; race

Shorty, Davide, 31

Taylor, Charles, 267, 273n7, 273n9

terrorism, 57, 84. *See also* Islam

Tolu, Mista. *See* Kuti, Tommy.

Tunisia, migration to, 1

unification, Italy's, 1, 25

Vorpsi, Ornela: biographical details, 200, 206, 211n9, 269; feminist writings, 201, 205–206, 206–207, 209–210; use of languages, 199, 200–201, 211n2, 211n4, 212n12, 269; writings on Albania, 205–206, 207

xenophobia, 2, 32, 61

Yan, Mo, 46

About the Contributors

Basir Ahang is a poet, journalist, and actor born in Ghazni, Afghanistan. He graduated from Kabul University in Persian history and literature. He founded and worked as a radio producer for Radio Malistan and for other media in Kabul. Due to his journalistic work, Ahang received death threats from the Taliban and was forced to flee the country. In 2008 Ahang obtained political refugee status in Italy, where he worked as an interpreter and cultural mediator. In 2009 he went to Greece, where he made a documentary *La Voce di Patrasso / Patrassos' Voice* (On the Plight of Refugees). He has worked with the United Nations Agency for Refugees (UHNCR), and his articles have been published in BBC Persian, Deutsche Welle, Radio Zamaneh, and Frontiers News. Many of his poems have been translated into Italian, English, and Spanish. In 2014 he was awarded the special critics prize for poetry from the International Festival of Sassari "Ottobre in Poesia." In 2015 he published his first poetry collection *Sogni di Tregua* (Dreams of Truce).

Ashna Ali is a queer non-binary Bangladeshi diasporic poet, researcher, translator, and educator raised in Italy and based in Brooklyn. Their research is featured in *Minnesota Review, Journal of Narrative Theory, Texte Zur Kunst,* and elsewhere. They hold a PhD in comparative literature from the Graduate Center, CUNY and is assistant professor of literature at Bard High School Early College Manhattan. Their chapbook of poetry, *The Relativity of Living Well* (The Operating System Open Access Designs) is forthcoming.

Ubah Cristina Ali Farah was born in Italy to a Somali father and an Italian mother. She grew up in Mogadishu, where she attended an Italian school. Her family moved to Hungary to flee the Somalian Civil War, and later moved back to Verona, her birthplace. She earned her BA in Letteratura italiana at La Sapienza University in Rome. Farah is president of the *Migra news agency* and a contributor to many Italian newspapers and magazines such as *La Repubblica, Il Caffè, Malepeggio, l'Europeo, Carta, Magiordomus, Accattone*, and *Liberazione*. In 2007 she published her first novel *Madre piccola* (Little Mother) and in 2014 her second novel *Il comandante del fiume* (The Commander of the River).

Adrián N. Bravi moved to Italy from Argentina in the late 1980s to continue his studies, and he graduated in philosophy from the University of Macerata. He worked as a librarian at the same University, dealing mainly with the cataloging of ancient books. In 1999 he published his first novel in Spanish and in 2000 he started to write in Italian. He has written several books for children and has published articles and stories in various magazines. His books have been translated into English, French, and Spanish. He lives in Recanati, Italy.

Simone Brioni is associate professor in the Department of English and Affiliated Faculty in the Departments of African Studies and Women, Gender and Sexuality Studies at Stony Brook University. His research focuses on migration studies and postcolonial theory with a particular emphasis on contemporary Italian culture. His articles have been published in edited volumes and peer-reviewed journals including *Altreitalie, Cinergie, Écritures, Incontri, Science Fiction Studies, Studi Culturali*, and *The Journal of Italian Cinema and Media Studies*. His most recent publications include the co-written book (with Shirin Ramzanali Fazel) *Scrivere di Islam. Raccontare la diaspora* (2020; Writing about Islam: Telling the Diaspora).

Jennifer Burns is professor of Italian studies at the University of Warwick in the UK. Her research engages with contemporary Italian literature and culture. It has moved from investigating political commitment in literature and the ethics of reading and writing in postmodernity to a focus on recent literature by migrant and mixed-ethnicity writers in the Italian language. Inquiring into questions of mobility, identity, language, and emotions in transnational narratives, her work has been published as a number of journal articles, essays, and a monograph, *Migrant Imaginaries* (2013). Both independently and as part of a major collaborative research project, "Transnationalizing Modern Languages," her current work explores the shared and heterogeneous spaces of language, creativity, and everyday cultural practice which challenge the notion of discrete and bounded national cultures and invite a deterritorialized perspective on literary and cultural production.

Ryan Calabretta-Sajder is an assistant professor of Italian at the University of Arkansas, where he teaches courses in Italian, film, and gender studies. He is the author of *Divergenze in celluloide: colore, migrazione e identità sessuale nei film gay di Ferzan Ozpetek* (2016; Celluloid Divergences: Color,

Migration, and Sexual Identity in the Gay Series of Ferzan Ozpetek) and editor of *Pasolini's Lasting Impressions: Death, Eros, and Literary Enterprise in the Opus of Pier Paolo Pasolini* (2018). His research interests include the integration of gender, class, and migration in both Italian and Italian American literature and cinema. In 2017 he was awarded one of four Fulbright awards for the Foundation of the South to conduct research and teach at the University of Calabria, Arcavacata. He is currently working on two book-length projects, one on the Algerian Italian author Amara Lakhous currently titled *Beyond the Margin or Within the Canon: The Novels of Amara Lakhous*, and a second exploring work of the Italian gay American author Robert Ferro.

Marta Cariello is an associate professor of English literature at Università della Campania "Luigi Vanvitelli," Italy. She has published extensively on postcolonial literature, with a focus on Anglophone Arab women writers. Her current research focuses on postcolonial Mediterranean studies and nationhood. She is co-author with Iain Chambers of *La questione Mediterranea* (Mondadori, 2019) and is co-founder and co-director of the academic journal *de genere: Journal of Literary, Postcolonial and Gender Studies*.

Clarissa Clò is professor and chair in the Department of European Studies at San Diego State University, where she is also director of the Italian Studies Program. Her research interests include feminist and queer theory, migration and postcolonial studies, literature, film, music, popular culture, and transmedia storytelling. Her work has appeared in numerous journals, including *Ácoma,Annali d'Italianistica, California Italian Studies, Diacritics, Diaspora, Forum Italicum, Italian American Review, Italian Culture, Italica, Research in African Literatures*, and *The Journal of Italian Cinema and Media Studies*. She has contributed to book collections such as *The Cultures of Italian Migration, Postcolonial Italy, Italian Political Cinema, Encounters with the Real in Contemporary Italian Literature*, and *Cinema and Cinema of Exploration*. She has co-edited a special double issue of the journal *Studies in Documentary Film* and edited a special double issue of *Il lettore di provincia*. She is the editor of the critical edition of the translation of Amir Issaa's autobiography *Vivo per questo*, forthcoming in English with SDSU Press.

Daniele Comberiati is associate professor at the Université Paul-Valéry Montpellier 3, France, where he is head of the Department of Italian Studies. He has published *Scrivere nella lingua dell'altro. La letteratura degli immigrati in Italia* (2010, Writing in the Other's Language: The Literature of Migrants in Italy); *"Affrica". Il mito coloniale italiano attraverso i libri di viaggio di esploratori e missionari dall'Unità alla sconfitta di Adua* (2013; The Italian Colonial Myth Through the Travel Books of Explorers and Missionaries from Unity to the Defeat of Adua), and *"Nessuna città d'Italia è* *più crepuscolare di Roma".* Le relazioni fra i simbolisti belgi e il cenacolo romano di Sergio Corazzini (2014; "No City in Italy Is More Crepuscular than Rome": The Relations Between the Belgian Symbolists and the Roman Cenacle of Sergio Corazzini).

Lidia Curti was honorary professor of English and former dean at the University of Naples Orientale, where she conducted the research group "Feminist Futures." She researched and published on Shakespearian drama, contemporary British theatre, women in film and television, women's literature between feminism and postcoloniality, Indian cinema, migration theory and culture. Her interests were Italian diasporic literature, migration in the visual arts, and feminist counter-genealogies. Among her recent publications are *Dal fondo del tempo. Epiche di esilio e di migrazione* (2014, From the Beginning of Time: Epics of Exile and Migration); *Literary Citizenship and Migrating Belongings* (2015); *Sognare in afro. L'estetica nera negli scritti di Stuart Hall* (2015, Dreaming in Afro: The Black Aesthetic in the Writings of Stuart Hall); *Tra presenza e assenza, o dell'ambivalenza* (2016, Between Presence and Absence, or on Ambivalence); and *Il soggetto imprevisto. Simone de Beauvoir tra femminismo e postcoloniale* (2017, The Unexpected Subject: Simone de Beauvoir Between Feminism and Postcolonial).

Vera Lúcia de Oliveira was born in Brazil and now lives and works in Perugia. She is a poet, writer, and professor at the University of Perugia, where she teaches Portuguese and Brazilian literature. Her works have been published in Brazil, Italy, Portugal, Spain, the United States, France, England, Romania, and Germany. She has received numerous literary prizes, including the Premio Sandro Penna (1988), the Premio Nazionale di Poesia "Senigallia Spiaggia di Velluto" (2000), the Premio di Poesia dell'Accademia Brasiliana di Lettere (2005), and the Premio "Popoli in cammino" (2005).

Shirin Ramzanali Fazel is an Italian writer of Somali and Pakistani origin whose works have been studied both in Italy and abroad. She was born in Mogadishu in 1953. In 1971, with her husband and young child, she had to leave her country for Novara, Italy, joining the first wave of Somali refugees. She currently lives in Birmingham, UK. Her first novel, *Lontano da Mogadiscio* (*Far from Mogadishu*), describes her experience of migration to Italy and the effects of Italian colonialism in her native country. It was revised in 2013, expanded in both Italian and English, and translated by the author. Her second novel, *Nuvole sull'Equatore* (*Clouds over the Equator*), deals with the issue of meticciato and racial discrimination.

Silvia Guslandi is a humanities teaching fellow at the University of Chicago, where she earned her PhD in romance languages and literatures in 2020. She also holds a PhD in comparative literature from the University of Genoa,

Italy. She has published articles on Emanuel Carnevali, Maria Luisa Spaziani, Elio Vittorini, and John Steinbeck. Her work as a translator includes English translations of works by Adriana Cavarero, Carla Lonzi, and Giovanni Pascoli, as well as the Italian translation of John Dos Passos's *War Journals*.

Gëzim Hajdari was born in Albania in 1953 and migrated to Italy in 1992. Poet and translator, he has published multiple volumes, and won numerous literary prizes, including Italy's most prestigious poetry award, "Premio Eugenio Montale" (1997). He is the president of the Centro Internazionale Eugenio Montale and honorary citizen for literary contributions of the city of Frosinone. He directs the poetry series "Erranze"(Wanderings) in Rome. He lives both in Italy and in England.

Ron Kubati was born in Tirana, then moved to Italy in 1991 and the US in 2008. He holds two PhDs: one in modern and contemporary philosophy from the Università degli Studi di Bari and one in Italian studies from the University of Chicago. He has published a collection of poems in Albanian (1992) as well as four award-winning novels in Italian: *Va e non torna* (2000, Goes and Doesn't Come Back), M (2002), *Il buio del mare* (2007, The Darkness of the Sea), and *La vita dell'eroe* (2016, The Hero's Life). His interests include modern and contemporary Italian literature, transcultural studies, Italian cinema, modern and contemporary philosophy, and migration studies. His articles have been published in edited volumes and peer-reviewed journals including *Moderna, Modernitá Letteraria, Forum Italicum*, and *NEMLA Italian Studies*. His books in progress are *The Transitional Human Being: Literary, Journalistic and Cinematographic Representations of Contemporary Italy* and the novel *The Intruder*.

Gabriella Kuruvilla is a writer, journalist, and painter born in Milan in 1969 to an Indian father and Italian mother. She has published the novels *Media chiara e noccioline* (as Viola Chandra, 2001, Light Beer and Peanuts) and *Milano, fin qui tutto bene* (2012, Milan, So Far So Good); the children's book *Questa non è una baby-sitter* (2011, This Is Not a Babysitter); and the short story collection *È la vita, dolcezza* (2008, That's Life, Sweetheart). Her newest novel was published in 2020, *Maneggia con cura* (Handle with Care).

Amara Lakhous is an author, journalist, and anthropologist. He was born in 1970 in Algiers to a Berber family. He graduated from the University of Algiers with a degree in philosophy and obtained a degree in cultural anthropology from the La Sapienza University in Rome. Lakhous wrote his first book, *The Bedbugs and the Pirates*, in 1993, written in Algerian dialect and published in a bilingual Arabic-Italian text in 1999. He started working as a reporter for the Algerian national radio in 1994 but left the country for Italy following death threats from Islamists. He worked in Italy as a cultural mediator and translator with a focus on immigration. In 2001 he wrote an Arabic language novel based on his early years in Rome, titled *How to be Suckled by the Wolf without Getting Bit*, which has been translated into English (Clash of Civilizations over an Elevator in Piazza Vittorio), French, and Dutch. A film released in 2008 was also based on this novel.

Marie Orton is professor of Italian at Brigham Young University, where she teaches courses in Italian culture and language and global women's studies. Her research areas include issues of migration and cultural shift and contemporary Italian literature and cinema. She has recently published articles on the documentaries of Fred Kuwornu, cinema of Andrea Segre, writings of Laila Wadia, and so-termed cinema of migration. Her English translation of Kossi Komla-Ebri's *Imbarazzismi* and *Nuovi imbarazzismi* was published as *EmbaRACEments: Daily Embarrassments in Black and White . . . and Color* in 2019. She has recently completed a translation of Monica Miniati's *Italian Jewish Women in the Nineteenth and Twentieth Centuries* (Palgrave, 2021) and is researching the intersections of migration and constructed cultural memory in the medium of museums.

Graziella Parati is the Paul D. Paganucci Professor of Italian Literature and Language at Dartmouth College. She is an expert in migration studies and the Mediterranean and teaches in comparative literature, Italian, and women's and gender studies. She has served as chair of French and Italian, comparative literature, and studio art departments and programs. She has also been director of the Leslie Center for the Humanities for the past four years. Her scholarly interests are reflected in the books she has published: *Public History, Private Stories: Italian Women's Autobiography* (1996), *Migration Italy: The Art of Talking Back in a Destination Culture* (2006), *Mediterranean Crossroads: Migration Literature in Italy* (1999), *New Perspectives in Italian Cultural Studies. Volume 1 Definitions, Theory, and Accented Practices* and *New Perspectives in Italian Cultural Studies. Volume 2: The Arts and History* (2012); *Italy and the Cultural Politics of WWI* (2016); and *Migrants Writers and Urban Space in Italy: Proximities and Affect in Literature and Film* (2017). Professional collaborations have engendered a series of co-edited books: with Ben Lawton *Italian Cultural Studies* (2001), with Rebecca West *Italian Feminist Theory and Practice: Equality and Sexual Difference* (2002), and with Marie Orton *Multicultural Literature in Contemporary Italy* (2007). She has published articles that focus primarily on migration issues. Her books in progress are *Un-becoming Fascists: Autobiography, Politics, and Nation Building* and *Italy and Libya: Literature, Architecture, and the Politics of Space*. She is the board of advisors of New Hampshire Humanities; SRM University in Amaravati, India; and the Jahjaga Foundation in Kosovo.

Eleanor Paynter studies displacement, asylum, and migrant testimony, focusing on Mediterranean mobilities and the colonial present in the Italian context. She draws on narrative and ethnographic methods and is at work on a book that engages migrant testimonies to challenge emergency and crisis framings of migration. As a translator, she has worked with literary, artistic, and journalistic texts. She holds an MFA in poetry from Sarah Lawrence College and a PhD in comparative studies from Ohio State University. She is a postdoctoral associate with Cornell University's Migrations initiative and the Mario Einaudi Center for International Studies.

Fulvio Pezzarossa was Professor of Sociology of Literature at the University of Bologna. In the last two decades, his research and teaching has focused on the critical analysis of literary works written in Italian by migrant authors. He is Editor-in-Chief of Scritture migranti (https://scritturemigranti.unibo.it/index), the first peer-reviewed academic journal dealing exclusively with the subject of migrant literature, which he founded in 2008. Since 2007 he has directed the first laboratory of intercultural creative writing in Italy. For several years, he was the chair of the jury of Eks & Tra, a competition dedicated to unpublished works written by migrant writers. He promoted and coordinated the International Conference Leggere il testo e il mondo. Vent'anni di scritture della migrazione in Italia, held in Bologna in October 2010. The conference proceedings were published in 2011 by CLUEB (Bologna). Prof. Pezzarossa has also worked on Renaissance literature in Florence and Bologna, young adult literature and anthropological themes in the writings of Pier Paolo Pasolini.

Wendy Pojmann is professor of history at Siena College in Albany, New York. She is the author of *Immigrant Women and Feminism in Italy* (2005), *Italian Women and International Cold War Politics, 1944–1968* (2013), and *Espresso: The Art and Soul of Italy* (2021); lead author of *Doing History: An Introduction to the Historian's Craft* (2016); and editor of *Migration and Activism in Europe since 1945* (2008). Her articles have appeared in such publications as the *Journal of Women's History, Gender, & History* and *Ricerche di Storia Politica.* She teaches courses in modern European history and gender and women's studies.

Lidia Radi is an associate professor of French and Italian at the University of Richmond. She has a dual doctorate from Rutgers University and the Université Stendhal-Grenoble in France. She has published extensively in the field of early modern studies. As a "first-wave" Albanian émigrée who has frequently presented on Italian literature of migration, her current research explores the Albanian culture of diaspora in Italy and other European countries. Her recent work "Scrittori senza frontiere: il caso di Elvira Dones" (Writers without Borders: The Case of Elvira Dones) will appear in *Multilin-*

gualism in Contexts of Migration and Refuge, a special edition of Arizona State University's *Journal of Critical Multilingualism Studies*.

Lucia Re is professor of Italian and the director of graduate studies with an appointment in the UCLA Department of Gender Studies. Her interests include poetry and the novel, women writers and artists, feminist theory, futurism and the avant-garde, Italy and the Mediterranean, race studies, and literary translation. She has published more than eighty scholarly articles and essays on authors ranging from Gabriele d'Annunzio to Anna Maria Ortese. Her book *Calvino and the Age of Neorealism* won the 1992 Marraro Prize of the Modern Language Association. For Amelia Rosselli's volume of poetry *War Variations* (translated with Paul Vangelisti), she was awarded the 2006 PEN USA literary translation award, as well as the Flaiano Prize for International Italian Studies.

Kevin Regan-Maglione completed his MA at Georgetown University in Italian studies and is currently a PhD candidate in romance languages at the University of Oregon, where he is finishing his dissertation, "Unbreaking Bonds: Queer Prison Testimony from the Holocaust to Today."

Caterina Romeo is associate professor at Sapienza Università di Roma, where she teaches literary theory, comparative literature, and gender studies. She is the author of *Riscrivere la nazione. La letteratura italiana postcoloniale* (2018, Rewriting the Nation: Italian Postcolonial Literature) and *Narrative tra due sponde: Memoir di italiane d'America* (2005, Between Two Shores: Memoirs of Italian American Women). She has coedited *Postcolonial Italy* (2012) and *Postcolonial Europe* (special issue of the *Postcolonial Studies Journal*, 2015). She has translated the works of numerous Italian American women writers into Italian. Her essays on Italian American literature and culture, Italian postcolonial literature, postcolonial feminism, and constructions and representations of Blackness in contemporary Italy have been published in national and international journals and edited volumes. Her most recent book, *Gender, Race, and Intersectionality in Italian Postcolonial Literature* is scheduled to be published by Palgrave in 2021.

James Walker, PhD, first began studying, translating, and celebrating italophone literature of migration in the mid-1990s while researching for his doctoral dissertation, *Figures of Difference: Race, Nation, Gender and African-Italian Literature*. Currently faculty mentor for the Norlin Scholars Program at the University of Colorado–Boulder, he is a proud co-founder of MOTUS Theater and a longtime arts-activist, performer, and diversity educator.

Enrico Zammarchi is assistant professor of Italian in the Modern Languages & Literature Department at Gonzaga University. He holds a Ph.D. in

Comparative Studies from The Ohio State University, where he wrote a dissertation on the development of hip-hop culture in Italy. His work analyzes the connections between music and politics, with a particular interest in 1990s popular and protest music, social movements, and radicalism in Italy.